ARCTIC INSTITUTE OF NORTH AMERICA

ANTHROPOLOGY OF THE NORTH:

TRANSLATIONS FROM RUSSIAN SOURCES

Editor: HENRY N. MICHAEL

Advisory Committee

CHESTER S. CHARD, University of Wisconsin, Madison, Wis.

ROBERT C. FAYLOR, Arctic Institute of North America, Washington, D.C.

F. KENNETH HARE, McGill University, Montreal, P.Q.

LAWRENCE KRADER, The American University, Washington, D.C.

HENRY N. MICHAEL, Temple University, Philadelphia, Pa.

DEMETRI B. SHIMKIN, University of Illinois, Urbana, Ill.

MARIE TREMAINE, Editor *Arctic Bibliography*, Washington, D.C.

HENRY B. COLLINS, Smithsonian Institution, Washington, D.C. (Chairman)

T0312569

ARCTIC INSTITUTE OF NORTH AMERICA

ANTHROPOLOGY OF THE NORTH:

TRANSLATIONS FROM RUSSIAN SOURCES / NO. 1

The Ancient Culture
of the Bering Sea and
the Eskimo Problem

S. I. RUDENKO / *Translated by Paul Tolstoy*

PUBLISHED FOR THE ARCTIC INSTITUTE OF NORTH AMERICA
BY UNIVERSITY OF TORONTO PRESS

Copyright, Canada, 1961, by
University of Toronto Press
Reprinted 2017
ISBN 978-1-4875-9257-8 (paper)

INTRODUCTION

WITH THE PUBLICATION of this first volume, the project ANTHROPOLOGY OF THE NORTH: TRANSLATIONS FROM RUSSIAN SOURCES[1] of the Arctic Institute of North America, offers a work which in the field of Arctic archaeology has been often cited not only in Soviet publications but also in those of many English-writing archaeologists. The latter, for the most, have had to be satisfied with a study of the illustrations (Rudenko's work contains 38 plates) and with abstracts.

Although published fourteen years ago, Rudenko's archaeological work has been selected by the Advisory Committee because it constitutes one of the basic contributions to Eskimo archaeology from the pen of a contemporary Soviet investigator who has done most of the field work himself.

The project has been fortunate in securing the services of Dr. Paul Tolstoy whose contributions and translations in the field of Soviet archaeology are well-known. Dr. Henry B. Collins of the Bureau of American Ethnology, Smithsonian Institution, has critically read the translation and has made valuable suggestions particularly in regard to terminology—by no means an easy or a settled issue in Arctic archaeology.

In transliterating place names and references, the transliteration system of the United States Board on Geographic Names was used with the minor modifications of not rendering the Russian "soft sign" with an apostrophe ('), and of contraction of "yy" to "y" and "iy" to "i." However, in this particular work of Rudenko, his own transliterations (suggested parenthetically) are used in those cases where they were so suggested. Thus: Uwelen and not Uelen, and so on. Statements or words appearing in square brackets [ ] in the text are either the translator's or the editor's. A few additional editorial remarks are in the form of footnotes.

In an encompassing work such as this, based on multilingual sources, minor and sometimes major errors of translation and interpretation are apt to occur on the part of the author. No attempt is made here to evaluate the material, the content. This is the prerogative of the reviewer. However, in order to avoid unnecessary confusion or delay to the reader, attention is brought to several potentially misleading points by editorial remarks attached to the passages in question.

Within approximately a year, four additional volumes of translated works are planned for publication. Volume 2 will contain sixteen articles on ethnogenesis of the nations and tribes of Siberia, volume 3 will be M. G. Levin's *Physical Anthropology and Ethnogenetic Problems of the Peoples of the Far East*, volume 4 will contain six articles on shamanism and volume 5 will be A. P. Okladnikov's *The Distant Past of the Maritime Province*.

May, 1961   HENRY N. MICHAEL

[1]Generous financial support of the National Science Foundation for this project, NSF 11411, is gratefully acknowledged.

S. I. RUDENKO *Professor at the*
University of Leningrad

General Editors

ACADEMICIAN L. S. BERG
and
PROF. V. I. RAVDONIKAS
Corresponding Member of the
Academy of Sciences of the USSR

The Ancient Culture of the Bering Sea and the Eskimo Problem

PUBLISHING HOUSE OF THE MAIN NORTHERN
SEA ROUTE
MOSCOW–LENINGRAD 1947

The present volume was prepared by the author on commission from the N. Ya. Marr Institute of the History of Material Culture and the Arctic Scientific Research Institute of the Main Northern Sea Route (Glavsevmorput), and approved by them for publication.

AUTHOR'S FOREWORD

THE PROBLEM OF THE SETTLEMENT of the Arctic by man and of ethnic interrelationships in this marginal area is not only unsolved at the present time, but has not even been formulated adequately. Just how little we know of the past of the arctic peoples has become clearly evident from a number of international congresses and specialized conferences organized by the Section of History and Philosophy of the Academy of Sciences of the U.S.S.R. While we have varying amounts of data on the ethnology, linguistics, and some aspects of the physical anthropology of the peoples of our Arctic, we have no archaeological information whatever for most of its areas. And yet we know that, however skilful the hypotheses of ethnic history we base on the three aforementioned disciplines, they need the support of archaeological data. Many hypotheses as to the origin of specific groups have been radically modified following new and often unexpected archaeological findings. A case in point is to be seen in the problem of the origin of the Eskimos and of their culture.

Over the past twenty years, archaeological investigations have been taking place on a broad scale on the islands of Bering Sea, in Alaska, in Canada, in northeastern North America, and in Greenland, in connection with the problem of the peopling of America and, specifically, the problem of the origin of Eskimo culture. In broad outline, a sequence of stages in the development of Eskimo culture, their geographic distributions, and, in some measure, their placement in time have now been sketched. However, since some part of continental Asia has been suggested as the place where this culture arose and underwent its earliest development, a pressing need has arisen for archaeological investigations in Asia and particularly, in its extreme northeast.

In the summer of 1945, acting at the request of the Leningrad Section of the Institute of the History of Material Culture of the Academy of Sciences of the U.S.S.R., in conjunction with the Arctic Institute of the Main Office of the Northern Maritime Passage, I investigated the coast of the Chukchi Peninsula from the village of Uwelen in the north to the village of Sirhenik in the south. We managed to carry out archaeological explorations in the villages of Uwelen, Nuukan, Dezhnevo, Yandygay, on the island of Arakamchechen, at Cape Chaplin, in the village of Kiwak, at Cape Chukchi, near the village of Avan, in Plover Bay, and in the village of Sirhenik. In addition, a study was made of materials provided by I. P. Lavrov from his explorations near the villages of Nunligran and Enmylen that same summer.

In working up for publication the materials of this first entirely archaeological expedition to the Chukchi Peninsula, I have also made use of the archaeological collections of N. P. Borisov and D. Ye. Bettak from the peninsula, which acceded in 1910 to the Ethnographic Section of the Russian Museum, today the State Museum of Ethnography in Leningrad. The publication of all materials available to date in the U.S.S.R. on the archaeology of the Chukchi Peninsula should, in my estimation, shed light on the prehistoric past of our eastern Arctic and should be instrumental, if not in the final solution, at least in the correct formulation of ethnological inquiry in the Pacific Far North.

CONTENTS

6   *Contents*

THE ESKIMO PROBLEM

THE PACIFIC ETHNOLOGICAL problem, the problem of the date of migration of man from Asia to America, and that of subsequent ethnic relationships between Asia and America has been already attracting the attention of scientists over many decades. Particular interest is being shown in the Eskimos, in view of their distinctive culture, adapted to life under severe arctic conditions, with its Neolithic cast and, as is supposed, certain survivals of Mesolithic or even Paleolithic traditions.

In the West, a theory of the origin of the Eskimos was first formulated by Cranz (Cranz 1770). According to the theory of Cranz, the Eskimos were originally an Asian people, related to the Kalmyk and other tribes of central and northeastern Asia. Having moved north under the pressure of neighboring tribes, they migrated to northeastern Siberia, crossed Bering Strait into Alaska, and, moving eastward, eventually reached Greenland in the 14th century of our era.

Almost a century later, Markham likewise sought the origin of the Eskimos in Asia, on the northern shores of Siberia. According to Markham, the Eskimos earlier lived along the coast of northeastern Siberia, but were compelled to migrate during one of the periods of political unrest in Central Asia as a result of pressure from the south (Markham 1865). Like Wrangell (Wrangell 1841) and Nordenskiöld (Nordenskiöld 1882) he saw proof of the former settlement by the Eskimos of the arctic shore of Asia in the remains of pit-houses from Chaun Bay to Bering Strait, and in certain Chukchi traditions, according to which these pit-houses had been inhabited formerly by the Nomallo or Onkilon, a maritime people pushed out by the Chukchi to distant, as yet unknown islands in the Arctic Ocean.

Suppositions as to the cultural or even genetic connections of the Eskimos with the Upper Paleolithic inhabitants of western Europe were made a long time ago by Larte (Larte 1864), Pruner Bay (Pruner Bay 1868), Hamy (Hamy 1870), Dupont (Dupont 1872), and Boyd Dawkins (Boyd Dawkins 1872), and have been backed by a number of authors: Sollas (Sollas 1911), Boule (Boule 1913), and others. This conception received its greatest elaboration from Sollas, who pointed out the similarities, particularly of detail, between a number of objects characteristic of the Paleolithic Magdalenian and the Eskimo cultures.

Schrenk (Schrenk 1883; I:256–261) formulated the problem more broadly, and considered the Eskimos, along with the Kamchadal, Koryak, and Chukchi, as northeastern, Paleo-Asiatic people having some relation also to a number of tribes of northern and northwestern North America. However, Schrenk believed that the Nomallo Eskimo tribe, which had inhabited the Asian shore of Bering Strait south of Cape Dezhnev nearly to the mouth of the Anadyr River, had come there from America. Yet, this migration, as Schrenk saw it, was only a return to Asia of part of the Eskimos, since, in view of their facial features and their traditions, the Eskimos were of Asiatic origin. Like Chamisso (Chamisso 1821), Veniaminov (Veniaminov 1840; I:112–113) and others, Schrenk considered Bering Strait as the point of entry of the Eskimos from Asia into America.

Basing himself on linguistic data, Thalbitzer (Thalbitzer 1904:266) considered the Bering Sea region as the place of origin of the Eskimos. Later he brought forth a number of considerations in favor of his supposition that the original home of the Eskimos was to the west at Bering Strait, where they had arrived from the coast of Siberia (Thalbitzer 1914:717–718).

Kroeber shared this point of view (Kroeber 1923:289–290).

The theory of Rink was the first to take into consideration cultural traits and conditions under which these might have originated (Rink 1887:4–5). According to Rink, the Eskimos were originally an inland people, who had followed the rivers to arrive at the coast. There, they transformed and adapted their culture to new environmental conditions, and only after that did this new Eskimo culture acquire its distribution over the vast territory that it now occupies. Rink held that the most favorable area for the development of what he considered the typically sub-arctic Eskimo culture was the mouth of the Yukon River in Alaska. Having adapted themselves to the new conditions of the maritime coast, a small part of the Eskimos crossed Bering Strait into Siberia, while the remainder spread eastward to occupy the long strip of arctic coast extending from Alaska to Greenland.

In opposition to Rink, who believed that Eskimo culture took form in interior Alaska, Murdoch pointed out that the culture of the Alaskan Eskimos was highly specialized rather than primitive, whereas the primitive Eskimos were those of the central portions of North America (Murdoch 1888:129–130).

The theory of the American origin of the Eskimos was also defended by Boas who considered their original home the inland area west of Hudson Bay. At the same time, he viewed the Alaskan Eskimos as relatively recent arrivals from the east (Boas 1888b:39; 1905:91–100; 1910).

The view of the American origin of the Eskimos was elaborated by Steensby in a number of papers, particularly his anthropo-geographic study of the origin of Eskimo culture (Steensby 1916).

Steensby's theory is interesting in that it is the first attempt to establish a sequence in the development of Eskimo culture.

According to Steensby's theory, Eskimo culture first appeared in the treeless country between Hudson Bay and Coronation Gulf (the Mackenzie River area), as a result of the adaptation to arctic conditions of the culture we find among the Woodland Indians. This culture, the culture of the Barren Grounds hunters, upon penetrating to the northern coast, gave rise to a maritime phase and spread east and west, to Greenland and to Siberia. Steensby termed this original coastal Eskimo culture "Paleo-Eskimo." Under the influence of the Paleo-Asiatic and Pacific peoples in the Bering Strait area, a "Neo-Eskimo" culture appeared, with such traits as the women's boat (umiak) and kayak. It was a highly distinctive littoral culture, which subsequently spread eastward and added a new overlay to the older "Paleo-Eskimo" culture.

Birket-Smith, a participant of the Danish fifth Thule expedition, emphasized in his writings the difference between the littoral culture of the "maritime coast" and the "inland" culture (Birket-Smith 1924, 1929, 1930). While the culture of the maritime coast is characterized by the hunting of sea mammals, the inland riparian culture features ice fishing on lakes and rivers. The primitive character of the inland riparian culture was a basis for presuming its existence over a long period of time in the circumpolar area. The culture of the Central Eskimo, according to Birket-Smith, is a typical inland ice-hunting culture, a modified survival of the ancient cultural stratum which may be termed "Proto-Eskimo."

Accepting the hypothesis of the origin of the oldest Eskimo culture in central North America, Birket-Smith presumes that, prior to their adaptation to the sea, the Proto-Eskimo probably lived in the Mackenzie region, clustered perhaps about one of the lakes between the Great Bear and Slave Lakes and Lake Athabaska. It was there that the foundation was laid for the whole of Eskimo culture. Birket-Smith follows Steensby in calling this foundation Paleo-Eskimo. Like Steensby, Birket-Smith considers the Eskimo cultures in western Alaska and to the east as more recent or Neo-Eskimo.

The division of Eskimo culture into two sequential stages also found favor with Hatt, though he supposed that the coastal culture which Steensby called Neo-Eskimo was in reality the older Eskimo culture, while the inland culture, called Paleo-Eskimo by Steensby, was more recent. Hatt believed that the northern coast of North America was first exploited by peoples of the older coastal culture, which was unquestionably related to the Paleo-Asiatic culture of northeastern Siberia and which contained precisely those traits that are now partially lacking in the central area (the umiak, the gut cape, tanning with urine, quadrangular dwellings, *et al.*). This ancient coastal culture probably incorporated various cultural and racial elements from the regions between Hudson Bay and the Mackenzie River, which spread along the northern coast of North America, and came to dominate and partially transform the older culture (Hatt 1916a, 1916b).

The theories so far enumerated of the American or Asiatic origin of the Eskimos and their culture were purely speculative in nature, and were not derived from any profound or many-sided studies of the problem.

An important turning point in the study of the Eskimo problem was marked by the archaeological excavations of the Thule expedition under Rasmussen, particularly by those of Mathiassen in the Central Eskimo area. It is true that a number of ancient sites had been excavated earlier in the Aleutian Islands (Pinart 1875, Dall 1878, Jochelson 1925), but the published materials contain few data that throw light on cultural phases and chronological relationships in connection with the problem of the origin of Eskimo culture.

Mathiassen's excavations (Mathiassen 1927) revealed an ancient Eskimo culture to the north of Hudson Bay which Mathiassen called the Thule culture. As Mathiassen pointed out, this culture was found to be not primitive but, on the contrary, developed and specialized, and containing all the most characteristic traits widespread throughout the area occupied by the Eskimos.

This culture was typical for people engaged in hunting sea mammals, particularly whales, who lived predominantly in permanent houses, and who made use of a wide variety of tools of highly elaborate form. The Thule culture is typically arctic and, at the same time, coastal: it must have originated on a coast abounding in large game, particularly whales. In addition, wood [driftwood] must have been abundant on the coast for the construction of umiaks (since it is either impossible or very difficult to throw a whaling harpoon from a kayak) and of dwellings. Permanent conditions of this kind prevailed only in the west.

In emphasizing the close relationship between the Thule culture and that of the Central Eskimo on the one hand, and that of the Eskimos to the west at Point Barrow, on the other, Mathiassen notes that the connection between them was even closer and more direct in the past. The problem remained of the place of origin of the Thule culture, of whether it was in the central area or to the west, and of the direction of its spread. Mathiassen came to the conclusion that this culture, with all of its specifically whale-hunting traits, originated somewhere in the west, in the Arctic, where whales had been abundant and where wood [driftwood] occurred in sufficient quantity, that is, on the coast of Alaska or in eastern Siberia, north of Bering Sea. There, all the conditions requisite for the formation of this culture were to be found, and it is from there that it spread eastward as far as Greenland. Among the finds in the central area, Mathiassen pointed to a whole series of traits whose occurrence was known only in western regions and which, therefore, could have come only from there. Of Birket-Smith's three phases, two, in the opinion of Mathiassen, were unquestionably valid and were represented by the Thule culture and that of the modern Central Eskimo. The third, oldest phase so far remained hypothetical. Inasmuch as the Thule culture found by him was not primitive but, on the contrary, highly developed and specialized, it must have followed, perforce, a long course of development and could not be viewed as the initial Eskimo culture.

In opposition to Birket-Smith, Mathiassen made the supposition that a group of Eskimos, arriving from the west to the coastal region between Coronation Gulf and Bathurst, transformed their culture in this barren area upon encountering there large herds of caribou. The culture of the Caribou Eskimo should thus be considered impoverished rather than primitive. In that case, wrote Mathiassen, the movement from west to east represented by the Thule culture becomes less questionable, and we can look to the west for the cradle of Eskimo culture.

After the excavations of Mathiassen, the study of Eskimo culture entered a new phase, which began with systematic archaeological excavations in northern Alaska. In 1926, Jenness, who had discovered the ancient Dorset Eskimo culture in the south of Baffin Island (Jenness 1925) the previous year, carried out excavations at Cape Prince of Wales and on Diomede Island in Bering Strait and found the remains of an ancient Eskimo culture that had formerly existed there. This culture was related to that of the modern Alaskan Eskimo, though notably different from it in certain respects. In kitchen middens near Bering Strait, Jenness found a considerable number of artifacts, including "fossil" walrus ivory, elaborately decorated and providing evidence of a culture which had attained a more advanced stage of artistic development many centuries ago than any other culture known hitherto in the arctic regions.[1]

Jenness dated this Bering Sea culture to a time preceding the beginning of our era (Jenness 1928a:78), on the premise that the Thule culture of the eastern Arctic is at least one thousand years old, while its oldest phase at Point Barrow, Birnirk, is to be placed in the first centuries of our era (Jenness 1933:387).

In those same years, Hrdlička was engaged in studies of physical anthropology along the coast of Alaska from Norton Sound to Point Barrow, and came across several ancient art objects, darkened from prolonged burial in the ground, principally from St. Lawrence Island. These objects, which constituted evidence of advanced native art, characterized by engraved curvilinear designs, occurred, Hrdlička found, from Point Hope in the east to the mouth of the Kolyma River in the west, and were infrequent to the north and south of Norton Sound. Their center was St. Lawrence Island and part of the Asiatic shore of Bering Sea, the Diomedes, and Seward Peninsula.

The discoveries of Mathiassen, Jenness, and Hrdlička provided new historic perspectives for solving the Eskimo problem and stimulated interest in archaeological investigations, which proceeded apace in the years that followed. In 1926, Geist (Geist and Rainey 1936) began investigations in the Bering Sea area, on St. Lawrence, and on the Punuk Islands. The year 1928 marked the beginning of the investigations of Collins, first on the Punuk Islands, then on St. Lawrence

---

[1]Similar objects had found their way much earlier (1910) from the Bering Sea coast of the Chukchi Peninsula to the Ethnographic Section of the Russian Museum in St. Petersburg, but failed to attract due attention and were not published.

(Collins 1937), at Cape Kialegak, and later in the northwestern portion of the island, near the settlement of Gambell. The excavations near Gambell allowed Collins to trace in detail the sequential changes of Eskimo culture on the island, and to establish a chronological succession of stages for this culture.

The earliest stage, which Collins called "Old Bering Sea," begins in the last centuries before our era and comes to a close at the end of the first millennium A.D. The following stage, the "Punuk," ends approximately in the 17th century. The last stage of Eskimo culture on St. Lawrence Island comes close to the present and begins about two hundred years ago.

It was found that the Old Bering Sea people lived in semi-subterranean houses of moderate size, with long and narrow entrance passageways. Their stone tools were mostly chipped, though they also made implements of ground slate. They used pottery. They subsisted mainly on the hunting of sea mammals, though Collins believes they did not hunt whales. They had dogs, but did not use them for transportation.

An amazing feature of the Old Bering Sea stage was the occurrence of a large number of objects, sometimes even utilitarian in purpose, bearing the attractive curvilinear designs characteristic of this period.

In the following Punuk stage, life was based largely on the same mode of subsistence as earlier. Dwellings became larger, but followed the same plan. Changes occurred in art, in some harpoon heads, and chipped stone implements were replaced almost entirely by ones of ground slate. Many new types of tools made their appearance and these Collins believes to be of Siberian origin.

The last stage of Eskimo culture on St. Lawrence Island, close to the present in time, is characterized by objects introduced rather recently from Siberia, among them dog sleds with bone runners, bird, mammal, and human figures carved out of walrus tusk, beads, and various metal objects.

Thus, the excavations on St. Lawrence Island threw considerable light on the problem of Eskimo prehistory, though they did not provide its definitive solution. Eskimo culture at the Old Bering Sea stage was found, in many respects, to be more highly developed and more specialized than in later stages. Therefore, Collins believes that we must probe more deeply into the past to find the simple beginnings of this ancient culture, and that there is no doubt as to the direction in which these beginnings are to be sought. We must look toward northern Eurasia, where Collins sees many amazing parallels to Eskimo culture, as well as geographic conditions suitable for the formation of a maritime culture. As for the immediate origins of Old Bering Sea culture, Collins sees its area of first appearance as eastern Siberia, somewhere between the mouths of the Anadyr and Kolyma rivers.

Meanwhile, as excavations proceeded on St. Lawrence Island, Hrdlička (Hrdlička 1935) spent several seasons investigating Kodiak Island in the sub-Arctic zone. Mason reported on excavations at Point Barrow (Mason 1930), Weyer worked near Port Möller in Alaska (Weyer 1930), and de Laguna had begun her excavations in Cook Inlet (de Laguna 1934), which Birket-Smith (Birket-Smith and de Laguna 1938) later continued in Prince William Sound. In the eastern Arctic, Jenness and Wintemberg (Wintermberg 1939) continued the study of Dorset remains from Baffin Island south to Newfoundland, while Mathiassen (Mathiassen 1930b, 1936), Larsen (Larsen 1934, 1938), and Holtved (Holtved 1938) completed extensive investigations along the entire coast of Greenland. Finally, Rainey, in collaboration with Larsen and Giddings, conducted investigations at Point Hope and then, once again, on St. Lawrence Island (Rainey 1941a).

In 1940, two summary articles appeared, "Prehistoric Culture Waves from Asia to America," by Jenness, and "Outline of Eskimo Prehistory," by Collins.

In the article cited, Jenness notes that excavations in the Bering Sea area apparently indicate no large-scale migration through Bering Strait from Asia to America, if we do not count the Eskimo migration of the beginning of our era. In addition, the development of Eskimo culture is suggestive of gradual evolution rather than alien intrusion. On the other hand, citing Nordenskiöld (Nordenskiöld 1931) and others, he observes that, although a few Polynesians may have fortuitously reached American shores, there has likewise not occurred any large-scale trans-oceanic migration, at least not on such a scale as to be reflected in the physical type of the natives of the New World or in the development of their culture. Jenness also excludes the possibility of migration from Asia to America from Kamchatka by way of the Aleutian Islands. Thus the only route that remains still is through Bering Strait. This conclusion, in the opinion of Jenness, ties in well both with the results of linguistic research—in particular that of Rivet (Rivet 1925a)—and with ethnographic data (Jenness 1940).

Jenness agrees with Collins in considering the ancient Dorset culture of eastern North America as Eskimo, and believes it branched off from Proto-Eskimo prior to the development of Old Bering Sea. The time of the migration of the Dorset people from Asia to America would be the first or perhaps, and even more probably, the second millennium B.C.

Jenness supports in its entirety Collins' view of the evolution and devolution of Old Bering Sea culture up to recent times, and agrees that the Birnirk phase of Point Barrow is the direct heir of Old Bering Sea culture. However, for a variety of reasons, he supposes that the Birnirk culture and its offshoot, Thule, are not immediately derived from Old Bering Sea, but are both derivative from some little-advanced culture which had existed on the northeastern coast of Siberia in the region of the Kolyma and Indigirka rivers. From there, the original (initial) hypothetical culture could have sent its offshoots eastward. One branch crossed Bering Strait and moved north along the shore of Alaska to Point Barrow. Another branch colonized the coast of Siberia south of Cape Dezhnev [East Cape] and then or later established a small outpost on St. Lawrence Island. Gradually, Jenness thinks, the southern colony on the Siberian shore of Bering Strait, subjected to strong influence from southern sources (particularly, perhaps, from China), revolutionized its art style and adopted certain traits such as pottery and the bow-drill which, seemingly, were not known in the earlier period.

Thus, according to Jenness, the original home of the Eskimo is not in America or in northeastern Siberia but at the mouths of the Kolyma and Indigirka rivers. He writes that he would not be surprised if it is precisely there, rather than in Alaska, that the homeland of Eskimo culture will be found. He concedes that he may have defined this area too narrowly, and that it may have to be extended westward. He also admits the possibility, referring to a communication by Chernetsov (Chernetsov 1935), that, during our era, an Eskimo-like people moved westward out of this area as far as the Yamal Peninsula and even further into northern European Russia, where the kayak and the bidarka were noted as early as the sixteenth century, according to an article by MacRitchie (MacRitchie 1912).

If the forerunners of the Old Bering Sea, Birnirk, and Dorset cultures are to be discovered on the arctic coast of western Siberia, as Jenness hopes, the gap would be greatly reduced, both in absolute time and in space, between the historic Eskimo cultures and the history of the Epi-Paleolithic peoples of northern Europe.

In his paper "Outline of Eskimo Prehistory," Collins (Collins 1940) presents a detailed survey of everything known at the time about Eskimo archaeology, and arrives at the following conclusions. Archaeological discoveries in the north, instead of yielding direct evidence on the origin of Eskimo culture, have shown that, to establish this origin, further work is required. Excavations in the Bering Strait region reveal a lengthy sequence of cultural change, tending more toward simplification than toward progressive development. The Old Bering Sea culture is, in many respects, more advanced than the present-day culture of the Alaskan Eskimo. The excavations of de Laguna in southern Alaska have shown that the oldest stage of Eskimo culture in that area was simple and generalized in nature. Moreover, since the most ancient Eskimo culture of Alaska was not under the influence of the culture of the Northwest Coast Indians, the same situation may be expected in the Bering Strait region. Archaeological excavations confirm these expectations. We see that, in prehistoric times, the highly developed culture around Bering Strait was in no way the result of influence from the American Northwest coast. The influence from this area, noticeable in the culture of the Alaskan Eskimos, appeared, it would seem, in recent times.

"It is highly significant that we find all the basic traits of Old Bering Sea culture," writes Collins, "in Europe or in Asia at the present time or in the past. Furthermore, these traits, widespread in the Old World, are found in America only among the Eskimos and in contiguous areas to which Eskimo influence has probably extended."[2] Like Jenness, Collins draws from this the natural conclusion that, inasmuch as the traits that form the basis of Eskimo culture have their origin in the Old World, it is there, rather than in America, that the roots of Eskimo culture must be sought.

In the article under discussion, Collins emphasizes particularly the significance of the inserted stone side-blades in ancient Eskimo harpoon heads which, he believes, serve as links connecting Eskimo culture through the Siberian Neolithic to the European Mesolithic.

In 1941, Rainey described the interesting Okvik site, discovered on one of the Punuk Islands (Rainey 1941d). This site differs from all other Eskimo sites previously investigated in that no house remains, mounds, or depressions visible on the surface occurred. Only the somewhat greener shade of the vegetation at the site, and a few bones scattered on the shore near-by testified to a former settlement. The site was discovered by Eskimos from St. Lawrence Island, who visited it on special expeditions to obtain fossil walrus ivory and various objects. A substantial collection from the site was acquired by Geist in 1931 and 1934, and by Rainey in 1937. In the same year, Collins' monograph on the archaeology of St. Lawrence Island appeared, and Rainey noted the fact that the style of ornamentation typical of the majority of objects from the Okvik site was identical to that found by Collins on objects from the oldest layer of the Old Bering Sea culture on St. Lawrence, and which he described under the name of Old Bering Sea style 1. In 1939, Rainey visited St. Lawrence Island with the object of spending some time in the Punuk Islands and investigating the Okvik site, but did not find it possible to carry out his intention. However, in the autumn of the same year, his companion Giddings discovered the remains of a dwelling with a culture apparently identical to that of Okvik near Gambell on St. Lawrence Island. Inasmuch as may be judged from the stone flooring, the dwelling was rounded in shape and probably had a covered entryway, and was probably semi-subterranean.

[2]Actually this is a condensation of Collins' statement. For full text see Collins 1940:586–7 —Editor.

In it were found a large number of objects (about 950), mostly implements of chipped stone and, in smaller numbers, of ground slate, as well as pottery sherds, wooden objects and a limited number of objects of bone, walrus ivory, and baleen. Some of the implements of bone and walrus ivory bore engraved designs, all in typical Okvik style.

Rainey believes that the dwelling of the Okvik culture excavated by Giddings is older than all of those excavated near Gambell by Collins.

Unfortunately, the collection of objects obtained from that dwelling is still unpublished, and the material which Rainey used in describing the Okvik culture consists almost entirely of objects purchased from Eskimos. Okvik differs from other Eskimo cultures primarily in its special style of ornamentation, which is simpler and sketchier than the curvilinear Old Bering Sea style, as well as in a distinctive type of harpoon head with a multi-pronged spur. A whole series of objects typical of Punuk but unknown in the Old Bering Sea Culture were found at the Okvik site. These include whaling harpoon heads, a number of arrowhead types, salmon spear prongs, shoe-shaped adze heads of walrus ivory, and others. Rainey presumes that the absence of these objects in the intermediate Old Bering Sea stage is fortuitous.

The culture designated as Ipiutak was discovered in 1939 at Point Hope and investigated in 1940 and 1941. The vast material from the many excavations of ancient dwellings and burials at the site of Ipiutak has not yet been published,[3] though it is already possible to gain some idea of this culture from preliminary reports (Rainey 1941 a, b, c; Stefansson 1944). Rainey considers the Ipiutak culture as preceding the types of Eskimo culture already known to us on the arctic coast. However, since it was not primitive and differed from typical Eskimo culture in a number of features, it is thought that its origin must lie somewhere in eastern Asia outside of the arctic area.

This culture is characterized, first of all, by quadrangular houses of very small size, in the construction of which neither stone nor whale bone, but only wood was used. Pottery is absent in the houses, but was found in accumulations of kitchen refuse and in graves of the Okvik culture. Most remarkable were burials where in the eye sockets were found artificial eyes of walrus ivory with pupils of agate, and the mouth was covered with a special mouth-cover, also of walrus ivory. In one instance, the nose was found to contain plugs in the form of bird-figures of walrus ivory. Objects found at Ipiutak are made of ivory, bone, antler, and stone, materials which are generally in wide use among the Eskimo, though tools of rubbed slate were absent. As for the nature of the objects, these belong on the whole to types common in Eskimo culture, with the exception of certain special types of arrowheads and dart heads, and a number of artifacts of carved ivory. Rainey considers the proportion of arrowheads to harpoon heads most notable in Ipiutak; this proportion is 500 to 50, i.e., the inverse of that usually observed in Eskimo collections. On the other hand, a number of objects characteristic of sea mammal hunters are absent. The predominance of arrowheads and the absence of many typical Eskimo tools designed for hunting along the coast lead Rainey to the conclusion that the occupants of Ipiutak were essentially an inland people, who hunted mainly land mammals and who traveled to the coast for seasonal sea mammal hunting.

After the discovery of Ipiutak culture, Rainey feels that it is obvious that there is no hope of finding a simple, primitive form of arctic culture attributable to the ancestors of the Eskimos. It is more probable, he writes, that Eskimo culture, as

[3]Eventually published in 1948—Editor.

we know it as a result of its adaptation to the arctic coast, is the culture of a people from more southern latitudes, probably to the west of Bering Strait in eastern Asia.

In his latest paper to reach us—"Eskimo archaeology and its bearing on the problem of man's antiquity in America"—Collins deals with two problems of interest to us: the Ipiutak culture and the resemblance between the Eskimo and the Meso-Neolithic and Paleolithic cultures of Europe (Collins 1943).

To Collins, the exact position of the Ipiutak culture among the other stages of the development of Eskimo culture in general remains undetermined. However, he presumes that the Ipiutak and Old Bering Sea cultures occupied the same area and were separated by a short interval of time. Rainey, as we saw, while recognizing the resemblance between Ipiutak and Old Bering Sea art, nevertheless sees Ipiutak as an independent pre-Eskimo culture. Collins argues against a number of Rainey's deductions in favor of this conclusion and notes that, on the contrary, a relatively recent age is suggested for the Ipiutak site by its topographic location and by a number of artifacts of walrus ivory, particularly the artificial eyes and the nose plugs from the burials. These testify to Chinese influence, perhaps no earlier than the Chou or Han dynasties.

The sporadic distribution throughout the Eskimo area of bone arrowheads and knives with stone side-blades and their abundance in Central Siberia and the Urals, in connection with the presence of similar implements with inset blades in Mesolithic sites of the Old World, reveal, in Collins' opinion, the ultimate origin of this type of Eskimo tool. Furthermore, basing himself on the findings by Okladnikov of Neolithic cultures in the Baykal area having bone implements equipped with stone side-blades (Okladnikov 1938), Collins concludes that it was precisely these cultures that were one of the primary sources from which Eskimo culture was derived.

In spite of the vast amount of foreign literature devoted to the Eskimo problem, of the existence of voluminous monographs on the ethnology of the American and Greenland Eskimo, and despite the numerous archaeological excavations, which have yielded many tens of thousands of objects, bourgeois scientists still have not solved the Eskimo problem. The origin and content of the Dorset culture, considered eastern Eskimo, are not clear. Neither the chronology nor the development of such stages of Eskimo culture as Birnirk, Ipiutak, or Okvik have been adequately clarified. The relations between the Punuk stage in the Bering Sea area and the synchronal Thule of Canada have not been elucidated. The territorially very restricted Old Bering Sea stage is in somewhat sharper focus, though even here a number of debatable points remain. Despite the abundance of factual material, the problems of the social structure and the development of Eskimo society and ideology through the various stages of their history remain not only unsolved, but unformulated by bourgeois scientists.

Here in Russia, except for the case of Jochelson, who sided with the theory of the American origin of the Eskimos, the dominant theory has been always that of their Asiatic origin. Scientific support for it was provided in the Soviet period.

Steller, in 1741, was the first to express an opinion on the Asiatic origin of the inhabitants of Kayak Island, which he visited. In the matter of the origin of the Eskimos, a similar position was held, as we have seen, by Veniaminov and Schrenk. On the basis of his investigations on Chukchi Peninsula, V. G. Bogoras (Bogoras 1904) pointed out that there were many reasons to conclude that in ancient times, long before the arrival of the Russians, the Asiatic Eskimos were more numerous and were distributed far to the west and south of their present habitat. Bogoras adduces toponymic evidence as proof of the widespread distribution of the Asiatic Eskimos in ancient times. He believed that the Asiatic Eskimos represent remnants of a very ancient people, as evidenced by the existence of three different dialects in a population numbering barely one thousand. However, he repeatedly stated his conviction (Bogoras 1904:226; 1925) that the Eskimos are not aboriginal to the Pacific coast, and supposed that the spread of·the Eskimos was from Eurasia to America, from west to east, and southward rather than northward along the Pacific coast.

Later (Bogoras 1936:249), basing himself on the view that fishing historically preceded the hunting of sea mammals, Bogoras wrote that

a series of fishing tribes on the northern Pacific coast formerly extended as a continuous arc from Asia to America, and included the Gilyak and Kamchadal in Asia, and a number of northwestern tribes in America: Haida, Tsimshian, Kwakiutl, Salish, and others. The Eskimo broke the continuity of this series, moved in from the north through Bering Strait, at a period which, though ancient, is relatively more recent than that of the first passage of human groups from Asia to America across the so-called Bering bridge.

This position was shared by A. M. Zolotarev (Zolotarev 1938b:13–14,23), who believed that pursuit of land game was not the major occupation of the ancient post-glacial population of northern Asia. This population spent the entire year on the broad coastal strip and on river flats. In the spring and autumn they hunted moose and reindeer at river crossings. They fished in open water, and through the ice in winter. Their dwellings were pit-houses, they used pottery, clothed themselves with fish, bird, and partly, reindeer skins, and were active dog-breeders. Their social organization, evidently, was matriarchal. This cultural stage involved totemism, sun worship and female clan shamanism. Such a culture was a necessary stage in the historical development of all northern tribes of Asia and America. The transition from the ancient culture of the "winter fishers" to that of the woodland hunters took place, apparently, not so long ago.

In the matter of the origin of the Eskimo, Zolotarev arrived at the following conclusions on the basis of all ethnological and archaeological data available at the time.

The most ancient proto-Eskimo culture is the Bering Sea culture, whose formal archaeological features are clear to us at the present time, though its socio-economic aspects are still obscure. This culture entered the area of Bering Strait from the west, in all probability, moving from west to east along the Arctic coast of Siberia. It retained a vigorous Paleolithic tradition in its art, and had not yet achieved a developed Neolithic level of material production (Zolotarev 1937:51–52).

This supposition finds support in the similarity of the Nenets [Samoyed] and Eskimo languages.

Turning to the data of physical anthropology, Zolotarev criticizes the view of Hrdlička that the western Eskimo has preserved the ancient Eskimo (brachycephalic) type, considerably modified among the central and Greenland Eskimo as a result of environmental adaptation to maritime arctic conditions. As a result, the long-headed Eskimo type would be a secondary and later phenomenon, while the broad-headed type would be the original proto-Eskimo form. This theory, as we know, allowed Hrdlička to relate the Eskimo to the Paleo-Asiatics and the Indians of western North America (Hrdlička 1930).

Zolotarev rightly points out that a number of skeletal finds in Alaska show that the Old Bering Sea culture was associated with a dolichocephalic type, which only later gave way to a brachycephalic population, and emphasizes that "the skulls of the ancient inhabitants of Alaska are unusually high-vaulted, narrow and long; they are highly reminiscent of crania from southern Greenland" (Jenness 1933).

On this basis, Zolotarev concludes:

the oldest and basically homogeneous Eskimo type is dolicho-cephalic, with a high keel-shaped cranium, and it evidently originated in Asia. In Alaska, it was supplanted in relatively late times by a round-headed type of tall stature, approximating the Paleo-Asiatic type. The recognition of the long-headed type as that of the most ancient Eskimo once again raises the problem of the connection of the Eskimo with the long-headed population of the Upper Paleolithic.—(Zolotarev 1937:53).

In his next article dedicated to ethnic relationships in northeast Asia, Zolotarev establishes three stages of economic and cultural development in northeast Asia:

The first stage is a sedentary culture of sea-mammal hunters. The second is that of a mixed economy, combining maritime hunting with reindeer herding on a small scale. The third stage is marked by the differentation of this combined economy into two distinct and (economically) specialized variants, mutually dependent by barter—the maritime hunting and the reindeer-breeding variants.

These three stages of economic development [he writes] provide us with a key to the understanding of the ethnic history of northeast Asia. Initially, northeast Asia (we are speaking here of the Chukchi and Koryak areas) was settled by sedentary coastal tribes. The culture of these tribes was of the ancient Eskimo type (Thule or Bering Sea). It spread at least from the Novosibirskiye [New Siberian] Islands to Bering Strait and further into America both along the Arctic and the Pacific shores, where its influence was felt far to the south. . . . The language of this ancient population was generally Eskimo-like, though divided into a large number of dialects. . . . The inception of reindeer herding put an end to this culture.—(Zolotarev 1938a:83–84).

Zolotarev supposes that the Koryak-Chukchi culture was formed on the basis of reindeer herding and that the Chukchi and Koryak are the descendents of the ancient Eskimos, who had become reindeer herders. In conclusion, he writes:

The original inhabitants of northeastern Asia and northwestern North America were Eskimo tribes of sea mammal hunters, living in the stage of the Thule or Bering Sea cultures. . . . The development of the reindeer herding economy caused the process of formation of the Chukchi-Koryak tribes, which pushed out and absorbed the Eskimo population. At the same time, the maritime Eskimo culture continued to exist and to develop in the Bering Strait region and thereby limited the spread of reindeer herding to the east. . . . Therefore, the Alaskan Eskimos are not a wedge, entering from the east to separate the Chukchi from the Indians, but the ancestors of ancient tribes which formerly lived on both sides of Bering Strait, whose culture developed on the basis of maritime hunting and separated, as a result, from the reindeer herding culture of the Chukchi-Koryak.

The homeland of the Eskimo is in Asia.

Over the last ten years, exceptionally productive archaeological work has been conducted in central and eastern Siberia by A. P. Okladnikov. The study of Paleolithic settlements and among them of one of the most remarkable Paleolithic sites in Russia, Buret, led him to consider the often raised problem of the connection between the ancient Paleolithic culture of Siberia (late Solutrean or early Magdalenian) and the Eskimo culture.

Excavations on the Angara River at Buret have shown that people contemporary with the mammoth and the rhinoceros lived in permanent settlements similar to those of the Eskimos. Their dwellings are amazingly similar, in shape and structure, to the winter houses of the Eskimos, with the only difference that mammoth and rhinoceros bones, rather than whale bones were used in their construction. Their clothing, like that of the Eskimo, was in the form of a tight-fitting one-piece suit with a hood (Okladnikov 1941b). Their art which consisted of engraving on bone and of sculpture, was similarly developed, with the only difference that mammoth ivory, rather than walrus ivory, was the raw material. Resemblances between the two cultures have been noted also in other features: in subsistence and household implements, in the economy and in religion (the cult of a female deity and sculptured female figures connected therewith).

Nevertheless, Okladnikov has arrived at the conclusion that here we are dealing with a case of convergence, in which similarity in basic traits is due to shared environmental conditions: (1) Abundant game, entailing a special mode of life for arctic hunters with permanent settlement at the most advantageous sites; (2) severe climatic conditions; and (3) the absence of wood for construction. As for the derivation of Eskimo culture itself, Okladnikov comes to the following conclusions in his report on the dwellings at Buret (Okladnikov 1941b:30–31).

In its origin, ancient Eskimo culture is connected not with the west, but with the southeast, and not with the Paleolithic, but with the Neolithic. It represents but the extreme northern link in a chain of Pacific coastal cultures, belonging to sedentary tribes whose main occupation was fishing combined with the hunting of sea mammals. The basic features of Eskimo culture have a wide distribution in the Pacific area. They are: (1) An economy involving the hunting of sea mammals and fishing; (2) corresponding specific implement forms including the toggled harpoon with socket and basal spurs, as well as distinctive slate points, unknown in Siberia and, generally, north of the Amur and of the Great Wall of China; (3) permanent villages in which the principal dwelling unit is the pit-house; (4) spiral or curvilinear ornamentation; (5) the cult of female ancestral deities and related totemic concepts of the wedding of the deity to a dog. These features are known since remote antiquity in Kamchatka, in the Amur area, in the Kurile and Japanese islands (the ancient Ainu culture), in southern China and, in part, even further south, as far as the Philippines and New Zealand.

In holding this view, the evidence for which was gathered through a study of Neolithic sites in the Far East, the Amur area, and the Japanese islands, Okladnikov has argued strongly against Zolotarev's view of the derivation of Eskimo culture from a special Neolithic culture of "winter fishermen" of inland Asia and America (Okladnikov 1935, 1939). Okladnikov does not believe that any such culture existed. On the contrary, the study of Neolithic sites in the Baykal region (Okladnikov 1938) led him to the conclusion that the Baykal Neolithic grew directly out of local Paleolithic culture,[4] and that in it hunting predominated for a long time over other means of subsistence (Okladnikov 1938, 1941). It is only toward the very end of the Neolithic that a shift took place in favor of the greater importance of fishing, and involved a number of important changes in the mode of life, in social structure, and in beliefs.

It is thus all the more important, in his estimation, that the Neolithic stage is marked by the development, in varying geographic environments, of a whole series of distinctive local cultures, each of which corresponds to a specific ethnic group of the Stone Age, with its own mode of life, characteristic beliefs, art, etc.

These groups were: (1) Plains hunters, later pastoralists, (2) hunters of Baykalia and Mongolia, (3) Uralian fishermen, (4) fishermen of the Amur and of the Far East, including Kamchatka, whose relationships were with the cultures

[4]A view that was since abandoned by Okladnikov—Editor.

of the Pacific islands and southeast Asia (including southern China, and Indochina). The latter were characterized by:

(a) Fishing, rather than hunting, as the principal occupation; (b) a sedentary existence, involving villages of settled fishermen, living in large pit-houses rather than in tents of light construction such as those of the Baykal hunters; (c) pottery with flat rather than pointed bottoms; (d) fundamentally different art: unexpectedly ornate curvilinear ornamentation, related to that of the Ainu and Maori, on the one hand, and that found at Neolithic sites in China (the Yang-shao culture) and in the Japanese islands (the Jomon culture), on the other.

It is this latter Pacific area in the broader sense that, as noted earlier, Okladnikov believes to be the homeland of Eskimo culture, the area from which it draws its most important features.

The investigations of Okladnikov in recent years in the valleys of the Lena and Kolyma rivers, to which we will yet have occasion to refer, allowed him to establish the existence, in the Neolithic and Bronze periods of northern Yakutia, of certain cultural ties with ancient Eskimo culture, in particular as regards shared pottery types and arrowheads.

Thus, the problem of connections between the ancient population of inland areas of northern Asia and that of the Chukchi Peninsula has been examined by Okladnikov on the basis of vast factual material. It is also he who was first to provide a survey of the history of the ancient Eskimos on the basis of a Marxist-Leninist understanding of the historical process with account of archaeological sites at that time known on the territory of the USSR (Okladnikov 1939; III–IV:513–526).

The publication of a portion of the archaeological collections gathered by Bettak and Borisov on the Chukchi Peninsula is to be credited to A. V. Machinski (Machinski 1941). As a result of an examination of these collections, he showed that Eskimo culture in the Old Bering Sea period was similar in nature and similarly developed in northeastern Siberia as on the coast of Alaska and on the islands in Bering Strait. However, he directed attention to the occurrence of nephrite objects in these collections and raised the problem of connections between Eskimo culture and the culture discovered by Soviet investigators at the mouth of the Ob River and on the Yamal Peninsula (Chernetsov 1935).

Our archaeological survey on the Chukchi Peninsula provided new material, in the light of which we shall return to the problem under discussion in the concluding section of this report.

ARCHAEOLOGICAL FINDS ON
THE ARCTIC COAST

The westernmost point along the shore of the Arctic Ocean where remains of ancient Eskimo houses have been found is Chetyrekhstolbovy Island [Four Pillar Island], in the Medvezhi [Bear Islands] group, opposite the mouth of the Kolyma. During the cruise of the ship "Maud" in the Laptev and East Siberian seas, Sverdrup (Sverdrup 1930:213) discovered six mounds with central depressions on Chetyrekhstolbovy Island: three on the northern side and three on the southern side of the island. Numerous sherds were found scattered around two of the southern mounds. On closer investigation, Sverdrup found several fragments of stone knives, two stone spear-like points, two walrus ivory harpoon heads, and numerous walrus bones. These harpoon heads, illustrated in one of Mathiassen's reports (Mathiassen 1927; 2:180, Fig. 12), have an open socket with a slot for the socket lashing, an asymmetric basal spur and one projecting barb with an opposing stone, inset side-blade. Harpoon heads of this type are characteristic of the ancient Eskimo culture stage of Birnirk, discovered near Point Barrow on the arctic coast of North America, and to some extent date the Eskimo settlements on the Medvezhi Islands.

Sverdrup saw similar remains of ancient Eskimo houses (in 1920) on Ayon Island (Sverdrup 1930:238). There he found sherds, two or three fragments of stone knives, and the bones of reindeer, seal, and birds. At that time, the ground on the island was frozen so that it was not possible to conduct excavations.

In 1946, the Arctic Institute in Leningrad received several objects from the polar station situated on the northwestern shore of Ayon Island. They were from an ancient settlement located 0.7 km east of the station. The objects included a large rubbed slate woman's knife (ulu), a bone spear or dart head, and pottery sherds. Judging from the pottery and the other objects, the village of Ayon Island yielding the objects is later in time than that on Chetyrekhstolbovy Island, and belongs apparently to the Thule phase of Eskimo culture.

Billings' companion Sarychev (Sarychev 1811:95–96) wrote of ancient dwellings on the north side of "Baranov Rock" (Cape Bolshoy Baranov). There he found (in 1787) collapsed earth houses at short distances from one another on the side of a stream. "They were built above ground and appeared round, about three *sazhens* [about 6 meters] in diameter. Upon digging the ground in the middle, seal and reindeer bones were found, along with many sherds from broken clay pots and two triangular stone knives in the form of a geometric sector, the arched side being sharpened, the other two sides straight and thick." It is clear that we are dealing here with typical Eskimo women's knives, found in ancient semi-subterranean houses.

In 1946, A. P. Okladnikov found the remains of ancient dwellings of Eskimo type in four small inlets to the west of the high point on Cape Bolshoy Baranov. The largest number of dwellings was found in the inlet where Sarychev had excavated. Of the five houses in this inlet, Okladnikov partially excavated two, as well as one dwelling in the neighboring inlet to the east. The collection from these excavations has not yet been analysed but, judging from the harpoon heads and other objects, the village at Cape Bolshoy Baranov, like the houses on Chetyrekhstolbovy Island, belongs to the Birnirk period of Eskimo culture.

One hundred years after Sarychev's account, Nordenskiöld's companions made limited excavations, in 1878, of an ancient settlement at Cape Severny [North Cape], now Cape Schmidt, or as its name was given to Nordenskiöld, Chukchi-Ikarpi, on the coast of the Arctic Ocean.

On the spit which joins Cape Ikarpi to the mainland we saw ruins which were the remains of dwellings that had belonged to the tribe of the Onkilon, who had lived formerly at that site and had been expelled several centuries ago by the Chukchi. Alqvist and Nordqvist excavated in the remains of these houses. The houses were built partially of whale bones and were half underground. Accumulations of refuse contained the bones of various genera of cetaceans, such as the white grampus, as well as the bones of seal, walrus, reindeer, bear, polar fox, dog and various birds. In addition to

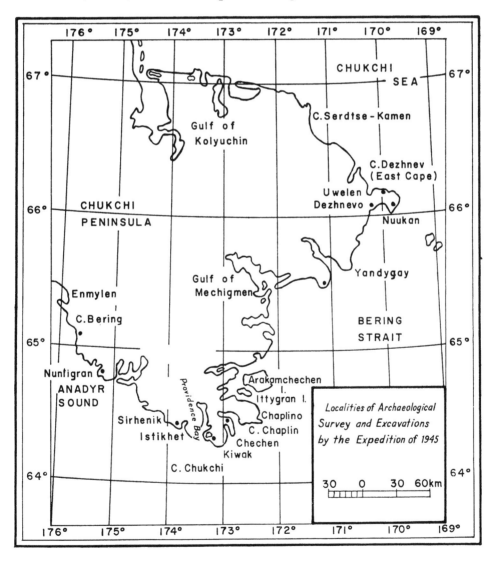

this evidence of hunting, objects of stone and bone were found. Notable among these were stone axes, secured to their hafts of wood and bone. Even the straps by which the axes were fastened to their handles were in a state of excellent preservation. Walrus ivory was, to these former inhabitants, as it is to the Chukchi today, a material out of which spear heads, arrows for bird-hunting, fish hooks, axes for cutting wood, etc., were manufactured, at times more effectively than out of flint. Cetacean bones likewise were used in great quantities. The remains of ancient houses were also found high above sea level on the gravels on Cape Ikarpi (Nordenskiöld 1882; 1:403–405).

A special plate in Nordenskiöld's report provides illustrations of a number of objects from the excavations at Cape Schmidt. Notable among them is a bone harpoon head of Mathiassen's Thule 2 type, a flat bone spoon of ovoid shape with a long handle, of a type characteristic of the ancient culture of the Central Eskimo, a stone adze in a bone haft, women's knives of argillaceous slate, and a large stone spear point. Althogether, the complex from Cape Schmidt appears typical of the Thule culture, as we think of it from the excavations of Mathiassen in Canada (Mathiassen 1927).

Nelson, who visited the arctic coast of northeastern Asia, reported on ancient sites discovered by him near Cape Vankarem, which he described as pertaining to the Eskimo (Nelson 1899:265–266). According to his description, the remains of the ancient houses had the appearance of mounds with a central depression and a trench (corridor entryway), oriented seaward and indicating the position of the entrance. Numerous whale ribs and jawbones were scattered about in the vicinity, and the eroding end of a whale jaw projecting above the top of one of the mounds indicated the material used in building these houses. Nelson made no excavations, and a number of considerations which he brings to bear on the relative age of the village at Cape Vankarem are based on the topography of the ancient houses.

These archaeological data, though very modest, are evidence of the fact that an ancient maritime population once extended from Cape Vankarem in the east along the arctic shore of Asia westward beyond Capes Schmidt and Shelagski, Ayon Island, Cape Bolshoy Baranov, to the Medvezhi Islands. The cultural remains, it is true, are thus far exceedingly few, but indicate that this part of the arctic coast was settled as early as the Birnirk stage of the development of Eskimo culture, though most of the finds apparently belong to the later Thule stage.

DESCRIPTIVE PART

The Ancient Settlement at Uwelen

EVEN BEFORE our arrival in the Eskimo-Chukchi village of Uwelen (Eskimo Ulak, Chukchi Uwelen) on the Chukchi Sea coast, we had heard that local Eskimos and Chukchis already had been excavating systematically for several years the site of an ancient settlement, not far from the modern village. There they obtain ancient walrus ivory (that has been underground for a long time), highly prized in America, and trade it through the intermediary of American Eskimos who visit our coast on the Chukchi Peninsula. And, indeed, upon arriving in Uwelen, in addition to the ruins of ancient semi-subterranean houses ("nynglu" in Eskimo) among the buildings of the present-day inhabitants of the coastal spit, we discovered also the site of an ancient settlement. It was found to be located relatively high, southeast of the modern village, on the eastern margin of the lagoon. There, on the slope of a hill rising from the lagoon, a large area had been dug over, though not continuously, but in isolated sections separated by undisturbed areas (Fig. 1). At three points we uncovered a cultural deposit over a total area of about 10 sq m in areas which had not been dug over and which were covered with a thin layer of sod. It was found that the cultural deposit here was not thick, measuring 0.4 to 0.6 m in depth, though it contained numerous objects of bone and stone in addition to the bones of walrus, ringed seal, bear, and reindeer.

The slope of the hill covered by the cultural deposit is rather steep and therefore is not likely to have been convenient as a permanent dwelling place, though we do know of a number of Eskimo villages in similar topographic settings, such as, for example, Nuukan near Cape Dezhnev and the old Eskimo village in the north of Ratmanov Island (Big Diomede). No evidence was discovered of houses, either subterranean or semi-subterranean, in the area described, nor were there any indications of meat storage pits. Also unusual is the location of an Eskimo village not on the sea shore but on the shore of a lagoon, separated from the sea by a bar several kilometers in length. However, it is quite possible, particularly if we consider the uninterrupted epeirogenic rise of the arctic coast of the Chukchi Peninsula, that the lagoon was not cut off from the sea in ancient times by a gravel bar, at least not in its eastern part, and that the ancient village was then on the sea shore. In this connection, we may note that the rather wide spit on which the village is situated today is markedly lower in its eastern portion where it joins on to the high rocky mainland.

SEA-MAMMAL HUNTING EQUIPMENT

We will begin our description of the objects found at the ancient site of Uwelen in the course of excavations and in part, acquired and forwarded to us by V. M. Leontyev (12 objects out of a total of 168) with the harpoons and, in first place, the toggling harpoon heads, inasmuch as these constitute the most typical and, to some degree, a temporally diagnostic trait of Eskimo culture.

A toggling harpoon head is complex (Fig. 2), and the following features are

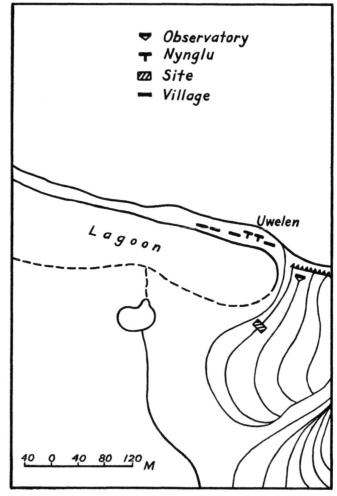

Observatory
Nynglu
Site
Village

Uwelen

Lagoon

40 0 40 80 120 M

FIGURE 1

usually considered: the socket, the slots or grooves for the lashing which covers an open socket and holds in place the shaft inserted into it, the spur, the line hole, the presence or absence of barbs or stone inset [side-] blades, and the presence or absence of a stone end-blade in a corresponding slit. In addition to being structurally complex, toggling harpoon heads vary in the material out of which they are made (walrus ivory, reindeer antler, bone) in the size, form, and proportions of their component parts, in the combination of the component parts, in technique of manufacture, and in decoration. All these features allow the establishment of types and their recognition in cultural complexes.

Harpoon Heads

In describing harpoon heads, we will first indicate their structural features, and then give their secondary characteristics. The first include: (1) closed or open socket at the lower end of the head, to hold the end of the foreshaft; (2) in the case of an open socket, slots or other features for the socket lashing to secure the shaft in the socket; (3) taper of lower end or spurs; (4) central opening in harpoon head or line hole, used to fasten the head to the line; (5) presence or absence of lateral barbs or inset stone blades (side-blades); (6) presence or absence of slit at forward end for insertion of end-blade.

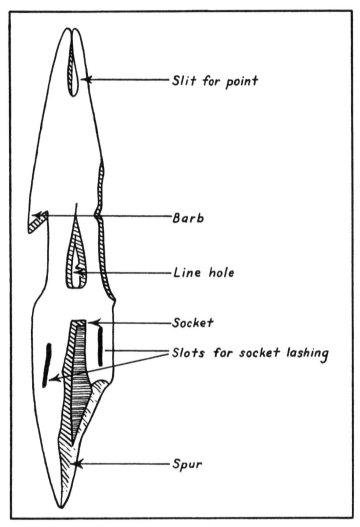

FIGURE 2

Secondary characteristics include the material, the proportion and shape of various portions of the head, technique, and other traits of diagnostic value, as well as decoration.

The harpoon head represented in Plate 1, no. 1, has a broad but flattened socket for the foreshaft end; there is one slot and an opposing groove for the socket lashing; the basal spur is broken off; the line hole is round, drilled conically, with a shallow groove on one side only; the grooves for stone blades are short and deep, in the same plane as the line hole and situated directly above the hole; the anterior pointed end is four-sided, rhombic in section; the deep groove for the socket lashing is grooved lengthwise to secure more firmly the lashing of baleen fiber. The harpoon head described is made of reindeer antler, and has acquired the hue of burnt coffee as a result of remaining in the ground a long time. The decoration consists of diagonal deeply incised lines.

Another similar harpoon head (Plate 1:2) differs from the one described only in being considerably smaller, in being light brown in color, and bearing somewhat different decoration.

While these two harpoon heads do not retain their lower portions or spurs, a third one (Plate 1:3) is broken in its forward portion but the lower half is in good condition. This head has a broad, open socket, two slots for the socket lashing, close to one another on the side opposite the socket, a round line hole, and a triple, asymmetric basal spur. The material is antler, and the decoration consists of simple deeply incised lines.

In view of their distinctive characteristics, these harpoon heads may be assigned to the Birnirk type, so typical of that ancient Eskimo site, also on the arctic coast, near Point Barrow. Similar harpoon heads have been published by Collins (Collins 1935, Plate 11:7) from Point Barrow and by Jenness from Little Diomede (Jenness 1928a, Plate 12:d).

Exceptional interest attaches to a series of harpoon heads which are typical only of the ancient site of Uwelen in their shape and decoration. All these harpoon heads have broad and shallow open sockets for the foreshaft with one slot for the socket lashing and one opposing groove; the line hole is drilled conically or biconically; one or two deep grooves are present for stone side-blades, or else a slit is provided for an end-blade; the asymmetric spur is often highly complex, though sometimes simple; typical decoration consists of deeply incised lines, sometimes a schematic representation of the beluga, and at times the basal spur is shaped to resemble the head of an animal (Plate 1:7).

The harpoon head shown in Plate 1:4 is one of the best specimens of the Uwelen series. The socket is open and broad, there is one slot and an opposing groove for the socket lashing, the line hole is round, the spur is asymmetric and multiple. Unlike other similar harpoon heads, there is only one groove for a stone side-blade, an it is deep and situated in the plane of the line hole. The material is walrus ivory. Apart from deeply incised lines, interesting features of the decoration are graphic representations of two figures, probably beluga, an arched line with a number of spurs, and a shaping of the spur to make it appear as an animal head in profile.

The harpoon head shown in Plate 1:5 is complex and unusual in design. It differs from the preceding in the presence of two lateral grooves for side-blades in the plane of the line hole and, in addition, an end-blade at right angles to the line hole. The shape of the spur, like the decorative motifs, are the same as those of the harpoon head illustrated in Plate 1:4. The material is reindeer antler.

Plate 1:6 represents a harpoon head with an open socket, one slot and an opposing groove for the lashing. The line hole is round, the spur is asymmetric and highly complex, and the slit for the end-blade is in the plane of the line hole. The shape of the harpoon head in cross-section is ellipsoid with a slight median constriction. The material is reindeer antler. Deeply incised lines provide the decoration. The collection includes another similar harpoon head (Plate 1:7), but with a simpler spur, with a profile resembling the head of an animal, and with somewhat different decorative motifs.

All the harpoon heads described above are relatively small in size, from 7 to 9 cm in length, and were probably intended for seal hunting.

The harpoon head shown in Plate 1:8 is considerably larger, about 12 cm in length, and was probably intended for walrus. It does not differ from the preceding in type: it also has an open socket, a round line hole, a multiple asymmetric spur, and a slit for the end-blade in the plane of the line hole. The material is reindeer antler. A distinctive detail of the ornamentation of this harpoon head is a triangular decorative incision above the line hole and one below the socket lashing.

A very interesting series of harpoon heads differs from the preceding in the simple design of the asymmetric spur. Of six such heads, made of walrus ivory, three are illustrated. The first (Plate 1:9) is characterized by a narrow open socket, the presence of grooves below the round line hole, a simple spur flaring outward, in shape resembling the head of an animal. The slit for the end-blade is in the plane of the line hole. A distinctive characteristic of the decoration, as in the second harpoon head in this series (Plate 1:10) is the presence, in addition to deeply incised diagonal lines, of deeply indented broad notches above the line hole, i.e., between it and the end-blade slit, on the specimen represented in Plate 1:9, or else nearly at the forward end of the head, as in the specimen shown in Plate 1:10. The slot for the end-blade is in a plane perpendicular to that of the line hole. The third harpoon head in this series (Plate 1:11) differs in being smaller in size and bearing more simple decoration.

In the type under examination must also be included a very large specimen (18 cm long) of walrus ivory, probably a whaling harpoon head (Plate 1:13). Here too the socket is open, and there is a slot and an opposing groove for the socket lashing. The biconically drilled line hole is round, the spur is simple and bent outward, and the slit for the end-blade is in the plane of the line hole. Of particular interest is the decoration by means of zigzag-like incised lines in a style which, as we shall see, is highly typical of the Uwelen site and unknown from any other region occupied by the Eskimo.

This, the most numerous group of harpoon heads from the ancient Eskimo site on the hill slope at Uwelen, has relatively close analogies among harpoon heads of the Birnirk type (Collins 1935, Plate 11:5) but, above all, with some of the harpoon heads from the Okvik site on one of the Punuk Islands. The harpoon heads published by Rainey from that site (Rainey 1941d, Fig. 5, items 2–5, 7–9; Fig. 7, items 3, 5–7) without doubt belong to the type described. The resemblance between the Uwelen and Okvik harpoon heads is not only of type, but also extends to details of decorative style.

The harpoon head in Plate 1:12 (purchased) was found, according to statements by Eskimos, at the ancient site. The socket is open and narrows slightly at the top; there is one groove for the lashing, but it is on the flat face opposite the socket, rather than to the side, and has lateral grooves; there is a short and pointed basal spur, and another rudimentary one; the line hole is round, conically drilled, but is situated not at the center of the harpoon head, as is usually the case, but asymmetrically, on the side opposite that of the basal spur; neither stone side-blades nor a slit for an end-blade are present; where slots for side blades might be expected, there are some notches that are purely decorative in nature. The harpoon head is flattened and shaped like a laurel leaf. The material is ivory, strongly patinated from having been on the surface of the ground for a long time. This aberrant harpoon head of unusual design may be considered as derivative from the Birnirk type.

Somewhat special status must be assigned also to a harpoon head (Plate 4:16) of walrus ivory, whose front end is broken off. It has a broad open socket, one slot and a groove for the socket lashing. The line hole is round, and a double asymmetric spur is present. The slit for the end-blade is in the plane of the line hole. This short harpoon head comes close to the Birnirk type, but its style of decoration by means of thin scratched lines is Old Bering Sea. Similar decoration is known from harpoon heads from the Okvik site (Rainey 1941d, Fig. 6, item 9).

The harpoon heads with *closed sockets* are all of walrus ivory and belong to three distinct types. The first of these (Plate 1:14) has a closed socket which is conically drilled in the base of the head, and a biconically drilled round line hole. The triple basal spur is asymmetric, and is of Bering Sea type, with a long median spur and two blunted lateral ones, at the bases of which a pair of additional small spurs occurs. Of particular interest is the presence in the extreme forward portion of deep grooves for stone side-blades. It would have been enough to cut through the tip of the harpoon head some 6–7 mm more to obtain the usual end-blade slit instead of slots for side-blades. The decoration consists of simple incised straight lines. Typologically, this harpoon head is similar to some published by Collins from Little Diomede (Collins 1937, Plate 27:5,6).

The harpoon heads represented on Plate 1:15,16 have a closed socket, a round hole, and grooves below the hole on both sides of the head. The basal spur is simple, and the slit for the end-blade is, in one case, in the plane of the line hole and, in the other, at right angles to it. Their cross-section is ellipsoidal. Decoration is by means of deeply incised lines. They differ from the harpoon heads illustrated in Plate 1:9,10 only in the design of the socket for the foreshaft.

Of interest are some unfinished harpoon heads which give an idea of the technique of manufacture of these weapons. One walrus ivory blank (Plate 1:17) was intended for a harpoon head of the type represented in Plate 1:1. By successive cuts with a stone blade, the blank has been given a hexagonal form in its lower portion and a quadrangular form (rhombic in section) in its upper part. The lower part has been shaped in preparation for a multiple spur. The conically-drilled line hole has been made before cutting out the socket and shaping other parts of this complex device.

Another blank is more finished in form (Plate 1:20), and is also of walrus ivory. It is intended for a harpoon head of the type represented in Plate 1:9. The harpoon head has already been shaped, and the details of its form are all blocked out. There remains only to hollow out the socket, to cut a groove for the socket lashing, to drill the line hole, to cut the slit for the end-blade, and to apply the decoration, whose general features have been already indicated.

A blank for a large, perhaps a whaling harpoon, is shown in Plate 1:24. The line hole has been drilled already and we have indications of the open socket and of the position of the slots for stone side-blades.

Only one *foreshaft* for holding the harpoon head was found at the ancient village of Uwelen (Plate 1:21). This foreshaft is of ivory, rather long (12.2 cm), quadrangular, flattened with rounded corners in cross-section. The butt end, which fits into the foreshaft receiver, has the form of a truncated cone. The fore end, which fitted into the socket of the harpoon head, is flat and chisel-shaped, and specially designed for a shallow open socket. In its lower third, close to the butt end, a narrow triangular hole has been cut to receive the line, and it has two lightly marked grooves, directed downward.

No bone or ivory *foreshaft receivers* were found at the Uwelen site. As we shall see later, these are not often found in excavating Eskimo sites. In part, this may be explained by the fact that the foreshaft, bearing the harpoon head, was often set directly into the wooden shaft. Also, damaged foreshaft receivers were often re-worked into other artifacts.

We have six specimens of harpoon *ice picks*. They are all made from distal ends of tusks of young walrus, and are moderate in size (their average length is about 10 cm). They are ellipsoidal in cross-section. The upper part of the pick, the tang, which fits into the lower end of the harpoon shaft, is relatively long, and bears deep transverse cuts, made with a stone adze, for more secure attachment to the shaft. Plate 1:22,23 shows two typical ice picks from the ancient site of Uwelen, with beveled and blunted points. In type, the Uwelen ice picks are closest of all to the Old Bering Sea and Birnirk specimens, as well as those which Rainey considers Okvik.

Plugs for sealskin floats, made of wood or walrus ivory, were used by the ancient and modern Eskimos alike to plug holes (natural orifices or wound rents) in sealskins used for harpoon floats. A plug of this type, made of walrus ivory, from the ancient site of Uwelen is shown in Plate 1:18. It is oval in shape (2.8 by 4.2 cm, 1.5 cm thick), with a broad and deep groove. Similar plugs are known from the Okvik site and from St. Lawrence Island, where they occur in the artifactual assemblage of the Old Bering Sea stage of Eskimo culture.

Float bars. To secure the line to the sealskin harpoon float, the Eskimos of the Bering Sea coast attach a special bar at one end of the float. One such float bar of walrus ivory from the Uwelen site is illustrated in Plate 1:19. It is a small shank, oval in cross-section, with knobs and deep grooves at either end which prevent the loop of the line from sliding off the bar. The entire surface of the bar between the knobs is covered with deep cuts whose purpose is similar, that of providing a more secure hold. As a result of remaining for a long time in a refuse deposit, the bar has acquired a dark brown color.

LAND HUNTING EQUIPMENT

No remains of bows or wrist guards used in shooting with the bow were found at the ancient site of Uwelen. However, many arrowheads of bone and reindeer antler did occur.

The first *Uwelen arrowhead type,* represented only by three specimens, is shown in Table 2:1. It is long (13.7 cm) and thin (0.7 cm in diameter), round in cross-section, with a sharpened tang, rhombic in cross-section, and a blunted point.

A frequent (15 specimens were found) and apparently major type was one of simple arrowheads of round cross-section, slit at the fore end for the insertion of an end-blade. Two variants of this type may be distinguished: one with a conically beveled tang, which was inserted into the shaft, and another with a split, forked tang.

The first variant of this type, represented in Plate 2:2,3,4,5, varies considerably in size, from very long (18.3 cm) and thin (0.8 cm in diameter) arrowheads to short (8.9 cm) and thick (0.9 to 1.4 cm) ones, flattened in cross-section. All arrowheads of this variant are thicker in the upper than in the lower half.

Arrowheads of the second, more common variant of this type (Plate 2:6,7,8) differ less from each other in size. In length, they vary from 9.6 to 12 cm and their maximum transverse diameter ranges from 0.8 to 1.2 cm. The split in the butt end of the arrowhead is in the same plane as the end-blade slit. The depth of the end-blade slit is rather constant and varies between 2.0 to 2.6 cm. While the deepest point of the upper slit, designed to receive the base of the end-blade, is rectilinear, the lower slot, into which the shaft must fit, is so designed that the shaft end must be forked. In view of the considerable length of the lower slot, this, probably together with the use of outside lashing, resulted in a very firm connection between the arrowhead and the shaft. As in the first variant, the diameter of arrowheads of the second variant is greater in the upper than in the lower half.

Decoration by means of deeply incised longitudinal lines is typical for arrow-heads of this type, though in somewhat lesser degree than for harpoon heads. Of particular interest is the combination of incised linear decoration with spiral surfaces in the manner of screw threads on one arrowhead (Plate 2:9) and one harpoon head (Plate 1:1).

We are not aware of arrowheads of the Uwelen types just described in any Eskimo collection, either from the Bering Sea or Alaskan areas, or from the Central Eskimo or Greenland areas. Apparently these are specifically Asiatic types, whose analogies are found to the west only in late Neolithic and early Bronze Age burials of the Middle Lena and, to the south, on the Kamchatka Peninsula and in the Kurile Islands.

A third arrowhead type from the ancient site of Uwelen is made of ivory, has a blunt tip and cylindrically-drilled socket in its base to receive the arrowshaft (Plate 2:10). Unlike the simple acorn-shaped and egg-shaped blunt bird-points which become widely distributed among the Eskimos beginning with the Thule-Punuk stage of their cultural development, this arrowhead is trilobate in form. Apparently, we are dealing here with a relatively ancient type of arrowhead, known both from the Okvik site and in the Old Bering Sea complex of St. Lawrence Island.

In addition to bird-points, the ancient inhabitants of Uwelen also made use of *darts* with one central and several side-prongs, secured to the lower third of the dart shaft, similar to those in use among the Bering Sea Eskimos until recently. Unfortunately, only a few whole prongs of such darts were found.

A small center-prong for a dart or fish spear (Plate 2:11), made of bone, is round in cross-section and bears two asymmetric barbs. The point is blunted, and the tang is sharpened.

Center-prongs of bird darts, all of them damaged, are made of walrus ivory. One of them is oval in cross-section (Plate 2:12), the others are triangular (Plate 2:13). Their lateral barbs are arranged asymmetrically The fragment of the center-prong shown in Plate 2:15 gives an idea of the form of the tip of such a prong.

The surface decoration of the prong shown in Plate 2:13 is worthy of note, and consists of a pattern of deeply incised longitudinal lines entirely similar to that seen on harpoon heads, for example the specimens in Plate 1:9,10.

Points which we consider to be side-prongs for bird darts (Plate 2:16,17) differ from center-prongs in all of them being made of bone and, technically they are of simpler design. It is possible that some of them, particularly no. 17 in Plate 2, served as fish spear prongs.

The complete prong shown in Plate 2:17, as is consistent with side-prongs, is flattened and somewhat bent, and has three unilateral barbs. The prong shown in Plate 2:16 (the point is broken off) apparently also had three unilateral barbs. The base of this prong has a special notch for securing it to the lower third of the dart shaft.

The prong represented in Plate 2:18 shows the same typical, frequently noted Uwelen decoration by means of deeply incised lines.

Comparing center- and side-prongs of bird darts from the Uwelen site (Plate 2:12,13,18) with similar artifacts from other ancient Eskimo sites, we find our closest analogies again in Okvik and Old Bering Sea materials from St. Lawrence Island.

We deal with *snow goggles* after hunting weapons inasmuch as they are connected with spring hunting. The Uwelen site yielded only one specimen of such goggles, and a damaged one at that (Plate 2:14). They are of the usual form among the Eskimos, with thin eye slits and slots for attachment. The decoration on the outer surface of these goggles is of interest: deeply incised lines are made to form circles or lozenges of irregular form with dots in their centers, as well as crow's feet, a widespread element in Eskimo decoration. In form and style of decoration, these goggles are closest to those found in the excavations of Ipiutak at Point Hope on the arctic coast of America.

FISHING GEAR

First, we must note a small *harpoon head* of the type commonly used by the Eskimos in fishing for salmon (Plate 2:19). The socket is closed, the line hole is round with a groove directed downward, the basal spur is simple and the slit for the end-blade is in the plane of the line hole. It is decorated in Uwelen style with deeply incised transverse and diagonal lines.

Among other fishing implements, a *spear side-prong* of very large size (about 26 cm in length), made of reindeer antler, deserves mention. The point of this prong is sharp (Plate 2:26). The lateral barb near the point is turned inward. The butt end, which joins the shaft, is flattened, and bears three deep notches on the opposite, outer side to allow secure lashing to the shaft.

Of particular interest are some *barbs* of compound salmon spears, found at the ancient site of Uwelen, which belong to a type rarely found at ancient Eskimo sites. A distinctive feature of Uwelen barbs (Plate 2:20,21) is the fact that the longitudinal slot for lashing the barb to the shaft is disproportionately long as compared with the barb tip. While both are identical in form, one of the barbs is of bone (Plate 2:20), the other is of walrus ivory (Plate 2:21). Similar compound salmon spears were known both in ancient times and in the later stages of Eskimo culture almost throughout the entire area populated by Eskimos, including Greenland. However, barbs of Uwelen type such as we illustrate are known only from the Okvik site in the Punuk Islands and, as we shall see later, from the south of the Chukchi Peninsula.

In fishing, the ancient inhabitants of Uwelen probably made use of *compound fishhooks*. Plate 2:24 illustrates the barb of such a compound fishhook. The upper end of the barb is carefully sharpened, while the lower end, which is flattened, has numerous notches cut into it for lashing to the fishhook shank.

Several massive fish line *sinkers* were found at the site. They are all made of walrus ivory. The sinker shown in Plate 2:27 is oval in cross-section and narrower at the upper and lower ends. Line perforations at the ends of the sinkers are drilled in different planes, at right angles to each other.

In addition to the larger sinkers, there are two miniature specimens (3 and 3.6 cm) of bone, which are so small that there is doubt whether they were used as fish line sinkers or as some kind of pendant. One of them (Plate 2:23) is elongate and oval in cross-section, the other (Plate 2:22) is shorter, and bears characteristic Uwelen decoration by means of deep incised lines. In both, the line holes are in the same plane.

A one-piece hook of bone (Plate 2:25) is round in cross-section and flattened at its upper end, where an elongate perforation has been cut. It is possible that it was used in fishing, since similar hooks are described as fishhooks from the Okvik site in the Punuk Islands.

VARIOUS TOOLS AND UTENSILS

Picks and mattocks. Numerous massive picks or mattocks for excavating soil, made of large walrus tusks, have been found at the ancient site of Uwelen.

It is with good reason that the local inhabitants dig over this site to obtain precisely such artifacts of ivory. The largest of these tools (Plate 2:30) is 37 cm in length and 7 cm across, and is made of a walrus tusk which has hardly been worked, bearing only four adzed circular grooves in its upper portion for hafting the mattock to a handle. The inner surface of this implement bears deep transverse cuts in its upper portion adjacent to the handle, to ensure better lashing.

Mattocks of smaller size (about 32 cm in length, 6 cm in width), of which one is illustrated in Plate 2:29, differ from the specimen described above in having a single, broad, circular groove. Finally, there are several quite short picks or mattocks (about 16 cm in length), with greatly worn working ends, one of which is represented in Plate 2:28. The inner surface, facing the handle, is flat, while the outer surface is convex, with a broad groove cut in its upper end with a stone adze.

All these walrus ivory tools, as stated earlier, were used to excavate frozen, often gravelly and rocky ground, in house building and in chopping ice. This is the reason for the pronounced wear of the working ends of all of them, without exception. In type, these tools have much in common with similar ones from the Okvik site and from the Old Bering Sea layers in the excavations on St. Lawrence Island.

Ice staff ferrules. Two interesting objects of walrus ivory are illustrated in Plate 3:1,2. We know of no analogies to them either in archaeological or in ethnographic collections from the Eskimo. Without doubt, they served as tips for some kind of tool, judging from their forked upper ends, into which was fittted the wedge-like beveled end of a shaft. These tips were fastened securely to the shaft by means of holes drilled in their upper portions. The lower thickened portion was cut in the shape of a blunt wedge. It is quite blunt, worn, and bears evidence of strong blows. Both of these tips were no longer in use, inasmuch as large pieces, are broken off, precisely in their lower portions. The purpose of these objects is evident from Nelson's description of the ice staffs of the western Eskimos. Nelson writes (Nelson 1899:214–215, Fig. 67) that hunting or traveling on sea ice always involves the risk of falling through wherever thin ice is concealed under snow. To protect themselves from this danger the Eskimos customarily carry with them, in certain seasons, a strong wooden staff with a solid walrus ivory ferrule mounted on the end of the staff and lashed to it by strong sinews.

Several specimens of walrus ivory *wedges* were found at the site, and range from relatively large (Plate 3:7) to quite small (Plate 3:6). They were usually made from the distal ends of walrus tusks, though some made from the central portion occur. To give them the required shape, the working end was carefully pared with a stone adze, and then polished at the very tip. The poll ends of all the wedges that have been in use are smooth and rounded and bear star-shaped scars from blows by a stone hammer. Walrus ivory wedges could also be used, naturally, for splitting logs, though this was not their principal function. Bone, antler, and walrus ivory were widely used by the Eskimos for a variety of objects.

In rare instances, a bone and especially a walrus tusk would be sawed through into separate pieces or plates. Usually, however, bone or ivory would be cut into with a stone adze and then broken or, more often, partly sawed through from one or two sides and then split in two with the aid of a walrus ivory wedge.

Bone adze heads. We found no stone adzes in our excavations at the site, though we did find two adze heads for such adzes, one of them of antler (Plate 3:8), the other of whale bone (Plate 3:9). They both belong to the same type of flattened pentagonal adze heads, with the lower edge being the wider one, into which a socket has been cut for the adze, and a relatively narrow gabled upper edge. Square orifices, in one case narrow (Plate 3:8), in the other, broad (Plate 3:9), have been cut closer to the upper edge to receive the handle. The adze head in Plate 3:8 has a small round aperture on one side, perhaps to allow the removal of the remains of a broken adze blade from the head.

Bone drills. Of the implements that can be considered drills, we illustrate two bone specimens (Plate 3:3,4). One of them is in the form of a cylinder wider at the top (Plate 3:3), expanding in the upper third, the other (Plate 3:4) is flattened and has a conical wedge-like sharpened bit. Both of these points were used as drills, hafted to a wooden shaft, as is clearly evident from a close examination of their bits.

Drill rest. In drilling and making fire with a drill, it is essential to use a special rest for the upper end of the drill shaft or stick used in fire-drilling. One such rest from the Uwelen site is shown in Plate 3:14. It is made of a slab of whale bone. It is last-shaped and bears deep cuts at one end for suspension. One of the sides of the drill rest is completely smooth, while the other has a deep pit in the middle to receive the drill shaft. The presence of this type of drill rest is evidence that the ancient inhabitants of Uwelen used a bow-drill for drilling holes and making fire, since they had to use one hand to hold the drill rest.

In making fire by drilling, the inhabitants of the Uwelen site made use of rather long, round wooden sticks, several examples of which were found with charred lower ends.

Awls and reamers were found in considerable numbers and, with few exceptions, they are all of walrus ivory. Plate 3:5,11 illustrate two awls. One of them (Plate 3:11) is made of bone and was apparently, a multi-purpose tool, inasmuch as the blunt end opposite the point is cut and shaped in the form of a spatula.

The function of a reamer is to dilate or to smooth the rim of a perforation in leather, wood, and sometimes bone. Its working edge is near-cylindrical in form. Plate 3:10 illustrates an example of such a reamer.

Knives and knife-handles. The Uwelen site yielded one miniature knife made of a thin plate of walrus ivory with two well-sharpened cutting edges (Plate 3:12). Only a handle fragment remains of another small bone knife (Plate 3:13). No women's knives of polished slate (ulu), so common at Eskimo sites, were found. Even if the absence of women's knives in our collection from the ancient site of Uwelen is attributed to chance, the relatively slight use of knives of argillaceous slate by the inhabitants of the site is still worthy of note. Indeed, we have only one man's knife blade of argillaceous slate from this site (Plate 3:15). It is of the usual leaf-shaped outline and has a rather long tang. In relation to its total length of 5.9 cm, this blade is rather thick (0.5 cm), and is polished in such a manner that, when the cutting edges are sharp, a short crest is formed on both faces of the fore end.

A second man's knife blade is made of silicified tuff (Plate 3:16), is rhombic in shape, and is only partly polished.

Of particular interest are some long and narrow knives which are inserted in handles as side-blades and which are typical of the Uwelen site while being absent, to our knowledge, from other ancient Eskimo sites.

An excellent example of such a knife is shown in Plate 3:17. The long blade of argillaceous slate is set in an elaborately shaped handle of walrus ivory. The handle is decorated on both sides with pairs of oblique, deeply incised lines, which alternate with scratched broken lines. The blade of a similar knife without the handle is shown in Plate 3:21. This blade is of agrillaceous slate and has been pressure-flaked over its entire surface, particular care being lavished on retouching the convex cutting edge. Another similar flint blade with a straight cutting edge is shown in Plate 3:22. Knives of this type were in wide use among the inhabitants of Uwelen, as may be concluded from the numerous handles of such knives found at the site. Plate 3:18,19,20 illustrate three short handles of walrus ivory, belonging to knives similar to that reproduced in Plate 3:17. They are all decorated in the distinctive Uwelen style by means of patterns of deeply incised and thin double and broken lines intersecting one another at acute angles.

In addition to the short knives, long knives were also in use, as may be seen from their handles (Plate 3:23,24). The walrus ivory knife-handle shown in Plate 3:23 bears two deep slots or sockets for two stone blades. An antler handle (Plate 3:24) has one continuous deep slot for the knife-blade. These last two handles are even more elaborately decorated in the same style by means of deeply incised lines meeting at acute angles or double lines separated by broken spurred lines or commas.

However, more simple handles for such long knife side-blades were also in use, as illustrated in Plate 3:22. These were either simple bone handles of the type shown in Plate 3:25, or wooden handles, of the kind shown in Plate 4:1. This latter specimen is a large (26 cm long) handle of oval cross-section with a long (about 13 cm) lateral slot for a stone blade.

In addition to those already described, long and narrow double-edged knives were used at Uwelen. These had continuous rows of stone side-blades. We gain an idea of these knives from their handles, one of which is nearly intact (Plate 4:2), while the other two (Plate 3:26,27) have only the grip and part of the rib preserved. Knives of this type had no less than three pairs of stone side-blades, and the end of the handle was perforated with a hole for a loop or for suspension. Deep longitudinal cuts were made in the flat surfaces on both sides. In some cases, the handles of these knives were also decorated in the familiar Uwelen style.

The types of knives with side-blades just described are not known in the cultural assemblages of other ancient Eskimo sites. While such types could have been inferred from isolated chance findings from the Okvik site in the Punuk Islands, from Point Hope, and Southampton Island in Hudson Bay, they have not been found heretofore as series within a specific complex of implements.

The next, rather numerous type of bone knife-handle, well known also from St. Lawrence Island and from ancient sites of the Central Eskimo, consists of two halves which are lashed together. Of the five handles of this type found, four are of walrus ivory and one is of antler. Plate 4:3,4,5 illustrate three of them. The ends of these handles have a short (1.2–1.6 cm) and narrow (2–4 mm) slot into which a small blade was set. To hold the lashing of the two halves of such handles in place, the forward end of the handle always has a more or less pronounced projection and a circular groove. From a technological point of view, these handles are of interest inasmuch as they provide a clear idea of certain details of bone-working technique. In cases when the material was bone, each half was obtained by the simple sawing of a prepared blank. In cases when the handle was to be of walrus ivory, the blank was partially sawed through from one or two sides, then split in two with the aid of a wedge. All walrus ivory handles retain wedge marks on the cleavage planes, as well as smooth sawed surfaces and rough cleavage surfaces.

We are dealing here with well-known Eskimo tools which Murdoch describes as "antler chisels" and Mathiassen calls "whittling knives." Murdoch wrote (1892:173) that he never had occasion to see them in actual use, though he was informed by Point Barrow Eskimos that these tools were intended especially for working reindeer antler. It should be noted however that Murdoch's antler chisels had steel blades, a feature we can hardly suppose to occur in tools from the ancient Uwelen site. On the other hand, handles of this type have been found at such ancient Eskimo sites as Okvik in the Punuk Islands and Miyowagh on St. Lawrence.

It is possible that the ivory object represented in Plate 4:6 was a knife-handle. From the same site we also have the fragment of a jasper blade which, judging from its massive proportions, is that of a spear rather than of a knife.

Scrapers for removing fat from intestines are represented by several specimens from the Uwelen site. They are all of walrus ivory and have the form of shallow elongate cups. One of these scrapers is shown in Plate 4:13. It is oval and has sharp, though not cutting, edges. Another similar scraper, carefully shaped (Plate 4:19), was found on the site by Eskimos. Its distinctive feature is the presence of a small ear for suspension. Such cup-shaped scrapers of walrus ivory for fat removal are particularly characteristic of the early stages of Eskimo culture, Okvik and Old Bering Sea on St. Lawrence Island.

MISCELLANEOUS OBJECTS

Under this heading we will describe objects which, because of their rarity, cannot conveniently be assigned to special categories of their own.

Bone handles or fasteners are more or less flat bone plaques with a longitudinal slit in the center. One of these handles made of walrus ivory is represented in Plate 4:20, while another one, of bone, is shown in Plate 4:21. The latter is decorated by means of deep incised lines — typical of the Uwelen site. Judging from its beveled ends, and the long and narrow slit for suspension, it may be supposed that we are dealing here with the handle of a woman's bag.

There is no doubt that another similar object (Plate 4:22) was indeed the handle of woman's bag. It is made of a slab of walrus ivory, is of much greater length, and has a narrow central slit. The trapezoidal object of walrus ivory shown in Plate 4:23 is described by our colleagues abroad as a fastener or a drag-line handle, of the kind so widely used by the Eskimos to pull boats ashore, drag in dead walrus, etc. Similar handles, sometimes with drilled central openings, are known also from other ancient Eskimo sites.

No pottery vessel fragment of significant size was found at the site. This may be accidental. However, the absence or in any event the extreme scarcity of pottery remains has been noted previously at a number of the more ancient Eskimo sites on the arctic coast of North America. Yet, the presence of pottery among the ancient inhabitants of Uwelen is indicated by the finding of a tool (Plate 4:25) which, in our opinion, was used for imparting decoration to the outside of pottery vessels. It is a slab of walrus ivory (5 × 17 cm, about 1 cm thick), completely covered on one side with deeply incised diagonal lines. The other, smooth, side is covered with numerous, often intersecting minute striations, which are scratch marks left by a very fine cutting edge. While the grooved surface may have served as a paddle for finishing pottery vessels, the smooth side was probably used as a cutting board.

Buttons or beads of walrus ivory. The first of these, which has a large opening in the center (Plate 4:11), has the shape of an ellipse, one half of which is divided into a series of ridges by means of little grooves, while the other half is divided in half by a deeper groove, which goes from one side of the opening to the other on the opposite side of the button. The second button or, more exactly, bead (Plate 4:12) is barrel-shaped, perforated, and is decorated by two parallel lines with spurs projecting alternately on either side of them.

The wooden tablet shown in Plate 4:9 served as a *pendant*, and is unlikely to have had any practical use. It has a miniature hole drilled through its upper edge.

Plate 4:14 illustrates a cap for some kind of object. It is made of walrus ivory and has a deep socket.

The walrus ivory tablet shown in Plate 4:17 is pointed at one end and has a side notch. It may have been used for untying knots or as a twister.

The flat decorated *tablet* in Plate 4:24 is made of walrus ivory and has a miniature suspension hole. The decoration covering this tablet on both sides is of interest, and is in the familiar Uwelen style. One side bears single and multiple incised lines and commas, while the other side has three rows of broken lines and, at the upper end, the familiar "crow's feet" and rows of commas.

Another decorated object the purpose of which is unknown to us (Plate 4:15), is a tube of walrus ivory, oval in cross-section. The thickened end of this tube bears ten drilled openings, of which four are complete. Some of the openings contain inserted pins in the form of small rods of baleen. Above these openings there are two bands of parallel lines with alternating spurs facing inward, which create the impression of cord-decoration. The opposite end is decorated with a circular band with a row of teeth projecting from it.

CARVED FIGURINES

Of exceptional interest is a remarkable carved representation of a polar bear of walrus ivory, reproduced at natural size in Plate 4:8. The bear is shown in spread-out posture, as if swimming. The head and neck are disproportionately large, and only the head is shown realistically, while the remainder of the figure is conventionalized. The shortened body is unnaturally constricted in the area of the waist. The forelimbs and hand limbs are stretched forward. The entire upper surface of the figure to the rear of the crown of the head is covered with an engraved design. The face bears only a few sketchy ornamental lines, which serve to emphasize its form. The eyes are represented by circles with dots in their centers, and the short ears are rendered in the round. The partially open mouth has projecting fangs. The decoration covering the body is executed so as to emphasize the conventionalized parts of the body. The under surface of the figure is flat, and bears only a central quadrangular depression about 4 mm in depth, apparently for setting the figurine on some kind of support. The decoration here is very simple, and consists of punctate outlines. Another depression in the neck region is so placed as to make it possible to pass a cord or a thin strap through the open mouth from below. We do not know the actual function of this figure, though it was not merely decorative, but served some kind of special magic or a ceremonial purpose. The decorative style of this figurine differs in its simplicity and expressiveness from that of all other similar figurines found in excavating ancient Eskimo sites.

Another figurine is that of a human being (Plate 4:7), carved out of ivory. It was found at the same site and purchased from the local inhabitants. The head is exaggerated in height and sits on a short neck. The eyes, nose, and mouth are crudely indicated. The body is narrow, exaggerated in length, with short legs. The figure is male. It wears a belt with trimming above the navel, and some sort of triangular ornament is indicated on the chest by deeply incised lines. Deep lines indicate the shoulder blades on the back, and the spinal column is shown by one longitudinal line and short transverse ones. Arms are lacking, but deep notches occur where the shoulders articulated with the arms. We know of similar carved figurines of ivory only from the ancient site of Okvik in the Punuk Islands.

A distinctive human head carved out of ivory (Plate 4:10) was also found in the course of the excavations at the ancient site of Uwelen. It has a typically elongated face with a very long nose, and clearly marked eyes or, more exactly, eyebrows. On one-half of the head, the hair is indicated by a series of deeply incised lines, while, on the other half, it is shown by rows of punctate lines. Analogies to this head occur only among the Okvik carvings.

The total inventory of objects found at the ancient Uwelen site is distinctive enough to stand out among all other hitherto known remains of Eskimo culture. The ancient inhabitants of Uwelen did not live, apparently, in subterranean or semi-subterranean dwellings. They hunted sea mammals, among them walrus and, perhaps, whales. At the same time, they hunted land mammals, above all reindeer, as well as bears, bones of which have been found at the site. Their complex and highly distinctive harpoon heads have analogies only among those of the Okvik site, though some of the types are similar to those found on the arctic coast of America, at Point Hope and Point Barrow. The arrowhead type is distinctive and archaic. It is notable that only at Okvik do we find salmon spear prongs identical to those from Uwelen. Of great importance in the finding of large numbers of knives with stone side-blades and the near-absence of polished slate knives. We do not even commonly find the widespread woman's knife (ulu). Pottery is also absent.

The Uwelen decorative art style is highly original, and is known from no other place except for its occurrence on certain objects, again, from the Okvik site. Yet at Uwelen this style was very widely used to decorate a great variety of objects. Several objects found at the Uwelen site were similar in type and decoration to artifacts of the Old Bering Sea stage, but not a single object was found pertaining to the late Thule or Punuk stages of the development of Eskimo culture. This cannot be said of the Okvik site, as we know it from Rainey's publication (Rainey, 1941d), where quite a few clearly late objects of the Punuk stage occurred. Thus, we may suppose that the ancient site on the slope of the hill at Uwelen is, if not the oldest, at least one of the oldest known settlements of sea mammal hunters on the arctic coast.

Nynglu in Uwelen

On the easternmost portion of the Uwelen gravel spit, which divides the lagoon from the sea, near the mainland, there are remains of ancient semi-subterranean houses (*nynglu*) and meat storage pits. These houses are clearly visible as high mounds with steep sides, covered with a dense growth of weeds. Soil for a hothouse had been removed from a deep pit on the south side of one of these mounds. Availing ourselves of this cut, we tested the mound. Having cleaned the vertical wall of the pit (about 5 m in width and 1.5 m high) we proceeded some 50-60 cm toward the center, and removed 4 to 5 cubic meters of dirt. Here we found about 160 objects among kitchen refuse, and bones of seal, walrus, whale, and reindeer. Below, we describe the more characteristic of these finds.

SEA HUNTING EQUIPMENT

Harpoon heads. Only two of the harpoon heads found in excavating the pit-house were of walrus ivory, the remainder being of bone. They belong to late types, characteristic of the Thule-Punuk stage of Eskimo culture.

The harpoon head shown in Plate 5:2 has an open socket with straight sides, one slot and an opposing groove for the socket lashing, a single asymmetric spur, a triangular central line hole, and two symmetric barbs. The material is ivory, and the specimen is undecorated. This is the well-known barbed toggling harpoon head type, Mathiassen's Thule 2, Collins' Type IV. This specimen differs from Central Eskimo heads in the presence, as we have seen, of one slot and an opposing groove instead of the usual two slots or two drilled holes for the socket lashing.

The harpoon head in Plate 5:3 has an open socket expanding toward the base, two slots for the socket lashing, a simple pointed basal spur, a round line hole, and an end-blade slit in the same plane as the line hole. The material is bone. The cross-section is a flattened oval. There is no decoration. The harpoon heads shown in Plate 5:1,4 belong to the same type, and differ only in a few details. Both of them are hexagonal in cross-section. The more important differences are in socket design. The shorter harpoon head (Plate 5:1), which is made of ivory, has one slot and an opposing groove instead of two slots for the lashing. In addition, the open socket is trapezoidal in cross-section, with a wider inner floor and a narrower outer opening. The long bone harpoon head (Plate 5:4) has two pairs (one is broken off) of small drilled holes, made with a metal drill, instead of slots for the socket lashing. Another similar bone harpoon head was found in the same dwelling. It has two pairs of holes for the socket lashing, but is short, and has a triangular, rather than round, line hole. In addition, the fore end of the harpoon head (Plate 5:4) has a hole drilled for the stem of a rivet, which holds the end-blade in place. The perforations in all these harpoon heads, both for the lashing and for the rivet, are of highly regular cylindrical form, only 2–2.5 mm in diameter, and were undoubtedly made by a drill with an iron bit. The end-blade secured by the rivet was also probably of iron.

The harpoon head in Plate 5:5 is of simple form, has a closed socket and round line hole with grooves directed downward away from it. The basal spur is simple. The material is ivory. The form is flattened, oval in cross-section. There are neither stone side-blades nor end-blade.

We have two specimens of whaling harpoon heads of walrus ivory from this dwelling. One is unfinished (Plate 5:6) and still lacks a socket and a slit for the end-blade. The other was in use over a long period of time and is very worn. The socket for the foreshaft in this latter specimen is conically drilled and is closed, as in all Eskimo whaling harpoon heads. The line hole is large and elongate, and is intended for a thick line of walrus hide. The end-blade slit is at right angles to the line hole.

No *foreshafts* of the smaller seal and walrus open-socket harpoons were found. However, there are some damaged foreshafts of whaling harpoons. They are all of ivory and of the usual spindle shape, with a longitudinal slot for the loop.

The harpoon shaft *socket pieces* are of ivory and all of the same type. There are large ones for walrus-hunting harpoons, and relatively small ones for sealing harpoons, one of which is illustrated in Plate 5:7. They are cylindrical in form, and have a conical socket at the fore end for the foreshaft. The butt end is steeply beveled, and was fastened to the shaft by three bone dowels, fitting into round holes drilled in the lower beveled portion of the socket piece.

A socket piece of unusual form, made of ivory, served simultaneously as a foreshaft for mounting the harpoon head. This specimen (Plate 5:16), which has a cleft base, was mounted on the wedge-shaped beveled fore end of the shaft and was secured there by means of two bone rivets and a perforation drilled in the center of the socket piece.

The harpoon *ice pick* in Plate 5:8 is of ivory. In its upper portion, adjacent to the shaft, it is cut down to half its width, and is covered on the outside with rows of transverse notches. The pick was fastened to the shaft by means of a rivet and a lashing, for which two holes have been drilled in the lower portion of the pick.

The dwelling yielded several wooden *float bars* for securing the line to a sealskin harpoon float. One of these is shown in Plate 5:18. They are all of the usual form, round in cross-section, with flanges at either end.

LAND HUNTING EQUIPMENT

Bow and arrow. A model bow was found in the excavation of the Uwelen house (Plate 5:9). It is similar to those often found in excavations of ancient Eskimo sites on St. Lawrence Island. Such small bows have been described usually as children's toys. I doubt whether these miniature bows are toys. Toys must allow shooting as an exercise of skill and strength so as to produce actual results and make it possible to hit a selected target. The miniature bow in question, which is a model of a real bow, was doubtless prepared for traditional ceremonies during feasts, in the manner still observed today among the Asiatic Eskimos and the sedentary Chukchi. Judging from this model, the bow was thickened in its central portion and had special notches cut at either end for fastening the bow string.

In addition to simple bows, the inhabitants of the Uwelen house also made use, apparently, of the composite reinforced bow, as evidenced by the remains of the wooden components of such a bow (Plate 5:10) and by special bone strips.

The arrow heads were wooden, of one piece, with thickened fore ends (Plate 5:12) or with blade-like or blunt bone points. Plate 5:11,13,14 illustrate a flat, tanged arrow point of triangular cross-section and two acorn-shaped blunt points of walrus ivory with basal sockets for hafting to the shaft.

Arrow shafts were nearly round in cross-section (about 1 cm in diameter), slightly flattened, with the usual notch for the bow string (Plate 5:19).

In addition to blunt arrowheads, the inhabitants of the Uwelen house apparently made use of bolas for bird-hunting. At the present time bolas are extensively used for the same purpose in Uwelen. Plate 5:15 illustrates one of the balls of a bird-bola, made of a walrus tooth.

FISHING GEAR

The *center-prong of a spear* of ivory (Plate 5:21) and a net sinker (Plate 5:24) of the same material constitute the only fishing gear found. The spear prong, broken in its lower portion, has two pairs of side-barbs. The sinker is a slightly worked segment of walrus tusk with two suspension holes on one of the longer sides.

Wooden spindles for *fire-drilling* were found in large numbers in excavating the house. They were all of the same, as it were, standard, shape, shown in Plate 5:17.

These spindles are 8 cm in length, 8 mm in diameter at the upper end, and 14 mm in diameter at the lower slightly charred end.

The sandstone spindle rest for fire-drilling illustrated in Plate 5:20 was held in the mouth. This type of rest (the "mouthpiece for bow-drill" of American authors) is known from St. Lawrence Island and among the modern Alaskan Eskimos. When using the mouthpiece, held between the teeth, both hands are free during the fire-drilling process, and the use of a bow-drill is therefore not obligatory: The spindle may be rotated by means of a simple thong, whose ends are held in the hands.

Six specimens of walrus ivory *wedges* were found, despite the small volume of dirt moved. Two of them are illustrated in Plate 5:22,23 and show signs of prolonged use.

No stone adzes were found, though two *sockets* for such adzes were recovered, one of them of whale bone, the other of reindeer antler. The reindeer antler adze head was lashed to the handle by means of two deep cuts in the poll (Plate 6:1). The other adze head, made of bone (Plate 6:2) was lashed with the aid of a row of drilled holes. Judging from the shape of the holes in the poll of the latter, they were perforated by a drill with an iron bit.

Knives and knife-handles. The house yielded the blade of large knife or spear made of walrus ivory (the front end is broken). This blade (Plate 5:25) is triangular in cross-section, and has sharp cutting edges and a flat tang which fits in a handle or shaft.

Plate 6:3 illustrates an unfinished man's knife of silicified tuff, while Plate 6:4 shows the forward half of a polished knife of argillaceous slate. Many fragments and several whole women's knives (ulu) of argillaceous slate were found. An example is shown in Plate 6:5.

The bone *spoon* in Plate 6:13 is flat and thin (about 1 mm in thickness), ovoid in outline; it lacks a handle and has a small round hole for suspension.

A wooden *bottom* represents the remains of a small container of baleen (Plate 6:8).

Plate 6:9 illustrates the handle of a wooden ladle or dish with a triangular opening for suspension. The bone disk inlay is of interest, and was apparently a fashion of the time. The excavation of the same house yielded two bone insets of semi-lunar form for just such an inlay (Plate 6:11,12), of which one is decorated on the outer face with a dotted line and points, while the other bears a deeply incised line paralleling its outline.

Numerous fragments of pottery *vessels* (pots for cooking food) and oil lamps were found. Judging from the sherds, the vessels were of large size (25–35 cm in diameter), with very thick walls (1 to 1.6 cm thick); near the hemispherical bottom the thickness reaches 2.5 cm. The paste is coarse with considerable admixture of fine gravel and crushed shell. The firing is so poor that organic tempering materials such as grass and hair are not only not burnt out, but in places are not even charred.

For transporting loads, the inhabitants of the Uwelen house used heavy sleds, and also had light dog sleds, of which bone sled shoes are preserved.

For traveling they used kayaks. A wooden model of one of them, also probably intended for ceremonial use, is shown in Plate 6:10. They also traveled by umiak, judging from the finding of an ivory block used in umiak rigging (Plate 6:23),— see Nelson 1899:218, Plate 78:19—and from umiak bone keel plate (Plate 6:19).

The bone hook, probably that of a boat hook (Plate 6:6) is unusual in shape, square in cross-section.

Armor plates found in the excavation of the dwelling, belong to two types: one of smaller size (Plate 6:18) with three pairs of elongate rectangular perforations, and a larger type (Plate 6:17), with round holes, drilled with a metal bit.

A *back scratcher* (Plate 6:20) is in the form of a round plate of walrus ivory with a hole in the center. Such back scratchers, mounted on long sticks, are used today by the Eskimos of Chukchi Peninsula. Apparently, a plate of baleen (Plate 6:22) square in shape, with rounded corners and a round hole in the center, was also used as a back scratcher.

A wooden *nail* with a head (Plate 6:21) may have been used as a wound plug, though the form is not typical for the latter.

A *human figure* cut out of larch bark (Plate 6:14) is of a type known from excavations on St. Lawrence Island (Collins 1937, Plate 59:16) and in the Central Eskimo area (Mathiassen 1927; 1, Plate 62:7), usually described as a children's toy. This figure has a disproportionately large head, and indications of eyes, nose, and mouth. The shoulders are outlined, but arms are lacking. The legs are set apart. The chest has a perforation, probably for suspension. The figurine was undoubtedly of apotropaic significance, and was worn as a protection.

A very schematic sculptural rendering of a polar or common fox with extended tail (Plate 6:15) is made of ivory and is an amulet or a representation of a "guardian."

All the objects recovered in the excavation of the dwelling on the Uwelen spit clearly indicate a very late date for the construction of that dwelling. With the exception of the Thule-type harpoon head (Plate 5:2), all the objects from the house pertain to protohistoric times, immediately prior to the arrival of the Russians or, perhaps even to the 17th or beginning of the 18th century. In any case, it was a time when the inhabitants of Uwelen were not only thoroughly familiar with iron, but also made wide use of metal tools and even equipped their harpoon heads with iron end-blades.

Cape Dezhnev [East Cape] Area

The Eskimo village of Nuukan (Niwogak in Eskimo) is situated south of Uwelen and of Cape Dezhnev. West of it, we find the village of Dezhnevo, today inhabited by Chukchi. Earlier, the site of the village of Dezhnevo was occupied by the Eskimo settlement of Enmittaun (Enm(i) Tag(i)n).

In 1924, Rasmussen acquired in Nuukan an archaeological collection consisting of 168 objects, which was published by Mathiassen as a collection from East Cape, i.e. Cape Dezhnev (Mathiassen 1930a).

We too conducted limited excavations in the settlement of Nuukan.

The Eskimo have come to occupy the modern site of Nuukan in relatively recent times. Earlier, they lived closer to Cape Dezhnev. This apparently explains the fact that neither Rasmussen's collection, nor our own finds from Nuukan, as we shall see below, include any Old Bering Sea or Birnirk types. Yet, as mentioned earlier, the Ethnographic Section of the Russian Museum received in 1910 from D. Ye. Bettak a small (44 objects) but most interesting archaeological collection, mainly from the Eskimos of the village of Enmittaun. Some of the objects in the collection given at the same time and to the same museum by N. P. Borisov were also found to be from the Cape Dezhnev area. Finally, I acquired certain objects in the village of Dezhnevo, and these, like the objects in the Bettak and Borisov collections, pertain to an early period of Eskimo culture on the Bering Sea coast.

During my short stay in the Cape Dezhnev area, I had no opportunity to investigate the coast or to establish the location of the ancient settlement which yielded the objects described below. Nevertheless, these are interesting enough to merit special description.

SEA MAMMAL HUNTING EQUIPMENT

Harpoon heads. Particular interest attaches, in the Cape Dezhnev area collection, to two large, probably walrus, harpoon heads of unusual form, both of them of ivory. The first of these (Plate 7:1) has an open, very large trough-shaped socket, typical of Old Bering Sea harpoon heads. Two slots on the dorsal side and two lateral grooves are provided for the socket lashing. The basal spur is triple, symmetrical, with the central prong longer than the two side-prongs. This is typical of Old Bering Sea harpoon heads, though in this case the central prong is much longer than usual, judging from the decoration that remains. The central line hole is round, but is drilled not at right angles to the plane of the spur, but parallel to the latter. The deep side-blade slots are situated directly above the line hole and in the same plane. The fore end is broken off. The decoration is in the earliest Old Bering Sea style (Collins' Style I) which, according to Rainey, already existed at the Okvik stage in the Punuk Islands. Despite the damage to this harpoon after it had ceased to be used, there is doubt as to its original appearance. Its stylistic and decorative characteristics make it quite clear that the form of this ancient harpoon head is not accidental, but one that was fully worked out.

The other harpoon head is also, apparently, very ancient (Plate 7:2). It is somewhat simpler, but does have a number of design features in common with the one represented in Plate 7:1.

Its open socket is likewise broad and trough-shaped. There are no slots for the lashing, but only one deep circular groove. The single basal spur is centrally placed, and its inner (ventral) face is ornamented by means of a row of transverse ridges. The spur has no clearly defined side-prongs, though the design of the spur retains vestiges of the side-prongs of a triple spur. The line hole is triangular, and is asymmetrically placed. It is accompanied by a second one, also asymmetric, in the form of a narrow slit below the socket. Instead of stone side-blades, there are two lateral barbs above the upper line hole and in the same plane with it. The fore end is broken, but without doubt was pointed. The head has acquired a dark brown stain as a result of being buried in the ground over a long period.

There are four harpoon heads of classic Old Bering Sea type (Collins' Type I) in the collection, and they are all of ivory. Two have decoration, and two lack it. We shall describe two of these heads below. The first (Plate 7:3) is rather large, and has a broad open socket. The two slots for the lashing come close together on the dorsal side. The asymmetric triple spur has a long central prong and short side-prongs. There are two round line holes, above and below the lashing slots, and these are connected with a deep groove on the dorsal face. Stone side-blades are set in deep grooves in the same plane as the line holes. The specimen lacks decoration, with the exception of the central spur prong, the outer surface of which bears a transverse decorative molding, while the lower surface has an additional false spur. The cross-section of this harpoon head is nearly round.

The second harpoon head of similar type (Plate 7:6) is of moderate size, flattened in shape, and decorated. Here again the socket is open and trough-shaped. There are two slots for the socket lashing. The basal spur is triple, symmetric, with a long central prong. There are two round line holes, above and below the lashing slots, and they are connected by a deep groove on the dorsal side. The stone side-blades are set at right angles to the line holes. The decoration is in Old Bering Sea style.

Apart from damaged specimens, we have five excellently preserved harpoon heads of Birnirk type from the area, all of them of ivory. Their diagnostic features are as follows: broad, shallow, trough-shaped open socket, two lashing slots which come close together on the dorsal side of the harpoon, a triple asymmetric spur with a longer central prong, a round line hole with oblique grooves directed downward, stone side-blades in deep slots directly above the line hole and parallel to it. The cross-section is nearly round, and decoration is in Old Bering Sea style or is absent. This is Type II of Collins.

The harpoon head of this type represented in Plate 7:4 is short and thick and, apart from its general form, differs from the others in having a relatively short central spur prong. The specimens shown in Plate 7:5,7 are distinctive in having flattened fore ends, resulting in a quasi-triangular profile. Like the preceding example, they lack decoration.

The harpoon head in Plate 7:8 is one of the best examples of this type of artifact, and is finely decorated in Old Bering Sea Style 3.

The harpoon head represented in Plate 7:13 differs from all others in this group in the presence of only one lashing slot with opposing groove. The decoration is in Old Bering Sea Style 2.

The bone and antler harpoon heads illustrated in Plate 7:9,10 are of Birnirk type, though somewhat different from those described above. One of them (Plate 7:9) has a broad, shallow, trough-shaped open socket with two lashing slots close together on the dorsal face, an asymmetric two-pronged blunt basal spur, a round line hole with grooves directed downward, stone side-blades set directly above the line hole, far from the fore end of the harpoon head and at right angles to the line hole. The shape is flattened and decoration is lacking. The second specimen (Plate 7:10) has many features in common with the earlier described Uwelen-Okvik type from the ancient Eskimo site in Uwelen. It has an open socket, and one lashing slot with opposing groove. The spur is asymmetric and multiple. Stone side-blade slots occur above the round line hole. The material is antler, and decoration is by deeply incised lines.

There are some curious harpoon head fragments (Plate 7:11,25) the type of which is difficult to determine. They are of interest in that, while having an open socket, and two lashing slots, there is only one stone side-blade over the round line hole instead of the usual two, with a small opposing rudimentary barb.

With reference to the technique of manufacture of harpoons of the Birnirk type just described, it is interesting to note two blanks and one broken harpoon head. One of the blanks (Plate 7:14) is intended for a harpoon head of round form. The general outline has been blocked out. The base has been outlined but not yet divided into spurs, a central line hole has been drilled, and the place of the open socket has been faintly indicated. Another blank (Plate 7:15) is intended for a flat harpoon head. Apart from the line hole, the triple asymmetric spur has been broadly outlined, the socket is indicated, together with the positions of the lashing slots and the slots for the stone side-blades.

The broken specimen (Plate 7:12) is interesting in that it reveals details of the interior design of the stone side-blade slots.

The next type, Collins' Type III, occurs in two variants. The first (Plate 7:16) has a narrow open socket with straight sides, two lashing slots, one simple lateral basal spur, a triangular line hole with grooves directed downward and a slit for the end-blade in the same plane as the line hole. The material is ivory, and decoration is absent. The second variant (Plate 7:17) has a narrow open socket with straight sides, two lashing slots, one higher than the other, placed close together on the dorsal side, a simple asymmetric projecting spur, a round line hole, and a slit for the end-blade in the same plane as the line hole. The material is ivory. The overall shape is hexagonal, flattened, with shoulders and a constriction in the lower third. As Collins has shown, this type is characteristic on St. Lawrence Island of the Punuk stage of Eskimo culture.

Special mention must be given to the bone harpoon head in Plate 7:18. It is very short, sub-triangular in shape, and triangular in cross-section. The socket is open, with straight sides and two lashing slots. The line hole is round, the basal spur is two-pronged and asymmetric, and the end-blade slit is in the plane of the line hole. Only one similar harpoon head, lacking however the end-blade slit, is known to us, and it is part of Rasmussen's collection from the Cape Dezhnev area (Mathiassen 1930a:78, Plate 18:6).

Our collections contain specimens of apparently rare and not widely found toggling harpoon heads that are both barbed and equipped with end-blades. They were used to stab "dead" animals, walrus, or seal. The first of these (Plate 7:19) is of reindeer antler, and is flattened in form. The socket is open and narrow, with straight sides. There are two lashing slots placed far apart and at different levels, one pointed, projecting asymmetric basal spur, a triangular line hole, two sharp symmetrical lateral barbs, and a slit for the end-blade in the plane of the line hole. The decoration is by means of straight lines that meet at an acute angle. The other barbed toggling harpoon head (Plate 7:24) is of ivory. It is oval in cross-section, the socket is open, narrow, with straight sides. The two lashing slots are at different levels and come close together on the dorsal side of the head. The line hole is triangular. There is one asymmetric pointed basal spur. The two pairs of barbs are placed symmetrically one above the other. The end-blade slit is in the plane of the line hole. Harpoon heads of this type (Collins' Type IV) belong to Punuk times. They are known from St. Lawrence Island (Collins 1937:206, Plate 70:6) and from Point Hope in Alaska (Mathiassen 1930a, Plate 12:5).

Finally, there are some quite simple toggling harpoon heads of Collins' Type V (Late Punuk), or the Thule Type 3 of Mathiassen. One of them is illustrated in

Plate 7:21. The socket is open, with straight sides. There is one lashing slot with opposing groove. The spur is simple and asymmetric. The line hole is triangular, and there are neither side-blades nor end-blade. The material is ivory.

The harpoon head shown in Plate 7:22 has a closed socket, a simple basal spur, a round line hole with grooves directed downward, and an end-blade slit at right angles to the line hole. The material is ivory. The cross-section is rhombic. The decoration retains the basic features of late Old Bering Sea Style 3, with nodes within concentric circles and diverging lines, though in this specimen the decoration is crude, the lines are deeply incised, and the degeneration of the style is apparent.

Another closed socket harpoon head (Plate 7:23), also of ivory, is typologically similar to the one described above, but is smaller, better finished, and decorated in classic Punuk style.

The large whaling harpoon head of ivory in Plate 8:1 is of the usual late form with closed socket, simple basal spur, a large elongate line hole, and an end-blade of slate at right angles to the line hole. The polished end-blade is arch-shaped, with a straight base.

The collection of harpoon heads we have just examined has the undoubted interest of including all the types discovered in the course of intensive excavations over a period of many years on St. Lawrence Island. What is more, it includes the most ancient harpoon heads that preceded Collins' Old Bering Sea Type 1, and that have Old Bering Sea Style 1 decoration (Plate 7:1), which Rainey assigns to the earlier Okvik culture stage on that island.

The *foreshaft* for a harpoon head (Plate 8:2) is made of bone, and is oval in cross-section. The base is flattened, and the fore end is round in section. It is intended for a closed socket harpoon head. There is a round line hole placed below the mid-point, toward the butt end.

Harpoon *ice picks* from the Cape Dezhnev area are of two types: very massive ones of ivory (Plate 8:3), with a short poll and lateral perforation for lashing to the shaft, and relatively light ones (Plate 8:4,5,6), also of ivory, with the upper end, which fits on the lower end of the shaft, cut away half-way down, and round holes for bone rivets above and below for fastening the pick to the harpoon shaft.

Wound pins. The artifact of ivory in the form of an awl or pin with a head, illustrated in Plate 8:7, is interpreted by Sollas (Sollas 1911:326, Fig. 193:2,3) as a pin used by the Eskimos for pinning together the edges of wounds on dead seals and other large animals for the purpose of preserving the animal's blood, the loss of which is undesirable. According to Sollas, the Eskimos carried with them special cases on their hunts for sea mammals. The cases contained a supply of such pins.

MISCELLANEOUS OBJECTS

Dart and spear heads. The short ivory point illustrated in Plate 8:9 we consider to be the prong of a bird-dart. It is oval in cross-section, thickened at the base, and has two pairs of asymmetric barbs. A long and thin specimen, also of ivory, is shown in Plate 8:10 and has three asymmetric barbs (the fore end is broken). In all probability, the two long specimens in Plate 8:11,12 were fish spear prongs. They are of walrus ivory. One has a single end barb, the other has three unilateral barbs. Both prongs are pointed on the butt end, which fits into the shaft, and the specimen in Plate 8:12 has, in addition, a double protuberance for hafting to the shaft.

The fine walrus ivory dart or spearhead shown in Plate 8:13 is oval in cross-section and has a pointed tang and very sharp, carefully worked unilateral barbs. The upper end is broken off.

Stone spear points. One of these, shown in Plate 8:14, is made of rubbed slate. It is leaf-shaped in outline, has a broad stem, and was probably the blade of a "bear" lance. As in the whale lances of the Koryaks and the bear lances of the Eskimos, the point was set in the splayed fore end of the shaft and secured by means of special baleen lashing. Another spear point (Plate 8:15) of silicified tuff is bifacially chipped and worked over by pressure flaking. It has shoulders and a long stem.

Knives and knife-handles. In the settlement of Dezhnevo, I acquired an unfinished man's knife of flint (Plate 8:18) with a broad stem. It has been chipped to the desired shape, and needs only to be finished by rubbing. Another man's knife of similar form (Plate 8:17) is made of slate. It is well rubbed and has a leaf-shaped outline and a broad stem.

The woman's knife of slate (ulu) set in an ivory handle (Plate 8:16) was acquired in the settlement of Dezhnevo. I also acquired there a magnificently worked bone handle (Plate 9:1) decorated with deeply incised diagonal lines. The characteristics of this handle and the nature of its decoration indicate that, if it does not originate from the ancient site of Uwelen described earlier, it belongs at least to the same cultural complex.

Stone scraper. Plate 9:2 represents a flint scraper for the working of skins, acquired by me in Nuukan. It has the oval shape typical of two-handed scrapers, and is excellently finished by means of pressure flaking. Its edges have been smoothed and polished from lengthy use.

The ivory *paddle* shown in Plate 9:7 was used, we believe, in applying a pattern in the finishing of clay vessels. The paddle has a well-defined handle, and its inner somewhat concave face is covered completely with deep diagonal grooves, quite like those we have seen on the slab from the ancient site of Uwelen (Plate 4:25). Subsequently, in our examination of ancient Eskimo pottery, we will have occasion to come across pottery sherds bearing designs applied with these tools. A similar paddle, though of wood and less carefully made, was found by Collins in an old Bering Sea deposit on St. Lawrence Island (Collins 1937, Plate 47:17).

A *boat hook* or meat hook is shown in Plate 8:8. Nelson writes that the western Eskimo used similar hooks in traveling by kayak along the coast or the edge of the ice pack. (Nelson 1899:222, Plate 80:45). The hooks are highly useful, particularly to people in kayaks landing on a rocky shore or on ice. Similar hooks are used in carrying pieces of walrus or whale meat and whale blubber. This particular hook is of a shape common among Eskimos, and has a broad hole and a deep notch on its fore end to allow fast lashing to a shaft.

Winged object. In the settlement of Dezhnevo, I acquired a walrus ivory winged object of very large size. Its purpose is not clear, though it was probably the representation of a bird or, more likely, a butterfly, with added head and tail, which was suspended on straps during a whaling ceremony. The object in question, illustrated in Plate 9:11, was covered on the outside with a design in characteristic Old Bering Sea Style 2, subsequently rubbed off in large part. The round holes drilled in the central and wing portions are of later origin. There is a deep depression in the middle of the body for affixing the head. A slot in the back is probably intended to receive a tail. The triangular openings under the wings meet in the middle of the body. The lower ventral surface bears simple decoration by means of deep incised lines. The complex design just described points to a lengthy process of preparation of this specialized type of object.

A carved *bear figurine* of ivory is an example of the high level of artistic achievement of the ancient inhabitants of the coast of the Chukchi Peninsula. The bear (Plate 9:9) is represented "at bay." The ears are carved in relief, and the eyes and nostrils are shown as deep pits. The digits and claws on the front paws are shown as incisions. The surface of the figurine is covered with a typical curvilinear Old Bering Sea design. A perforation through the body with very worn and smoothed edges indicates that this bear figurine was worn for a very long time, probably as an amulet.

STYLE OF DECORATION

The decorated piece of ivory (Plate 9:10) which I acquired in Nuukan and whose purpose is not clear to me is of interest because of its engraved design. It is not an arrowhead or a dart head, and may have had some ceremonial function. Its antiquity is beyond doubt, since it has the characteristic dark brown color acquired by walrus ivory only from prolonged burial in the ground. The broad surfaces of the piece, which is oval in cross-section, bear the same design, in the form of a pattern somewhat resembling a horned mask, rendered by deeply incised lines. The two patterns are separated by means of deep lines carved on the narrower sides and extending nearly over the entire length of the object. This design motif first appears on Old Bering Sea objects. In style, the decoration has nothing in common with Old Bering Sea, and is closer to the decorative style of objects from the ancient site of Uwelen.

In our examination of the harpoon heads and other objects from the Cape Dezhnev area we have already seen a number of examples of the remarkable curvilinear decorative style of Old Bering Sea. Such is also the style of the decoration of a damaged open-socket harpoon head, shown in Plate 9:3, and of a closed-socket harpoon head, like the preceding, of ivory, with a simple spur, a round line hole, a slit for the end-blade at right angles to the line hole, and rudimentary barbs (Plate 9:4). The following objects are decorated in elaborate Old Bering Sea Style 3, with raised circles enclosing baleen inlays as dots, combined with other lines so as to suggest an animal face, and animal faces carved in the round: (1) a harpoon head (Plate 9:5); (2) a harpoon head with a closed socket and a round line hole (Plate 9:8); and (3) the fragment of some very large object, made like the preceding of ivory, perhaps the head or socket piece of a harpoon (Plate 9:6), though we know of no parallels to it in other collections.

Nuukan

Repairs on the Nuukan school in the center of the settlement involved an excavation of considerable size, resulting in a cut about 1 m. in depth through a cultural deposit (Fig. 3). The clearing of a small portion of this cultural deposit yielded a certain number of bones of walrus, ringed seal, and bearded seal, as well as various objects which permit conclusions as to the date of occupation of Nuukan and the cultural affiliation of its ancient inhabitants.

HUNTING AND FISHING GEAR

Two types of harpoon heads were found in the excavations. One of these (Plate 10:1) has an open socket, a side slot and opposing groove for the socket lashing, a simple pointed asymmetric spur, a triangular line hole, two asymmetric barbs, and a slit for the end-blade parallel to the line hole. The material is bone and decoration is absent. This is the well-known Thule 2 type of Mathiassen or IV of Collins. The arrangement of the socket is worthy of note. The socket has the form of a truncated cone and is hollowed out in such a manner that the edges of the slot come together and largely enclose the socket, thereby ensuring a stronger connection between the head and the foreshaft. It is enough to say that the actual diameter of the socket is twice the width of its open portion. The second type of harpoon head at Nuukan (Plate 10:2) has an open socket, two slots for the socket lashing, coming together on the back of the head, a simple asymmetric spur, a round line hole, and no barbs or end-blade. The material is ivory, and the dimensions are unusually large (the length is 12 cm) for harpoon heads of this type, which is Mathiassen's Thule 1 and Collins' V. Another variant of this type is exemplified by the specimen in Plate 10:3, also of ivory. Apart from its small size, it is distinctive in the arrangement of the socket lashing. Instead of two slots, there are two pairs of drilled holes, connected on the dorsal side by deep grooves.

A whaling harpoon head (not illustrated) of ivory has a closed socket, and a large and elongated triangular line hole. A similar head from Nuukan has been published by Mathiassen (1930a; Plate 18:1).

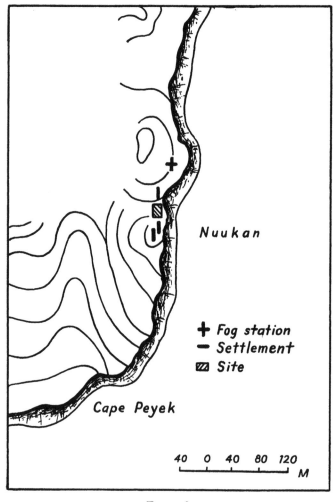

Nuukan

+ Fog station
— Settlement
▨ Site

Cape Peyek

40   0   40   80   120

M

FIGURE 3

Slate *end-blades* for harpoon heads are of the usual type for whaling (Plate 10:4) and sealing (Plate 10:5) weapons.

A harpoon *socket piece* (Plate 10:7) of ivory is cylindrical in shape, somewhat flattened in its upper portion. The lower end is beveled on both sides: on one side the bevel is continuous, on the other, it is stepped. We may conclude from this that the fore end of the shaft had a deep indentation to receive the socket piece. The body of the socket piece contains a drilled perforation for attachment to the shaft. The fore end has a deep conical socket for the foreshaft.

The *foreshaft* in Plate 10:6 is of the usual form, and is similar to that from Nuukan published by Mathiassen (1930a, Plate 19:1). It has conically sharpened and beveled ends, is round in cross-section, and has a line hole in its upper half, with two grooves leading downward away from it.

The harpoon *ice pick* in Plate 10:8 is made of walrus ivory, and is beveled in the upper portion adjacent to the shaft, where a round hole is cut out to receive a bone rivet. A triple perforation has been drilled in the lower portion of the pick for lashing to the shaft.

The *arrows* from the excavations in Nuukan are either one-piece and of wood, or else are of wood with bone heads. The one-piece wooden arrows (Plate 10:14) usually have blunt tips and were used in bird-hunting. We have no whole ones, and therefore do not know their lengths. The shaft is oval in cross-section (0.7 cm by 1 cm) and expands toward the lower and bearing the notch for the bowstring.

Arrowheads are of two types. The first is exemplified by bone arrowheads of a form characteristic of the latest protohistoric culture of the western Eskimo. Such arrowheads are well known from ethnographic collections of the last century, particularly in its first half. This type is massive (Plate 10:9), oval in cross-section, with a conical tang, three unilateral barbs and a slit for an end-blade at the fore end. Judging from the opening drilled in the fore end to receive a rivet, the end-blade may have been of bone, though it was more probably of iron. A diagrammatic representation of a reindeer is engraved on the lower edge of one of the flat sides. We know that such arrows were used for hunting reindeer and in warfare.

The second type consists of the usual blunt bird-hunting arrowheads of bone. Some of them are made of walrus teeth.

A *wrist guard* used in shooting with a bow (Plate 10:13) and worn on the left hand above the wrist, is of usual form, but is made of baleen. Longitudinal slots for lacing occur along the long edges of the wrist guard in its central portion.

Bird bola weights were found in considerable numbers, and they are all roughly of the same shape (Plate 10:12).

Sinkers for fishing are of two kinds: for fish lines and for nets. The fish line sinker of ivory in Plate 10:15 is in the shape of a fish with its head pointing downward. Apart from the usual perforations at the upper and lower ends for the line, there is an additional hole for the hook.

The net-sinker in Plate 10:19 is made of a large waterworn segment of walrus tusk, with two drilled suspension holes.

The wooden object shown in Plate 11:22 was probably used as a float.

VARIOUS TOOLS AND UTENSILS

The bone *pick* in Plate 10:16 for digging up edible roots is hexagonal in cross-section and has a blunted working edge.

Stone *adzes* from Nuukan are of two types, both of which were hafted in bone adze heads. One of the types (Plate 10:11) is made of nephrite, and is only partially ground at the cutting edge. The other (Plate 10:17), of siliceous slate, is polished on both faces and has a steeply ground bit. It is possible that this adze, like the adze-like scrapers described by Collins (1937:152–153), was used as a scraper.

The unusual adze-like implement of reindeer antler shown in Plate 10:18, whose precise purpose is not clear, was used either as an adze or as a scraper, judging from the nature of the working edge.

A shouldered and stemmed shovel-shaped *scraper* of siliceous slate was used in working hides, hafted to a curved wooden handle as shown in Plate 10:20.

Men's knives are of two types. One of these includes the flint knife shown in Plate 11:1, shaped by broad flaking, and pressure-retouched along the cutting edges. Judging by its short butt, it was held directly in the hand when used. A tool of this kind could be used not only for cutting, but also for sawing wood and bone. The second type of man's knife, represented by several examples, consists of flat and broad two-edged stemmed blades of rubbed slate. One of these, shown in Plate 11:2, is very thin (about 5 mm) and relatively large. Another (Plate 11:4), with its lower end broken off, is lozenge-shaped in cross-section, and is as much as 10 mm thick but relatively small. Some of these types of knives have conically and bi-conically drilled holes near the stem for hafting to the handle (Plate 11:3).

The type of *handle* used with men's knives is represented by the specimen shown in Plate 11:5. It is oval in cross-section. It has a slot for the blade at its forward end and, for the lashing, broad and shallow grooves on the surface, bounded by sharply cut edges. The proximal end has a drilled suspension hole.

Women's knives of argillaceous slate are numerous, of varying size, and of the usual form. Of the wooden handles of women's knives, we illustrate only one example of moderate size (Plate 11:12).

An *awl* or *drill* for enlarging perforations already made with an awl or drill is shown in Plate 11:7. The technique of its manufacture was simple. A triangular rod was detached from a walrus tusk by two sawings roughly at right angles to each other. The rod was then sharpened to a fine point and polished on one end.

Holes were drilled in wood, and perhaps in bone, by means of *drills with bone drill points*. Plate 11:8 shows a drill point with a cylindrical bit and an upper portion which fits into a shaft and which is square in cross-section .

Bone spindles for *fire-making* by drilling were found in considerable numbers. Most of them have the usual form of short rods, round in cross-section, hemispherical and broader at the lower end, and narrower at the top. These rods are quite similar in size and shape to those found in excavating the dwelling at Uwelen (Plate 11:6).

CONTAINERS

Excavations in Nuukan yielded a large wooden ladle (Plate 11:20). It is deep, ovoid in form, and has a long handle. The site also yielded a very shallow, oval wooden saucer measuring 8 cm by 10.8 cm. Finally, judging from preserved wooden bottoms and baleen sides, the inhabitants of Nuukan made wide use of baleen boxes of moderate size (4 cm by 5.5 cm and 8 cm by 10 cm) of a form common among the Eskimos.

The flat piece of wood with a small depression, shown in Plate 11:21, was probably used as a ladle.

MISCELLANEOUS OBJECTS FROM EXCAVATIONS

Walrus ivory *blocks* of large size (Plate 11:16) may have been used in umiak rigging, while smaller ones (Plate 11:15) are, in all probability, parts of a dog harness.

Drum handles. One of these is made from a large long bone (Plate 11:23), and still retains part of a broad rim of whale bone. The rim is wedged in a slot in the handle with the aid of a special bone wedge, and is riveted from the top. The lower end of the handle has a perforation for suspending the drum. Another drum handle is also of bone and is of the same type though smaller in size (Plate 11:24). In addition to a wedge, the handle has a special drilled perforation to receive a rivet for attaching the rim.

A *bull-roarer* with serrated edges is made of a plaque of baleen (Plate 11:14). It is known among the Eskimos as a children's toy (Murdoch 1892:378–379, Fig. 377; Birket-Smith 1924:421, Fig. 299), though we know that it has a wide distribution throughout the world and is often used in religious ceremonies. It is possible that it had a similar use among the ancient Eskimos.

Among wooden objects, we have a bird effigy, which was hung up during the whaling ceremony and on other ceremonial occasions.

PURCHASED OBJECTS

We acquired from the Eskimos in Nuukan several objects which went out of use a long time ago. They include a small walrus ivory closed-socket harpoon head, with one projecting asymmetric spur and a triangular line hole with grooves directed downward. Small holes for a rivet have been drilled at the edge of the slit for the end-blade.

A harpoon *finger rest* of walrus ivory (Plate 11:11) has a concave base and a triangular hole for lashing to the shaft.

The *mouthpiece* of a sealskin float in Plate 11:9 is made of ivory.

The *flint arrow point* in Plate 10:10 is leaf-shaped in outline, shouldered and stemmed, and lozenge-shaped in cross-section.

Three *drill rests* of ivory are of the same type but differ in details (Plate 11:13,17,18). Like the stone drill rest from Uwelen (Plate 5:20), the Nuukan specimens were placed in the mouth and held between the teeth.

Quite apart from the purchased objects, the entire complex of objects from the Nuukan excavations points to the late settlement of the location now occupied by the modern Eskimo village. It took place, apparently, at the time of the occupation of the dwelling excavated in Uwelen, in Late Punuk and partly in protohistoric times, prior to intensive trade contacts with the Russians.

Yandygay

The village of sedentary Chukchi, Yandygay, is situated on the steep shore between Cape Krigugon (Novosiltsev) and Cape Khargilakh, which lies south of Lavrenti [Lawrence] Bay. In this village, at the very edge of the coastal cliff, there is a rather large number of caved-in semi-subterranean dwellings and long-abandoned meat storage pits, apparently of various age (Fig. 4).

The exposed cultural deposit here was found to be thick, in places 4 m deep. Transportation conditions precluded our staying at this site for any length of time. As a result we had to content ourselves with small excavations of the exposed cultural deposit in two places. In addition to the bones of walrus and

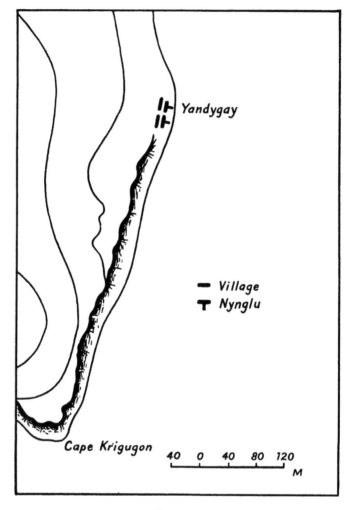

Yandygay

➖ Village
⊤ Nynglu

Cape Krigugon

40   0   40   80   120

M

FIGURE 4

bearded seal and, in fewer numbers, those of whale, the deposit yielded a series of objects, the description of which follows.

The *harpoon head* of walrus ivory (Plate 12:4) has an open socket, two slots for the socket lashing, which come together on the dorsal side of the head. There is one asymmetric basal spur. The line hole is round, and the slit for the end-blade is in the plane of the line hole. The cross-section is oval.

Foreshafts for hafting harpoon heads are of two types: long ones (11.2 cm), oval in cross-section, with rounded butt ends and flattened fore ends, and a lateral line hole below the mid-point. The short ones (less than 7 cm), are round in cross-section and spindle-shaped in outline, with a central line hole near the mid-point of the foreshaft. Both types are of ivory. The short foreshafts fit closed-socket heads.

A walrus ivory harpoon *ice pick* is of the usual type, with a wedge-like beveled upper end and transverse notches on the flat surface fitting on the shaft.

Arrowheads fall into three types: (1) a long bone arrowhead (Plate 12:1) with a single barb and a conical tang; (2) a short ivory arrowhead (Plate 12:2) also with a single barb, in this case an end-barb, and a conical tang with a shoulder; and (3) a wooden arrow with a broad spatulate, pointed tip (Plate 12:3).

The only fishing gear found was a line *sinker* of ivory (Plate 12:5). Its form is a common one, round in cross-section and thickened at the end. The upper end has a triangular line hole. Unlike other similar sinkers, this one has holes for attaching hooks not at the lower end, but in the middle.

The walrus ivory *mattock* is interesting in view of the manner in which it is hafted. For hafting purposes (Plate 12:6), the face fitting against the handle is beveled, while the remainder of the surface bears two deep grooves and is provided with a relatively small longitudinal slot.

Fragments of large *women's knives* were found in great number. Some have conically and bi-conically drilled perforations for lashing to the handle.

The size of these knives may be gauged from their wooden handles, illustrated in Plate 12:12,13.

A *bow-drill* made of an antler tine is represented in Plate 12:10. The bone handle of a baleen bucket is shown in Plate 12:7.

In Yandygay, I purchased a walrus ivory *comb* of long (21 cm) and narrow shape (Plate 12:11) used for combing grass and, perhaps, in working deer skins. It was found in the exposed cultural deposit where we had been excavating. In addition to the special finger holds on the handle, holes have been perforated on the upper part of the latter on a lateral edge, and two deep pits (eyes) have been drilled, thus giving the handle the appearance of a dog's head.

Judging from the artifacts found, the cultural deposit, though deep, represents a late occupation, at least at the point excavated. Its date is no earlier than the Punuk stage of the cultural development of the Eskimo, and is probably terminal Punuk.

Arakamchechen Island

On the high bank (15 to 20 m above sea level) of Arakamchechen Island, which is uninhabited today, on the very shore near the lighthouse and east of a small lake, we found the remains of semi-subterranean houses and, next to them, on the edge of the cliff, meat storage pits (Fig. 5).

The semi-subterranean dwellings were found to be of a type common among the ancient Eskimos, square in ground plan, with an entranceway facing the sea, and whale bones used in construction projecting out of the ground in large numbers. Our test excavations took place at one of the meat storage pits and in the entrance deposit of the large (11 m by 12 m) northern pit-house. In uncovering an area of about 3 square meters to the depth of 0.5 m on level ground (below this the ground was frozen) and to the depth of 1 m along the edge of the shore bank, we came across a cultural deposit containing large numbers of whale, walrus, bearded seal, and seal bones, and occasional bones of reindeer and mountain goat. The most distinctive of the objects found here are described below.

Simple *harpoon heads*, made of bone and ivory (Plate 12:9,20), had open sockets, a simple asymmetric spur, a round line hole with grooves oriented downward, and a slit for the end-blade parallel to the line hole. In cross-section, the

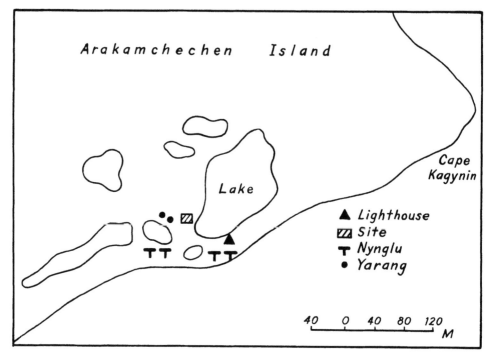

FIGURE 5

heads were oval. These specimens are interesting in that, while having open sockets, they have neither slots nor grooves for the socket lashing. In this instance, as in the case of a harpoon head from Nuukan (Plate 10:1), the foreshaft remained in the socket as a result of the narrowness of the opening relative to the width of the socket and therefore, of the foreshaft. Such harpoon heads are typical of Late Punuk, at which time they are particularly numerous.

Large *whaling harpoon heads* of ivory from Arakamchechen Island, of which one is illustrated in Plate 12:8, are of widespread type, with closed socket, one asymmetric spur, a large longitudinal slot for a line hole, and a slit for the end-blade at right angles to the line hole. The harpoon head is hexagonal in cross-section.

Spear prongs of ivory include a *center-prong* (Plate 12:17) with two pairs of symmetric barbs and a triangular hole near the base for lashing to the shaft, and a *side-prong* with one blunt barb, central holes, and a projecting knob on the lower end for fastening to the shaft.

A *bird bola weight* (Plate 12:15) of a walrus tooth has a small perforation for attachment.

A *weight* made from a large (8 by 12 cm) granite boulder with a deep central encircling groove (Plate 12:26) was used with a baleen *net* for catching saffron cod ["tomcod"] under ice in the winter.

A *mattock* of whale rib for sod removal (Plate 12:22) is nearly unworked, only the lower working end of the tool being slightly sharpened with an adze, and small notches and a series of transverse grooves being provided where the mattock is hafted to the handle.

A whale-rib *pick* for digging edible roots (Plate 12:21) shows careful workmanship. It bears deep cuts on the outer and inner surfaces to allow secure hafting to a handle by means of a system of lashings.

Wedges, as usual, are of ivory and fall into two types: (1) broad, massive specimens (Plate 12:16) and (2) narrow, chisel-like examples with a small suspension hole at the upper end.

Awls or reamers of ivory fail to exhibit any distinctive features. One (Plate 12:24) is large, with a flattened butt end, while another (Plate 12:25) is small and triangular in cross-section.

Fragments represent women's slate *knives* (ulu) of the usual type. No men's knives were found, though we have some very interesting handles, whose forward ends held the stone blades of men's knives. One such *handle* (Plate 12:23) of antler bears a deep slot for the blade stem at the forward end, while the other end has a diagonally drilled suspension hole. A distinctive feature of handles of this type is the presence of a longitudinal slot through the side of the handle into the socket, at a short distance from the leading edge of the handle. These handles held slate blades which were easily broken. The slot described was provided to make it easier to extract the stem of the broken blade from the socket. We are not aware of this feature in the design of sockets in bone knife-handles from either St. Lawrence Island or Alaska.

Another *man's knife-handle* is of ivory. Only its forward end is preserved, and it has a deep slot on one side for the insertion of a side-blade.

A *scraper* for removing fat from intestines (Plate 12:19) is made of a segment of long bone, concave in outline, with sharp, but not cutting, edges.

An *umiak keel plate* is in the form of thin broad plate of whale bone (Plate 12:28) with two pairs of drilled openings near the edges. These holes have been made with a metal drill, and are joined by deep grooves cutting through half the thickness of the plate for tying the latter under the keel.

A *handle* or *fastener* is made of ivory and has a central opening (Plate 12:14).

A bone *drum handle* (Plate 12:27) is of the usual form, distinctive only in the presence of two specially drilled holes and a longitudinal perforation for lashing it to the rim of the drum.

The square plan of the large houses with their entrance passageway, the house construction involving the use of whale bones, the harpoon head types, the occurrence of rubbed slate tools and the absence of chipped stone, and the entire range of objects found in the refuse from this house, indicate a Late Punuk occupation.

Also on Arakamchechen Island, on the shore, a few hundred meters southwest of the lighthouse mentioned earlier, the remains of yet another group of houses were found. These were also square in outline, with entranceways and meat storage pits nearby. However, they were not semi-subterranean, since the depressions in the ground were very shallow, not exceeding 20 to 30 cm in depth. The testing of the cultural deposit at the entrance of one of these houses showed that the occupation had been relatively recent.

The objects found included a harpoon head with an iron end-blade; an iron knife, identical to that found by Geist (Geist and Rainey 1936, Plate 23:2) in the excavation of one of the more recent Eskimo dwellings on St. Lawrence Island; a heavy, massive clay oil lamp with two ridges, of a type widespread until recent times among the Asiatic Eskimo and the maritime Chukchi, and wooden dishes, bowls, and other objects.

On the southern shore of the lake west of the lighthouse we noted an exposed layer a few centimeters in thickness formed of the shells of an edible mollusc (***Mytilus edulis* L.**), capped by a thin layer of humus. Having uncovered a small area, we came across fragments of women's knives of slate, pottery sherds, in no way different from modern materials, an oil lamp, identical to that found among the remains of the southern houses mentioned above, and a bone paddle, of the kind used today by the Eskimos for smoothing the snow after setting a fox trap.

Cape Chaplin

On Cape Chaplin, between the buildings of the polar and fog stations to the east, and the Eskimo village of Chaplino to the west, the remains of an ancient Eskimo settlement (Fig. 6) are marked by vertically standing whale jawbones, which catch the eye from a distance. Four houses of square outlines with corridor entranceways lined with whale bones form a distinctive group at this site. Here also we find several abandoned meat storage pits. On the southern shore of Cape

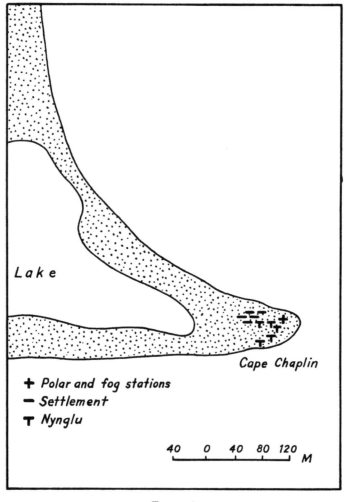

Lake

Cape Chaplin

+ *Polar and fog stations*
− *Settlement*
⊤ *Nynglu*

40   0   40   80   120
                              M

Figure 6

Chaplin, south of the fog station, on a portion of the coast eroded by the tide, there are also remains of ancient dwellings and meat storage pits, with an exposed cultural deposit from 1.5 to 2.5 m thick, extending over several tens of meters. The clearing of this deposit near two meat storage pits brought to light a considerable number of walrus, bearded seal, and ringed seal bones, whale bones and baleen, as well as a variety of artifacts. The more characteristic of the latter are described below.

HUNTING AND FISHING GEAR

The *harpoon heads* from Cape Chaplin belong to two types with which we are already familiar: Collins' Type III or Mathiassen's Thule 3, and Collins' Type V or Mathiassen's Thule 1.

The harpoon head in Plate 13:1 has an open socket, two slots for the socket lashing, coming together on the dorsal side of the head, one simple asymmetric basal spur, a round line hole, and a slit for the end-blade parallel to the line hole. The material is ivory. The cross-section is oval. Decoration is by straight lines and dots in Punuk style. Another harpoon head of the same type (Plate 13:2) differs from the one described in lacking slots for the socket lashing. The socket, though open, has an opening which is narrower than the floor of the socket. It lacks decoration, and differs somewhat in shape from the specimen illustrated in Plate 13:1.

The bone harpoon heads represented in Plate 13:3,4 are of the same type, and differ only in dimensions and in minor details. The sockets are open. There is one slot and an opposing groove for the lashing, an asymmetric basal spur, and a triangular line hole with the groove oriented downward. Side-blade slots and end-blade slits are lacking. Decoration is absent.

Plate 13:5 shows a rare, perhaps accidental, example of a small ivory harpoon head with an open socket and two drilled perforations: one for the socket lashing, the other for the line. This harpoon head could have been used only for large fish, of the kind that abound in the lake on the Chaplin sand bar. A similar harpoon head, though with a closed socket, was found by Mathiassen (1927; 1, Plate 12:7) in his excavations in the Central Eskimo area at the ancient site of Naujan, and was described by him as salmon-fishing gear.

Whaling harpoon heads (Plate 13:7) are of the usual type, with a closed socket, a large triangular line hole, and slit for the end-blade at right angles to the line hole.

Foreshafts of ivory to hold the harpoon head belong to a single type. They are round in cross-section, with a conical butt end and a flattened upper end. There is an elongated or triangular perforation at the mid-point or in the lower third of the foreshaft. The length is 11 to 12 cm.

The harpoon shaft ivory *socket piece* in Plate 13:6 is of unusual type, short, with a conical socket, similar to examples found by Collins (1937, Plate 31:12,13) on St. Lawrence Island in the Old Bering Sea complex.

A harpoon *ice pick* (Plate 13:8) of walrus ivory has a flattened triangular cross-section in its lower portion, and a beveled inner surface in its upper third, which fits the shaft.

Wooden float bars for fastening the line to a sealskin harpoon float are identical to those found in excavating the house in Uwelen and in the Nuukan excavations (Plate 1:19; Plate 5:18).

The inhabitants of the Chaplin site already used the compound reinforced *bow*. The proof of this is the presence of bone braces, one of them an end-brace with a notch for the bowstring (Plate 13:17), and several flat braces from the central part of the bow (Plate 13:23), as well as the occurrence of a twister for sinew or baleen strands. The twister (Plate 13:12) has the size and shape typical for this kind of tool, and ends bent in opposite directions. However, it has an unusual suspension slot in the center and is triangular in cross-section at that point.

Arrowheads are of three types.

The first is a long bone arrowhead, oval in cross-section with two sharp barbs, a conical tang, and a slit for an end-blade (Plate 13:11).

The second is also a long arrowhead with a conical tang, but has a pointed fore end and a single small barb, and may occur in two variants: a bone variant, lozenge-shaped in cross-section (Plate 13:10), and an ivory variant, triangular in cross-section (Plate 13:9).

The third type includes blunt bone arrowheads with a basal socket for fastening to a shaft. One of these is illustrated in Plate 13:13.

In shooting with the bow, inhabitants of Chaplino made use of bone *wrist guards* of the usual concave form. The wrist guard represented in Plate 13:16, apart from the openings drilled (with a metal drill) for lacing it to the hand, has perforations along the edges with baleen inlays, which are decorative in nature.

Bird bola weights were found in large numbers. They are all either carved out of ivory or made of walrus teeth modified merely by suspension holes through the roots. The more typical weights are shown in Plate 13:14,15,18,19.

The *bone paddle* shown in Plate 13:22 is similar to those used today by the Eskimos for erasing tracks in the snow when setting traps for arctic and other fox. It is narrow (2.5 cm) and long (33 cm), somewhat convex, with slight shoulders at the handle and a round suspension hole.

Hoop-net for catching saffron cod ["tomcod"]. Even today when catching saffron cod under the ice in winter, the Asiatic Eskimos make use of special nets, consisting of a baleen hoop about 40 cm in diameter, and a net, also made of baleen fibers, to the bottom of which is fastened a heavy weight in the form of an oblong boulder with an encircling groove around the middle. An example of such a net from Sirhenik is shown in Plate 23:1,2. The weights made from granite and gneiss boulders are exactly like the specimen from Arakamchechen Island, illustrated in Plate 12:26.

In making nets, the inhabitants of Chaplino made use of *shuttles* of the usual type. The smooth surface of such a shuttle (Plate 13:24) bears the scratched property mark of its owner.

Other fishing gear includes only line sinkers with line holes on either end, and the barb of a composite fishhook (Plate 13:21), flattened and diamond-shaped in cross-section.

The magnificent flint *spear blade* in Plate 14:1 was found in the cultural deposit on the shore bank and was given to us by an Eskimo, the mechanic at the polar station. This blade has been shaped by the removal of large chips and then retouched by pressure flaking.

VARIOUS TOOLS AND UTENSILS

A *device for gathering sea weed* (Plate 15:1) has been rather well preserved and is designed as follows. A boulder weight with a deep encircling groove around the middle is attached to the end of a stick by means of baleen lashing. A cluster of four sharp diverging bone spikes, notched at the base for better lashing, is attached with baleen to the same stick below the weight.

A whole series of bone and ivory *picks* and *mattocks* for digging up edible roots was recovered at Cape Chaplin. We illustrate some of the more typical examples.

The pick of antler tine in Plate 15:2 has a pointed lower end and a large perforation at its thickened upper end for hafting to a handle. A similar bone tool, triangular in cross-section, is represented in Plate 15:3.

The walrus ivory mattock in Plate 15:4 may have been used not so much for digging up edible roots as for excavating the ground in building houses or making meat storage pits. In the portion which is hafted to the handle, notches are provided above and below, and a large number of grooves have been made to ensure better lashing. The working end is blunted from prolonged use.

The mattock illustrated in Plate 15:6, which served for digging, is made of a very large walrus tusk. The upper end is altogether unworked, with the exception of a rather deep encircling groove for hafting to a handle. The lower end is beveled in the manner of an adze, and is smoothed from prolonged use.

Many ivory *wedges* of the usual form were found in the excavations on Cape Chaplin. As an example, we illustrate one of the larger wedges (Plate 15:5).

The *hammer* in Plate 15:7 is made of a granite boulder and bears a deep encircling groove for hafting. It differs from fish net sinkers of similar form in the much deeper hafting groove and the wear on the lower striking surface, in the form of minute chips and scars.

The ivory hammer shown in Plate 15:11 is of unusual form, as if imitating an iron hammer with a narrow end flattened from use. It has a spherical poll, below which the part of the inner surface adjacent to the handle, serving as the point of hafting, is carved out and bounded by deep grooves. Toward the lower end, the hammer is wedge-shaped, but blunted instead of sharpened. At the mid-point of the inner face, there is a round pit, indicating that it was used as a drill rest.

A *bone bow-drill* for perforating holes or for fire-making is illustrated in Plate 15:10.

An *adze* of moderate size (Plate 14:9) is made of a dense green stone, and has a well sharpened, slightly concave bit.

A bone *socket piece* for a stone adze is of a type similar to that found at Sirhenik (Plate 24:5). The upper end has a heel. The inner surface which fits against the handle is given a smooth finish and bears transverse cuts, while the remainder of the surface at the point of hafting is covered with a series of deep notches.

Plate 14:6 illustrates the unfinished *blade* of a large slate knife, while Plate 14:2 shows an unpolished man's knife of silicified tuff ground only on its front end at the cutting edge.

The large *bone points* described below are more correctly interpreted as knives than as dart points. The first of these (Plate 14:15) is nearly flat on one face and concave on the other, and has a wedge-like beveled tang which fits in a splayed handle. The second (Plate 14:16) is considerably larger in size, and has a slit for an end-blade. Finally, the third (Plate 14:14), unlike the two preceding, is of ivory and might be either a dart head or the blade of a dagger. It is diamond-shaped in cross-section, the tang is flat and pointed. An elongate perforation serves for hafting to a handle.

Bone handles of men's knives from Cape Chaplin are of three types. The first is already familiar to us from the excavations on Arakamchechen Island, and has a socket for the knife-blade stem at one end, and a suspension hole on the other. It is represented here in two variants: without a slot in the socket wall (Plate

14:17), and with a slot for extracting the blade stem in case of breakage (Plate 14:7,18). The second type of handle is a rare one. It consists of two halves, with notches at their fore ends for holding the blade stem. Special grooves on the outside (Plate 14:4) ensure a tight fit of the blade between the two halves of the handle. It is unlikely that such handles held slate blades. These blades were of bone, flint, nephrite or, more likely, iron. The third quite widespread type of man's knife handle is in the form of a simple bone rod with a side-slot at the end (Plate 14:19).

Women's knives of slate (ulu) are of usual, predominantly semi-lunar form (Plate 14:3), sometimes of very large size, as may be judged from their handles.

Whetstones of sandstone, such as that illustrated in Plate 14:11, were used to sharpen knives and polish stone and bone implements. The example shown has a last-shaped outline, rather characteristic of Eskimo whetstones.

The purpose of the bone point shown in Plate 14:20 is not clear. It is long, slightly curved, sharpened at one end, with a round hole at the other. It may have been used as an awl or reamer or to untie knots.

Awls or *punches* are shown in Plate 16:2,3. They are made of bone splinters and have sharp points, well-polished from long use.

The *needle-case* (damaged) in Plate 16:4 is made from the wing bone of a cormorant. It is decorated in Punuk style with unilaterally spurred encircling lines.

Scrapers for removing fat from intestines are of two types at Cape Chaplin. They are either cup-shaped ivory bowls or else asymmetric bowls, also of ivory, with only one working edge, as illustrated in Plate 14:8. Such a scraper could also be used as a drill rest, as evidenced by a round pit on its outer surface.

CONTAINERS

The cultural deposit at Cape Chaplin yielded a large number of semi-finished products of baleen, in the form of bundles of strips and fibers, and a number of artifacts of the same material. Apart from the net for the ice-fishing of saffron cod, mentioned earlier, we also found a large number of containers of baleen with wooden bottoms (Plate 15:9), sometimes with lids. Such boxes or buckets are usually oval, and measure 13 cm by 21 cm or 14 cm by 17 cm. Their height is from 10 cm to 12 cm.

Plate 15:8 illustrates one of these vessels. A strip of baleen is used for the side, which is fastened with a strip of the same material. We know of similar vessels in the Old Bering Sea stage of Eskimo culture on St. Lawrence Island. They are also well-known at the Thule stage of Central Eskimo culture.

An interesting *scoop* made of the palm of a reindeer antler (Plate 15:14) was used for removing boiled meat from cooking pots.

Clay pots, judging from the remaining sherds varied in size from 12 cm to 28 cm in diameter. They had thick walls, ranging from 1 cm to 1.5 cm in thickness and attaining 2 cm at the base. The latter was round. The rims curved in slightly. The paste consists of black clay with added coarse sand and organic fiber (hair and grass). Firing is very poor. Most of the pottery is undecorated. The surfaces of certain vessels bear traces of smoothing with a bunch of grass, while others show the imprints of a grooved paddle. One of the sherds bears indistinct check-stamping.

Oil lamps, judging from the fragments preserved, were of medium size, oval in shape, with transverse ridges for the wicks, of the type prevalent until recent times among the Eskimos of the Chukchi Peninsula.

Bone or, more exactly, *antler spoons* (Plate 14:12,13) are of a type well-known since Nordenskiöld wrote his description of the spoon found by him in excavations at Cape Schmidt on the Arctic coast. They are small and flat, with very long, usually somewhat-bent handles. They became widespread throughout the Eskimo area during the Thule-Punuk stage.

Special antler *hooks* were used to suspend vessels inside houses and, perhaps, over the fire. Plate 15:15,16 show two such hooks, one of them with a drilled suspension hole, the other with grooves and a lashing of baleen.

MEANS OF TRANSPORTATION

Bone ice creepers, attached to footwear under the arch for walking on ice, were of two types at Cape Chaplin. One (Plate 14:5) is a broad bone piece with conically drilled holes, into which were fitted sharp spikes of walrus ivory. Paired holes at the edges, connected on the outside by deep grooves, serve for attachment to the boot. The other type (Plate 14:10) is in the form of a single piece of walrus ivory, with three pairs of points or nubbins.

The *sled runners* in Plate 15:12,13 are very massive and wide, and typical of the Punuk stage of Eskimo culture on St. Lawrence Island. Particular note should be taken of the great width of the runner (up to 4 cm). Pairs of round holes are drilled along the upper edge to allow the attachment of cross-pieces.

Here, as on Arakamchechen Island, we found *umiak keel plates* of whale bone strips 8 cm in width and 0.5 cm in thickness (Plate 15:17). Pairs of holes connected by grooves serve for lashing to the keel.

The wooden *paddle model*, shown in Plate 16:1, was part of the paraphernalia in religious ceremonies. It is interesting in providing an idea of the type of paddle in use at the time.

So far, we have no indisputable evidence of the use of dogs for traction, if we exclude the walrus ivory block in Plate 16:5 which has two perforations at right angles to each other and which may have been part of a dog harness.

MISCELLANEOUS OBJECTS

A *bone shovel* for snow removal is of a type usual among the Eskimos (Plate 15:18) and is made from a walrus scapula. In addition to a large slit and round drilled holes for hafting to a handle, the shovel has a series of small mending holes along its interior broken edge.

A circular *back-scratcher* of ivory with a hole at the center (Plate 16:10) is similar to the one found in excavating the house at Uwelen.

Whale bone *armor plates* are of two types: large plaques (7 cm by 30 cm, 0.6 cm thick) with three pairs of longitudinal slits and round holes for joining the plates together (Plate 15:19), and smaller plates of the usual type, of which one is shown in Plate 16:15.

Wooden *drum handles* are of a type already described for Arakamchechen Island. Cape Chaplin yielded both large handles from real drums (Plate 16:7) and small ones, belonging perhaps to toy drums (Plate 16:6).

The *canines* of young walruses, dogs, and polar bears, perforated for suspension at the base of the root, were probably amulets (Plate 16:13,16,17).

The *figurine of a bear*, crudely and schematically carved out of walrus ivory (Plate 16:12) was more probably ceremonial than a toy.

Another figurine (Plate 16:20) was made of wood. It is rounded in shape, with no arms or legs; the face is flat, with indications only of eyes, mouth, and nose.

A *baleen strip* (Plate 16:8) cut out as a simplified representation of a man's knife with a side-blade at the fore end, had a ritual purpose or, perhaps, may have been part of the equipment of a shaman.

The object *plaited* from four strips of *baleen* (Plate 16:9) served, in all probability as a decoration or pendant, like the object of plaited baleen found at Kiwak (Plate 17:26).

An examination of the total inventory of objects from the excavations on Cape Chaplin provides convincing evidence that we are dealing here with a single and not very lengthy time span. The types of harpoon heads, of bow and arrow, the wrist guard, the bird bola weights, the men's knives and their handles, domestic utensils, the type of sled runners, the armor plates, the decorative style, and other details, all point to a late cultural phase of the Punuk phase, and Late Punuk at that. Our efforts to find remains of earlier settlements on Cape Chaplin were not successful. This disturbed us, inasmuch as the Eskimos of St. Lawrence Island, where the early phases of Punuk and Old Bering Sea are abundantly represented, trace their origins to Cape Chaplin, and ancient connections between the island and the cape, which is the closest point on the mainland of Asia, stand to reason. In this connection, we may point out that, according to Rainey (1941d:564), harpoon heads with Okvik decoration were found by Bogoras not only at Cape Dezhnev, but also at Cape Chaplin. They are kept at the present time at the American Museum of Natural History, but have not been published.

The trouble, apparently, is that the gravel bar of Cape Chaplin moves continuously as a result of wave action. Even at the present time, every bad storm leads to the erosion or deposition of large areas of the bar, extending tens of meters inland. It is highly possible that the remains of ancient Eskimo settlements on the cape have been washed away by the sea.

To determine the date of occupation of the group of dwellings mentioned earlier the remains of which lie between the polar station and the modern Eskimo village of Chaplino, one of the houses was cleared. In a shallow cultural deposit, no more than 40 cm in thickness, below a pebble layer, two skeletons (one male and one female) were discovered, as well as a number of objects. Brief notes on these objects follow.

A bone harpoon head (Plate 13:20) has a closed socket, a simple basal spur, a round line hole, and deep grooves below the latter. The iron end-blade was fastened in its slit by an iron rivet. A number of wooden floats were found (Plate 16:18), and probably belonged to a fish net. A short wooden adze handle is of a form well known from Eskimo ethnographic collections. The wooden and bone handles of women's knives (Plate 13:25) differ in no way from modern examples. Among the containers, note should be taken of a large wooden bowl, hollowed out of the knobbed growth of a larch, and a small baleen box of the usual type with a wooden bottom. Ivory ice creepers for traveling on ice are also modern in type and have four pairs of pyramidal spikes. A wooden arch from a dog-sled and a harness fastener (Plate 16:11) are evidence of dog transportation. The long-toothed ivory comb in Plate 16:14 is for combing hair. A wooden drum handle is of the usual type. A thick-walled pottery vessel, jar-like in shape and with a flat bottom, belongs to a type which went out of use recently. We saw similar vessels at the Eskimo cemetery in Nuukan, where the dead had been buried within memory of the village inhabitants.

All the objects enumerated indicate the recent occupation of these houses. According to the traditions of the Eskimos at Chaplino, it took place in the middle or the third quarter of the last century.

Kiwak

Kiwak, the southernmost Eskimo village on the Chukchi Peninsula, is located near Cape Nizmenny [Low Cape] or, more exactly, between Cape Nizmenny to the south and Kiwak Lagoon to the north. Two meat storage pits have been exposed on the southern edge of the modern village, on the very shore, and at the present time have been largely destroyed by the sea. The cultural deposit here measures about 2 m in thickness. Directly west-southwest of the meat storage pits are found the remains of two square semi-subterranean houses (Fig. 7). One of these (the northern one) measures 8 m by 8 m and is about 1 m deep. It has an entranceway from the sea side 10 m in length and 1.5 m in width. The second (southern) semi-subterranean house is somewhat larger, measuring 9 m by 9 m, and has an entranceway of about the same size.

Limited work at Kiwak was done at two points: on the disrupted shore where the northernmost of the storage pits is exposed and to the right of the entrance of the first house.

The shore near the storage pit is vertical, and rises about 4 m above sea level. The upper 1.5 m to 2 m form a thick cultural deposit, black in color, containing large numbers of bones of walrus, bearded seal, ringed seal, and whale, shells of molluscs (*Mytilus edulis* L.), various artifacts of bone and stone, and pottery sherds. A small portion of the deposit, hardly more than 1 cu m was cleared away.

The excavation of the pit-house entranceway took place a few meters away from the storage pit, and at a distance of 2 m from the entrance to the house. The latter, as stated earlier, is the smaller of the two. The entranceway has two side-chambers, each about 4 m square, at a distance of 4 m from the end. The walls both of the house and of the entranceway are held by whale bones set upright. Kitchen refuse has accumulated to the right and left of the house entrance. The excavation near the entrance to the house was moderate in size, about 2 m square, and was carried to a depth of 55 cm, to permafrost. This kitchen refuse yielded bones of the same animals that were found in the shore cut, with the exception of whale bones.

Despite the very modest size of our tests, these provided quite a clear picture of the culture of the ancient inhabitants of the Cape Nizmenny houses.

Unfortunately, we did not find a single harpoon head. The only harpoon part we have is an ivory *ice pick*, dark brown, nearly black in color, like all bone objects taken out of the Kiwak excavations. This ice pick (Plate 17:4) is oval in cross-section. Its lower end is somewhat blunted. Its upper half (tang), which fits the shaft, is sharpened and is entirely covered with minute transverse ridges. Similar picks are known from the Okvik site on Punuk Island (Rainey 1941d, Fig. 11, item 11), and from the Old Bering Sea Hillside site on St. Lawrence Island (Collins 1937, Plate 29;6,7).

Three bone *arrowheads* were found at Kiwak. Two of them are whole and well preserved; the third has the top half broken off. One of the whole specimens is a one-piece arrowhead (Plate 17:3), short, tanged, with a round cross-section, broader at the base and gradually narrowing toward the tip. The second arrowhead is large (Plate 17:1), and of a type known only from the Okvik site and in Old Bering Sea deposits on St. Lawrence Island. It is thus characteristic of the earliest phases of the development of Eskimo culture. It is oval in cross-section, has a conical tang, and the fore end is provided with a slit for an end-blade. Two pointed symmetrical barbs are at the very base of the arrowhead. As on

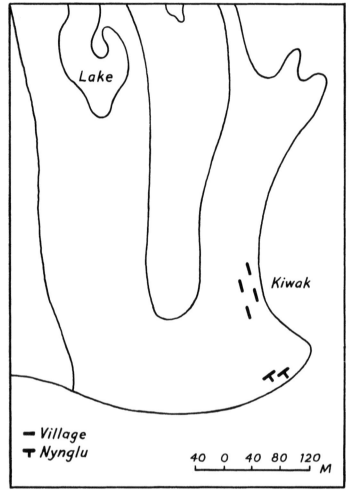

Lake

Kiwak

━ *Village*

┳ *Nynglu*

40 0 40 80 120
                M

similar specimens from Punuk Island (Rainey 1941d, Fig. 14: 1–3) and St. Lawrence (Collins 1937, Plate 29:6,7), four grooves start near the mid-point of the arrowhead, two to each flat face, and continue downward, becoming progressively deeper, down to the tang, where they meet in depth to form the two barbs mentioned above, which diverge outward from the shaft. The flat surfaces of this arrowhead are decorated with three slightly inclined, deeply incised lines, such as we have seen on the arrowheads from the ancient site of Uwelen.

The *dart or spear head* of walrus ivory in Plate 17:2 is flattened in shape, with three pairs of barbs. The tang has a wedge-like taper.

The *lance point* of slate in Plate 17:5 (the forward end is broken off) has a sharp cutting edge and a biconically drilled hole for lashing to the shaft.

Men's knives are of two kinds: unground knives of silicified tuff of a humped type (Plate 17:8), or of the usual form for end-blades (Plate 17:6), and polished leaf-shaped knives of slate, with a tang and mid-rib (Plate 17:7,9).

Slate *women's knives* are represented by several examples, of which two are illustrated: one is a small whole specimen (Plate 17:12), the other is the fragment of a very large broken one (Plate 17:11).

The knife shown in Plate 17:10 is unusual in form, and was purchased from the Eskimos.

The *adzes* from Kiwak are of two types. One of these is represented by a large nephrite adze, symmetrically beveled at the bit like an axe (Plate 17:21). The other adze is short and broad, and made of silicified tuff. While the second must, perforce, have been hafted in a bone socket piece in order to be attached to a handle, the first may have been lashed directly.

The walrus *mattock* in Plate 17:25 for digging up edible roots and other purposes has two grooves deeply cut with an adze on its frontal surface for lashing to a handle. The working edge is sharpened from two sides.

A long *bone rod* (made of the os penis of a walrus) illustrated in Plate 17:24 has a deep socket on its thickened forward end to receive a stone drill.

To *obtain fire* by drilling, the inhabitants of Kiwak made use of wooden spindles identical to those described from the excavations at Uwelen, Nuukan, and Cape Chaplin. They are short rods, 8 cm in length, round in cross-section, 1.5 cm in diameter at the lower end and 1.1 cm wide at the top. Both ends are hemispherical, and the lower one is usually charred.

Household utensils at Kiwak are represented by the following: a fragment of a rather large dish made from a whale scapula, measuring only 1.3 cm in depth; a small box with baleen sides and a wooden bottom, oval in shape and measuring 9.5 cm by 19 cm; a large hook of reindeer antler (Plate 17:20), with a suspension hole; a very shallow whalebone spoon with a short handle (Plate 17:16), and, numerous pottery sherds.

The pottery sherds, examples of which are shown in Plate 17:15,19, represent very crude thick-walled vessels. The usual wall thickness is 1 cm – 1.5 cm near the base, attaining 2 cm – 2.5 cm at the rim. The vessels were tall jars with rounded bases. The characteristic decoration of these vessels consisted of rows of diagonal ridges imparted with a special paddle series of deep diagonal grooves, such as the one found in the area of Cape Dezhnev (Plate 9:7).

Means of transportation are represented only by walrus ivory sled runners of two types. One type consists of very massive runners 4 cm in width and up to 8 cm in height, made of whole, slightly adzed tusks. The other type is that of narrow runners, less than 1 cm in width. The first (Plate 17:28) has large longitudinal slots with notched edges cut through from both sides for the lashing of cross-pieces. The second has small holes drilled along the upper edge for the same purpose. Since the lashing of cross-pieces to such narrow runners would present difficulties, the upper edges of the runners retain a rather broad platform, about 2 cm in width, with projecting ledges.

Among other objects, note must be made of two wooden specimens, the purpose of which is not quite clear. The first of these (Plate 17:23) is the grooved end of some kind of a handle. The second (Plate 17:13) is a small wooden cylinder, 2.8 cm in length, with a circumferential groove near the middle and tinted with red ochre. Identical cylinders, some of them also colored with red pigment, were found by Collins on St. Lawrence Island at the site of Miyowagh, in an Old Bering Sea cultural deposit. Collins suggests that they were used as floats for small bird snares of looped baleen (Collins 1937; 174; Plate 57:18,19).

A remarkable find made during the excavations at Kiwak is the wing (Plate 17:14) of a large winged object, exactly like the one obtained at Point Hope in

1880 (Collins 1929, Plate 6), and similar to one found in the course of excavations on St. Lawrence Island (Collins 1937, Plate 20:1). The outer surface of this wing, like the analogous examples from Point Hope and St. Lawrence Island, is covered with elaborate curvilinear decoration, typical of the Old Bering Sea style of Eskimo art.

The house type and the entire complex of objects found in the excavations at Kiwak, particularly the arrowheads, the ice pick, the stone adzes, the pottery, the sled runners and, finally, the winged object, indicate, without a doubt, that the dwelling investigated at Kiwak dates from the Old Bering Sea period of the development of Eskimo culture.

Cape Chukchi

A few hundred meters west of Cape Chukchi, there is a clearly defined stratum of black soil in a coastal cut. It is capped by a mound, overgrown by an intensely green grass cover (Fig. 8). Closer examination revealed that here, at an elevation of 10 to 12 m above sea level, on the side of stream issuing from a lobe of a higher snowfield, were located the remains of a group of nine small semi-subterranean houses. The central one was somewhat larger than the rest, and joined to them by passageways. Abandoned meat storage pits are located close by the mound formed by this collective dwelling, on the side toward the undercut shore.

The cultural deposit throughout this flattened mound, composed of oily black soil, does not exceed 1.5 m in depth, judging from the existing cut. Pits, covering an area no greater than 1 m square, were excavated at two points: at the cut on the edge of the storage pit, and at one of the entranceways to the house. They yielded a small number of bones, principally of walrus and bearded seal, and only a few objects. In the cut, the pit was carried to a depth of 1 m, while excavation was halted at 0.6 m at the house entrance because of permafrost.

Of the objects found, two flint blades of *men's knives* are of interest. They are unpolished, and probably served as side-inserts. One of them is illustrated in Plate 17:22.

Here also we found two stone *adzes* in good condition, made of dense igneous material. As may be seen from their drawings (Plate 17:17,18), they have been given the desired form by chipping and subsequent pressure retouching, only the bits being ground (Plate 17:17). It is worth noting the very steep bevel of the adze bit illustrated in Plate 17:17, which approaches a right angle and is similar to that on the Old Bering Sea adze-like scrapers described by Collins (Collins 1937:152–153, Fig. 16).

Both adzes, doubtless, were used hafted in bone socket pieces.

The same site yielded a large walrus ivory *wedge* (Plate 17:29) and pottery sherds with a ridged surface finish such as we observed on the Kiwak sherds.

In view of the small amount of earth moved, we can hardly expect to find objects that would date accurately the settlement described. Yet, in view of the absence of ground slate knives, even women's knives, the presence of small square dwellings connected by passageways, and the characteristics of the pottery, we may presume that we are dealing here with a settlement of the Old Bering Sea stage of Eskimo culture.

Between Cape Chukchi and Gidrograficheskoye Lake, but closer to the latter, there also occurs an exposed cultural deposit in the undercut shore. It is relatively shallow, from 1 to 1.5 m in thickness. Limited clearing of this deposit yielded several objects, some of them of undoubted interest, in addition to bones of walrus, bearded seal, and reindeer.

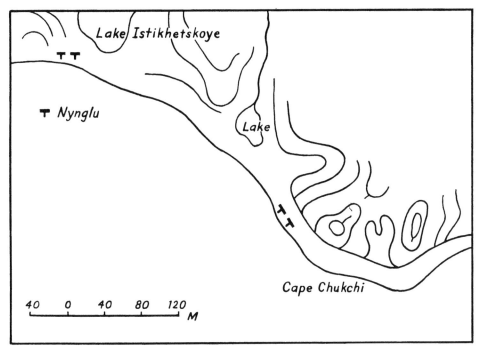

FIGURE 8

The whaling harpoon head of walrus ivory was of the usual type, with a closed socket, a simple basal spur, a large elongate line hole and a slit for an end-blade at right angles to the line hole. Of much greater interest are the *objects of baleen.* Among these, we must first note a small fish cut out of baleen (Plate 17:27), with a small suspension hole drilled in its head. We also found a small box with baleen sides and a small oval wood bottom measuring 6 cm by 8.4 cm. Finally, there is a bone sinew twister, used in making reinforced bows, enclosed in a special baleen case (Plate 17:26). The design of the lower portion of this case is of particular interest, inasmuch as it is plaited of four baleen strands in a manner technically similar to that exemplified in the square plaited objects from the excavations of Geist (Geist and Rainey 1926, Plate 36:11) and Collins on St. Lawrence Island (Collins 1937, Plate 56:8,9).

On the basis of the objects found, it may be supposed that the site near Gidrograficheskoye Lake, whose cultural deposit we tested, belongs to the Punuk stage of the development of Eskimo culture.

Avan

Istikhetskoye Lake is located between Chukchi Bay and Provideniya [Providence] Bay, on the very coast (Fig. 8). This lake, which covers about 20 sq km, has been extending southward and is separated from the sea only by a narrow gravel bar. The Eskimo settlement of Avan existed until recently on the western end of this bar and on the adjacent low-lying terrace. Remains of typical square Eskimo semi-subterranean houses with entranceways and side-chambers near the [inside] entrance to the passageway are preserved on the terrace-like platform mentioned earlier, among the remainders of round *yarangs* of recent times. As in all Eskimo dwellings of this kind, the construction materials included whale bones, principally the jawbones.

Judging from the good state of preservation of the pit-houses, some of which retain the roofing of the very low entranceway, these must not be very old. Limited clearing of the cultural deposit at the entrance to one of these dwellings confirmed this supposition. The only finds were fragments of clay pots, rubbed slate women's knives, and a harpoon head of very recent type.

Remains of older dwellings and meat storage pits were discovered in the coastal cut. A superficial cultural deposit 2 m to 2.5 m in thickness stands out clearly in the eroded shore because its black color. The clearing of this cultural deposit yielded a number of objects, in addition to the bones of hunted animals, principally walrus and ringed seal. Below the more characteristic of these objects are described.

Only one *harpoon head* was found. It was of the whaling type, made of ivory (Plate 18:1), with a closed socket, simple basal spur, an elongated line hole and a slit for the end-blade at right angles to the line hole. Several slate end-blades were found, both from walrus-hunting and whaling harpoons (Plate 18:2,10). A *foreshaft* was also found.

Hunting weapons also include a wooden arrowhead with asymmetrically placed barbs (Plate 18:14) and the usual bird *bola weights* of sections of walrus tusk.

Among the tools, an adze fragment of compact sandstone (Plate 18:12) with a well-preserved bit, carefully ground and sharpened, deserves mention. This *adze*, like the adze-like scrapers of which two were found, was used hafted in a bone socket piece or head. A very typical artifact found at the site is a small *wedge* of walrus ivory, with a sharply beveled bit end and a poll scarred by blows from a hammer.

The series of *men's knives* found is numerically large and varied. The knives are ground with varying degrees of care, and some of them are illustrated in Plate 18:3,4,11.

Also numerous and varied are the *women's knives* of slate—ulu (Plate 18:16, 17). Some of them have biconically drilled holes for lashing to the handle. The site also yielded *obsidian chips*, some of them retouched along the edges.

A wooden tablet (Plate 18:19) with drilled and charred pits is evidence of *fire-making* by drilling.

The whalebone *pick* in Plate 18:21 is highly typical. As usual, it is a large tool (43 cm in length) slightly concave in outline, with a smooth inner surface and a row of deep grooves on the convex side for hafting. The lower working end is blunted from long use.

Among other bone artifacts, we must mention a whale-rib paddle, probably for beating the snow out of clothing, and antler *hooks* for suspending utensils (Plate 18:24).

Of great interest is the humerus of a dog with round holes drilled in its extremities (Plate 18:15) which, by analogy with one found by Collins on St. Lawrence Island with an attached barb (Collins 1937, Plate 79:8), should be probably considered a shank of a fishhook. A considerable amount of baleen was found in the cultural deposit at Avan, both in the form of blanks (Plate 18:20) and as artifacts, mainly boxes with baleen sides and wooden bottoms.

Judging from the size of the wooden bottoms (7.5 cm by 16 cm and 14 cm by 25 cm), some of these box-like buckets were of considerable size.

Pottery in Avan is not as coarse or thick-walled as at Kiwak. The paste is of better quality, and the sand added to the clay is fine. The pottery consists largely of rather tall round-bottomed pots with outside perforated lugs for suspension (Plate 18:23). In rare instances, wall thickness attains 1.5 cm, but it is usually less than 1 cm. Rims are straight, though just slightly incurving and slightly thickened at the lip. Decoration by means of ridges imparted with a paddle, typical of older Eskimo pottery, was not found. The diagonal marks which may be detected on the surfaces of some of the sherds result from smoothing the outside of the vessel with a bunch of grass.

Among other objects, we must mention a bone *toggle* (Plate 18:5); a half of *snow goggles* of fine and careful workmanship, made of ivory (Plate 18:18), with a narrow eye slit and a side loop for tying on and bone *armor plates* with paired holes for joining; these holes are small and were drilled with a metal bit (Plate 18:22).

In the absence of a series of diagnostic types, it is difficult to define more precisely the time of occupation of the Avan village, though it is clear that it pertains to the Punuk stage of the development of Eskimo culture, probably its latest phase.

Plover Bay

Bearing in mind the harpoon head from Plover Bay published by Collins (Collins 1929:5, Fig. 1), which is of undoubted Old Bering Sea date, I devoted particular care to investigating the remains of Eskimo dwellings in this small bay. However, my hopes of finding there the remains of an ancient Eskimo settlement were not realized.

There are numerous easily seen remains of old houses and meat storage pits on the bar which shields Plover Bay from the southwest, near the entrance to Providéniya Bay. Here also, the pit-houses were of the usual square shape, with entranceways. Test pits were carried down to depths of 0.5 to 0.6 m at two points near the entrance to a pit-house, ground-water preventing deeper excavation. The objects recovered from the cultural deposit in the test pits indicate a late date for these houses. Some of them (the southeastern group) may date to proto-historic times, while the majority (on the northwestern part of the bar) belong to the quite recent past.

The most interesting of the objects found in Plover Bay are the following: pressure-flaked arrowheads (Plate 18:8) of silicified tuff; a small concave scraper of flint (Plate 18:6) and an obsidian end-scraper (Plate 18:7); men's and women's rubbed slate knives, the former large to medium in size (Plate 18:9). Some of the women's knives have biconically drilled holes for lashing to the handle. Judging from the sherds, the pottery is the same as at Avan, consisting of large round-bottomed pots of rather large size, with walls measuring 1.5 cm in thickness, and as much as 2 cm at the rim. Such pots have outside suspension lugs (Plate 18:23). The narrow sled runner in Plate 18:13 is of walrus ivory and measures only 4 cm in height. The upper edge of the runner has elongate perforations for lashing the cross-pieces. A broad strip of whale bone, similar to those found on Arakamchechen Island and at Cape Chaplin, served as an umiak keel plate.

Thus, we may suppose that the Old Bering Sea harpoon head from Plover Bay published by Collins does not come from that bay. More probably, it was found at some other place and merely purchased from the Eskimos living at the bay.

Sirhenik

The modern Eskimo settlement of Sirhenik ["Success"] is located on a rather broad terrace-like platform, bounded on the south by the sea, and on the east by the stream of Sirhenik-keyvuk, beyond which rise immediately the vertical cliffs of Cape Ulakhpen. To the west, the platform on which the village is located meets the high cliffs of Yakun, which rise precipitously from the water, while to the north, it comes up against the continental tableland. The modern Eskimo village occupies the eastern part of the platform. The remains of ancient settlements are to be found on the southern edge, which drops off vertically into the sea (Fig. 9). A thick cultural deposit, in places exceeding 4 m in depth, extends over several tens of meters and stands out by its black color from the light-grey background of the coastal cut.

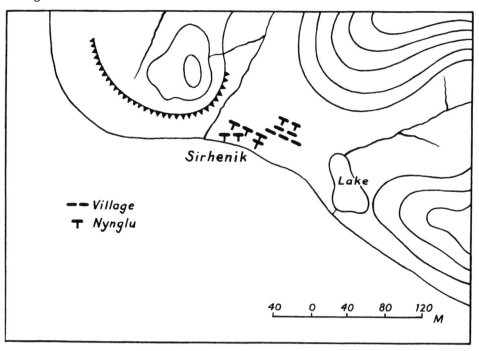

FIGURE 9

Remains of ancient dwellings and of associated meat storage pits occur at three points: in the north, at the base of the ridge and adjacent to the houses of the modern settlement; in the center of the terrace, also near the modern settlement; and in the western part of the terrace. The semi-subterranean houses north of the modern village were not investigated, though a number of considerations suggest that they constitute the latest of the ancient settlements in Sirhenik. The central houses, which include two pit-houses better preserved than the rest, must be assigned to the Punuk stage of the development of Eskimo culture on the basis of our tests. The western group, in which the remains of four pit-houses are clearly distinguishable, is, on the basis of all data, the oldest, and pertains to the Old Bering Sea stage of Eskimo culture.

Excavations in Sirhenik took place on a relatively greater scale than at other points on the peninsula. Tests were initiated there by I. P. Lavrov, and further excavations were conducted by me. In the eastern part of the exposure of the cultural deposit, approximately 25 cu m of soil were removed, while in the western part, the volume of earth moved was only about 4 cu m. The uncovered portion of the cultural deposit in the eastern portion also included in part the meat storage pits associated with the two pit-houses of the central part of the terrace, mentioned earlier, which are located nearby. These pit-houses are imposing structures, in which whalebone has been used to the utmost. They are large in size, each one covering an area of about 200 sq m, with a narrow, though long (14 m) entranceway from the sea side. Having dug out the depressions for these houses, the builders then set up continuous rows of white whale (beluga) skulls both along the walls of the house itself and along the entranceway, so that both houses together made use of about 150 skulls.

The cultural deposit in this eastern part of the settlement contained, in addition to the bones of whale, walrus, bearded seal, and ringed seal, the remains of bear, reindeer, Arctic fox, common fox, rabbit, dog, various birds and fish, as well as a considerable amount of baleen, which occurred in places as a continuous layer. The lower levels of the cultural deposit were underlain by accumulations of mollusc shells (*Mytilus edulis* L.). The number of objects found in this sector is also large, exceeding 1100, not counting fragments of various objects, stone and bone chips, and pottery sherds. The lower levels contained objects characteristic of the Old Bering Sea stage of Eskimo culture, while the middle levels yielded objects typical of Early Punuk, and the top levels pertained to Developed Punuk.

In the western sector, as already stated, the remains of four pit-houses were well preserved. Of these, one was situated near those described above, while the other three were further west. These semi-subterranean houses are smaller in size, do not protrude as markedly above ground surface, and are covered with sod and a thick grass cover. Unlike the eastern houses, where not only whale skulls, but also many other whale bones are exposed, mostly lower jaws were used as elements of the frame. In the western houses there are not [readily] visible whale bones, and these become apparent only upon a thorough inspection of the surface. The entranceways to the pit-houses are duly oriented seaward, and small side-chambers occur at some distance from the entrance of the passageway.

The cultural deposit uncovered on the bank near the meat storage pits associated with the western houses yielded objects typical only of the Old Bering Sea stage of Eskimo culture. It should be noted that here, in the western sector, typical Old Bering Sea objects appeared in the uppermost level of the exposure, at depths of 1 m to 1.5 m from the surface, whereas in the eastern sector they occurred at considerable depths, at about 4 m below surface.

The resulting impression is that, in Old Bering Sea times, the Eskimo inhabited the western, somewhat higher part of the terrace, and that their kitchen refuse spread over the somewhat lower southeastern part. In Punuk times, structures were built to one side of the already collapsed older pit-houses, and the older cultural deposit was covered with later strata varying from 2 to 4 m in thickness.

The description of the objects found at Sirhenik is ordered independently of their provenience from the eastern or western sectors, but provenience is given for typologically important items.

Harpoon heads. Blanks for harpoon heads have been found at other sites, but in Sirhenik they occurred in large numbers. They are all segments of the distal ends of the tusks of young walrus, and present similar features. At a certain distance (6 to 16 cm) from the tip on the inner side of the tusk, the end was cut through with an adze to three-quarters of its thickness and then broken off. Thus, the tusks of young walrus (the distal ends of which are never worn or ground down) provided blanks for harpoon heads of various sizes (7 cm to 15 cm), in accordance with need. The length of the blank along the outer convex surface is naturally greater than along the inner face (Plate 19:1,2). Subsequently, the basal spur was shaped on the outer longer side of the broader end of the blank. A sharp flint blade was then used to impart a hexagonal or some other desired form to the blank (Plate 19:3,4), and the line hole was drilled (Plate 19:5). Then, as we see from the example in Plate 19:5, the socket was hollowed out. Finally, the harpoon head was given its definitive shape, and the decoration was applied.

The large ivory harpoon head (11 cm in length) of Old Bering Sea type in Plate 19:9 differs somewhat from those previously found. It has a wide, shallow, trough-like open socket, similar to the sockets of the harpoon heads from Cape Dezhnev, described earlier (Plate 7:1,2,13). There are two narrow but long slots for the socket lashing. The triple symmetric spur has a long center-prong and short side-prongs, the tip of the spur being bent outward (backward). The round line holes are two in number, one in front of the socket, the other in its lower part, rather than below it. These line holes are not connected by a deep groove on the dorsal side, as they are typically on harpoon heads of the Old Bering Sea type (Plate 7:3,6). The specimen has yet another distinctive feature. Whereas all Old Bering Sea harpoon heads with triple spurs hitherto known to us are provided with stone side-blades, this one lacks side-blades, but does have a broad slit for an end-blade in the plane of the line holes. This harpoon head was found in the eastern sector of the refuse area, not in the lowermost layer, but in the middle level (at a depth of 3 m below surface)—apparently as a result of secondary deposition. The fact is that this harpoon head bears decoration in the Old Bering Sea style, preserved only on portions of its surface, and was deposited originally within the high tide area, where water action rounded all of its formerly sharp features and erased its decoration almost entirely. Later, it was gathered up off the beach, and happened into the deposit where it was found.

An ivory harpoon head found in the western sector of the refuse area at a depth of 1.5 m below surface also belongs to the Old Bering Sea stage of the development of Eskimo culture (Plate 19:10), though we know of no exact parallels to it. The open socket is broad, shallow, and trough-like. There are two slots with edge-grooves for the socket lashing, but these slots do not come together on the dorsal side, as is usually the case in Old Bering Sea harpoon heads of Collins' Type I, but merge in such a manner that we have three openings instead of four for the lashing. The basal spur is triple, symmetrical, with a longer center-prong. The line hole, which still retains baleen strands, is drilled biconically, not in the usual direction from the ventral to the dorsal side of the head, but in the plane of the spur and of the side openings of the socket lashing.

The two flint side-blades are set in slots which are at right angles to the line hole. The entire surface of the head, with the exception of the socket and the ventral side of the spur, is decorated in Old Bering Sea style.

The harpoon head described differs, therefore, from heads of Collins' Old Bering Sea Type I in the presence of only one line hole, instead of two, and a distinct lashing arrangement. A number of considerations allow us to suppose that this harpoon head is older than the heads of Collins' Type I.

The fragment of another similar harpoon head was found, also in the western sector and in the same layer as the specimen described above. In view of the small size of the fragment, the typological characteristics of this head cannot be given. We illustrate it in Plate 19:12 because of its splendidly preserved decoration.

At a depth of 4 m in the lowermost layer of the eastern sector we found a bone harpoon head of Birnirk type (Plate 19:11). Its diagnostic features are as follows: open socket with straight edges, a single slot and opposing groove for lashing, a double, vaguely divided, asymmetric spur, a round line hole directly above the socket, and two small shell side-blades set in slots. The projecting portions of these side-blades have been broken off, but their remains are firmly implanted in the slots. Decoration consists of two lines forming an angle, the apex of which is between the side-blades, while the diverging sides go as far as the socket lashing. One technical detail must be noted: a narrow transverse slot has been cut at the upper edge (apex) of the socket, and into it has been set, like a brace, a narrow strip of walrus ivory.

The harpoon head shown in Plate 19:13 also belongs to the Birnirk type. It was found together with the bone specimen described above. It has an open socket with straight edges, two slots for the socket lashing, in which the lashing itself, made or twisted baleen strands, has been preserved in good condition, a double asymmetric basal spur, and a round line hole. The forward end of the head bears a sharp barb, on the side opposite the spur. This type is common among the ancient harpoon heads from Point Barrow. Similar heads were found by Sverdrup (Mathiassen 1927; 2:180; Fig. 12) in his excavation on Chetyrekhstolbovy Island in the Medvezhi group, opposite the mouth of the Kolyma. It differs from the one represented in Plate 19:13 only in the presence of a slot for a side-blade opposite the barb.

At a depth of 2 m below surface in the eastern sector of the refuse area, we found several bone harpoon heads of Mathiassen's well-known Thule 2 type or Collins' Type IV. Two of them are illustrated in Plate 19:7 and 19:8. The open socket in these harpoon heads is in the form of a truncated cone. There is one slot with an opposing groove for the socket lashing, or else merely a circular groove. The line hole is round, elongate, or triangular. There is one asymmetric spur and two symmetrical barbs. Decoration is absent.

An unfinished harpoon head of similar type (Plate 19:6) is of interest, inasmuch as it shows that the basal spur and side barbs were shaped prior to the perforation of the line hole and the hollowing of the socket.

In the middle layer of the eastern sector of the site (from 2 m to 3.5 m below surface) we found a series of harpoon heads typical of Early and Developed Punuk. Particularly numerous are harpoon heads of Collins' Type III(a)x, differing from one another only in size and details (Plate 19:14,15,16,19,20,21). Their typological features are as follows: an open socket with straight edges, slightly wider toward the bottom; one slot for the lashing with an opposing groove (Plate 19:14,16) or, more often, two slots, one usually considerably higher than the other (Plate 19:15,19,20,21); one simple basal spur, a round line hole biconically drilled, with grooves directed downward, and a slit for the end-blade in the same plane as the line hole. The material is usually bone, more rarely ivory. Decoration is by means of distinctly drawn lines, characteristic of Early Punuk, or by means of dots and lines meeting at acute angles, typical of Developed Punuk.

The harpoon heads represented in Plate 19:17,18 differ from those described above mainly in the design of the basal spur. These heads have an open socket, a single slot and opposing groove for the socket lashing, a double or triple spur, vaguely divided, a round line hole with grooves directed downward, and a slit for the end-blade in the plane of the line hole. Decoration is by means of simple lines. Of the ten harpoon heads of this type, four are of ivory and six of bone.

Only three harpoon heads with closed sockets were found, all of them of ivory. Two of them are shown in Plate 19:22,23. The first (Plate 19:23) has a sharp basal spur, a round line hole and a slit for the end-blade in the plane of the line hole. The cross-section is oval, with a constriction just above the line hole. The decoration is typical of Developed Punuk and consists of dots and incised lines. The second harpoon head (Plate 19:22) is somewhat different in shape, has a slit for the end-blade at right angles to the line hole, and lacks decoration.

A quite diminutive (less than 6 cm in length) bone harpoon head found at a depth of 2.5 m below surface, is very simple typologically: it has an open socket with straight sides (Plate 22:25), one short longitudinal slot and an opposing groove for the socket lashing, a simple lateral spur, and a line hole which is not round, but in the form of a transverse slot just above the socket. The forward end is pointed, and the cross-section is flattened. This harpoon head is closest to Mathiassen's Thule I type or Collins' Type V. By its size, it is too small to have been used for hunting sea mammals. A harpoon with a head of this kind would have been used probably in fishing.

Only two whaling *harpoon heads* were found at Sirhenik, of which one is unfinished. The other one is also typical inasmuch as it lacks a slit at the forward end for an end-blade, though having a closed socket, a side-spur, and a large elongate line hole.

Harpoon *end-blades* of slate were found in considerable numbers at Sirhenik. They are all triangular in outline, with straight bases (Plate 20:1–5,10–12). In rare instances, they are chipped and trimmed by pressure retouching (Plate 20:4). In most cases, however, they are thoroughly ground (Plate 20:2,11) and thin (as thin as 1 mm). Thick ones are not as frequently found (Plate 20:1,3), and number only five. Their edges are ground bilaterally, and a short longitudinal ridge occurs at the point.

The number of harpoon *foreshafts* found at Sirhenik is not great. Among them are the usual Eskimo spindle-shaped foreshafts flattened at the fore end and with a round line hole (Plate 20:14). The foreshaft represented in Plate 20:15 is of ivory, round in cross-section, with two small perforations or slots for attachment, one at the base, the other near the middle. The fore end, which fits into the socket of the harpoon head, is cut and beveled from two sides.

Harpoon *ice picks* of ivory, characteristic of Old Bering Sea sites on St. Lawrence Island, were found in the middle and lower levels of the eastern sector and in the western sector. The picks found in the eastern sector (Plate 20:7,9) are both made of tusks of young walrus, with a sharpened fore end and a conically beveled butt, made to fit the harpoon shaft, and covered with transverse grooves which extend nearly half-way down the piece. The ice pick found in the western sector (Plate 20:6) differs from the preceding in being somewhat larger, and in having a different arrangement for hafting to the shaft. While the conically beveled tangs of the first two picks described were designed to fit into the end of the harpoon shaft, this pick has a flat side cut away at the upper end so as to fit against the shaft, to which it was fastened by a special binding. For more secure attachment, the upper half of this pick was also transversely corrugated. The same mode of attachment to the shaft was used for the bone ice pick found in the upper level of the eastern sector (Plate 20:8), which, in addition, bears two drilled holes, one at the top, through the mortised portion, for the insertion of a bone rivet, the other toward the bottom, for tying to the shaft.

The ivory bone point from the eastern sector shown in Plate 20:13 is unusual in form. It may have served both as an ice pick, and as a probe for gauging the thickness and strength of the ice.

Wooden inflation *plugs* for sealskin *floats* at Sirhenik are of the usual form, which occurs in two variants: tall (Plate 20:21) and flat (Plate 20:20). These plugs have a deep circular groove for lashing in the mouthpiece of the float. Round holes are drilled for inflation, and are plugged with stoppers of wood or bone.

Float bars for the attachment of the line to the float (Plate 20:22) are wooden, of the usual type, in the form of short rods with knobs at the ends.

Objects not directly connected with the harpoon complex though relating to the hunting of sea mammals include seal scratchers and wound plugs.

Several examples of wooden *seal scratchers* were found. They are all in the form of slightly curved wooden paddles with four prongs (Plate 20:16), to which seal claws were attached. A perforation in the center is for the claw lashing. These scratchers and their use in seal hunting have been described in detail by Nelson (1899; Plate 52:10,11) and Murdoch (1892:253–254, Fig. 253). Five-fingered scratchers entirely similar in form were found by Geist in excavations on St. Lawrence Island (Geist and Rainey 1936, Plate 43:7).

Wooden *wound plugs*, varying considerably in size and shape, were also found in considerable numbers. The more typical ones are represented in Plate 20:17, 18,19. Plugs were found both in the eastern and western sectors of the refuse area.

Spear points occurred at Sirhenik in large numbers. They are made of silicified tuff or slate. One such point, not completely finished, is represented in Plate 20:23.

About ten ground spear points of slate were found. Their size is too large for them to have been harpoon end-blades, even in whaling harpoons, and their concave bases are not such as to allow their use as knives. It is interesting that they should all have biconically drilled holes for lashing to the fore end of a shaft. A whole point of this kind, with one hole for lashing to the shaft and a concave base, is shown in Plate 20:24. Another, also intact, has an unusual stemmed base and two lashing holes. Eight of these points are represented only by halves, usually the bottom halves (Plate 20:25,26), the fracture always having taken place in line with the drilled lashing holes.

BIRD AND MAMMAL HUNTING EQUIPMENT

Bird dart heads were few in the eastern sector at Sirhenik, though some quite typical ones were found. The center-prong of a walrus ivory dart, represented in Plate 22:16, is flat and has a tang which fits into the shaft and a longitudinal hole or slot for attachment. The tip is very sharp. Five pointed barbs are placed asymmetrically, two along one edge, three along the other. Another similar dart-head (Plate 22:15), also of ivory, differs only in its greater length and the presence of four symmetrically placed barbs. A third ivory dart head (Plate 22:18) is simpler than the two described above, and has only two symmetrical barbs.

The point with two unilateral barbs represented in Plate 22:17 served, in all likelihood, as a side-prong on a bird dart.

A *throwing board* for darts and, perhaps, light harpoons, is incompletely preserved (Plate 20:27). Judging from the remaining portion, which was held in the hand (the drawing shows the hole for the thumb), this board was of a type typical of the western Eskimo of Alaska, and was similar in form to the one found by Geist on St. Lawrence Island (Geist and Rainey 1936, Plate 48:1).

Bows and arrows. No well-preserved one-piece bows were found at Sirhenik, though four small wooden bows were. Of these, two are children's toys, and two are small-scale models of real bows. The illustrations (Plate 21:1,2,3; 2 is of baleen) allow some idea of the form of real bows. However, apart from such simple bows, the inhabitants of Sirhenik apparently also had composite, reinforced bows. This conclusion is motivated by the finding of a number of bone strips and individual wooden parts which may be viewed as components of a composite bow. As an example, we illustrate a carefully finished slightly concave wooden piece (Plate 21:10), one of the end-pieces of a composite bow. A similar object was also found by Geist (Geist and Rainey 1936; Plate 65:10) in excavations on St. Lawrence Island. The only difference is that, in our specimen, one end is shouldered to retain the bowstring, while the other is wedge-shaped to fit into the adjacent piece, which is splayed, whereas the Geist specimen has one end shouldered to retain the bowstring, while the other is splayed, and fits a wedge-shaped piece.

The *twister* for sinew or baleen strands is an indispensable tool in making a bow, and is usually used as one of a pair. It is represented by one specimen from Sirhenik (Plate 21:9), made of wood, an unusual material in this case.

Wrist guards, protective plates worn on the left wrist in shooting with a bow, are represented at Sirhenik by a very interesting series of five specimens: two of them (Plate 21:4,5) are from the lower levels of the eastern sector of the refuse area, two are from the middle level (Plate 21:7,8), and one is from the upper stratum (Plate 21:6).

The wrist guard shown in Plate 21:5 is of ivory, large in size (3.5 cm by 11 cm, allowing for the broken portion), and has the slightly curving shape with rounded corners typical of such objects. Two slots are provided in the central narrower portion for lacing to the hand. The decoration on the outside of this wrist guard is of interest. It consists of paired curved lines and concentric circles with radiating spurs. The cross in the center, the concentric circles, and the curvilinear patterns formed by pairs of parallel lines are all motifs of the Old Bering Sea style. The technique, however, is different. Instead of the thin scratched lines of Old Bering Sea engraving on bone, we have rather deeply incised bold lines, such as were usual in the engraving of Punuk times. For this reason, I am inclined to assign this object to Early Punuk, a period transitional between the Old Bering Sea stage and Punuk.

The other wrist guard from the lower levels (Plate 21:4) is made of bone, and is comparable in size to the preceding. It is undecorated. It is of unusual form and has details of design which I had not seen hitherto on similar objects, which have a very broad area of distribution in Siberia. The bone plate out of which this wrist guard is made has the customary trough-like shape, but both of its ends are somewhat uplifted. Two deep cuts of unusual shape are in its central portion. Small narrow slots along the edges are provided for attachment to the arm, two on one edge, and one on the other. Decoration is lacking.

The wrist guards from the middle levels are moderate in size. One of them is of ivory (Plate 21:8), the other of bone (Plate 21:7). Both are decorated in Punuk style and probably date from that period. Both wrist guards are provided with one narrow slot on each edge for attachment to the arm.

The wrist guard from the upper level (Plate 21:6) is of ivory and has three narrow slots for tying on, two near one edge, and one on the other. It is undecorated.

No whole *arrows* were found. The numerous shafts and arrowheads indicate that the length of arrows varied from 60 to 70 cm. Some of the arrows were made from one piece of wood. These were mainly arrows with a thickened blunt tip. Most arrows however, had bone arrowheads. Arrow shafts average about 50 cm in length. They are round in cross-section, about 1 cm in diameter, or else slightly flattened (6 to 9 mm by 11 mm). The proximal end of the shaft (Plate 21:14) is somewhat wider where the notch for the bowstring is cut (13 to 13.5 mm). In one instance, the proximal end of the shaft was made of bone (Plate 21:12). Thickened distal ends of one-piece wooden arrows occur in several variants, as shown in Plate 21:11,13,15. The diameter of the thickened distal ends of such arrows varies from 13 to 20 mm.

Bone arrowheads are numerous and varied. Only two bone arrowheads were found in the lower levels of the eastern sector (Plate 21:23,25), the remainder nearly all being from the middle levels (from 1.5 m to 4 m below surface). The arrowhead in Plate 21:25 is very similar in type and decoration to one found at Kiwak (Plate 17:1). This long arrowhead, oval in cross-section, is provided with a slit for an end-blade at the tip, but has a forked butt rather than a conical tang like the Kiwak specimen. Just like the latter, it has two symmetrical barbs reaching down to the butt, and decoration consists of a row of deeply incised lines. The second arrowhead from the lower levels (Plate 21:23) differs from the preceding in the absence of barbs and of decoration, its round cross-section, a thickening near the middle, and the presence of a conical tang.

Stone end-blades of silicified tuff, of the kind inserted into the tip of this type of bone arrowhead, are illustrated in Plate 21:23,25.

Arrowheads from the main occupation layer may be reduced to several types. Long flattened bone arrowheads diamond-shaped in cross-section, have a splayed base (Plate 21:17) or a conical tang (Plate 21:19). Flattened arrowheads, also of bone, oval to round in cross-section in their lower half, and triangular or diamond-shaped in the upper, have a distinctly shouldered conical tang and one (Plate 21:21) or, more rarely, two barbs (Plate 21:16).

Relatively short and flat arrowheads with two symmetrical barbs and a flat pointed tang occur in several variants (Plate 21:20,22,26). Finally, a tanged arrowhead with a laurel-leaf shaped distal end is shown in Plate 21:24.

Blunt arrowheads may be divided into two groups: tanged bone arrowheads, and walrus ivory or tooth arrowheads with a socket for mounting to the shaft.

The first group is illustrated by an unfinished example of a short, blunt arrow-head, which provides some idea of the technique of manufacture of such an object (Plate 22:1). Three types may be distinguished in this group: (1) a simple arrowhead, round in cross-section, with a splayed base (Plate 22:2); (2) an elongate pyriform type with a conical tang (Plate 22:3), and (3) a type which is round in cross-section with a splayed base and a thickened trilobate tip (Plate

22:4). We know of a similar trilobate arrownead from the ancient site of Uwelen. Another one, but with a wedge-shaped tang, is known from Rasmussen's Point Barrow collection (Mathiassen 1930a; Plate 7:13) and probably belongs to the Birnirk complex. The same type survived as late as the 19th century among the western Eskimos of Alaska (Volkov and Rudenko 1910, Fig. 12m; Nelson 1899, Plate 59b:16), where, as at Uwelen, it had a socket for mounting on the shaft. Simple ivory blunt arrowheads with a socket for mounting on the shaft of egg and acorn shapes are represented in Plate 22:5,6,7.

The upper level yielded long bone arrowheads with one (Plate 22:9) or two (Plate 22:8) sharp unilateral barbs, and with tangs that are knobbed rather than pointed at the very tip.

As a parallel to the miniature bows, Sirhenik has yielded a whole series of wooden and two bone miniature arrows. These are about 8 cm in length, about 5 mm in diameter, with simple pointed, blunt or barbed tips (Plate 22:10,11,12). Like the bows, they had a ritual purpose and were prepared for ceremonial occasions.

Bird bola weights were found in large numbers, and do not differ in type in any way from those found at other ancient Eskimo sites. They are all (Plate 22:19,20,21) made of walrus teeth or segments of walrus tusks and have drilled suspension holes.

In Sirhenik, as at Kiwak, we found small wooden cylinders (Plate 22:22) with a central circular groove, some of them colored red. A baleen line (Plate 22:30) in conjunction with such a cylinder formed a device for snaring ducks.

FISHING GEAR

Salmon harpoon heads. The harpoon heads shown in Plate 22:23,24 were found in the middle level layer of the eastern sector. They are both miniature in size and made of ivory. The first is very similar in size and shape to the one we described from Cape Chaplin (Plate 13:5), but lacks the finishing touches; there is no socket, while the line hole is disproportionately large. The other specimen has a closed socket and one blunt lateral spur. The line hole is round, biconically drilled. The distal end is leaf-shaped, and constricted in its upper third. The lower half of this flattened harpoon head is oval in cross-section, while the forward leaf-shaped half is diamond-shaped, as a result of the occurrence of ridges running from the tip toward the line hole on both faces. Similar miniature harpoon heads of ivory have been found on St. Lawrence Island by Collins (Collins 1937, Plate 59:18–21) and Geist (Geist and Rainey 1936, Plate 74:8) in Old Bering Sea deposits, and were interpreted as children's toys. One cannot agree with this interpretation, if only because these harpoon heads show marks of long use, and have worn, and sometimes broken, distal ends. Harpoons with such heads were used in catching fish.

Spear points. The middle levels in the eastern sector yielded several beautifully preserved bone points, too large to have served as prongs of bird or other darts. It is better to consider them as fish spear prongs, especially since similar fish spear points and prongs are known from ethnographic collections (Murdoch 1892, 268; Birket-Smith 1924:359, Fig. 259).

First, we must note two splendid flattened bone points (Plate 22:31,32) with two pairs of sharp asymmetric barbs, a pointed tang designed for insertion into a shaft, with a small opening at the tang for attaching to the shaft. The point in Plate 22:31 even retains some of its baleen lashing.

The flattened bone spear side-prong in Plate 22:40 is very large (38 cm in length), has two barbs on its slightly incurving inner side, and an elongated opening at the beginning of the tang for lashing to a shaft.

The ivory point in Plate 22:39 apparently was a spear prong. It has two barbs and a tang which is flat on its inner surface.

I believe the points shown in Plate 22:33,34 also to be fish spear center-prongs, since they are too large and their barbs are too blunt for considering them bird dart points. One of these points is made of bone, flattened, with one convex and one concave side (Plate 22:33). It has three pairs of asymmetrically placed barbs and a hole for lashing near the tang. The other point is of ivory, has a diamond-shaped cross-section (Plate 22:34), two pairs of asymmetric barbs, and a pointed tang, designed to fit into the shaft.

It is possible that the point fragment of ivory in Plate 22:35, with a series of unilateral barbs, and the long miniature bone point, also with a row of unilateral barbs (Plate 22:13) are fish spears.

Barbs or *hooks* of compound fish spears were found at Sirhenik both in the lower levels of the eastern sector, and in the western sector (Plate 22:36,37,38). They are all moderate in size, made of bone, and identical to those found at the ancient site of Uwelen and at the Okvik site in the Punuk Islands. Similar barbs of composite salmon spears, though somewhat different in shape, were found by Mathiassen in his excavations in the American Central Eskimo area (Mathiassen 1927, Plate 12:10,11; Plate 43:1,3,5).

Fishhooks, which were found mainly in the middle layers of the cultural deposit, are of two types. The first consists of a bone shank, similar to a fish spear point, with a row of unilateral barbs, to which a bone barb was attached at an acute angle by means of baleen strands (Plate 22:14). This type of fishhook is described for Old Bering Sea times by Collins from St. Lawrence Island (Collins 1937, Plate 56:3), and is known from Mathiassen's excavations on northern Baffin Island (Mathiassen 1927;1, Plate 43:11). The other type is represented by compound fishhooks with a wooden (Plate 22:26), bone, or ivory (Plate 22:27) shank with three barbs. At the upper end, the shanks of such hooks have a line hole, while the lower thickened end has three radially placed longitudinal slots for the barbs, and a circular groove below them for lashing the barbs to the shank. The barbs were of wood, bone, or ivory (Plate 22:28,29).

Fishhooks of this type were found on St. Lawrence Island at relatively late Punuk sites (Collins 1937, Plate 75:45; Geist and Rainey 1936, Plate 54:9). They persisted among the western Eskimos of Alaska to the end of the last century. Rainey has described them in the inventory from the Okvik site in the Punuk Islands (Rainey 1941d, Plate 15:6).

Fish line sinkers are all of one type, made of ivory, elongate in form, with line holes at both ends. Sometimes, in addition to the end-holes, side-holes occur toward the middle of the sinker. The sinkers differ from one another only in shape and size (Plate 23:15,16,17,18).

Apart from lines, the inhabitants of Sirhenik also used hoop-nets made of baleen in fishing for saffron cod under the ice, of the type described from Arakamchechen Island. The rims of such nets were made of wood or strips of baleen. An elongate boulder with a circular groove around the middle served as a heavy weight, fastened to the bottom of such a cone-shaped hoop-net (Plate 23:1,2; Plate 12:26; Plate 28:1).

In addition to the hoop-net, another type of net was used in fishing, but the small size of the fragments, made of baleen, precludes any knowledge of their nature or shape. Many sinkers of ivory of various shapes used with nets were preserved. Examples are shown in Plate 23:20,21,22.

The antler piece represented in Plate 28:2 may have served as a spool for winding a fish line. At least among the western Eskimo (Nelson 1899:193–194, Plate 77:22,23) similar objects served that purpose.

A very interesting scoop is of rather complex design and was probably used for skimming [floating] ice from the holes made in the ice. The bottom is made from a trimmed deer antler, reinforced by a net of rootlets (Plate 28:3).

VARIOUS TOOLS AND UTENSILS

The *hammer* in Plate 28:4 is made from a segment of the main stem of an antler, the handle being a tine of the same antler. The latter has a perforation for suspension. Initially, we considered this a fish club, but we then found an illustration of an identical object in Birket-Smith's work on the ethnography of the Greenland Eskimo (Birket-Smith 1924, Fig. 288), where it is described as a blubber mallet.

Before being used as fuel in a lamp, frozen blubber is first pounded with such a mallet on a flat stone or a piece of wood. This probably was also the purpose of the mallet made of the os penis of a walrus, shown in Plate 28:5.

The flat *mattocks* from Sirhenik for the removal of sod are entirely like those described from Arakamchechen Island and Cape Chaplin. They are of very large size (40 cm–50 cm in length) and wide (up to 10 cm). As may be seen from Plate 28:6,7, their lower, working ends are shovel-like. Broad and deep grooves are provided at the upper end for hafting to a handle.

The *picks and mattocks* for digging up edible roots, made of bone and ivory, are numerous and varied. Some of them are similar to those represented in Plate 2:28–30 and Plate 15:6. An ivory pick with a worn lower end and a well preserved upper portion is shown in Plate 28:8. The four hafting grooves are clearly visible. There are also some quite short specimens of ivory. Plate 28:9 shows an example from the western sector, Plate 28:10 one from the eastern.

The pick shown in Plate 28:11 is of interest in view of its hafting arrangement.

The ivory *adzes* are typologically close to the shorter mattocks. They were hafted directly to the handle, and occur in two variants, shouldered (Plate 28:13) and unshouldered.

The ivory *wedges* are of the usual form which one finds at all ancient Eskimo sites. As an example, we illustrate a wedge (Plate 28:12) from the western sector. A wedge from the eastern sector was also used as a drill rest.

We have a whole series of stone *adzes*. Of these, only two are from the western sector, including the one shown in Plate 24:4, the remainder being from the eastern sector. The adze in Plate 24:4 is of moderate size and is made of silicified tuff. It is only slightly ground and has a sharply beveled bit. Adzes are represented in the eastern sector by four examples of various sizes: a large one (Plate 24:1), two medium-sized ones (Plate 24:2, and 3), and one quite small, of silicified tuff.

As examples of the bone *socket pieces* of stone adzes, we illustrate one specimen designed for a large adze (Plate 24:5) and another for a smaller one (Plate 24:35).

A characteristic feature of the cultural deposit in the western sector and the lower levels in the eastern sector is the abundance of various chipped, but not ground, stone tools. Obsidian fragments and flakes were found in large numbers.

Some of them are retouched, others lack retouching, but have sharp edges slightly blunted from use (Plate 24:24,27). Flakes of flint and siliceous slate have cutting edges, also with traces of use (Plate 24:9,28), the latter being retouched along the edge. Blades of the same materials occur (Plate 24:8,15,16) and occasionally have a finely retouched cutting edge (Plate 24:8,14).

Small and large *scrapers,* used in working skins, are highly varied. Plate 24:6 shows a large skin scraper, crudely worked through the removal of large flakes. Another similar scraper (Plate 24:20) has two working edges. There are also smaller scrapers of finer workmanship, representing a great variety of types. We will enumerate the more typical kinds: thick end-scrapers (Plate 24:7,11) of flint and silicified tuff; double end-scrapers (Plate 24:13); concave scrapers of flint (Plate 24:23,25) and obsidian (Plate 24:30); a side-scraper (Plate 24:26); and thick humped scrapers (Plate 24:12,29).

There is a very interesting series of stone tools from the western sector, not highly specialized in form, which may have been used as *reamers,* but could also have served as scrapers or knives (Plate 24:17,18,19,20), all of them of silicified tuff. An excellent example of a stone *drill* is shown in Plate 24:21. The fragment of a similar drill is illustrated in Plate 24:22.

In addition to the stone examples, bone drills were also used for making holes. One such drill was found fastened to a wooden shaft (Plate 23:10). The bone drill bit (7 cm in length, about 0.6 cm in diameter) was set in a notch on the end of a long wooden shaft (27 cm in length, 2 cm in diameter) and bound with a lashing of baleen strands. Another similar shaft was found without the drill bit (Plate 23:9).

There are several drills of bone and ivory. Some of them have a cylindrical working end (Plate 23:3), others are flattened and wedge-like in form (Plate 23:4,5).

Bow drills are wooden, rather large (Plate 23:25) or else smaller and of bone (Plate 23:26). Identical drills were used in fire-drilling.

Wooden *fire-making spindles* were sometimes large (as long as 20 cm), sometimes quite small (7–8 cm). Most frequently, the spindles were of medium size, such as those illustrated in Plate 23:23,24.

Drill rests for the spindles included casual objects such as wedges, but more often were the astragalus bones of reindeer, which have a natural depression in the form of a round pit.

The most numerous stone tools in Sirhenik were knives. They include, first of all, stone side-blades. Examples of such blades of flint and silicified tuff are shown in Plate 24:36,38,39,40. There are also some knife end-blades (Plate 24:37). The handles holding the stone side-blades were of wood or bone. Plate 25:16 illustrates an antler tine handle with one deep and one shallow slot for stone side-blades, and two narrow suspension slots.

Men's knives of slate and siliceous slate form another large group. These knives, like the slate women's knives, occurred mainly in the middle and upper layers of the eastern sector. One such knife, having a broad stem set in a slot in the fore end of a wooden handle, was found together with the latter (Plate 25:1). The remainder of the knives and handles were found separately. The most typical forms of men's slate knives are illustrated in Plate 25:2,3,4,5,6,7,10,11,12,14. Typical handles for such knives are represented in Plate 25:26,27,28,35. Large wooden handles (Plate 25:26,27) held the blades of large knives or blades with broad stems (Plate 25:10), whereas blades with narrow stems (Plate 25:5,12) were inserted into small wooden (Plate 25:28) or bone handles of a type already familiar to us, with (Plate 25:18) or without (Plate 25:17,19,20) a special slot for extracting the stem in case of breakage of the blade.

Either metal blades or very small stone blades, such as the one shown in Plate 25:12, were hafted in small handles of walrus ivory consisting of two halves (Plate 25:21), with a narrow slot for the insertion of the blade. Only two such handles were found at Sirhenik.

We found only one asymmetric single-edged man's slate knife (Plate 25:13).

A very large number of women's slate knives and wooden and bone handles for them were found, almost all of them in the eastern sector. Plate 25:15 illustrates one of these knives, found associated with its handle. The variety of shapes and sizes among women's knives and their handles is apparent from their illustrations: Plate 25:23,25,30,31,32,33, showing knives, Plate 25:22, showing a bone handle, and Plate 25:24,34 and Plate 26:1,2,3,4,5, depicting wooden handles.

In case of damage and cracking, wooden handles of women's knives were not discarded, but mended. A deep groove was cut, and a tight lashing of baleen fiber was applied.

Few *bone knives* were found. A knife of this kind can be a large double-edged tool of walrus ivory with a suspension hole, as illustrated in Plate 25:29, or a very small bone knife with a thin blade and with or without a suspension hole, as shown in Plate 23:13,14. The latter two are probably women's knives for tailoring and other fine work. Ivory knives made from broken bird darts (Plate 23:6,7) probably served the same purpose. Both of them have been sharpened at their distal end to wedge-like and chisel-like forms, respectively, while the proximal ends are provided with suspension holes.

The object represented in Plate 24:31 is a well-known type of *flaker*, used in manufacturing stone tools. It consists of a carefully made antler handle with a long and deep open socket, into which a bone rod, the flaker proper, was inserted. As a result of the shape of the socket, the rod does not fall out, but moves freely within it, and may be set further in or out as desired. An outside flange on the forward end of the handle held in place the lashing used to hold the rod in the socket. This handle design allowed its use in combination with various flaker tips. Similar flakes are described by Murdoch (Murdoch 1892:288–289, Fig. 281) for the western Eskimo of Alaska.

Awls are numerous and varied. They are in the form of pointed bones and bone splinters (Plate 27:13,13,20,21), pointed flat pieces (Plate 27:12), or ivory points with eyes or a knob on the end opposite the sharp tip.

Two types of bone *needles* were found: relatively long and thick ones (Plate 27:18), and thin ones (Plate 27:19).

The *needle-case* in Plate 23:11 is simple in design, made of a tubular bird bone, and lacks decoration.

Needle-cases, awls and small knives were customarily tied by the Eskimo to women's bags, which were used for keeping strips of fur or leather, and various small items and adjuncts to women's handwork. The handles of such bags were made of ivory and were frequently decorated. A handle of this kind, undecorated, is shown in Plate 23:8. The lower edge of the handle has special depressions to provide a more convenient hold for the hand.

No *thimbles* have been preserved, though these were probably made of seal-skin, as among the modern Eskimos. Thimbles were kept on a strap, with a bone holder at one end. One such thimble holder is shown in Plate 29:4. A thimble-holder of similar type has been published by Mathiassen from his excavations in the north of Baffin Island (Mathiassen 1927:1; Plate 63:6).

HOUSEHOLD CONTAINERS

Spoons at Sirhenik are of two types: ovoid with a short handle, and a long-handled type. Short-handled spoons are of bone (Plate 26:8,9) and wood (Plate 26:7), very shallow, no deeper than 2–4 mm. The end of the handle always has either a hole or grooves for suspension. The long-handled spoons are of antler (Plate 26:10), of a type already familiar to us from the excavations at Uwelen and Cape Chaplin. Long-handled wooden spoons of crude workmanship also occur. A small wooden scoop was also found in the eastern sector.

Two very interesting scoops, one of which is shown in Plate 26:16, were found in the lower levels of the cultural deposit of the eastern sector. They are made of whale bone (beluga jawbone). The handle is long and narrow, with a suspension hole at the end. The broad part of the bone has been cut through and one edge of the cut has been superimposed over the other to produce the concavity of the ladle. The two edges are tightly bound together with a strip of baleen. A similar scoop was found by Collins in association with objects of the Old Bering Sea complex in excavations on St. Lawrence Island (Collins 1937;166, Plate 47:16).

Numerous baleen buckets (Plate 28:15) with wooden bottoms (Plate 26:6,11; Plate 28:14) were found. While they are all of elliptical shape, the bottoms vary considerably in size, from the smallest measuring 2.7 cm by 4 cm to the largest, which measure 16 cm by 20 cm. In some cases, the sides were attached to the bottoms with baleen. The handles of such containers are usually curved, with small holes at the ends for attachment, and may be of wood or bone, for example, the rib-bone of a ringed seal (Plate 26:12). Sometimes, the handles were straight (Plate 26:14 and 15).

The ivory handle shown in Plate 26:13 has a round biconical opening in its central portion, in addition to holes at the ends.

Various kinds of antler *hooks* were used for suspending containers. Examples are shown in Plate 28:16,17.

There is an interesting large-mesh strainer of baleen, shown in Plate 26:17. The rim consists of several strips of baleen, forming several layers, tied together with baleen strands. Similar strands form the cribwork of the strainer itself.

The *pottery* from Sirhenik is of particular interest. Numerous sherds were found in the western sector of the refuse area, and most particularly in the middle and lower levels of the eastern sector.

The vast majority represent crudely made vessels of tall shape with convex bases. As a rule, the vessels have thick walls, from 1 cm to 1.5 cm in thickness, which become thicker toward the rim (Plate 26:20), where the thickness attains 2 cm. Paste color is a deep black (that of oily soot) throughout the sherd, as a result both of the composition of the paste and low firing temperature. Temper consists of fine sand, pea-sized gravel particles, vegetal fibers and hairs. Decoration consists of groups of diagonal, parallel lines (Plate 26:20,21) imparted with a paddle or some similar tool (Plate 26:19) on which were carved parallel grooves, producing a ridged surface, or a *design of checks* (Plate 26:22,23,24), applied with a special stamp (Plate 26:18).

This check-stamped decoration of pottery vessels had, as we know, a wide distribution in eastern Asia. It has been found by Collins in his excavations on St. Lawrence Island (Collins 1937:169, Fig. 17). The walrus ivory slab with deeply carved diagonal lines for decorating the outer surfaces of pottery vessels from Sirhenik (Plate 26:19) is identical to the one we already know from Uwelen

(Plate 4:25). The shape is roughly the same, though the size is smaller. The longitudinal grooves along the narrow edges are the same. The bone stamp shown in Plate 26:18 is one used in applying check-stamped decoration.

Both in the eastern and western sectors of the refuse area at Sirhenik, we find sherds of pottery vessels bearing decoration of a different kind. The nearly smooth surface of these vessels was effected with a bunch of grass, which produced rows of shallow, though discernible, parallel or criss-cross streaks.

MEANS OF TRANSPORTATION

From Sirhenik there are several types of *sleds* with ivory runners. We must first note some very heavy, massive runners found in the western sector and in the lower levels of the eastern sector. These are very large, measuring 40 cm in length, up to 8 cm in height, and about 4 cm in width, and are made of the tusks of old walrus (Plate 28:19). To fasten the cross-pieces of such sleds, small transverse notches were cut on the upper surface of the runner with an adze, and wide elongate openings were hacked out directly below them in the upper half of the runner (Plate 28:20). In some cases, these openings are replaced with biconically drilled pairs of holes over 1 cm in diameter. Entirely similar runners are known from Old Bering Sea sites on St. Lawrence Island (Collins 1937, Plate 44:3; Plate 45:1,2). Together with such heavy runners, belonging to sleds used in transporting heavy loads, light sleds with thin runners, likewise of ivory, were also used. In the western sector of the refuse area at Sirhenik, we found a splendidly preserved pair of light runners of walrus ivory of distinctive form (Plate 28:21). These runners had a normal length of 40 cm. Their middle and rear sections are 5 cm–6 cm in height, whereas the forward portion rises steeply, following the natural curvature of the walrus tusk, and narrows toward the end. The width of these runners is only about 1 cm, except for the parts grooved for cross-pieces, where the width of the runner attains 1.8 cm. Rather large longitudinal slots have been made under these cross-piece supports. The forward ends of the runners are provided with long longitudinal grooves and notches for drag lines. Apart from the dark brown, nearly black color of these runners, which is characteristic of the oldest objects at Sirhenik, we may note the distinctive and undoubtedly very ancient style of the decoration on the visible side, consisting of carved lines meeting at acute angles. A portion of a similar runner (Plate 28:23), also from the western sector, bears a different design, likewise of deeply carved and thin straight lines, combined with vertical spurs. That this type is not accidental is confirmed by the finding of a fragment of yet another similar runner, which differs from the first specimen described in having two holes instead of a lengthwise slot under the groove for the cross-piece (Plate 28:22). Here again the outer surface is decorated with incised lines.

Runners of both the heavy and light types were also found together at the Okvik site in the Punuk Islands (Rainey 1941d, Fig. 16:2), and there also the runners bear decoration in a style close to those from Sirhenik described above.

The Eskimos of the village of Sirhenik explained to me that sleds with heavy runners were used only to transport heavy loads, such as meat or umiaks. Similar sleds with light runners such as we have just described had a special use. They served in seal-hunting from kayaks. When a seal had been killed, it was lowered into the hatch of the kayak, for which purpose it was placed on a light sled of this type and pulled into the bow end of the kayak. Then, while the carcass of the seal was held down with the end of a harpoon shaft, the sled was pulled out from under it. The next carcass was stored in similar fashion in the stern of the kayak. Thus, an Eskimo could kill up to three seals without pulling up to the shore or ice.

The walrus ivory sled runners generally found in the middle levels of the eastern sector are of a type which we know from excavations on Arakamchechen Island and Cape Chaplin. They are of moderate height (about 4.5 cm), rather narrow (1.5 cm in width), with two round perforations near the upper edge. In some specimens, the perforations retain bindings of baleen strands (Plate 28:24). Runners of this type are common in Eskimo settlements of Punuk times.

I hesitate to answer definitely the question of whether the ancient inhabitants of Sirhenik had dog sleds and whether they used the dog as a draft animal. However, the finding of a number of objects in the upper levels of the eastern sector that could be interpreted as wooden runners of dog sleds (Plate 28:18), as curved wooden sled braces and finally, as a buckle from a dog harness (Plate 27:2,3,4) allow the supposition that the inhabitants of Sirhenik in late times did have dog traction. To this evidence should also be added the occurrence of swivels. Parts of such swivels of ivory are shown in Plate 27:5,6.

A miniature *boat* of larch bark probably served as a child's toy (Plate 27:11). It is similar to the one found by Collins in excavations on St. Lawrence Island, but provides no idea of the boat type (Collins 1937, Plate 59:6). The two boat models, one of ivory, the other of wood, shown in Plate 27:9,10, are another matter. They are from the eastern sector, and clearly represent the umiak. The bow and stern portions of the boat are easily recognized in these models. In addition to the examples described, the inhabitants of Sirhenik also made true umiak models, i.e., models made of skin stretched over a wooden frame. We found several wooden cross-pieces belonging to the frame of such a small umiak (Plate 27:7,8). Entirely similar cross-pieces were found by Collins on St. Lawrence Island in association with objects of the Old Bering Sea complex and described by him as cross-pieces of a toy umiak (Collins 1937, Plate 59:2). A similar cross-piece, this time of normal size, has been published by Geist and Rainey from St. Lawrence Island (Geist and Rainey 1936, Plate 36:11). As for the purpose of these boat models, it is more likely that they were made for ceremonial occasions than as children's toys.

Boat hooks or meat hooks at Sirhenik are of three types, all of them of ivory. The first type (Plate 27:31) is a large hook with a round hole and a deep indentation on the front end for secure lashing to a shaft. The point is long and sharp. The second type (Plate 27:30) has three round holes and a notch at the forward end for lashing to the shaft. The point is short. Finally, the third type (Plate 27:29) is of moderate size, with one longitudinal opening for lashing to the shaft.

For fastening lines when dragging an umiak ashore, and for pulling loads, such as walrus carcasses or pieces of whale meat, various kinds of *fasteners* and *handles* were in use. We illustrate some of the more typical examples.

From the western sector, we have a quite simple handle to hold the loop of a drag line (Plate 27:23), in the form of a piece of ivory, round in cross-section, slightly curved, with circular grooves in the central portion for the line. The middle layers of the eastern sector yielded a walrus ivory handle of the same type (Plate 27:24), though carefully finished, with a broad circular groove for the line at the middle. It is decorated in Punuk style. Various levels have yielded small, crudely made fasteners of the same simple type (Plate 27:25,27), or of triangular or trapezoidal shape, like those from the ancient site at Uwelen, or else of elongate form, with a hole at the middle and a notch on one or both long side for the line (Plate 27:26,28). Similar fasteners have been found at the Okvik site in the Punuk Islands (Rainey 1941d, Fig. 35:1–3).

Ice creepers of ivory, worn under the boots when walking on ice, are of only one type at Sirhenik (Plate 27:1), with a central longitudinal slot, two holes connected by a groove at one end, a single hole for attachment at the other end, and eight pyramidal spikes.

An *ice staff ring* in the form of a ring of baleen strips twisted together measures 10 cm in diameter, and contains a second inner ring only 4 cm in diameter. Both rings are wound with a thin strip of baleen and are joined in such a manner that the result is somewhat like the ring on present day ski poles (Plate 23:19). According to Nelson, the western Eskimos of Alaska mounted these rings on one end of their ice staffs (Nelson 1899:214–215, Fig. 67). When walking on ice over a doubtful spot, Nelson writes, the traveler strikes a sharp blow with his staff in front of him before taking a step. If the ice is thin, the tip of the staff goes through the ice, but the ring coming in contact with the surface of the ice, prevents the staff from sinking deeper.

MISCELLANEOUS OBJECTS

A *button* and a *bead* of ivory were found in the middle level of the eastern sector. The button is oval in shape, with a loop on the inner side, and a reticulate decorative pattern cut in on the outer surface (Plate 29:3). The bead, shown in Plate 29:2, is decorated with straight lines of Punuk style.

Two *toggles* were found: one of ivory (Plate 29:1), the other of wood.

A *back-scratcher* consists of a flat wooden disk with a round hole in the center for mounting on a stick.

It is surprising that only one *armor plate* should be found in the upper levels of the western sector at Sirhenik. There are two longitudinal slots along its narrow side for binding to other plates.

The ivory *rod* with a number of circular grooves shown in Plate 27:17 in all probability served as the handle of a woman's work-bag or as a fastener, similar to one published by Nelson (1899, Plate 45:12).

A number of artifacts of baleen were found, the purpose of which is not entirely clear. Of these, we illustrate: a bundle of baleen strips (Plate 30:9); a special plaited object (Plate 30:22) of four baleen strips, of the kind already known to us from the excavations at Cape Chaplin (Plate 16:9) and Cape Chukchi, as well as from the excavations of Collins (Collins 1937, Plate 56:9) and Geist (Geist and Rainey 1936, Plate 36:11) on St. Lawrence Island. The lower jaw of an arctic fox (Plate 30:19), lashed to two sticks with baleen, may be a scraper, used in working small skins.

ART

We have described above a number of decorated objects from Sirhenik, which already give some idea of the decoration on objects from the site. Here, we will provide some additional examples of the graphic and plastic arts of the Sirhenik inhabitants.

Plate 29:5 shows the fragment of a thin plaque of walrus ivory with punctate decoration. Plate 29:23 illustrates a walrus tusk segment with a conical perforation, partly decorated with incised lines.

The walrus ivory plate shown in Plate 29:22 is similar in shape to a wrist guard and is decorated in the same style as a wrist guard of Punuk date from St. Lawrence Island (Collins 1937, Plate 65:9–11). A series of decorated walrus ivory handles is of interest. One of these is decorated with simple lines, meeting at an angle (Plate 29:29). Another, shown in Plate 29:28, is also decorated with simple lines and is carefully shaped. The decoration of the objects shown in Plate 29:21,26 is of particular interest. Fundamentally, it is already Punuk, though still exhibiting a number of traits characteristic of Old Bering Sea decoration: curved lines edged with a number of spurs. The decoration of a fragment of an ivory object shown in Plate 29:27 is typically Punuk. It consists not only of lines that are parallel or that meet at sharp angles, but also of dots, undoubtedly drilled with a metal bit.

Associated with the decorated objects described above in the middle levels of the eastern sector, we also found a *trident* (Plate 29:24), of a type well known from occasional finds and from excavations on the islands of Punuk and St. Lawrence. Like all other similar tridents, this one has a socket drilled in the basal portion. The socket retains a piece of the shaft. Both sides are decorated with lines and dots in classical Punuk style, the design on one side differing somewhat from that on the other.

The same level as the one in which the trident occurred yielded the only metal tool, a miniature drill shaft with a miniature iron bit for drilling points in decorating various ivory objects. The small wooden shaft, shown in Plate 23:12, bears on one end a short bit, about 0.6 mm in diameter, which has rusted on the outside to such an extent that its shape can be hardly made out. An X-ray photograph of the shaft showed that the drill bit is set in the shaft at a depth not exceeding the rust layer on its surface.

No winged objects were found at Sirhenik, with the exception of one small unfinished specimen.

The middle and upper levels of the eastern sector yielded a fair number of *carved animal figures* of ivory. The examples found include bird figures (Plate 29:6,7), rendered in a manner typical of late Eskimo art; the representation of a fish (cod) with decoration in Punuk style (Plate 29:8); very simplified, yet expressive seal figures (Plate 29:9,10,16) and representations of arctic or common fox (Plate 29:11,14); an unusual representation of a polar bear (Plate 29:15) and a two-headed dog (Plate 29:12). Of particular interest are some carved representations of whales. One of these is simplified and schematic in the same manner as the seal figures (Plate 29:13), while another conveys more realistically the characteristic features of the animal (Plate 29:17). A third shows a degree of stylization (Plate 29:18) and is covered with decoration in Punuk style.

There is no doubt that, with rare exceptions (the birds), these figures were not toys. They served either as amulets, ensuring success in the hunt, or else were among the paraphernalia for ceremonial observances connected with hunting.

OBJECTS OF CEREMONIAL FUNCTION

Apart from the animal figures described above, the eastern sector of the refuse area yielded various *amulets*. Notable among these are bear canines (Plate 30:11) and, especially, the tusks of small walrus with perforations drilled through the root and special lashing for suspension (Plate 30:1,2,3). Apparently, individual bones were kept or worn as amulets: examples include a walrus astragalus (Plate 30:7), a walrus phalanx (Plate 30:6), a bird tibia (Plate 30:5), walrus scapulae with baleen bindings at the narrow end, and, finally, vertebral disks of whales (Plate 40:4,8) perforated at the center and similar to those hung even today by the Eskimos as charms around the necks of young children.

Water-worn vertebrae, which have acquired the form of hemispherical pendants with large, round perforations (Plate 29:19,20) were also probably amulets.

The *drum handle* in Plate 29:25 is remarkable for its flawless shaping and its fine and careful workmanship. It differs somewhat from run-of-the-mill specimens in its massiveness and its flattened form, designed to provide an easier grip. A distinctive feature is a ring for suspension at the lower end. The decoration in classic Punuk style, with nucleated circles made with a metal drill and containing baleen plugs, covers its entire surface.

From the excavations at Cape Chaplin and Cape Chukchi, we are already familiar with representations of a knife and of a whale, made of baleen. There are over thirty similar objects from Sirhenik. Some of them undoubtedly represent fishes (Plate 30:15,16,17,20), others are obviously knives (Plate 30: 14,19,21), while still others are shaped like spoons (Plate 30:12) or unidentifiable objects. Nearly all these objects at Sirhenik came from one and the same spot. Entirely similar objects were found by Mathiassen (1927; 1, Plate 35:10,11,19; Plate 52:2; Plate 79:13) in excavations in the Central Eskimo area, and by Collins on St. Lawrence Island (Collins 1937, Plate 56:4–7). The former describes them as utilitarian objects, while the latter considers them children's toys. I cannot agree with either interpretation of their function. I believe they are models of various objects, intended for use in some kind of ritual.

Excavations in Sirhenik have shown that Eskimos lived at the site from the Old Bering Sea stage onward, probably nearly continuously down to present times. The western portion of the area investigated was occupied first. The eastern sector, where most of the excavation took place was occupied later. The occupation of the northeastern portion of the site took place still later, and it is there that the Eskimo dwell at the present time. Objects characteristic of the Old Bering Sea stage are relatively few, as a result of the small scale of the excavations in the western sector. Most of the material dates from Punuk times, inasmuch as the work was concentrated mainly in the eastern sector of the refuse area, directly adjacent to the later houses. Highly valuable results may be definitely expected from further excavations both of the western Old Bering Sea houses and of the eastern Punuk dwellings at this archaeologically important site.

Nunligran

The formerly Eskimo, now Chukchi, settlement of Nunligran (Nunligren) is located south of Preobrazheniya [Transfiguration] Bay, on Cape Achchen. Remains of ancient dwellings occur on both sides of a depression, the bottom of which is occupied by a stream emptying out of a lake into the sea (Fig. 10). The house remains are situated roughly midway between the village of Nunligran to the south and the trading station of the Office of the Northern Maritime Passage in Preobrazheniya Bay, to the north. I. P. Lavrov tested the cultural deposit near the houses situated on the west side of the stream, and then the deposit near the houses east of it.

WESTERN SITE

The pit-houses of the western site occupied a large knoll, one slope of which faces the sea, the other the stream. All told the remains of about fifteen houses were discovered on the knoll. Some of them show such good preservation that the main wall supports and even portions of the roof are discernible. The knoll is densely overgrown with grass. Meat storage pits are situated on the lower slopes of the hill, some of them still being used for their original purpose at the present time.

A few test pits in one of the refuse heaps sloping toward the stream revealed a cultural deposit, in which a trench 1.5 m in width was excavated down to permafrost level, from the periphery of the deposit to the foundation of one of

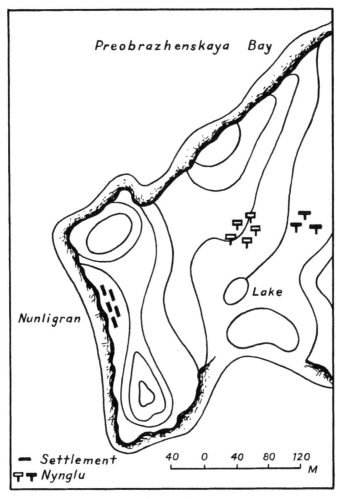

FIGURE 10

the houses. The cultural deposit began directly below the sod, and consisted mainly of mollusc shells (**Mytilus edulis L.**), the bones of walrus, ringed seal, reindeer, and birds, pieces of wood, pottery sherds, and various artifacts of bone and stone.

HUNTING AND FISHING GEAR

Harpoon heads. The western site yielded two bone harpoon head blanks and eight harpoon heads, of three types. One of the blanks is of moderate size, only about 6 cm in length, of flattened shape, and was intended for a small salmon harpoon head (Plate 31:1). The other blank is of normal size (about 9 cm) and intended for a sealing harpoon, with a well defined spur and a slit for the end-blade, but lacking a line hole and a definite socket (Plate 31:2).

The harpoon head shown in Plate 31:3 is of the laurel-leaf shaped, flattened Thule 1 type of Mathiassen–Collins' Type V. It has a partially open socket, a circular groove for the lashing over the socket, a single simple asymmetric spur, and a round line hole. Neither side-blades nor an end-blade are present. Three such heads were found, all of bone.

Another type of harpoon head from the same dwelling is a derivative of the first. It is of Thule 3 type, with a half-closed socket (Plate 31:4), without slots or grooves for the socket lashing, with a simple asymmetric spur, a round line hole, and a slit for the end-blade in the plane of the line hole. All four harpoon heads of this type are of bone.

The harpoon head represented in Plate 31:5 is of ivory and belongs to the group of earlier mentioned small harpoon heads used in catching large fish. It is toggling and barbed at the same time, though the barbs are blunt. The socket is closed and shallow. The point of the short asymmetric barb opposite the socket bears a narrow slot for a line which was lashed to the foreshaft, thereby ensuring more secure attachment of the head. The line hole is round. The fore end is blunted from prolonged use and is partially broken.

The *ice pick* in Plate 31:27 is of bone (made from the os penis of a walrus), oval in cross-section, pointed at the lower end and somewhat flattened at the upper, where it was fastened to the shaft. The upper third of this ice pick, where it was attached to the shaft, is entirely covered with transverse indentations. Two other picks, of which one was of bone, the other of walrus ivory, are represented only by their upper portions.

Finger rests, one of which is illustrated in Plate 31:6, are of ivory, in the form of pegs with a groove fitting on the harpoon shaft and an elongate hole for lashing to the shaft.

The *hook* or peg of a wooden harpoon throwing board is shown in Plate 31:10. Its flat base was fastened to the front end of the throwing board, and the peg served as a stop.

Arrowheads are of two types: simple arrowheads of bone, flattened in shape, as shown in Plate 31:7, with a conical tang and a circular indentation (shoulder) at the base of the tang, and blunt arrowheads. The latter are of bone (Plate 31: 8,9) or ivory with broad sockets corresponding to the considerable width of the arrow shafts (up to 1.2 cm). They are varied in form: some are acorn-shaped, others egg-shaped with a pointed or rounded fore end, still others cylindrical. A very interesting arrowhead, shown in Plate 31:19 has a partially broken socket rim, thereby clearly revealing the structure of the socket. We note the nubbin at the center of the bottom of the socket, indicating that the socket was drilled either with a hollow tube or, more probably, with an asymmetrical drill bit.

The ivory arrowhead blank in Plate 31:17 is of interest. In its final form, it was to be a three-flanged arrowhead with a tang, reproducing the shape of a well-known type of bronze or iron tripartite arrow point. It is the only arrowhead of its kind ever found among the Eskimos.

The small *wrist guard* of ivory in Plate 31:11 is of somewhat unusual quadrangular form, with two narrow slots on the longer sides, a continuous row of small pits drilled along one edge of the outer surface, and one similar decorative pit near the center. All of these precisely executed round pits were produced with a metal drill.

Bird bola weights. The large variety of these weights at Nunligran testifies to the extensive use of bolas in catching birds. All (Plate 31:12,13,14,15) are of ivory, with the exception of one (Plate 31:16), for which walrus tooth was used. Their form is varied: some are quadrangular with a pyramidal apex, others are nearly spherical, still others have the accidental shapes of tusk fragments. The shape of the holes for the string is as varied as that of the weights themselves. At times, these holes are round, narrow or wide. In other cases, they are triangular or consist of two deep slots meeting at a right angle inside the weight (Plate 31:14).

Fishing gear includes only hooks and net sinkers. *Fishhooks* are of two types: compound and one-piece. Compound fishhooks are represented by several barbs (Plate 31:25), all of ivory, flat, and carefully sharpened to a point. The lower ends bear a deep notch for lashing to the shank.

The western site yielded two one-piece fishhooks of walrus ivory, one of which is illustrated in Plate 31:26. These hooks have an elongate eyehole at the upper end of the shank and three barbs. Fishhooks of this type are not known in ancient Eskimo cultural complexes but are quite widespread in protohistoric times, and are well-known from ethnographic inventories of the Eskimos of western America and of Asia.

A *fish net weight* made from the distal end of a walrus tusk is of the usual elongate type, with a pair of biconically drilled openings for suspension at both ends on the upper side.

A knife-like *blade* of ivory with blunted edges (Plate 31:23) may, by analogy with similar tools in use until recently, be considered a marrow extractor for picking molluscs out of their shells and marrow out of bones.

The *awl* in Plate 31:24 is made of a walrus ivory splinter, flattened in shape and of small size.

The large *needle* of bone in Plate 31:31 lacks an eye, but has a deep notch at the upper end, whence it may be concluded that it was used for sewing in the form in which it was found.

Walrus ivory *wedges* are of the usual shape. One is illustrated in Plate 32:28.

There is a conspicuous absence of chipped stone implements. Stone tools from the western house site include only women's knives of rubbed slate of the usual type (Plate 31:37).

An elaborately made ivory *handle* of a small *woman's knife* bears two decorative excisions in its upper half (Plate 31:36).

Handles of men's knives are represented by a whole series. They are all of bone, and fall in two types, well known to us from excavations at Cape Chaplin and Sirhenik.

Bone handles of the first type, with a deep socket at the fore end for the blade stem and a deep slit through one of the socket walls for its extraction in case of breakage occur in two variants: single-bladed (Plate 31:40,41) and two-bladed (Plate 31:42). Certain differences of detail occur. In view of the thinness of the stem socket and, as a result, not infrequent cases of breakage at the upper end of the socket, a circular groove is present, as a rule, to hold a special binding, designed to strengthen the haft.

In other cases, when a crack appeared, special openings were cut for a binding, as may be seen in Plate 31:41. For suspending the handle from the butt end, a round hole was drilled (Plate 31:41), or a notch was cut on one side (Plate 31:42). In some cases, several such notches were made (Plate 31:40).

Handles of men's knives of the second type are composite, and consist of two halves. One half of such a composite handle, made of ivory, is illustrated in Plate 31:39. The slot for the blade is very narrow (2 mm in width) and relatively shallow (4 mm in depth). Another handle is made of bone (Plate 31:38), and has a rather small and narrow socket for the blade stem, which was held in the socket by a tight lashing without a second half being used, though perhaps with an added piece with a small groove corresponding to the socket groove.

A small *spoon* of ivory (Plate 31:35) is of interest; it is unusually deep and has a long handle.

Pottery from the western house, to judge from a few sherds, was relatively thin-walled, about 4–5 mm in thickness, of well-kneaded clay, and rather well fired.

A flat *comb* made from a plate of ivory (with the teeth along one of its shorter sides) is shown in Plate 31:32. Judging from the slipshod workmanship of the teeth, some of which are broken, it may be supposed that this comb served not for combing hair, but for craft purposes, such as working hides. The short side of the comb opposite the teeth is so beveled and sharpened that it may well have been used for cutting.

Another dentate plaque (Plate 31:29) is so thin that the thickness of its toothed edge is but a fraction of a millimeter.

An interesting *ear ornament* of ivory is oval in form, with a convex outer surface, and a short stem, which was inserted in the ear lobe (Plate 31:33). The end of the stem has a small hole for some sort of pendant. Ear ornaments of this type were widely used until recently by the western Eskimo of Alaska (Nelson 1899, Plate 24:4,9,10,15).

The function of the two ivory objects shown in Plate 31:21,30 is not entirely clear. One of them (Plate 31:30) is in the form of a shaft, round in cross-section, with a circular groove at one end for suspension, and a hemispherical, highly polished surface at the other end. It may be that we are dealing here with a polisher for smoothing seams when sewing together hides or prepared strips of walrus intestines. The other rod (Plate 32:21) is part of some object with a longitudinal slot-like opening at the point of breakage, and decoration at one end in the form of three encircling lines with spurs vertical to them.

An ivory *back-scratcher* is in the form of a disk (Plate 31:20) about 1.5 cm in thickness, with a round cylindrical opening at the center.

Figurines carved out of walrus ivory include a rabbit in sitting position (Plate 31:34) and a seal (Plate 31:15). The latter has a small perforation in the tail for suspension.

Of particular interest is the representation of a woman (Plate 31:22) carved of ivory, which apparently has been worn over a long period of time as an amulet. While the human figure here is highly conventionalized, the breasts and hips are clearly indicated and emphasize the sexual features of this figurine.

Despite the rather limited number of objects found in excavations of the western site at Nunligran, taken together, these constitute a complex that is so homogeneous, that we may, without hesitation, date the time of occupation of the site as the Late Punuk phase of the development of Eskimo culture, chronologically pertaining already to protohistoric times.

EASTERN SITE

The site which was discovered on the eastern bank of the stream has a less accentuated relief than the western site. The slopes are more gentle. The grass cover is thick, but of unequal height. The house pits are indistinct. The whale bones hardly protrude above ground level, are covered with moss, and are discernible with difficulty.

Testing was started at the foot of the hill, near one of the houses, and progressed gradually toward the house pit. The cultural deposit was encountered directly below the sod layer, and consisted of bones of walrus, ringed seal, deer, and dog. Shell deposits were not encountered, though we found thin black fragments of mollusc shells (*Mytilus edulis* L.) which had disintegrated with time. We found numerous pottery fragments and artifacts of bone, stone and baleen.

The *bone harpoon head* in Plate 32:1 has a closed socket, a simple asymmetric basal spur, and a round line hole, with downward-oriented grooves. Unfortunately, the distal end is broken, precluding thereby a definite identification of the harpoon head as to type. However, in view of the nearly imperceptible false barbs and the nature of the decoration by means of incised lines, we may suppose that we have here, if not an Okvik type, at least an example pertaining to a period no later than Early Punuk.

The ivory harpoon *foreshaft* found at the eastern site is of the usual form, and is not distinctive enough for chronological purposes.

The ivory harpoon *ice pick* (Plate 32:17) is of simple design. It is wedge-shaped at the lower end, while the upper end, fitting the harpoon shaft, is entirely covered with deep transverse grooves for better lashing. Typologically, it comes close to the ancient Okvik Old Bering Sea forms.

The bone *arrowheads* are of considerable interest. One is almost intact (Plate 32:19), while the other (Plate 32:20) is represented by a fragment, which, however, is enough to give an adequate idea of its type. These arrowheads are oval in cross-section, with very sharp lateral barbs, a conical tang designed to fit in the shaft, and a slit at the distal end for an end-blade. The pairs of sharp, symmetrical barbs are highly distinctive. One of them occurs at the very base of the arrowhead, while the other pair, or one single barb, occurs near the middle. The type and shape of the barbs, as well as the deeply cut decorative lines, serve to identify these arrowheads as Okvik-Old Bering Sea in type, of the kind already known to us from finds at the ancient site of Uwelen, at Kiwak, and at Sirhenik.

Together with these arrowheads, we also found an *end-blade* (Plate 32:2) of silicified tuff, leaf-shaped in form, with a very finely worked straight base, and some arrow shafts (Plate 32:28,29).

The walrus ivory *dart heads* are also of interest. One of these (Plate 32:26) has a broken fore end, an oval cross-section, a flattened butt fitting into the shaft, and an oblong lashing hole near the base. The preserved portion bears three small asymmetrically placed barbs. The other dart point, also damaged, is diamond-shaped in cross-section, tanged, and has one very sharp barb (Plate 32:21).

The center-prong of an ivory bird dart (Plate 32:18) is well-preserved. It has a flattened proximal end, designed to fit in the shaft, a longitudinal slot at the base for lashing, and five small, though sharp, asymmetric barbs.

Unlike the western site, the eastern site is distinctive in yielding a considerable number of *stone tools* which are not ground. These include flint blades of men's knives (Plate 32:3,9), short knife-like stone side-blades (Plate 32:10,14) of the same material, a kind of small chisel of silicified tuff (Plate 32:4), a fine end-scraper (Plate 32:15) and, finally, two drill points (Plate 32:5,13), both of flint. In addition, the site yielded a rather large number of obsidian and flint chips, some of which were used as concave scrapers (Plate 32:16), while most (Plate 32:6,7,8,11,12) have sharp edges, in some cases retouched, used for various kinds of work on bone.

Rubbed slate artifacts include only fragments of a triangular end-blade and of women's knives of the usual type (Plate 32:32).

The woman's knife is also represented by a well-preserved handle, shown in Plate 32:31.

The inhabitants of the eastern site also made use of small knife-blades, hafted in two-piece handles. One-half of such a handle, made of walrus ivory, is represented in Plate 32:30. The short and narrow slot on one side is intended for a small blade. The outer surface of the handle bears transverse grooves for lashing the two halves more effectively to one another.

The wedges, awls, and punches from the eastern site are of the usual type (Plate 32:22,23). Like the drill points, they are all of ivory. The drill points are cylindrical in form, with wedge-shaped bits (Plate 32:24,25).

No stone adzes were found, though we do have some well-preserved *adze socket pieces*, one of which is illustrated in Plate 32:33. The type of these adze heads is altogether identical to that of the examples from the ancient site of Uwelen, with a quadrangular socket for the handle.

A very interesting *vessel of walrus ivory*, a trough-like bowl, is shown in Plate 32:34. It is 16 cm. in length, 4.5 cm. in width and 3.2 cm. in height. There is an opening for suspension through one of the narrower sides. Similar vessels of smaller size, which served as fat scrapers, are known on the Chukchi Peninsula only from the ancient site of Uwelen.

Sleds, judging from preserved fragments of runners, were of two types: one with relatively high (5.5 cm) but narrow ivory runners, the upper edges of which are lined with a row of biconically-drilled holes for the attachment of cross-pieces, and another type, with lower (4.7 cm) though also narrow runners, in which narrow longitudinal slots were cut for lashing the cross-pieces. The outer edges of such runners, as may be seen from Plate 32:35, were decorated with horizontal, vertical, and diagonal deeply incised lines and diagonally hachured bands. This type, as we know, is characteristic of the oldest stage of Eskimo culture.

The eastern site yielded walrus ivory drag-line *toggles* of sub-triangular shape with a round center hole, of a type previously known from ancient sites, and a *walrus tooth* with a small hole drilled for suspension. This tooth may have been an amulet (Plate 32:27).

On the basis of the total inventory of objects from the eastern dwelling at Nunligran, it may be concluded that its occupation was coeval with that of the ancient settlement on the hillside at Uwelen. Despite the archaic characteristics of most of the objects found, not one is decorated in Old Bering Sea style.

Enmylen

The formerly Eskimo, now Chukchi, settlement of Enmylen has been visited by many investigators, as a result of its geographic location at Cape Bering. The Borisov collection includes a series of objects from Enmylen. The site was also visited by Sverdrup during the cruise of the ship "Maud." Limited archaeological testing of Enmylen was carried out by Lavrov. The topography of the settlement and ancient habitation sites (Fig. 11) has been described in some detail by Sverdrup (Sverdrup 1930: 325–326).

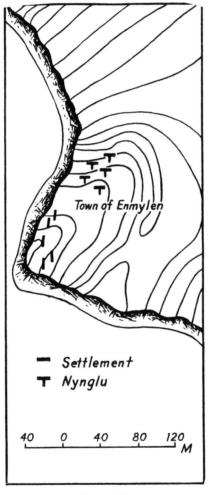

Town of Enmylen

— Settlement
T Nynglu

40 0 40 80 120
M

FIGURE 11

The modern settlement of Enmylen is on Cape Bering proper, on a small coastal flat at the foot of the cliffs. To the east, cliffs drop off sharply into the sea, so that the coast at that point is inaccessible from the water. A rather extensive plateau stretches out to the north. There is no communication between this tableland and the flat on which the settlement is located; they are separated by a cliff which faces the sea over a distance of 2 km. At the foot of the cliff, one runs across whale bones and accumulations of stones, which mark the emplacements of ancient dwellings. Sverdrup writes that an ancient beach line extends as a ridge at Enmylen somewhat above the low shore occupied at the present time by a large number of houses.

Lavrov found three groups of dwellings at Enmylen: (1) the modern settlement on the beach itself; (2) a relatively recent settlement with remains of round *yarangs* on an eminence to the west of the modern settlement, and (3) a group of ancient collapsed houses, also on an eminence, at the foot of the mountains between the first two groups of houses. The remains of about 20 dwellings were found here on a platform about 20–25 m above sea level. At that point, the sea cuts into the shore, and a steep incline begins 70 m from the water, leading to the platform, the edge of which is 200–250 m away from the foot of the cliffs. The rim of the platform is concealed by kitchen refuse, overgrown with dense grass. The houses clustered on this terrace in groups and apparently intercommunicated. One of the pit-houses stands out from the rest by its large size. Some of the dwellings are recognizable only from their outlines, while others are located by whale bones protruding above ground. Their structural features are different. The clearing of a small area 10 by 10 m on the slope between the houses and the sea uncovered a cultural deposit 40–45 cm in thickness, containing large numbers of edible molluscs (*Mytilus edulis* L.), and bones of walrus, bearded seal, ringed seal, and whale. Finds also include bones of dog, rabbit, and birds and numerous artifacts of bone, stone, wood, and baleen, as well as pottery fragments. The cultural deposit is underlain by a layer of shells 1–1.5 cm thick, lacking cultural remains. Below it, the soil, likewise culturally sterile, was frozen.

HUNTING AND FISHING EQUIPMENT

Enmylen yielded two bone *blanks for harpoon heads*. We draw attention to them because, together with other such blanks, they illustrate the process of manufacture of these implements. The blank shown in Plate 33:2 suggests the overall shape of the harpoon head and the area of the basal spur. It also has a conically drilled line hole and a sawed slit for the end-blade. However, a portion of the fore end was broken in manufacture, and the blank was discarded. The other blank (Plate 33:1) is intended for a harpoon head of the type represented in Plate 33:10. The bone has been given the required shape, the position of the multiple spur has been marked, and the line hole has been drilled.

The bone *harpoon head* shown in Plate 33:5 is of particular interest. The socket is open, with straight edges. There is one slot and opposing groove for the socket lashing. There is a triple asymmetric spur, a round line hole, and side slots for blades in the same plane as the line hole near the very tip of the harpoon head. Barely noticeable false barbs are indicated. Decoration is by means of deeply incised lines. This harpoon head is interesting because of its resemblance to certain specimens from the ancient site of Uwelen, from which it differs only in details of design. Harpoon heads closely related in type have been published by Rainey from the Okvik site in the Punuk Islands (Rainey 1941d, Fig. 4). Thus, we may suppose that we are dealing here with a rather ancient form.

The remarkable harpoon head illustrated in Plate 33:3 is unfortunately broken at the distal end. It is a splendid example of one of the more complex harpoon heads of the Old Bering Sea stage of Eskimo culture. The socket is open, with straight sides. There are two slots for the socket lashing, coming together in a deep groove on the dorsal side of the head. The line hole is round. The asymmetric triple spur has a center-prong which is much longer than the secondary lateral prongs. The slit for the end-blade is at right angles to the line hole. The material is ivory. Decoration is in elaborate Old Bering Sea style. It characteristically includes such features as false barbs on the sharp edges of the head, relief in the form of nodes enclosed in concentric circles, as well as the bird's head motif with "beak" and "eyes." A harpoon head of the same type from the Asian side of Bering Strait has been published by Sverdrup (Sverdrup 1930, Plate 25:2), though it differs from our specimen by the presence of true sharp barbs instead of false barbs. Similar harpoon heads are known from St. Lawrence Island (Collins 1937, Plate 24–25:15) and Little Diomede (Collins 1937, Plate 27:5).

The splendidly preserved harpoon head in Plate 33:4 has a shallow open socket with straight sides, two slots for the socket lashing coming together in a groove on the dorsal side of the harpoon head, a round line hole, a double spur, with a divided and asymmetric larger part, and a slit for the end-blade in the plane of the line hole. The material is ivory. Decoration is in Old Bering Sea style. On the basis of its type, this harpoon head may be assigned to the Old Bering Sea or Early Punuk stage of Eskimo culture on St. Lawrence Island. A similar harpoon head from the site of Miyowagh on St. Lawrence Island has been published by Collins (Collins 1937, Plate 27:5).

Plate 33:6 shows the spur of a harpoon head decorated in Old Bering Sea style.

The harpoon heads illustrated in Plate 33:7,8,10 have an open socket, one slot and an opposing groove for the socket lashing, a double asymmetric basal spur, sometimes with an extra rudimentary prong, a round line hole, and a slit for the end-blade in the plane of the line hole. The material is bone. The cross-section is flattened. Collins assigns this special type of harpoon head to Early Punuk. We may assign to the same period a harpoon head with an open socket and straight socket sides, two slots for the socket lashing, situated one above the other and coming together on the dorsal side, a round line hole, a simple pointed spur, a slit for the end-blade in the plane of the line hole, and a flattened shape, with a slight constriction near the middle. The material is ivory. Decoration is by simple incised lines.

Thus far, harpoon heads of the type shown in Plate 33:13,14 are known, on Chukchi Peninsula, only from Enmylen. These are of bone, toggling, and at the same time barbed, harpoon heads with two or three pairs of symmetrical barbs. The sockets are half-closed, with a circular groove for the socket lashing on one harpoon head, and a slot and opposing groove on the other. The line hole is narrow and triangular. The spur is simple. Neither side-blades nor an end-blade occur. Decoration is absent. Harpoon heads of this type are known from Point Hope (Mathiassen 1930a, Plate 12:2), where drilled holes replace the lashing slots, from the area of Point Barrow (Collins 1933:46, Fig. 45d) and to the east, in the Central Eskimo area (Mathiassen 1927; 1, Plate 37:9; Plate 39:4). Insofar as we know, this form of harpoon head is late in America, and dates from immediately before historic times. The conically drilled sockets of these heads are already half-closed, so that there is no absolute need for a socket lashing, and the latter may sometimes be lacking.

Harpoon heads with closed sockets are of two types at Enmylen. The first includes a small bone harpoon head, probably that of a sealing harpoon, with one simple spur, an oblong line hole and a slit for the end-blade in the plane of the line hole (Plate 33:11). The second type is represented by a small barbed toggling harpoon head of ivory (Plate 33:12), diamond-shaped in cross-section, with a narrow slot for the line. Like similar specimens described earlier, this one was intended for salmon fishing.

Other harpoon parts from Enmylen include two purchased harpoon shaft socket-pieces of ivory and a purchased ice pick.

The harpoon shaft *socket piece* represented in Plate 33:15 is oval in cross-section, with a conically drilled socket for the foreshaft and a wedge-shaped lower end sharpened from one side, designed to fit on the shaft; for fastening to the wooden shaft there is drilled one through hole and a lateral hole.

The socket-piece represented in Plate 33:16 differs from the preceding only in that its wedge-like lower end has been beveled from both sides to fit in a splayed shaft, and bears two eyeholes for lashing.

The *ice pick* shown in Plate 33:17 is semi-circular in cross-section, with a recessed upper half adjacent to the shaft and a round central lashing hole.

Apart from the specimen just described, purchased in Enmylen, there are several fragments of ice picks of more ancient type, with a conical butt end fitting into the shaft, covered over its entire surface with transverse grooves.

Of the two *dart heads*, one (Plate 33:26) is flat, triangular in cross-section, with two slots for lashing to the shaft, while another (Plate 33:18) is oval in cross-section, with a slot near the base and two notches for hafting. A third point, probably belonging to a fish spear, is unfinished, and has three pairs of asymmetric barbs (Plate 33:19).

A *lance head*, probably that of a whale lance, is made of argillaceous slate, and is a form already familiar to us (Plate 34:21) from the excavations at Sirhenik, with a concave base and two biconically drilled holes (on the line of fracture) for lashing to the shaft.

Arrowheads from the excavations at Enmylen are few, but typologically of great interest. One of these (Plate 33:21) is long, flat, made of bone, with a sharp barb at the base and a slit for an end-blade. The broad surfaces are decorated by means of two parallel lines and a broken line between them. This type comes close to that of the Old Bering Sea or Early Punuk arrowheads from St. Lawrence Island (Collins 1937, Plate 29:6; Plate 34:2).

A good example of a flint end-blade of a bone arrowhead is shown in Plate 34:13. It is a thin (2 mm) triangular blade, carefully retouched along the edges and with ground faces. Another similar triangular end-blade is broader in shape, with slightly convex sides and a barely concave base, similarly thin (Plate 34:14); it was more probably intended to fit a harpoon head, being too wide for an arrowhead.

There is an interesting miniature triangular end-blade, only 1 mm in thickness (Plate 34:19), more likely that of an arrowhead than a harpoon.

A second type of bone barbed arrowhead (Plate 33:20) is similar to one encountered at Sirhenik (Plate 21:26). Both are leaf-shaped at the distal end, and have two symmetrically placed barbs. The Enmylen arrowhead has a tang that is shorter and splayed.

A third type is of moderate size, barbed, and tanged. One is of bone, flat, with two unilateral barbs (Plate 33:9). Another is made of ivory, is quadrangular in cross-section at the base and triangular at the distal end, and has one barb (Plate 33:22).

A fourth type of arrowhead is flattened and laurel-leaf shaped, with a diamond-shaped cross-section (Plate 33:23).

Only the lower half with the tang remains of a long arrowhead, round in cross-section (Plate 33:24).

A very interesting wrist guard of walrus ivory (Plate 33:25) was purchased in Enmylen. It is rather large and of the usual form, with narrow slots along the longer sides for attachment. Its surface is covered with decoration in classical Punuk style, consisting of parallel lines and circles with dots in the center. Note should be taken of the geometric precision of the incised circles and drilled dots, which could have been achieved only with the aid of an iron tool.

Except for the fish spear point described earlier, fishing equipment from Enmylen consists only of the bone barb of a compound fishhook (Plate 34:1) and a purchased bone line sinker. This *sinker* (Plate 34:8) is oblong and quadrangular in shape, and thicker at one end. The upper end bears line holes, and the lower has perforations for attaching a hook. It should be noted that such a sinker could also be used as the shank of a compound fishhook, inasmuch as the lower thicker half bears sockets drilled through the edges for the attachment of a hook (cf. Collins 1937, Plate 75:15). If this is so, we are dealing here with a form which is apparently Late Punuk or protohistoric in time.

VARIOUS TOOLS AND UTENSILS

The refuse area excavated in Enmylen is characterized by the occurrence of a rather large number of stone tools which were not ground. However, before proceeding to describe the stone implements, mention should be made of the bone object purchased in Enmylen represented in Plate 34:2. It is a bone thumb ring. A similar ring is reproduced in Jochelson's work on the Koryaks (Jochelson 1908:608, Fig. 134B). According to that author, the Koryaks wore a ring of this kind on the thumb of the left hand in manufacturing stone tools, so as not to injure a thumb with the hammerstone when flaking a piece of stone held in the hand. Judging from its dark brown color, our finger ring is, without doubt, from an excavation. The upper rim of the ring bears a small lug which, so it was explained to us, was for a small thong connecting it to a bone ring worn on the index finger of the left hand (Plate 35:16).

Of the *stone tools,* we must note in the first place knife-like flakes of flint and silicified tuff, with sharp cutting edges, used in various operations on bone and wood (Plate 34:3,4,5,6). The edges of many of these flakes bear evident traces of use in the form of minute irregular chippings.

An interesting small chisel of silicified tuff (Plate 34:15) has a well-ground and sharpened cutting edge.

The two moderate-sized blades, one stemmed (Plate 34:9), the other unstemmed (Plate 34:10), despite their small size, should be interpreted as the *blades of men's knives,* since they are too thick (0.4 cm) to have served as arrow or harpoon points. They are both of silicified tuff, carefully worked over by pressure retouching. Plate 34:11 illustrates the fragment of a knife of flint, while Plate 34:12 shows one of silicified tuff.

The slat end-blades of men's knives are of the usual stemmed type (Plate 34:17,18). An unusual form is that of the long, single-edged slate knife with a broad back and a round biconically drilled hole in the stem for hafting to a handle, illustrated in Plate 34:20.

Men's knives are represented in the Enmylen excavations by bone handles, illustrated in Plate 34:31,32. The form is one already familiar to us, with a socket for the blade stem at one end, and an opening for suspension at the other. Again, we find an opening in one of the socket walls for extracting the stem in case of blade breakage. The handle shown in Plate 34:31 lacks decoration, whereas the one in Plate 34:32 is decorated by broad circular grooves with ridges between them.

Enmylen yielded many women's knives of slate, both whole and damaged. As examples, we illustrate two large whole specimens (Plate 34:24,25) and one of medium dimensions (Plate 34:23).

Of the damaged women's knives, some have conically drilled holes for lashing to the handle.

Scrapers are of two types: a long flint end-scraper (Plate 34:16) and a concave flint scraper, with a carefully retouched working edge (Plate 34:7).

The implement of silicified tuff represented in Plate 34:22 at first suggests a woman's knife. It is oval in form, the upper half being shaped only by detaching small flakes, while the lower working edge is ground on both faces. The considerable thickness and blunt working edge indicate that we have here a *scraper*, designed to fit in a special handle.

The range of bone tools is varied. First, we must note two *walrus ivory blades*. One of them was excavated (Plate 35:30), the other purchased (Plate 33:27). Both are of the same type, with a broad blade, triangular in cross-section, and a narrower handle, with a round suspension hole at the end. The exact function of these blades is not clear. They may have been used as daggers or as knives for dressing the carcasses of killed animals.

Wedges are represented by six specimens, all of ivory. The largest is 16 cm in length (Plate 34:26), while the smallest measures only 5 cm (Plate 34:29). They all have a striking surface considerably scarred from prolonged use and a sharpened lower edge. The wedge shown in Plate 34:26 has been sawed through, apparently after its use had been discontinued. One of its flat sides bears a broad (1.5 cm at the top) and deep (0.9 cm) sawed groove, though the piece has yet to be split into two parts. The smallest of the wedges (Plate 34:29) has been carved out of a walrus tusk splinter.

The ivory implement (purchased) shown in Plate 34:30 was probably used as an adze. Its upper narrow portion, where it was hafted to the handle, is covered on both sides with deep transverse grooves. Other bone implements include large awls of deer bone (Plate 34:33), some quite small ivory awls of simple type (Plate 34:27) or with a special head (Plate 34:34) and, finally, multi-purpose tools, with an awl or bodkin at one end, some kind of small knife or polisher at the other, with a well-sharpened cutting edge, and a suspension hole at the middle (Plate 34:28).

The two *needles* of ivory with broken eyes, one of which is represented in Plate 34:35 were found together with a needle-case. This *needle-case* (Plate 35:28) is remarkable in its workmanship. Instead of the usual long bone from the wing of a bird, the needle-case is carved out of ivory. Its inner cavity, despite its great length (10.5 cm) has been drilled with amazing precision.

Two types of bone *drill points* were in use: those with a cylindrical bit (Plate 35:1) and those with a flat or even grooved bit, as exemplified in the ivory drill point shown in Plate 35:2. The purpose of the flat, small tray of bone with a suspension lug shown in Plate 35:4 is not entirely clear. It may possibly be a scraper for removing fat from intestines. An interesting *scraper* for working intestines was purchased in Enmylen. It is made of a thin slab of ivory, with a specially worked handle (Plate 35:4). A similar Chukchi scraper has been published by Bogoras (1904–1909; 1:387, Fig. 180). According to that author, similar scrapers are used in working intestines not only by the Chukchi, but also by neighboring tribes. However, until recently, neither excavated materials nor the

scrapers in use at present among the western Eskimo included any such implement. Finally, we must mention two bone splinters (Plate 35:5,6): one with an
eye hole at the end opposite the point, the other in the form of a narrow paddle
with a distinct handle. Both were probably used in extracting marrow from bones
and shellfish from shells.

DOMESTIC CONTAINERS

The fragment of a bone *dish* found in the excavations at Enmylen is large
enough to judge the dimensions and shape of the whole piece. This dish, made
of whale bone, was oval in shape (about 12 cm by 22 cm) and very shallow (no
more than 2.2 cm deep).

Judging from the find of a wooden bottom (6 cm by 12 cm), containers of
baleen in the form of bucket-like boxes were also in use at Enmylen.

A wooden *spoon* found in the excavations (Plate 35:25) is very flat, with a
long handle and a triangular opening for suspension. A number of flat antler
spoons were purchased in Enmylen and, judging from their color, they had
undoubtedly come out of the ground. Two are shown in Plate 35:29,31. They are
all of a type pertaining to the Thule-Punuk stage of Eskimo culture and well
known from the excavations on Arakamchechen Island and Cape Chaplin.

The ivory bucket handle in Plate 35:22 was excavated. For attachment to the
bucket, one end of the handle bears a horizontal eyehole, while a round hole has
been drilled through the other end following breakage.

Particular interest attaches to a purchased ivory vessel in the shape of a boat
(Plate 35:23). Judging from its dark brown color, it was undoubtedly excavated
after having been in the ground for a long time. Its outer surface is decorated
with straight lines, parallel or intersecting at acute angels. A suspension hole was
drilled through one of the shorter sides. We know of no complete parallel to this
vessel, though we may suppose that it was used either as a ladle or as a scraper
for removing fat from intestines.

Pottery sherds from Enmylen indicate that vessels were thick-walled (0.7 cm
to 1.2 cm), of poorly kneaded clay with an admixture of pea-sized gravel and
hair as tempering material. Firing is poor, and all the pots are of intense black
color. The outer surface is striated as a result of smoothing with a bunch of grass.

MISCELLANEOUS OBJECTS

Excavations yielded four sled runner fragments of ivory. They are all of the
same type, narrow (0.7 cm to 1.1 cm thick) and low (maximum height 5 cm),
with a row of biconically drilled holes along the upper edge (Plate 35:21). Some
of the pieces attain 20 cm in length, and have nine perforations for the attachment of cross-pieces.

A flat bone *buckle* (Plate 35:18) with two round holes may have been part of
a belt.

A bone *armor plate* is brown in color from having been in the soil, and has
three pairs of elongate slots along the edges (Plate 35:27) for tying to other
plates.

A *toggle*, in the form of a flat bar of ivory with an oblong opening cut at the
middle (Plate 35:19) may have been part of clothing or of a dog's harness.

An ivory *drum handle* (purchased) is of the usual form, with two holes drilled
in it for lashing to the rim (Plate 35:24).

The small flat bone *tube* in Plate 35:8 is of unknown function, and has very
thin sides. Another bone tube, shown in Plate 35:15 is flat, like the preceding

specimen, and is decorated by means of four encircling ridges. Likewise, we do not know the purpose of the wooden object in Plate 35:7 and that of the tusk of a young walrus with a suspension hole at the distal end (Plate 35:32). Judging from the dark brown color of this tusk and its scarred surface, it may be supposed that it was used as a mallet.

The rectangular *block* of wood in Plate 35:14 has two transverse openings through it. The outer surface of the longer sides bears two parallel lines with inward facing dentations.

The excavations yielded several sandstone *whetstones* with longitudinal grooves, one of which is illustrated in Plate 35:13.

The *fastener* in Plate 35:11 is made of a short rod of ivory with a circular groove at the middel.

The dog *canine* in Plate 35:17 has a suspension hole drilled through the root.

STYLE OF ENGRAVING

In discussing the harpoon heads and other objects we have already noted specimens with Old Bering Sea and the more recent Punuk engraving. In addition, we illustrate five other artifacts of ivory recovered in the excavations and of interest because of their decoration.

Two pendants, one of a piece of ivory (Plate 35:10), the other of a walrus tooth (Plate 35:9) are covered with a very fine engraved design of incised broken and dentate lines in early Old Bering Sea style.

An interesting example of engraving occurs on one object (a fragment of a handle or a throwing board). It is also in Old Bering Sea style, and consists of concentric ellipses with dots in their centers and lightly incised curved lines with spurs (Plate 35:26).

Engraving in the Punuk style occurs on a bone splinter shown in Plate 35:20 and on a fragmentary object of ivory illustrated in Plate 35:12.

The collection from Enmylen, including the purchased objects, is not homogeneous. It includes objects which are indisputably early, pertaining to the Old Bering Sea stage of Eskimo culture at the time of its flowering, as well as objects from later stages, such as Early and Classic Punuk and, finally, objects of late protohistoric times. It is clear that Cape Bering was a site of almost uninterrupted occupation by sea mammal hunters. However, since all of the material is in the nature of chance finds, it is not possible to characterize fully any of the cultural phases represented. There is a pressing need for further excavations at this important locality on the Bering Sea coast of the Chukchi Peninsula. Such excavations promise to yield valuable finds for our knowledge of the history and of the sequential development of ancient culture in the Bering Sea area.

Chance Finds from the Coast of the Chukchi Peninsula

This section provides a description of the objects in the Borisov collection, of which we know only that it was gathered on the coast of the Chukchi Peninsula between Cape Serdtse-Kamen to the north and Cape Bering to the south. The objects from Cape Bering (Enmylen) have been described already in the preceding section. At the same time, we shall note all previously published chance finds of archaeological objects from the Chukchi Peninsula, and identify the place of their original publication. Our purpose is thus to provide in the present volume a complete presentation of all materials pertaining to the archaeology of the Chukchi Peninsula coast.

HUNTING AND FISHING EQUIPMENT

Harpoon heads. Plate 36:1 illustrates the fore end of a harpoon head of Old Bering Sea type, decorated in Old Bering Sea style.

Excellent examples of Old Bering Sea harpoon heads from the Asian shore of Bering Strait have been published by Sverdrup (Sverdrup 1930, Plate 25:2,4), as well as by Collins (Collins 1929, Fig. 1) and Mathiassen from Plover Bay (Mathiassen 1929, Fig. 10).

One of the harpoon heads published by Sverdrup belongs to the Old Bering Sea type with triple asymmetric spur and two holes for the socket lashing, the other to Collins' Type III, with a triple asymmetric spur. Both have open sockets. The harpoon head from Plover Bay, with a closed socket and an end-blade, is decorated in late Old Bering Sea Style 3. A third harpoon head published by Sverdrup has a closed socket, a simple spur, a round line hole, and a slit for the end-blade in the plane of the line hole. Decoration is in typical Punuk style. Three harpoon heads from the Borisov collection (Plate 36:2,3,4) belong to the same type, and differ from one another only in the arrangement of the lashing of the open socket, in details of spur design, and in their decoration by means of simple lines. Their date, apparently, is Late Punuk. The somewhat later (proto-historic) harpoon head represented in Plate 36:5 is reproduced here because of its exceptionally good state of preservation, including a slate end-blade.

Harpoon heads of a type rarely found on the coast of the Chukchi Peninsula include the bone barbed harpoon head shown in Plate 36:6, which has an open socket, two slots for the socket lashing, one asymmetric spur, a triangular line hole, and two asymmetrically placed barbs. This is Thule 2 type, but with asymmetric barbs.

Harpoon heads of Thule 1 type, characteristic of Late Punuk, of bone and rarely of ivory, with an open socket, flattened and laurel-leaf-shaped in outline, are represented in considerable numbers. We illustrate three such specimens from the Borisov collection. They differ from one another in details of the socket arrangement. In one case we have an open socket with straight sides and two slots for the socket lashing (Plate 36:7); in the second case, we have a socket with inclined sides, the inner edges of which are further apart than the other ones, and a single slot with opposing groove (Plate 36:8); in the third case, the socket is half-closed and there is only a circular groove for the socket lashing (Plate 36:9). A distinctive fragment shown in Plate 36:10 is that of a large harpoon head, probably that of a whaling harpoon, judging from its size. The line hole is rectangular. There is a large and deep slit for the end-blade, at right angles to the line hole. Decoration is in the form of deeply cut parallel lines. We may note in passing that this fragment has been used as a drill rest in drilling holes or fire-making, for which purpose a depression has been made on one of its flat sides.

Flint and slate *end-blades* of harpoons have been found on Ratmanov Island and at a number of points on the Chukchi coast. They differ so little in size and shape, that we illustrate only two (Plate 36:11,12).

Foreshafts to hold harpoon heads include specimens that are long, round in cross-section, made of ivory, with a slightly flattened fore end. As an example, we illustrate one such foreshaft for a whaling harpoon (Plate 36:23).

The most common shape of the harpoon shaft *socket piece* is cylindrical (Plate 36:22), with a shallow socket for the foreshaft and a beveled wedge-shaped butt. The shape of the walrus ivory *ice pick* in Plate 36:24 is somewhat unusual.

The lower end of the pick is pointed, while the upper portion is beveled where it meets the shaft, and has a slot cut through it for lashing.

A *dart or harpoon throwing board* of ivory is remarkable and, so far, unique. The information available states that it was purchased in the settlement of Chekhlyuk (Seklyuk) on the island of Ittygran, southwest of Arakamchechen Island. In shape, this throwing board is simpler than the more recent analogous devices of the western American and Asiatic Eskimos. As may be seen from the drawing (Plate 38:21), it narrows somewhat at the middle and toward the end. The handle is plain, oval in outline, and triangular in cross-section. There is a deep groove for the shaft of the projectile. The fore end is broken. However, the arrangement of the peg to engage the butt of the shaft is clear. Apart from the form, the decoration is of exceptional interest. The inner surface is decorated with very fine incised lines, parallel or meeting at an acute angle. The entire outer surface is covered by decoration in Style 1, the earliest of the Old Bering Sea styles, with which we are already well acquainted. Designs include concentric circles of irregular form with central dots; bunched and radiating lines issuing from these in the form of spikes or spurs; semi-circles and broken lines, always very finely incised. All the elements typical of this well-known ancient decorative style of the Eskimo are present. We know this style from the decoration on a number of objects from the Okvik site in the Punuk Islands (Rainey 1941d, Fig. 19, items 6–9; Fig. 24, items 6–7; Fig. 26, items 1–3), from the decoration of a "winged" object from St. Lawrence Island (Collins 1937:42, Fig. 4) and from one of the harpoon heads from the Cape Dezhnev area (Plate 7:1).

The side-prong of a *bird dart*, shown in Plate 36:14, is of ivory, flattened in shape, with a pointed base designed to fit into the shaft, and a longitudinal opening for lashing to the latter. There are two barbs on the outer edge.

An interesting dart or spear head from the Asian side of Bering Strait is illustrated by Sverdrup (Sverdrup 1930, Plate 25:3). Judging from the decoration, it is Late Punuk in date.

The dart or fish spear point of walrus ivory in Plate 36:38, has four asymmetric barbs. It is flattened in shape and very large.

Arrowheads may be divided into three groups: pointed arrowheads of bone or ivory, blunt arrowheads, and stone arrow points.

Sharp arrowheads are mostly of bone, flat, with a splayed, forked (Plate 36:15), or tanged base, without barbs (Plate 36:16,17). Three-sided specimens with a single barb also occur (Plate 36:19). All these arrowheads, judging from the stain of the bone and from typological features, are Late Punuk or even protohistoric in date. Such is also the date of blunt cylindrical, acorn- and egg-shaped arrowheads with sockets for hafting to the shaft (Plate 36:13).

I believe elongate, stemmed, and shouldered arrow points of flint or gray quartz are contemporary (Plate 36:20,21).

Sinew twisters for the reinforced bow are always used in pairs for applying a "cable" of sinew or baleen strands to the back of the bow. They are in the form of flattened rods with ends twisted in opposite directions, as may be seen from the one illustrated in Plate 36:25. Judging from the color of the ivory out of which they are made, these twisters are of recent date.

Bird bola weights are all of ivory, of varied but widely distributed shapes (Plate 36:26,27). Those in the shape of seal figurines are of interest (Plate 36:28,29). A bola from Point Hope with similar weights, in the form of polar bear, bird, and seal figurines, has been described by Nelson (Nelson 1899:134; Plate 51:8).

Fish line sinkers are of three types: relatively short ones, round in cross-section, wider in their lower third, and made of ivory or of slate, with round line holes at either end (Plate 36:33); sinkers of roughly the same shape, but considerably longer, made of ivory (Plate 36:35); and sinkers of flattened shape, widening toward the bottom, with a line hole at the upper end and openings near the middle for several hooks (Plate 36:34).

Net sinkers of walrus ivory are of the usual shape, with two suspension holes at the upper edge (Plate 36:32).

VARIOUS TOOLS AND UTENSILS

Not a single workshop used in manufacturing stone tools has yet been discovered on the Chukchi Peninsula. Kitchen refuse in cultural deposits and materials from the excavation of ancient Eskimo dwellings usually contain finished implements, occasionally flakes, also bearing traces of use as tools. Chance finds from the coast of the Chukchi Peninsula include only one prismatic *core* (Plate 36:30) from which very thin and narrow blades were detached.

Among finished tools, axes with transverse bits or adzes must rank first in importance in view of their role in the daily life of the ancient Eskimos.

The massive *adze* flaked on all sides illustrated in Plate 36:36 is made of silicified tuff and is partly ground. The bit is beveled and ground from one side and is blunted from prolonged use. There are interesting marks along one of the long sides, owing to sawing which, followed by a blow, served to detach the blank from a boulder. Two other adzes, one made of a jade-like stone (Plate 36:37), the other of silicified tuff (Plate 37:5), are well ground almost over their entire surface, and have the usual rectangular form, with a bit beveled from one side. In addition to the larger specimens, truly miniature adzes occur. These, like the nephrite blade represented in Plate 36:31, were hafted in bone socket-pieces.

A very interesting steeply beveled nephrite adze of moderate size, set in an antler socket piece, is shown in Plate 37:1. Another antler socket piece (Plate 37:2), to judge from the shape of the socket, was designed to fit a flat adze blade of large size.

Mattock handles which, as a rule, were made of wood, like the adze handles, rarely occur in excavations. For this reason, it is of interest to note, among chance finds, a wooden mattock handle (Plate 37:3) and an ivory adze handle (Plate 37:4), purchased in Nogakut. The handle of the mattock is widened and extended in length at its forward end. The surface in contact with the mattock is concave. A special triangular opening in the body of the handle and a notch near its middle supplement a notch on the upper edge of the handle for hafting the mattock. This type was known already in Punuk times (Collins 1937, Plate 79:1,2) and subsequently acquired a broad distribution both in the west and the east of the area occupied by the Eskimo. The ivory handle is more specialized in type. Here too, the distal end bears a special notch or groove for the adze socket piece, while the fore end of the handle bears two biconically drilled lashing holes.

An example of a *scraper* for working skins is shown in Plate 37:6. It is roughly flaked of silicified tuff and was hafted in a special handle when in use. Use was also made of flat ground stone *scrapers*, of which an example is shown in Plate 37:7.

The chalcedony knife in Plate 37:10 is leaf-shaped and rather crudely pressure-flaked. Its cutting edge is sharp, but wavy and uneven in profile.

The long single-edged knife of flint with a back and a broad stem shown in Plate 37:13 was hafted in the end of a long wooden or bone handle.

It is probable that blades such as the flint (Plate 37:9) and smoky quartz (Plate 37:8) examples illustrated were used as men's knives, though they may have served as spears or dart points.

The first of these is leaf-shaped in outline, with a broad and long stem, and is carefully retouched by pressure flaking. The second is also leaf-shaped, but with a short stem and a slight basal notch; it is retouched over its entire surface.

Men's knives of slate are all laurel-leaf shaped, with a broad stem designed to fit in a bone handle. As an example, we illustrate one knife of this kind from our excavations on Ratmanov Island (Plate 37:11). The others (Plate 37:12,16,22) are from various localities on the coast of the Chukchi Peninsula. One interesting laurel-leaf shaped blade is set in a bone handle (Plate 37:22).

An example of a man's knife, also of slate, but with a back, a single cutting edge, and a broad stem is shown in Plate 37:14.

An interesting slate double-edged knife shown in Plate 37:23 probably served for cutting whale blubber and meat; its fore end is broken.

Women's slate knives (ulu) are of the generally widespread type. Plate 37:15 illustrates a small knife of this kind set in a bone handle, and Plate 37:17 shows another, with biconically drilled lashing holes.

Some very interesting small nephrite knives have a convex back and a straight cutting edge, and show careful grinding. The stem of one of these (Plate 37:18) bears an incompletely drilled opening in the form of a conical depression. It is possible that, when used, these knives were set in bone handles with very narrow sockets.

The *hammer head* of ivory with a round socket for a handle (Plate 37:19) (purchased in Neyine-Knyskhven) is of a deep brown color from prolonged burial in the ground. It bears interesting decoration in Punuk style, in the form of deeply cut parallel lines.

Combs. A very interesting long-toothed comb of ivory from the Asian shore of Bering Strait has been published by Sverdrup (Sverdrup 1930, Plate 25:5). It has a distinctively shaped handle, decorated in Old Bering Sea style. The Borisov collection includes an ivory comb with a wooden grip from Vladimir station. It is of the same type, though much plainer. A row of long teeth form an elliptical pattern, and the comb is fastened to its handle by means of a bone rivet. Such combs are well known from Eskimo ethnographic collections both from the Asian coast and from America.

Two ivory combs with short, worn teeth (Plate 37:20,21) belong to a different type. These combs were probably used in working hides.

DECORATED OBJECTS OF WALRUS IVORY

Passing on now to an examination of a variety of ivory artifacts of interest primarily as art, we must mention first of all the model of a *kayak*. This small, keeled kayak is remarkable for the engraving on its upper surface. A low relief representation of a human face is cut out at the center of the manhole (Plate 38:6). The face is rendered schematically, with indications of the eyes, mouth, and nose. The remainder of the upper surface is entirely covered with the classic beak and eye motif of Old Bering Sea decoration, executed with very fine engraved lines. The underside of the kayak has a suspension hole at the prow end. Models of this kind, as we know, are commonly interpreted as children's toys. In this particular case, there is no doubt that we are dealing with a model intended for some kind of ritual custom connected with sea mammal hunting. This model is very ancient. This is indicated not only by its style, but also by its dark brown color, the result of remaining underground over a long period of time. Whatever the practical function of this model, it is important as a document which shows that as early as Old Bering Sea times the Eskimo had perfected the kayak in its definitive form, completely protected against the pentration of sea water into the hull.

An ovoid *spoon* of walrus ivory with a short and broad handle (Plate 38:18), apart from its form, is of interest for the decoration that covers the upper face of the handle. Two wavy lines occur along the center line, and from these issue series of straight parallel lines. An examination of these wavy lines easily reveals their stylistic similarity to the wavy line we observe on a bone brow band of Old Bering Sea date, found by Collins (1937, Plate 58:12) on St. Lawrence Island. This allows a conclusion as to the date of this spoon.

Apparently, the decoratively worked *dowels* of ivory (Plate 38:1,2), the purpose of which we do not know at present, are likewise very ancient. One of these has a crown resembling an opening three-petaled bud. The surfaces of both are cut with a groove descending in a spiral, indicating familiarity with the principle of the screw. In this connection, it is interesting to note that ivory rods with screw threads were found by Collins in an Old Bering Sea context in excavations on St. Lawrence Island (Collins 1937, Plate 59:15). In passing, we may note that both of these dowels have the dark brown color characteristic of excavated bone.

A *winged object*, the purpose of which has not yet been elucidated, resembles a butterfly in this case not only in shape, but also in size. This "butterfly" (Plate 38:3), like all winged objects, is carved out of ivory. The body and wings are clearly differentiated, particularly on the lower ventral side. Openings have been provided between the wings and the abdomen on the underside. In the neck area there is the usual shallow socket. The abdomen and the entire upper surface are covered with decoration, in the form of incised solid and broken lines repeating the outlines of the wings and accenting the shape of the dorsal area. Typologically, this "butterfly" is without doubt of early Old Bering Sea type. This conclusion follows both from the relative realism of the butterfly representation, and from the nature of its decoration. [This artifact should be] compared with "butterflies" from the excavations of Geist and Collins on St. Lawrence Island (Geist and Rainey 1936, Plates 60,61:3; Collins 1937, Plates 20,21). Its antiquity is confirmed by its dark-brown almost black, color.

Among objects decorated in Punuk style, we must note first the fragment (Plate 38:4) of a wedge-like "ceremonial" object, as Geist terms these artifacts, though the resemblance to a wedge is slight and relationships seem rather to be with the trident, an object we first came across in describing the materials from the excavations at Sirhenik (Plate 29:24). Like the trident, this object has a rectangular base, with a central cylindrical socket for holding a shaft, and three interconnected rising branches. Objects identical not only in shape but also in type of decoration are known from the excavations of Geist (Geist and Rainey 1936, Plate 62:4,5; Plate 72:1) on St. Lawrence Island. A similar object was acquired there by Collins (1937, Plates 68,69:6), and other similar objects have been described earlier (Collins 1929, Plate 10c,d,e; Hrdlička 1930, Plate 23b). Collins believes them to be Punuk versions of "winged" objects, inasmuch as here too we have a cylindrical basal socket for inserting a shaft, though the wings, instead of being free, are attached to the top of the central vertical shaft (Collins 1937:199). A complete parallel to our specimen may be found in an intact example illustrated by Geist (Geist and Rainey 1936, Plate 62:4). It is worth emphasizing the amazing constancy of form and decoration in all such ceremonial objects known to us.

A portion of a *needle-case* made from the wing bone of a bird and covered on the outside with characteristic decoration of parallel lines and spurs at right angles to them is represented in Plate 38:13. An entirely similar needle-case was purchased by Collins on St. Lawrence Island (Collins 1937, Plate 66:7).

A hook-shaped *thimble-holder* of ivory for thimbles of sealskin is reproduced in Plate 38:12. This thimble-holder, highly typical of Eskimo culture, is in the form of a plaque with a slit cut through its central part to three-quarters of its length, and a suspension hole. Both broad surfaces are decorated with concentric circles and parallel lines with rows of perpendicular spurs, such as are typical of Punuk times. Hook-like thimble-holders of this kind vary considerably in detail; numerous specimens have been described by a number of authors (Murdoch 1892:321, Fig. 328; Nelson 1899, Plate 44:1–9; Thalbitzer 1914:522, Fig. 250; Mathiassen 1930a, Plate 11:2–6; Plate 16:2).

A *bone buckle* (from the village of Nikhlan) is carved to represent the head and ears of a small animal (Plate 38:5). The back is decorated with dotted lines, while the ventral side has a loop for fastening.

The ivory *snow goggles* (Plate 38:7) with very narrow eye slits are of a type widespread among both Asiatic and American Eskimos, and are covered on the outside with decoration in Punuk style. Numerous examples of similar goggles have been published in the works of Murdoch (Murdoch 1892:260, Figs. 259–261) and Nelson (Nelson 1899, Plate 14), and have been found by Collins on St. Lawrence Island in the Old Bering Sea and Punuk complexes (Collins 1937, Plate 58:1,2; Plate 60:6; Plate 79:11). The dark brown color of these goggles, like that of the thimble holder described above, serve to confirm the fact that they were excavated.

The ivory handle (probably that of a woman's bag) in Plate 38:20 is an outstanding example of Eskimo artistic achievement. It is in the form of two whale heads opposed in heraldic fashion executed in the round, with a wide loop at the top and two smaller perforations below the heads. Except for the whale heads, the entire surface of the handle is covered with fine decoration in Punuk style, the component elements of which are well known to us from the excavations of Geist (Geist and Rainey 1936:180, Fig. 29) and Collins on St. Lawrence Island (Collins 1937, Plate 70:22).

Of the *carved figurines* found at ancient Eskimo sites on the Chukchi Peninsula, we must draw attention to the figure of a seal made of bitumen (Plate 38:16), that of a sea otter (Plate 38:14) made of ivory decorated with parallel lines and perpendicular spurs, and ivory figures of birds (Plate 38:15,17).

A *drum handle* of ivory of widespread type is interesting in view of its upper portion, shaped to represent the bill of a goose or duck and decorated with parallel lines in Punuk style (Plate 38:19).

An interesting *amulet* made from a wolf canine has a suspension hole and an eye carved on one of its surfaces, so that the result suggests the head of a bird (Plate 38:8).

Hrdlička has published a remarkable carved human figurine of ivory from the northeast coast of Asia (Hrdlička 1930, Plate 25). The specimens in the Borisov collection available to us are a far cry from the statuette published by Hrdlička. They are apparently amulets, three in number, carved of ivory, which render the human figure in highly schematic terms. They appear quite recent and it is possible that they represent modern Chukchi rather than Eskimo guardians (Plate 38:9,10,11).

COMPARATIVE ANALYSIS

Dwellings

THE TYPICAL permanent dwelling of the Asiatic Eskimo was the pit-house, in the construction of which whale bones were extensively used, for lack of driftwood.

The first notice of such semi-subterranean dwellings among the Eskimos appears in 1655 in a report of the Yakutsk governor, Stepan Dezhnev, who saw a settlement opposite Diomede and Gvozdev islands with "edifices of whale bone" (Berg 1920:15). Later, in 1711, Petr Popov, who came down the Anadyr River (on his way to Cape Dezhnev), wrote of the Chukchi (Eskimo–S. R.) dwelling on both sides of Cape Chukchi: "They dwell in earth lodges" (Berg 1920:38). In 1732, sailing from the mouth of the Kamchatka River to the Chukchi Peninsula, Ivan Fedorov and his companions landed north of Cape Chaplin, and there "examined two empty lodges built in the ground of whale bones, that were ancient and dug over." Somewhat later, at Cape Dezhnev, they inspected "six of these lodges, built in the ground of spruce wood" (*ibid.*, p. 48).

Permanent dwellings of the same type as that of the Eskimos existed among the Chukchi. Krashenninikov (Krashenninikov 1755:2:25–28) writes of them: "Like those in Kamchatka, they are built in the ground, but are incomparably larger; many people live in them." According to Billings' companions (Sarychev 1811:5), the winter houses of the Chukchi were similar to those of the Aleut. Their interiors had the form of an elongate rectangle. The roof was made of beams and whale bones, covered with grass and sod and heaped with earth. The entrance to the house was through a special opening in the roof. The hearth was in the middle.

Wrangel, who ran into remains of abandoned pit-houses everywhere, from Cape Baranov to Bering Strait and beyond it south along the Bering Sea coast, suggested that they had been inhabited once by Eskimos, who had since moved to America.

To the north and west of Shalaurov Island the headland rises to a height of fifteen *sazhens* [about 32 m—Translator]. Its western face slopes seaward, and is littered with whale ribs, which lie about here in small separate heaps. They are the remains of the huts of a people who once lived here and nourished itself on fish and sea mammals, mainly whales, and who used the giant ribs of the latter instead of logs and poles in building its huts.

Further, we read: "Judging from the remains of the huts, these were somewhat sunk into the ground and roofed with whale ribs and earth." (Wrangel 1841:295,333). Nelson is of the same opinion as Wrangel as to the assignment of the ancient pit-houses on the coast of the Chukchi Peninsula to the Eskimos (Nelson 1899:253–255). He saw ruins of ancient Eskimo villages along the Siberian shore of the Arctic Ocean, in particular at Cape Vankarem.

Hooper had seen partly destroyed semi-subterranean houses at Cape Vankarem as early as 1881.

Near the extremity of the cape we found the ruins of houses similar to those now in use by the Innuits, half under ground, with frames of the bones of whales. Probably they were former dwellings of Innuits, who for some reason crossed the straits and attempted to establish themselves on the Siberian side. . . . These houses, which have been found by different travelers at many places along the coast, are not all like those used by the Tchuktchis . . . (Hooper, 1884:63,99).

Bogoras saw a similar "dwelling of jaw bones" in the Chukchi village of Nunligran (Bogoras 1904–1909; 1:120–123). Judging from the detailed description of this dwelling, the pit-house had two entrances, the top entrance through the roof being used in the summer, whereas a long and narrow underground tunnel served as one in winter.

Dwellings only slightly sunk below ground level, having short, very low entrance corridors, the construction of which involves the use of whale bones in significant numbers, have been retained by the Eskimos of Ratmanov Island and in the modern village of Nuukan on the mainland.

On the basis of systematic excavations at Gambell on St. Lawrence Island, Collins distinguishes the following four types of Eskimo houses, three of them ancient and one modern (Collins 1937:260–261).

1. Houses of the Old Bering Sea period: small, square, semi-subterranean, with stone floor. The walls are made of small logs laid horizontally with occasional whale jawbones, held in place by wooden or bone stakes. The form of the roof is unknown. There is a long entrance passageway, situated below the level of the house floor, having a stone floor and walls and a log roofing.

1a. A modification of the Old Bering Sea house comes into use during the early phase of the succeding Punuk period. It resembles the older form in all basic features, but is nearly twice the size. The roof is made of timbers.

2. A different type of house pertains, apparently, to a late stage of Punuk. It is semi-subterranean, square in plan, with a stone floor and walls built of stones, walrus skulls and whale bones, which replace logs. The entranceway is now below or at the same level as the house floor, and is roofed with whale ribs or stones. There are round enlargements or compartments at the entrance.

2a. A modification of the form described above has walls made entirely of stone that are mainly above ground. There is no entrance passage; an inner wall forms a partition. The framework of the roof is sometimes made of whale jaws, and may have been covered with walrus hides. This is apparently a summer dwelling.

3. A dwelling differing from the preceding in certain fundamental features. It came into use during the Punuk period and persisted as late as 40 or 50 years ago. It is semi-subterranean and square. The flooring is made of well-fitted hewed planks or logs. The walls are of small logs and whale jawbones. There are low, wide sleeping platforms along two or three sides, and two to six heavy posts rising from the floor near the center, supporting two or three heavy whale jaw-bones, laid parallel, serving as roof beams. The central portion of the roof is flat, while the lower portions are inclined and completely covered with sod. There is a small smoke hole made of a whale vertebra. The entrance passageway is long and narrow, on the same level as the house. It is built and roofed with logs, and may have a stone floor.

4. Modern houses on St. Lawrence Island are octagonal and built above ground. The frame is wooden, and the roof is made of walrus hides. The interior sleeping chamber was introduced from Siberia, probably in the 18th century.

Descriptions of the houses of the Alaskan Eskimos by the first Russian travelers who visited Alaska in the beginning of the 19th century are of great value in gaining an idea of the former design of Eskimo dwellings. Khrostov and Davydov wrote:

The Koniags build their houses in the following manner. They set logs or split timbers in the ground sloping inward at somewhat of an angle, and make the roof flat or rounded. Then they cover it completely with grass and earth. This is their communal kitchen, which is entered through a small opening, covered with seal hide. They make fire in the middle of this hut and leave a hole in the roof above it for the smoke to escape. Instead of a floor, they lay down dry grass, and store certain household utensils along the sides. Some houses have sleeping benches, but this kind of hut is always most unclean. Through one side of the kitchen there is a small round opening, which barely allows one to crawl through it to enter the heated chamber which the Russians call *zhupan* and which is usually occupied by two or three families, and very rarely by one only. Each kitchen may have two or three such chambers [attached to it—P.T.], depending on the number of families living together. The floor of such a chamber is always below ground. Its walls slope and the roof rises above the ground. The roof or the wall have a window. Beaver intestines or other thin translucent intestines are used instead of glass, and four sticks serve as a window frame, and quite enough light enters the room. The *zhupan* is kept clean and is floored with boards, if timber is available near by, or, if such is not the case, is lined with dry grass and often with woven grass mats.

In each village, a hut called the *kazhim* is built in which games take place. Its roof is rounded and has a large window covered with sewn intestines, and there is a bench around the inside. (Khvostov and Davydov 1812; 2:19–21).

Zagoskin wrote of the houses of the Norton Sound Eskimo, the northern neighbors of the Koniag:

The natives of Norton Sound have summer dwellings that are different from their winter dwellings. Both kinds are built as follows. At the site of the winter house, earth is removed to a depth of 1 *arshin* [about 70 cm.—P.T.] or more. At the corners, reasonably thick posts are set, measuring 1½ to 2 *sazhens* [about 3 to 4 m.—P.T.] in height. The walls are assembled from split planks, which are likewise set on end and in line with the corner posts. The roof is built out of logs in the form of a pyramid. A special small frame is set in the opening that remains. It is stretched over with the guts of marine animals, and serves instead of a window. The frame is faced on the outside with planks or laths and the entire structure is then covered with earth so that the native huts appear from a distance as small mounds. As an entrance to the winter houses, a long and narrow passageway, 1½ to 2 *sazhens* in length, is excavated in the ground, lined with stakes, and also heaped with earth. A winter house is entered on all fours. There is a rectangular fire pit below the skylight. . . . In each native village there is a communal building, known as *kazhim*, as it is called in Kadiak. *Kazhims* are built like winter houses, but are larger in size. Some are 10 *sazhens* square [about 21 m. square —P.T.] and 4 or 5 high. Instead of sleeping platforms and shelves, these are lined on all sides with bunks, which are built in two or three tiers in some *kazhims* of Kwikpak and Kuskokwim. In addition to the usual entrance from the antechamber, which is narrow and long as in the winter houses, *kazhims* are provided with a special entrance from below through the fire pit, which may be as much as four feet deep. (Zagoskin 1848; 1:55–56).

Describing the houses of the Aleut, Veniaminov tells us that in former times they were very large in size, so that each held from 35 to 40 families (Veniaminov 1840:199). Of the ancient dwellings, he writes:

Often, and particularly in the more remote times, the ribs of large whales were used instead of posts, beams and laths. They were set along the wall with both ends somewhat buried, two others being placed over them, joined by girders or buttresses and lashed with thongs to form a semi-circle. Then, several logs were set on them at regular intervals, along the sides of the lodge and covered entirely with planks. At the top, between the elements of the frame, several skylights or openings were made, one of which served as an entrance to the house and as a window and smoke hole at the same time, while the others let through only smoke and light. (Veniaminov 1840:205).

We did not excavate any houses on the coast of the Chukchi Peninsula. Nevertheless, our archaeological tests in the vicinity of specific houses justify a number of conclusions.

First, we must answer a basic question: did the sea mammal hunters who formerly inhabited the coast of the Chukchi Peninsula dwell in pit-houses from earliest times? This question did not arise prior to the discovery of the Okvik site in the Punuk Islands and of the ancient settlement at Uwelen described earlier. Despite cultural deposits saturated with kitchen refuse and implements, neither the islands nor the mainland has yielded any evidence of semi-subterranean dwellings at the sites in question. It might be supposed that we have, in both places sites of a seasonal nature, used in the summer, in which dwellings were all above ground, and no storage pits were provided to preserve a meat supply for the winter. On the other hand, it seems no coincidence that both at Uwelen and at the Okvik site we have a distinctive and, apparently, the oldest stage of Eskimo culture in the Bering Sea area, rather than temporary camping sites of later and better known stages of Eskimo culture. It is true that Rainey writes that Giddings found the remains of a house of Okvik date on St. Lawrence Island (Rainey 1941d:468–471). However, this was not a typical pit-house. The dwelling was, apparently, round in plan, and the stone-lined floor was not sunk much below ground level. Furthermore, it is possible that this dwelling pertained already to the early Old Bering Sea stage of Eskimo culture, marked by Old Bering Sea Style 1.

Thus, it is entirely possible that further research will definitely show that the ancestors of the Eskimo arrived on the Bering Sea coast with some type of above-ground dwelling, and only gradually made the transition to semi-subterranean winter houses, as they adapted to the novel conditions of sedentary life in the Arctic.

At the Ipiutak, Birnirk and Old Bering Sea stages, the permanent winter dwelling of the inhabitants of the Bering Sea coast and neighboring tribes was the pit-house. At Point Hope, pit-houses were of very small size and relatively shallow. Typical Old Bering Sea houses were somewhat larger in size and were sunk more deeply into the ground.

On the basis of data in the literature, and without going into details, we can say that remains of pit-houses extend all along the arctic coast of Asia from Chetyrekhstolbovy Island to Cape Dezhnev. Beyond Cape Dezhnev, we have observed such remains along the entire coast from Bering Strait to Cape Bering. They are known also from the western and southern parts of Anadyr Gulf. Here, as on St. Lawrence Island, square pit-houses of small size are connected with cultural remains of the Old Bering Sea period. Pit-houses of this kind with entrance passageways occur both singly and in groups. We have seen the remains of such houses on Ratmanov Island, at Cape Nizmenny, near Cape Chukchi at Sirhenik, and at Cape Bering. It is quite possible that, as Khvostov and Davydov found it to be the case among the Koniag, the central unit of such a collective dwelling served as a communal kitchen, while the peripheral units, connected by passageways to the central house, were the abodes of individual families.

As on St. Lawrence Island, Eskimo houses on the Asian coast in later times, at the Punuk stage of Eskimo culture, were of large size as compared to Old Bering Sea houses. A striking feature that emerges from a comparison of Old Bering Sea and Punuk houses on the Chukchi Peninsula is the extensive use of whale bone as building material for houses in Punuk times. A particularly good illustration of this is provided at Sirhenik, where the construction of a single, albeit perhaps multi-family, house entailed the use of eighty whale skulls [probably of the beluga—Ed.] alone, not counting jawbones, ribs, and vertebrae [probably of the bowhead whale—Ed.]

Nowhere on the coast of the Chukchi Peninsula did we see the remains of structures standing out by their large size among other houses in an ancient Eskimo settlement. We may conclude from this that neither in Old Bering Sea times nor later did the Asiatic Eskimo have special communal structures or men's houses, similar to the *kazhim* of the western Eskimo of America. The explanation for this may lie in the fact that, as far as we know, the Eskimo population on the coast of the Chukchi Peninsula was never very large. Nowhere did we find ancient sites in which the number of pit-houses of the same type exceeded ten to twenty, and it is unlikely moreover that all such houses were ever occupied at the same time.

It is a problem for future research to determine what changes in the social structure of the Eskimo determined changes in house type. It is possible that the new type of house in Punuk time arose concomitantly with the patriarchal family, replacing the matriarchal family of the Old Bering Sea period.

We know too little as yet of the details of house construction. We cannot state definitely whether the ancient Asiatic Eskimos used the central skylight and smoke hole in the roof as an entrance, in addition to the passageway. It is certain only that the extensive use of whale bone as building material for houses was the natural consequence of the development of whale hunting that took place only in relatively late Punuk times.

The *tools* used by the Eskimo in *house construction* were: heavy ivory mattocks, mattocks of whale ribs, large ivory wedges for splitting tree trunks into planks, and stone adzes for finishing planks and whale bones. We shall deal with wedge and adze types subsequently.

Heavy mattocks of whole ivory tusks were a very common tool of the Old Bering Sea period on St. Lawrence Island (Collins 1937:160). On the Chukchi Peninsula, we have such mattocks from the ancient site at Uwelen (Plate 2:30) and from Kiwak (Plate 17:25). As stated, they were made from whole walrus tusks, in some cases from large segments thereof, and were intended for excavating the ground in building pit-houses and digging meat storage pits. It is possible that they were used also in chopping holes through the ice. The lower end of these mattocks is usually beveled from both sides. There were several methods of hafting them to a handle. Most frequently, the inner surface of the upper end, fitting against the handle, was cut in and transversely grooved for more secure attachment. Several transverse channels across that upper end served for lashing. In some cases, the upper end bears one broad notch instead of several transverse channels. Short mattocks usually have one or two hafting grooves.

Similar mattocks from sites of later times do not differ substantially from the Old Bering Sea specimens. We have entirely similar examples from such late sites as Nuukan, Arakamchechen Island, Cape Chaplin (Plate 15:6), Avan and the upper levels of the eastern sector at Sirhenik.

A second type of mattock, for removing the sod at the projected house site and for gathering sod to cover the pit-house, is made of a whale's rib, and, it would seem, appears later. It was not noted in Old Bering Sea inventories either on St. Lawrence Island or in our excavations on the Chukchi Peninsula. We did find such mattocks in late Punuk sites on Arakamchechen Island, on Cape Chaplin and in the upper levels of the refuse deposit in the eastern sector at

Sirhenik (Plate 28:6). Similar mattocks are characteristic also of the Thule culture in North America (Mathiassen 1927; 1:56, Plate 21).

For removing soil and shoveling snow, shovels made of walrus scapulae or whale bone were also used in ancient times. The walrus scapula shovels used for this purpose in Old Bering Sea times and later were hardly worked at all. They were merely given the required shape and provided with slits for lashing to a handle (Geist and Rainey 1936:105, Plate 24:6,7; Collins 1937, Plate 50:6; Plate 60:12). We found one such shovel in our excavations at Sirhenik. Snow shovels of whale bone of the type represented in Plate 15:18 from Cape Chaplin evidently appeared late in Punuk times and recent ones are also well known from ethnographic collections from the Chukchi Peninsula.

The Gathering of Plant Foods

Sea mammal hunting, as we know, was the subsistence basis of the ancient Eskimo. However, the large number of picks and mattocks of bone, antler, and more rarely ivory, for digging up edible roots, found at all ancient sites, are evidence that formerly, like today, the Eskimo gathered plant foods when they could. Bogoras gives a long list of plants, the roots of which were used as food on the Chukchi Peninsula (Bogoras 1904–1909; 1:198). Nelson also wrote of the gathering of roots and the collection of accumulations thereof from mouse burrows among the Alaskan Eskimos (Nelson 1899:268).

Picks for digging up edible roots differ from mattocks in their considerable length, combined with a small diameter and a pointed lower end. The simplest form of a pick, made from an antler tine and provided with an opening in its upper part, is shown in Plate 15:2. A flattened bone pick with a hafting groove is shown in Plate 15:3. These picks all differ in form and hafting arrangement (Plate 10:16; Plate 18:21). The form of the handles of picks for digging up edible roots may be judged from the wooden handle illustrated in Plate 37:3.

In addition to edible roots, the Asiatic Eskimos formerly, as they do today, made use of seaweed as food. A device for gathering the latter, found in the excavations at Cape Chaplin and dating from Punuk times, is rather complex in design. It is possible that less complex devices may have been used in ancient times for the purpose, though seaweed may always be gathered in the summer without difficulty on the beach, where it is left by the tide.

Sea Mammal Hunting Equipment

HARPOON HEADS

The overwhelming number of bones of sea mammals, such as walrus, bearded seal, ringed seal, and, later, whale, found in the kitchen refuse of ancient Eskimo sites on the coast of the Chukchi Peninsula, as well as the occurrence of pits for storing the meat of these mammals, point to the primary importance of hunting these animals. For this reason, we begin our survey of the means used by the Eskimo to obtain animal food with sea mammal hunting equipment and the most important weapon of the latter, the harpoon.

It appears that the shaft and other parts of the harpoon, apart from the head, changed little with time and, besides, they are not so well known. On the contrary, harpoon heads are numerous and, as a result of their variability in time and space, are superior diagnostic features for characterizing the stages of development of Eskimo culture.

Harpoons have been the subject of many specialized researches. Ancient Eskimo harpoon heads have been studied in particular detail by Collins. In addition to providing a classification, his work has produced a most useful scheme of the development at Gambell, on St. Lawrence Island, of open socket harpoon heads, the predominant class in the early stages of Eskimo culture (Collins 1937, Fig. 27 in the text). This scheme is not contradicted by our own observations on the Chukchi Peninsula. In a special paper (Rudenko 1947), I have had occasion already to review the harpoon heads of the Asiatic Eskimo. At this time, following excavations on the Chukchi Peninsula, our information on this remarkable weapon has been enlarged considerably by the discovery of a number of new types, which deserve special consideration.

Open-socket harpoon heads. The type which Collins has termed Old Bering Sea is distinguished, as we know, by the following features: an open socket for the foreshaft, two slots for the socket lashing, a triple symmetrical spur with a longer center-prong, two round line holes above and below the lashing slots, stone side-blades set in deep slots in the same plane as or at right angles to the line holes, and decoration either in Old Bering Sea style or else absent. The material is always walrus ivory. This type, broadly speaking, is very rare. Of the 417 harpoon heads excavated at Gambell on St. Lawrence Island, only 5 were found to be of this type, and only one was completely undamaged. Such harpoon heads were found in somewhat larger numbers by Geist (Geist and Rainey 1936, Plate 70:6,7,9,11,12,13, p. 206, Figs. 37,38,39 in the text) in excavations at Kukulik. Two harpoon heads of this type have been described by Jenness (1928a, Plate 13a; 1928b, Plate 3a) from Little Diomede. From Alaska, only three are known (Collins 1929, Plate 2f; Wissler 1916:410; Mathiassen 1929, Fig. 13b), and these are from the Point Barrow area. From the Asian coast, in the Bering Strait region, we know of five harpoon heads of Old Bering Sea type. One of these was published by Sverdrup (1930, Plate 25:4) and four are in the Museum of Ethnography in Leningrad, two of them published by us (Plate 7:3,6).

As far as we know, all harpoon heads of this type found to date were provided with stone side-blades. However, at Sirhenik, we found a specimen which differs in the presence of an end-blade in the plane of the line holes instead of side-blades (Plate 19:9). While having a broad trough-shaped socket for the foreshaft, generally typical of the harpoon head type under discussion, the Sirhenik specimen is distinctive in having lashing slots of equal size set far apart on the dorsal side, instead of being set close together in a groove. Partially preserved decoration in Old Bering Sea style precludes any doubt as to the antiquity of this harpoon head.

Harpoon heads of Old Bering Sea type, to judge from their decoration, are characteristic of the first half of the Old Bering Sea period of Eskimo cultural development. The presence of two line holes and related features of design serve to set these harpoon heads apart. The complexity of their design naturally invites a search for simpler antecedent forms. One such form, it seems to me, is represented by a harpoon head from the Cape Dezhnev area (Plate 7:1). Furthermore, the style of the decoration of this head (Old Bering Sea 1), apart from the features of its construction, is evidence that it is older than the classical Old Bering Sea type of harpoon head. The same must be said of the barbed harpoon head with stone side-blades from the same area represented in Plate 7:2.

Rainey, in describing the Okvik site, has shown that, simultaneously with objects and in particular harpoon heads decorated in Old Bering Sea Style 1 and, more specifically, bearing the motif which is clearly discernible on the specimen in Plate 7:1—a small circle with long radiating spurs—there occur harpoon heads of another type, well represented in our collections from the ancient settlement at Uwelen (Rainey 1941d). This type of head is genetically unrelated to the Old Bering Sea type, existed apparently earlier than the latter, and is genetically connected with harpoon heads of the so-called Birnirk type.

A representative of a special type, coeval with the Old Bering Sea and derived from the type represented in Plate 7:1, may be seen in a specimen from the western sector of the refuse area at Sirhenik (Plate 19:10). It has a very broad, trough-shaped socket, a double slot for the socket lashing, which merges into one on the dorsal side, a triple symmetrical spur with a longer center-prong, one line hole and stone side-blades. All these features, as well as the material (ivory), are equally characteristic of the types under comparison. Only the shape of the spur, the details of the arrangement of the slots for the socket lashing, the position of the side-blades in relation to the line hole and, above all, the style of the decoration, which is later in the Sirhenik specimen, justify a view of the latter as a special type, pertaining to the first half of the Old Bering Sea stage of Eskimo culture.

A harpoon head type characteristic of the Old Bering Sea or Early Punuk stage, which is Collins' Type II, the Birnirk type of Mathiassen, and types D and H of Geist and Rainey, is well represented on the coast of the Chukchi Peninsula. The diagnostic features of this type are as follows: open socket, two or more rarely one slot for the lashing, a triple or more rarely a double or multiple asymmetric spur with prongs of more or less equal length, though one of them usually projects further than the others, a round line hole, two stone side-blades set in deep slots in the plane of the line hole or at right angles to it. The cross-section of the body of the harpoon head is round in the case of a triple spur and flattened in the case of a double one. Decoration is in Uwelen-Okvik style, Old Bering Sea style, or absent.

The basic differences between this type and the classical Old Bering Sea are the presence of one line hole instead of two and the asymmetric position of the spur. The shape of the socket is entirely the same as in Old Bering Sea specimens, broad and trough-like, but the slots for the socket lashing, as a rule, are of unequal lengths and at different levels, one being higher than the other, so that the lashing that covers the socket is somewhat diagonal. In some cases, the two slots for the lashing are replaced by a single slot and an opposing groove. On the dorsal face, as in some Old Bering Sea specimens, at the point where the slots for the lashing come together, there is a deep groove leading from the line hole to the slots, and it is in this groove that the slots converge.

This type was first described by Murdoch (Murdoch 1892:22, Fig. 210) and Otis Mason (O. Mason 1902:277). It predominates in Stevenson's collection from Birnirk near Point Barrow and has been described in detail by Wissler (Wissler 1916). It also predominates in the Van Valin collection from the same site, where it has been described by J. Alden Mason (J. A. Mason 1930). Such harpoon heads are not infrequent on St. Lawrence Island, where they are found in several variants (Geist and Rainey 1936:204, Plate 69:7; Collins 1937:102–103, Plate 24–25:5–10; Plate 27:14; Plate 28:1,2). The type has been described by Jenness from Little Diomede Island (Jenness 1928, Plate 12), and by Rainey from the Punuk Islands (Rainey 1941d, Fig. 9). On the coast of the Chukchi Peninsula, harpoon heads of the same type, with a triple or multiple spur, have been found in rather large numbers and are confined, so far, to two areas: that of Bering Strait to the north and Cape Bering in the south.

In this group, we must note first some harpoon heads from the ancient settlement at Uwelen, which are the oldest, and are decorated in Uwelen-Okvik style (Plate 1:4) and similar harpoon heads from the Okvik site in the Punuk Islands (Rainey 1941d, Fig. 9 items 1–5). A large number with triple asymmetric spurs come from the Cape Dezhnev area (Plate 7:4,5,8,12,13), from Uwelen (Plate 1:3) and from Cape Bering (Plate 33:5). Harpoon heads of Birnirk type, flattened in shape, with a double asymmetric spur, have been found at Cape Dezhnev (Plate 7:9), at Sirhenik (Plate 19:11), and at Enmylen near Cape Bering (Plate 33:4).

Collins considers the harpoon heads of the type under discussion, the Birnirk type, to be derived from Old Bering Sea Type 1. We can hardly agree with this conclusion. The more ancient Uwelen-Okvik harpoon heads, with their highly complex spurs, their distinctive decoration by means of deeply cut lines, schematic representations of animals and modeling of the spur in the form of an animal head, were the predecessors of this type at Birnirk and in the Old Bering Sea stage of Eskimo culture.

Harpoon heads of the Birnirk type are decorated, as a rule, in late Old Bering Sea Style 3, characteristic of the late Old Bering Sea stage of the development of Eskimo culture. Mention has frequently been made in the literature of a distinctive feature of the Birnirk harpoon heads from Point Barrow, namely, that the two side-blades are replaced by a single blade, or by a single barb, or finally by a single barb and an opposing side-blade. We have an example of such a harpoon head with one side-blade and with decoration in Uwelen-Okvik style from the ancient settlement at Uwelen (Plate 1:4). Another example, also with a single side-blade, is from the Cape Dezhnev area (Plate 7:11). A flat bone harpoon head of Birnirk type with a double asymmetric spur and a single barb was found in the excavations at Sirhenik (Plate 19:13).

Harpoon heads of Birnirk type with a double spur, side-blades, one barb, and one side-blade, or without the latter, made, as a rule, of antler or bone have a distribution along the arctic coast from the mouth of the Kolyma—Sverdrup's find on Chetyrekhstolbovy Island (Mathiassen 1927; 2:180, Fig 72)—to Point Barrow, including Uwelen and Point Hope (Rainey 1941b). Collins considers their occurrence on St. Lawrence Island as fortuitous. However, finds of similar harpoon heads at the Okvik site in the Punuk Islands (Rainey 1941d) indicate that this variable type of harpoon head had a much broader distribution in ancient times than was formerly supposed.

As we have seen, most of the harpoon heads of the early stages of development of Eskimo culture were equipped with side-blades. However, even in early times, there were harpoon heads equipped with an end-blade instead of side-blades. We know of series of harpoon heads with end-blades (Collins' Type III) from the ancient settlement at Uwelen (where they are very numerous) and from the Okvik site. Series of harpoon heads with end-blades and bearing decoration in the Old Bering Sea style are known from St. Lawrence Island. Similar heads, decorated in Old Bering Sea style, have been found on the Asian coast: in the Bering Strait area (Sverdrup 1930, Plate 25:2) and at Cape Bering (Plate 33:3). It is apparent that even at the earliest known stages of maritime culture in the Bering Sea area, harpoon heads with stone side-blades coexisted with types having end-blades and that, exceptionally, harpoon heads with both an end-blade and stone side-blades occurred.

Mathiassen's Thule 2 type of harpoon head, Collins' Type IV, so widespread and typical in the culture of the western and, most particularly, the Central Eskimo of North America, is relatively rare on the coast of Asia. As we know, it includes barbed harpoons with open socket, one or two slots or a circular groove for the socket lashing, triangular line hole, and single asymmetric spur. The material is usually antler or bone. The classical form has two asymmetrically placed barbs, but we find some with two or even three pairs of barbs. The type occurs in two variants: with and without an end-blade. The latter is always in the plane of the line hole, inasmuch as we are dealing with a flat harpoon head. At the present time, the type is known almost throughout the entire territory inhabited by the Eskimos of America, though only at sites abandoned long ago: at Point Barrow in Alaska (Murdoch 1892:220, Fig. 209) and further east at Cape Atkinson and Barter Island (Mathiassen 1930a, Plate 1:1,5; Plate 5:1). In eastern North America, it is the type most frequently found in the Thule culture. It is the most common harpoon head at Naujan, where Mathiassen found no fewer than 31 examples (Mathiassen 1927; 2:16). It is also well known at other living sites of the Central Eskimo (Boas 1907:248; Jenness 1925; Wissler 1916:150), and is frequently found at sites of the northern portion of the west coast of Greenland (Birket-Smith 1924, Figs. 25,20b). Individual specimens have been found also on St. Lawrence Island (Geist and Rainey 1936:93–94, Plate 18:8; Plate 63:8; Collins 1937:205–206, Plate 70:4,6).

On the Chukchi Peninsula, the type of harpoon head in question with two symmetrical barbs but without an end-blade has been found on the arctic coast at Cape Schmidt (Nordenskiöld 1882; 1:404, Fig. 5) and in excavations of the house on the gravel bar at Uwelen (Plate 5:2), and on the Bering Sea coast in the upper levels of the cultural deposit in the eastern sector at Sirhenik (Plate 19:7,8). Harpoon heads of Thule 2 type with end-blades were present at Nuukan (Plate 10:1) and the Cape Dezhnev area (Plate 7:19). We have a specimen with two pairs of barbs and without an end-blade from Cape Bering (Plate 33:14), one with an end-blade from the Cape Dezhnev area (Plate 7:24) and one with three pairs of barbs and without an end-blade from Cape Bering (Plate 33:13).

Thus we see that harpoon heads of Thule 2 type and derivatives thereof are found sporadically throughout the surveyed portion of the coast of the Chukchi Peninsula, though, as in America, always in a relatively late context, corresponding on St. Lawrence Island to mature Punuk and to Thule on the American continent. At the same time, harpoon heads of this type cannot be considered typical of any stage of development of Eskimo culture on the Chukchi Peninsula. It is surprising at the same time that such seemingly specialized and rare harpoon heads as those with two or three pairs of symmetric barbs (Plate 33:13 and 14) should be found in the south of the Chukchi Peninsula, at Cape Bering, and as far east as Point Hope, northern Baffin Island on the arctic shore of North America and northwest of Hudson Bay (Mathiassen 1927; 1, Plate 37:9, Plate 39:4; 1930a, Plate 12:2). This can be explained only by intensive contacts at that time between the Bering Sea and arctic coasts of the Chukchi Peninsula and the arctic shores of North America, and the migration of individual families from one area to the other.

Small willow-leaf shaped points of Mathiassen's Thule 1 type and Collins' Type V, are well represented in our collections from the Chukchi Peninsula. The diagnostic features of this type are as follows: open socket, circular groove, one slot and opposing groove or two slots for the socket lashing, the lashing slots sometimes being replaced by a pair of drilled holes, triangular or round line hole, and one simple lateral spur. Neither side-blades nor end-blade are present. Decoration is absent. The material is antler or bone, more rarely ivory. Harpoon heads of this type with a circular groove for the socket lashing occur in several examples from the western site at Nunligran (Plate 31:3) and from the coast of Bering Strait (Plate 36:9). Outside the Chukchi Peninsula, such harpoon heads are known from St. Lawrence Island (Geist and Rainey 1936:93, Plate 18:7; Collins 1937, Plate 71:15,16,22), where they have been found in very small numbers. We know of only two similar harpoon heads from the Central Eskimo area (Mathiassen 1927; 1, Plate 1:1). Harpoon heads with one slot and opposing groove for the socket lashing (Plate 1:2; Plate 7:21; Plate 13:3; Plate 36:8) were found in the excavations at Uwelen, and from Cape Dezhnev to Cape Chaplin on the Bering Sea coast. We know of isolated specimens from St. Lawrence Island (Geist and Rainey 1936:93, Plate 18:5; Collins 1937:208, Plate 71:12,13). In this group, the specimen from the ancient settlement at Uwelen stands out (Plate 1:2). Unlike all the others, in which the slot for the lashing is through the longer edge of the head, the Uwelen has the slot through the median line. Furthermore, instead of the usual triangular line hole, we have a round one which is displaced over toward the short side of the head instead of being in the center. Judging from its stain and patina, the artifactual context in which this harpoon head was found, and the decoration—consisting of a plain deeply incised line—this specimen is much older than the others. It stands apart and may be considered as derivative from the Birnirk type of harpoon head.

Harpoon heads with two lashing slots that come together on the dorsal side number only three in our collection. Two have triangular line holes (Plate 36:2,7), the other has a round one (Plate 10:2). The latter is unusually large for this type (12.5 cm in length). The area of distribution is limited, and we know of none so far in areas other than the Bering Sea coast of the Chukchi Peninsula.

Mathiassen has published a harpoon head of this type from Cape Dezhnev in Rasmussen's collection (Mathiassen 1930a, Plate 18:2), which is distinctive in the presence of a pair of round holes instead of two slots for the socket lashing. A similar harpoon head with two pairs of round holes (Plate 10:3) was found by us in our excavations in Nuukan, in association with very late objects. Let us remember that this lashing arrangement in the socket is usual at late sites of the Central Eskimo and in Greenland. The round openings in such harpoon heads were drilled with iron drills.

Mathiassen believes that forms which appear simplest on typological grounds are also the oldest (Mathiassen 1927; 2:14). For this reason, he considered harpoon heads of the type just examined (Thule 1) as an older form than, for example, harpoon heads of Thule 2 type. Collins has shown that small harpoon heads of Thule 1 type without side-blades or end-blade are one of the late prehistoric types on St. Lawrence Island (Collins 1937:310). Our observations have confirmed the lateness of their appearance on the Chukchi Peninsula, in such complexes as those of the western site at Nunligran and the refuse deposit at Nuukan.

On the Chukchi Peninsula, as on St. Lawrence Island, the best represented group is that of open-socket harpoon heads of Mathiassen's Thule 3 type, Type C of Geist and Rainey, and Collins' Type III. This group is characterized by the following features: one slot and opposing groove or two slots for the socket lashing, a round line hole, an asymmetric simple, more rarely bifurcated, or trifurcated spur, and a slit for the end blade in the plane of the line hole. The material is bone or antler, more rarely ivory. Decoration is mainly in Punuk style or absent. On St. Lawrence Island, this type existed from the Old Bering Sea period to recent times. Harpoon heads of this kind from the Chukchi Peninsula likewise vary in date. We have examples decorated in Uwelen-Okvik style from the ancient settlement at Uwelen (Plate 1:9,13), as well as from the Okvik site in the Punuk Islands (Rainey 1941d, Figs. 4,6). One such harpoon head from the Cape Dezhnev area has been published by Sverdrup (Sverdrup 1930, Plate 25:2). It is a large head, probably that of a walrus harpoon, made of ivory, with triple spur and rudimentary barbs. The decoration is in Old Bering Sea style.

Massive harpoon heads with one slot and opposing groove for the socket lashing, and with a double or triple markedly projecting spur from Sirhenik (Plate 19:17,18) and Enmylen (Plate 33:7,8,10) pertain, in all likelihood, to Early Punuk. They are all decorated with simple lines in Punuk style. All four found at Enmylen are of bone or antler. Of the nine from Sirhenik, five are of walrus ivory.

Harpoon heads of this type with one slot and an opposing groove for the socket lashing but with a simple spur are found rarely on the Chukchi Peninsula. We have only a few examples from Sirhenik (Plate 19:14,16) and one from the excavations of the house on the spit at Uwelen (Plate 5:1). However, we have a very large series of specimens of this type with two slots for the socket lashing, in which the outer edge of the spur is the direct continuation of the edge of the head, at times with a negligible bulge at the base of the spur. The lashing slots come together and are most frequently on the same level on the dorsal side, while rarely being at the same level next to the open socket (Plate 10:2), the slot on the spur side as a rule being much lower than its opposite. We have such harpoon heads from the house excavations at Uwelen (Plate 5:3), from the Cape Dezhnev area (Plate 7:17), from Yandygay (Plate 12:4), from Arakamchechen Island, from Cape Chaplin (Plate 13:1), from Sirhenik (Plate 19:15,19), and from Cape Bering (Plate 36:3)—in a word, from the entire portion of the coast of the Chukchi Peninsula which we surveyed. Some of these specimens lack decoration, while the majority is decorated in typical Punuk style.

The latest, protohistoric, examples of this type were found in the excavations of the house on the coastal spit at Uwelen (Plate 5:3,4). Two of them have two pairs of holes about 2 mm in diameter drilled with a metal drill instead of lashing slots and one, in addition, has even smaller holes at the fore end for the rivet of an iron blade.

Harpoon heads of Type 3, which are relatively infrequent in the Old Bering Sea period, subsequently predominate in Punuk times. Of the 417 harpoon heads found near Gambell on St. Lawrence Island, 161 were found to be of Type 3. This type also predominates in Jenness' excavations at Cape Prince of Wales in Alaska. It is also familiar from Mathiassen's excavations in the Central Eskimo area of America and further east as far as Greenland.

A rare and distinctive form of flat harpoon head, known so far only from the Cape Dezhnev area, has an open socket, two slots at the same level for the socket lashing, a round line hole, a bifurcated symmetrical spur, and may have (Plate 7:18) or lack (Collins 1937:213–214) a slit for an end-blade in the plane of the line hole.

Closed-socket harpoon heads. Turning our attention to the shape of the open socket in Eskimo harpoon heads, we will note that it slowly and uniformly becomes narrower with time. The socket in Old Bering Sea harpoon heads is very broad and trough-shaped. It is even wider in harpoon heads which we believe to be pre-Old Bering Sea (Plate 7:1,2). A similarly broad and trough-like socket occurs in the more ancient harpoons of Birnirk type. During the Punuk period, the sockets of harpoon heads become narrower and are straight-edged and quadrangular in cross-section instead of trough-shaped. In Late Punuk, as Collins pointed out (1937:213–214), quadrangular sockets of equal width outside and inside begin to be replaced by sockets of trapezoidal cross-section. Whereas earlier the foreshaft was held in place only by the lashing, now the socket is carved so as to partially hold the foreshaft. This is achieved by a special preparation of the walls of the socket from the outside inward: the bottom of the socket is made wider than the top, and the foreshaft is held in place without a lashing even though the socket is not completely closed.

The wedge-like design of the socket evolves further as its opening at the top is narrowed, so that the groove becomes much narrower at the top than at the bottom. This change in the shape of the socket may be illustrated with a number of examples (Plate 5:1; Plate 10:1; Plate 12:20; Plate 13:4). In the end, the open socket acquires the shape of a cone or truncated three-cornered pyramid, enclosed in the body of the harpoon head, with a narrow slot in its outer wall. The lashing then becomes superfluous, as we can actually see in Plate 31:4. Thus, open sockets disappear altogether at a very late stage, in protohistoric times, and are all transformed into closed sockets.

Despite this very obvious evolution of the shape of the socket in Eskimo harpoon heads, it would be incorrect to consider as late forms all harpoon heads with closed sockets.

The closed-socket design, as we know from the excavations on St. Lawrence Island, was known to the Eskimos in the Old Bering Sea stage of the development of their culture. This finds confirmation from excavations on the Chukchi Peninsula.

Closed-socket harpoon heads are generally few in the early phases of the development of Eskimo culture, as compared with open-socket specimens. They become predominant late, only in protohistoric times. In historic times, open-socket harpoon heads go out of use altogether.

Plate 9:4,5,8 shows closed-socket harpoon heads with end-blades (Collins' Type III) decorated in excellent Old Bering Sea style. There is a closed-socket harpoon head from the ancient settlement at Uwelen (Plate 1:14), similar in form to open-socket specimens of Old Bering Sea date known from the Bering Strait shore (Sverdrup 1930, Plate 25:2) and from Cape Bering (Plate 33:3). In general, it must be noted that there is no type of open-socket harpoon head that does not find its parallel in shape and details among closed-socket specimens. Thus, the harpoon head in Plate 1:15 from Uwelen resembles a very similar specimen with open socket illustrated in Plate 1:10. The closed-socket harpoon head of Punuk type from Sirhenik (Plate 19:23) is similar to an open-socket specimen (Plate 19:16) from the same site. It is not hard to find counterparts to the closed-socket harpoon heads from the Cape Dezhnev area (Plate 7:22,23) among similar open-socket specimens. We may note in passing that all ancient closed-socket harpoon heads, like all whaling harpoon heads, to be discussed below, were made of walrus ivory. Only protohistoric and recent closed-socket harpoon heads, having a triangular or round line hole, a simple asymmetric spur, and an end-blade (for example, Plate 13:20; Plate 33:11) are with rare exceptions made of bone or antler.

Whaling harpoon heads. Finds of whaling harpoon heads are very few on the Chukchi Peninsula, as on St. Lawrence Island, compared to the number of seal and walrus harpoon heads. If we do not count those purchased from the Eskimos we have only four whole specimens of this kind and several damaged ones from our excavations. They were found at relatively late sites, belonging to the second half of the Punuk period: the house excavations on the Uwelen spit, Nuukan, Arakamchechen Island, Cape Chaplin, Avan, and one damaged specimen from Sirhenik. All of them have closed conically drilled sockets, a large triangular line hole, a simple straight basal spur and a slit for an end-blade at right angles to the line hole (Plate 8:1; Plate 12:8; Plate 13:7). They are flattened in shape, the material is ivory, and decoration is absent.

On St. Lawrence Island, whaling harpoon heads first appear in the Punuk period. Their late appearance, which is confirmed by excavations on the coast of the Chukchi Peninsula, is interpreted by Collins (Collins 1937:217) as indicating that whale hunting, on a small scale at that, began to be practised by the Eskimos only in Punuk times. At the same time, the absence not only of whaling harpoon heads, but also of whale bones at early sites of the Old Bering Sea period, in particular at the sites of Hillside and Gambell on St. Lawrence Island would seem to show, in the opinion of Collins, that the Old Bering Sea Eskimo failed to hunt whales altogether. The occurrence of whale bones at ancient sites is explained by Collins as follows: they were obtained from animals washed ashore by currents, after they had been killed, though we know not by whom.[1]

The problem of the date at which the Eskimo began hunting whales remains as yet unsolved. Rainey for example, believes that the ancestors of the Eskimos were already hunting whales at the Okvik stage (Rainey 1941d). The absence of whaling harpoon heads among finds of Old Bering Sea date is still not evidence for the absence of whale hunting. Among hundreds of harpoon heads in the cultural deposit at Sirhenik, we found only one whaling harpoon head, and a damaged one at that, though in Punuk times whales were hunted there most actively. In view of this ratio at Sirhenik, there is nothing surprising in the fact that we still have no whaling harpoon heads from Old Bering Sea sites, which are still not very numerous or thoroughly studied. On the other hand, the Eskimos could have hunted young animals or small whales such as the beluga (**Delphinapterus leucas** Pall.) using large walrus harpoons with heads such as the specimen illustrated in Plate 33:3 from Enmylen or the one published by Sverdrup (Sverdrup 1930, Plate 25:2) or, finally, large harpoon heads which seem more of the whaling than of the walrus type such as we have from the ancient settlement at Uwelen (Plate 1:13) or from Geist's excavations (Geist and Rainey 1936, Fig. 26 in the text) on St. Lawrence Island, decorated in Old Bering Sea style. Apart from harpoons, whale hunting also entailed the use of lances, the points of which do occur in Old Bering Sea artifact assemblages.

TECHNIQUES OF MANUFACTURING AND ARMING HARPOON HEADS

Excavations on the Chukchi Peninsula have yielded many semi-manufactured pieces, if we may use the expression, which provide a clear idea of the steps in manufacturing harpoon heads.

To begin with, it was necessary to obtain a *blank* of walrus ivory or deer antler. For this purpose, a selection was made of tusks of young walrus, the distal ends of which were still sharp and had not been worn down or blunted. At a certain distance from the tip, depending on the dimensions of the projected harpoon head, the tusk was cut at an angle two-thirds of the way through with a stone adze and the blank was broken off (Plate 19:1,2). The same procedure was followed with deer antler. The elliptical to round cross-section of ivory harpoon heads, and the flattened cross-section of antler specimens was largely predetermined, I imagine, by the shape of the blank. The oblique cut at the base of the

---

[1][Collins wrote: ". . . after having been killed by killer whales."–Ed.]

blank, resulting from the technique used in detaching it from the tusk, always initiated from the inner concave surface of the latter, determined the position of the spur.

The next step consisted in "faceting" the blank by removing the curved surfaces by use of a stone blade with a sharp cutting edge. It was at that stage that the blank was given the required form (Plate 19:3,4). Then, the line hole was drilled in what was usually a hexagonal blank (Plate 1:17; Plate 7:14; Plate 19:5; Plate 33:1,2). If a barbed harpoon head was required, the barbs were carved (Plate 19:6). The spur was carved into shape, the socket for the foreshaft and the slots for the socket lashing were outlined. At the same time, the slots for the side-blades or the end-blade were indicated (Plate 1:20; Plate 7:15). The shaping of the socket, followed by the polishing of the surface, the insertion of the side-blades or end-blade and, finally, the engraving of the surface completed the process of manufacture of the harpoon head.

Harpoon heads equipped with stone side-blades are characteristic, as we have seen, of the early stages of Eskimo culture, Uwelen-Okvik and Old Bering Sea. They occur in Birnirk and Early Punuk assemblages. In Mature Punuk, as well as in the Thule stage, they are already absent and have gone out of use.

The nature of the *stone side-blades* of harpoon heads is evident from the drawings in Plate 24:33,34. They are usually made of flint or chert, more rarely of silicified tuff or mollusc shells. In form, the side-blade is either an almond-shaped implement, very similar to an arrow point, carefully worked over its entire surface by pressure-flaking, especially along its cutting edge, or else a flint flake, carefully worked only along the outer edge, which protrudes from the harpoon head. Boas suggested that the side-blades were held in their sockets or slots with special cement (Boas 1907). Indeed, as a rule, side-blades are set very firmly in their sockets. Their outer edge is often serrated and very worn, while the blade itself remains as if welded to the ivory. I still doubt, however, that any kind of cement, glue, resin, or the like was used in securing side-blades in their sockets. No resin of any kind is provided by the environment on the Chukchi Peninsula. Glue cannot be used in a weapon employed in hunting aquatic mammals. It is my opinion that harpoon heads, like all small manufactures of bone, antler, or walrus ivory, were made of damp, fresh material, softened and humidified in warm water, in the manner observed in the manufacture of bone objects among a number of Siberian tribes. The side-blades were inserted in such freshly made harpoon heads and, after the bone had dried, became so firmly anchored that they could not by then be extracted from their socket without being broken.

We have quite a few ivory harpoon heads with broken side-blades, the remaining halves of which are firmly set in the sockets. Stone side-blades do not fit as firmly in antler harpoon heads, and these are usually found without their blades.

The *end-blades* of harpoon heads, unlike side-blades, very rarely remain in place. In excavations, it is rare that, among one hundred harpoon heads with slits for an end-blade, there should occur one with the blade in place. This is to be explained both by the design of these harpoon heads and the arrangement of the end slit, and by the brittleness of slate, the material usually employed in making the end-blade.

Originally, the end-blade of the harpoon was made of flint or silicified tuff, and was not ground. End-blades of this kind were found on Ratmanov Island (Plate 36:11), in Kiwak, at the ancient site in Uwelen, in the western (Old Bering Sea) sector of the refuse area at Sirhenik (Plate 24:32), and at Cape Bering (Plate 34:14). Most of them are of somewhat elongated, triangular shape with straight bases (Plate 24:32), are very flat, about 2 mm thick, and are very carefully retouched by pressure-flaking on both faces. Similar end-blades are known among the western Eskimos of America (Murdoch 1892:221; Fig. 212; Mason 1902:266; Fig. 61), among the Central Eskimo (Mathiassen 1927;1: Plate 74:1; Boas 1907, Fig. 284:a–c), on St. Lawrence Island, and in the Aleutian Islands (Jochelson 1925:50–55).

Harpoon end-blades of slate (Plate 20:1–3, 10–12) have roughly the same shape, but are carefully ground.

It has been noted earlier that end-blades are very rarely found *in situ* in harpoon heads. As already stated, this is to be explained by the brittleness of the material, slate, and the lack of firm attachment of the end-blade to the harpoon head. According to the Maritime Chukchi (Bogoras 1904–1909; 1:209), slate end-blades were inserted into whaling harpoon heads to replace damaged ones after each throw. Solberg in his work on stoneworking among the eastern Eskimos, is inclined to the view that slate end-blades set in bone harpoon heads appeared very late, contemporaneously with or even later than the spread of iron among the Eskimos (Solberg 1907:66–69). Solberg reaches this conclusion on the basis of the absence of any genetic link between the slate end-blade and earlier points of flint and other dense varieties of stone, of the inadequacy of slate as a material and the advisability of using it in this connection only as a substitute for iron in the absence of the latter, and of a number of comparisons bearing on the evolution of arrow points among North American Indians.

Murdoch comes closer to the truth in his belief that the iron end-blades of harpoons replaced earlier ones of slate (Murdoch 1884:219). Mathiassen rejects Solberg's opinion as to the late origin of the end-blades. The triangular end-blade of siliceous slate, he writes, is a form known in ancient times by all the Eskimos (Mathiassen 1927; 2:39).

The insertion of an end-blade in the tip of a bone harpoon head to increase its effectiveness, whatever the material out of which it is made, seems to me without a doubt to be a very ancient innovation. If the Uwelen-Okvik and Old Bering Sea bone arrowheads were equipped with end-blades, as we know they were, why could not harpoon heads be provided with similar end-blades? And indeed, we do know that harpoon heads at the ancient settlement of Uwelen and at the Okvik site (Rainey 1941d, Fig. 7) were equipped with end-blades. End-blades of rubbed slate were already in use at the Old Bering Sea stage of Eskimo culture, in any case in its later phase, as may be seen from the illustration of a harpoon head from Plover Bay (Collins 1929:5, Fig. 1) decorated in Old Bering Sea style. Still there is no doubt that the broad distribution of rubbed slate harpoon end-blades in the Bering Sea area dates from the Punuk stage of the development of Eskimo culture.

THE SHAFT AND OTHER HARPOON PARTS

No whole *harpoon shafts* have been found either in excavations on the Chukchi Peninsula or on St. Lawrence Island. For this reason, we do not know their length. We may gain an idea of their shape in cross-section only from the shape of the socket pieces of these shafts, in cases when they were made of ivory or bone, and from harpoon ice picks. Shafts were round or oval in cross-section. The fore end was thicker than the butt. In some cases, finger rests were provided; these are important when throwing the harpoon directly by hand. Apparently, some shafts were of one piece of wood, without a bone socket piece. In that case, the fore end was provided with a socket for the foreshaft which held the head.

Judging from the remains of shafts from St. Lawrence Island, where they were more numerous than on the coast of the Chukchi Peninsula, the later Punuk shafts did not differ in any way, it would seem from those of Old Bering Sea (Collins 1937:219).

No *harpoon socket pieces* of Old Bering Sea date have been found yet on the Chukchi Peninsula. Only three socket pieces from this period are known from St. Lawrence Island: one from Geist's excavations (Geist and Rainey 1936:215, Fig. 44b), decorated in Old Bering Sea style, and two from the excavations of Collins (Collins 1937, Plate 17:1), of which one is decorated in the same style. They are all oval in cross-section, with a shallow depression or socket (1.5 cm– 2 cm in depth) for the butt of the foreshaft. Similar decorated Old Bering Sea harpoon socket pieces are known from Little Diomede Island (Jenness 1928a, Plate 13c), and Point Hope (Mathiassen 1929, Fig. 15a,b) and Kotzebue Sound (Collins 1929, Plate 7c) on the coast of America.

The harpoon socket pieces from our excavations on the Chukchi Peninsula are all of late date, made of walrus ivory, oval in cross-section, with a shallow socket (about 1 cm deep), and a more or less steeply beveled lower portion fitting against the shaft. For firmer attachment, the portion in contact with the shaft is covered with transverse grooves and has either an eyehole (Plate 10:7) or specially drilled holes for rivets (Plate 5:7). Similar socket pieces have been found on St. Lawrence Island (Geist and Rainey 1936, Plate 20:8,9; Collins 1937, Plate 73:6,7). Unlike the Old Bering Sea examples, which are decorated and carefully made, harpoon socket pieces of later times are plain and simpler in design. Their tang, as Collins pointed out at the time, is neither conical nor splayed, but wedge-shaped, beveled from one side, as in the latest historical specimens. The harpoon socket piece from Cape Chaplin (Plate 13:6) is short and round, like late historical and some Thule-Punuk examples (Mathiassen 1927; 1. Plate 3:9,10; Collins 1937, Plate 33:26).

Foreshafts designed to hold harpoon heads are very scarce in excavations on the Chukchi Peninsula, both absolutely and in relation to the number of harpoon heads. This has been noted also on St. Lawrence Island (Collins 1937:124). The foreshafts from the Chukchi Peninsula are homogeneous in type, and vary but little in details, irrespective of harpoon head type. Old Bering Sea specimens are lacking so far, though their fore ends must have been considerably wider, to fit the diameter of the harpoon head socket, than later examples from the Birnirk or Punuk stages of Eskimo culture. The fore end of the Uwelen and Birnirk foreshafts (Plate 1:21), as in mature Punuk, when socket walls are straight (Plate 20:15), was flattened, rather than spindle-shaped and narrower at the tip as in foreshafts of later times, designed for closed socket heads. The butt of the foreshaft, as a rule, is much broader in diameter than the fore end.

We found no *finger rests* of harpoon shafts in the lower levels of our cultural deposits or at the older sites. The finger rests of notably different type from Nunligran (Plate 31:6) and from Nuukan (Plate 11:11) are characteristic of Punuk and protohistoric times.

Harpoon *ice picks* are numerous and varied in form. Without going into details, we may distinguish three basic types. Type one: short, usually made from the distal end of the tusk of young walrus. The upper portion or tang, fitting the shaft, is conical and textured by means of adze cuts over its entire surface. The lower end is pointed (Plate 1:22,24) or slightly flattened (Plate 17:4; Plate 20: 9). This type is characteristic of the older sites, such as the older Uwelen site, Kiwak, the western sector of the cultural deposit at Sirhenik and the eastern settlement in Nunligran. This same type has been found in the Old Bering Sea complex on St. Lawrence Island (Collins 1937, Plate 32:1–4) and at the Okvik site in the Punuk Islands (Rainey 1941d, Fig. 11, items 10,11). In general features, they are similar to the ice picks of Thule type in the Central Eskimo area of America (Mathiassen 1927; 1. Plate 4:3).

Type two is similar to the preceding, but is heavier and larger in size. Some of the picks of this type have well defined shoulders between the body and the tang (Plate 20:6,7; Plate 31:27; Plate 32:17), while the conical form of the tang is retained. Picks of this type were found at Nunligran and at Sirhenik.

Type three is the latest. It has an abrupt projecting shoulder and a beveled upper end (Plate 5:8, Plate 8:6; Plate 20:8; Plate 36:24). This form is characteristic of Late Punuk. It should be noted, that such picks are not infrequently made of bone (from the os penis of a walrus) and have holes for rivets drilled in their upper ends.

FLOAT MOUTHPIECES, PLUGS, AND BARS

Inflatable floats for light harpoons and buoys of whole sealskins for heavy harpoons are indispensable accessories of harpoons intended for hunting sea mammals. A special mouthpiece or plug with a bone or wooden stopper was inserted in the neck of such floats. Wooden mouthpieces of low (Plate 20:20) and high profile (Plate 20:21) were found at Sirhenik. In addition, the mouthpiece of ivory illustrated in Plate 11:9 also belongs to a sealskin float, to judge from its dimensions.

Wooden float mouthpieces of low profile, similar to the one illustrated in Plate 20:20, were found on St. Lawrence Island among objects of a late Old Bering Sea assemblage (Collins 1937, Plate 32:13–15). According to Collins (*ibid.*:130), this is an ancient type, which went out of use in Old Bering Sea times. Wooden float mouthpieces of high profile, like the one represented in Plate 20:21, appeared on St. Lawrence Island in Punuk times (Collins 1937:220; Plate 73:19). Similar mouthpieces are known also in later complexes (Geist and Rainey 1936, Plate 43:10) and sometimes, like one from Point Hope (Mathiassen 1930a, Plate 13:16), they were given the form of a human mask. The ivory mouthpiece is simpler, and belongs by its type with the latest protohistoric and modern forms.

Natural openings or wound rents in the sealskin intended for use as a float were closed with special plugs. Such plugs were of two types: of wood, similar to the mouthpieces, but without a central perforation, or else of ivory, similar to the one from Uwelen shown in Plate 1:18. Plugs of this kind have been found by Collins (1937, Plate 32:16–18) on St. Lawrence as part of the Old Bering Sea complex.

Float bars or handles for tying the line from the harpoon head to the float occur at all ancient Eskimo sites on the Chukchi coast. The most typical and oldest form of this type of bar is shown in Plate 5:18 and Plate 20:22; the specimens are from the house on the spit at Uwelen and from Sirhenik, respectively. On St. Lawrence Island, according to Collins, ivory float bars occurred only in the Old Bering Sea inventory, while wooden ones were found in Punuk (Collins 1937:221).

WHALE LANCE POINTS

Southern sites on the Chukchi Peninsula and most particularly Sirhenik have yielded a series of large, massive points of argillaceous or siliceous slate, up to 6 cm in width, which served apparently as the blades of whale lances (Plate 20:5,24,25,26; Plate 34:21).

With the exception of one specimen, which is thinner than the others, and an undamaged specimen from Sirhenik (Plate 20:24), which has one hole for lashing to the shaft, these are all thick, with smoothly ground surfaces and sharp edges, and have two conically drilled holes near the middle. The weakest part of these points is at the level of the holes, and it is there that they are usually broken. Some have straight bases (Plate 20:5), but in most of them the base is concave, the semi-lunar basal concavity at times being quite deep. The points with straight bases could have been inserted as end-blades in bone heads, but most were attached directly to the end of a shaft. Insofar as we know, points of this kind had not been found heretofore at ancient Eskimo sites. On St. Lawrence Island they were encountered in excavations of houses of recent date (Geist and Rainey 1936, Plate 33:20), while in the east they are known from the Thule culture (Mathiassen 1927; 1. Plate 44:1–3).

SEAL SCRATCHERS

Several examples of seal scratchers were found in the excavations in the eastern sector of the refuse area at Sirhenik. One is illustrated in Plate 20:16. Such scratchers were used by both Alaskan and Asiatic Eskimos to scratch the ice, so as to confuse the seals basking in the sun as the hunter crept toward them (Murdoch 1892, Fig. 253B). Slits on the dorsal side of the scratcher served to attach seal claws, fitted over wooden prongs (Nelson 1899, Plate 52:11). No such scratchers were found on St. Lawrence Island in ancient cultural deposits, though some do occur in collapsed houses recently abandoned by the Eskimos (Geist and Rainey 1936, Plate 43:7). To the east, in the American Central Eskimo area, they are known as part of the Thule cultural complex (Mathiassen 1927; 1. Plate 41:9,10).

WOUND PINS AND WOUND PLUGS

In the Cape Dezhnev area, we acquired an ivory pin of distinctive form, with a head. It is represented in Plate 8:7. A similar pin, so designated, has been published by Nordenskiöld from excavations at Cape Schmidt (Nordenskiöld 1882; 2:121, Fig. 2). Sollas, as we noted earlier, found out that such pins were used by the Eskimos to pin together the edges of wounds on killed seals and other large animals to preserve the blood of the animal, the loss of which is considered undesirable (Sollas 1911:326, Fig. 193:2,3). When setting out to hunt marine animals, the Eskimos carry with them special cases with a supply of such pins. Pins for closing wounds are known from excavations in the Central Eskimo area of America (Mathiassen 1927; 1, Plate 5:12–15; Plate 82:4; Plate 65:23; Plate 85:4) and among the modern Central (Stefansson 1914:7; Boas 1907, Fig. 475), and Greenland Eskimo (Birket-Smith 1924:329; Thalbitzer 1914, Fig. 155).

Another device of similar function, the wooden wound plug, was found at various relatively late sites, and occurred in particularly large numbers in the excavations of the eastern sector of the refuse deposit at Sirhenik (Plate 20: 17,18,19). On the subject of these plugs, known among the western Eskimos of Alaska, Nelson has written (Nelson 1899:130–131, Plate 52:19):

During the winter and late in the fall seals are usually fat enough to float when killed in the water, but in spring and sometimes at other seasons, they are so thin that they sink and the hunter loses them. To ensure their floating while being towed, it is common practice to make slits in the skin at various points and, with a long, pointed instrument of deer horn, to loosen the blubber from the muscle for a space of a foot or more in diameter. Then, by means of a hollow tube, made from the wing bone of a bird or from other material, air is blown in and the place inflated; wooden plugs are then inserted in the slits and driven in tightly to prevent the air from escaping. By the aid of several such inflated spots the seal is floated and the danger of losing it is avoided.

Boas (1888:410, Fig. 400a–c, 401) has written of the plugs, somewhat different in type it is true, used by the Central Eskimos for plugging wounds in the carcasses of animals pulled out of the water. They were also used by the Greenland Eskimos for closing wounds made with a harpoon.

In his excavations on St. Lawrence Island, Collins found plugs similar to those published by us among objects of the Old Bering Sea complex, though he does not emphasize their especially extensive distribution in Punuk times (Collins 1937:138, Plate 35:11–14).

Land Mammal and Bird Hunting Equipment

DARTS AND SPEARS

The very provenience of our collections from excavations is such as hardly to allow us to expect them to include whole spears or darts with shafts. In fact, we have only the stone or bone points of such weapons, and by no means in all cases is it possible to decide the purpose for which a given point or blade was intended. Wilson (Wilson 1897:947), Mason (Mason 1891), and a number of other authors (Fowke 1896:142), who have dealt with the classification of the weapons in question, mainly those of stone, have justly pointed out the difficulties encountered in differentiating the stone points of spears, darts, knives, and arrows. A small point may be that of an arrow; a large one of the same type may be the point of a dart if the shaft is light, or of a spear, if it is heavy. Points of the classes enumerated above may also serve as knives. It is easier to determine the purpose of such implements if a shaft or a handle is present.

Solberg (1907) found, in analysing the stone implements of the Eskimos, that it is always possible to decide whether we are dealing with a knife or a spear point. However, the criteria which Solberg proposes for that purpose (shape, degree of wear from use, etc.) do not always achieve their aim.

We know of several stone points of spears from the Chukchi Peninsula used in hunting bear (and perhaps deer). Two specimens, very carefully shaped by bifacial pressure flaking, of flint and silicified tuff with a long and a longer stem, respectively, are represented in Plate 14:1 and Plate 37:9. Spear points of flint and silicified tuff, some of which are apparently not completely worked, were found in various localities: Uwelen, Dezhnevo, Cape Chaplin, Avan, and Sirhenik. It may be supposed that a massive point of siliceous slate with a broken stem from the area of Cape Dezhnev also served as a spear point (Plate 8:14). We do not know of similar spear points from St. Lawrence or the Diomede Islands, no doubt because bears there are infrequent and deer are absent. On the other hand, such points are well known among the American Eskimos (Murdoch 1892:243–244, Figs. 241 and 246; Boas 1907:388, Fig. 182a). They are secured in the splayed distal end of the shaft by means of baleen lashing (Volkov and Rudenko 1910, Fig. 3a,b).

Stone points that could be regarded as the points of throwing darts are rarely found on the Chukchi Peninsula. As an example, we can cite only the point shown in Plate 37:8.

Bone dart heads are found more often, and include the one-piece specimen of ivory from Enmylen (Plate 33:26) and the dart head from Cape Chaplin (Plate 14:16), the end of which has a slit for a slate end-blade.

There are quite a few bone bird dart heads, nearly always of ivory, from the Chukchi Peninsula. They include very large, heavy heads from Enmylen (Plate 33:18), from Nunligran (Plate 32::21,26), and from the area of Cape Dezhnev (Plate 8:9,10), massive center-prongs of compound bird darts from the ancient site of Uwelen (Plate 2:13,15) and from Sirhenik (Plate 22:35), and light, very delicate specimens with sharp barbs from the older site at Uwelen (Plate 2:12), from Sirhenik (Plate 22:15,16), and Nunligran. Finally, side-prongs of bird darts are available from the older site at Uwelen (Plate 2:16 and 17), the coast of Bering Strait (Plate 36:14), and Sirhenik (Plate 22:17).

Judging from the specimens in our collections and, above all, from the excavations on St. Lawrence and the Punuk Islands, bird darts with three side-prongs on the lower third of the shaft appeared at an early stage of the development of Eskimo culture. We know of them at the Okvik site in the Punuk Islands (Rainey 1941d, Fig. 13) and at Old Bering Sea sites on St. Lawrence Island (Collins 1937, Plate 33, 1–10). Subsequently, they became one of the most widely distributed Eskimo implements in the latest stages of their culture, up to and including recent times.

Late sites, such as the house on the bar at Uwelen (Plate 5:25) and the house at Cape Chaplin (Plate 14:14), have yielded delicate, very long (over 25 cm) but thin (up to 3 cm in width) blades of ivory which may also belong to throwing darts. These blades have one flat side, while the other is humped in cross-section, with a clearly perceptible ridge in the center. The tips (broken) were pointed, and the ridges were sharpened. The flat bases fitted in a shaft.

These blades resemble closely the bone knives or daggers described below, but differ from them in their length and flattened base, possibly fastened to a long shaft.

THE THROWING BOARD

Throwing board is the term customarily employed in American literature to refer to a device for throwing the bird darts and light harpoons of the Eskimos. The Aleut wooden dart thrower is indeed in the form of a flat board, though the term is already inapplicable to the devices used today by the western Eskimo. From the Chukchi Peninsula, we have the remarkable dart or harpoon thrower from Seklyuk (Plate 38:21), which we have described in detail, and which is decorated in Old Bering Sea Style 1. Another wooden example, of which only a portion remains, is from Sirhenik (Plate 20:27) and is of a different type, of general distribution among the western Eskimo of Alaska (Volkov and Rudenko 1910, Plate 10 *et al.*).

Similar devices from St. Lawrence Island (Collins 1937, Plate 37:1–2), belonging to the Old Bering Sea period, differ from ours and from modern types (Nelson 1899:151; Murdoch 1892:117) and are closer to the Birnirk type (Mason 1930, Plate 1). In any event, the dart or harpoon thrower is one of the most ancient acquisitions of Eskimo culture. The considerable variability of recent forms and the scarcity of examples from excavations of ancient sites does not allow us, as yet, to trace the variation of this device through time.

THE BOW AND THE WRIST GUARD

No whole bows are available from excavations on the Chukchi Peninsula, though there is a considerable number of parts and models of bows. Miniature bows of wood and baleen are available from a number of coastal locations. Among them, two classes should be distinguished: small wooden specimens and miniature ones, of either wood or baleen. The first may have been children's toys (Plate 21:1). As for miniature bows of wood and baleen (Plate 5:9; Plate 21:2,3), they were prepared for special ritual purposes such as the "whale" ceremony and for others. Both classes, however, provide an idea of the type of the simple Eskimo bow.

Remains of the reinforced compound bow in the form of bone center- and end-pieces, as well as separate sections (Plate 21:10), are evidence of the occurrence of such a bow among the ancient Eskimos. The presence of the compound bow, reinforced by a winding of baleen or sinew strands, is confirmed also by finds of specialized twisters (Plate 13:12; Plate 21:9; Plate 36:25).

Simple toy and minature bow models have been found also in the excavations on St. Lawrence Island (Geist and Rainey 1936, Plate 47:2,3; Plate 50:3; Plate 65:5,9,10; Collins 1937, Plate 55:1,2; Plate 56:15; Plate 59:26,27), on the arctic coast of North America (Mathiassen 1930a, Plate 7:15) and in the Central Eskimo area (Mathiassen 1927; 1, Plate 8:1; Plate 66:5–7; Plate 75:7; Plate 79:7,8).

It remains yet to be determined when the compound bow appeared among the Eskimos. Collins (1937:134) supposes that the compound bow is later in origin and is characteristic of Punuk and subsequent stages in the development of Eskimo culture. On St. Lawrence Island, a bow of small size, reinforced with laths of wood and with baleen was found in an Early Punuk context in excavations at Miyowagh near Gambell. This small reinforced bow is, to date, the earliest evidence of this kind of bow among the Eskimos.

Wrist guards, as we know, have been found in considerable numbers on the Chukchi Peninsula and are varied in size, shape, and style of decoration. They include quite simple ones of walrus ivory or baleen (Plate 10:13; Plate 21:6), a large specimen of bone of unusual form, with central slits (Plate 21:4), wrist guards of ivory with round inlays of baleen or pits near the edges (Plate 13:16; Plate 31:11), and one of antler with lightly applied decoration along the longer sides (Plate 21:7). Of particular interest are three ivory wrist guards, decorated over their entire surface; two of them are from Sirhenik and decorated in Early Punuk style (Plate 21:5,8), the third is from Enmylen (Plate 33:25) and bears typical Late Punuk decoration.

We know of a number of wrist guards from the excavations of St. Lawrence Island (Collins 1937, Plate 22:10; Plate 65, Fig. 9–11; Plate 67:5,6). On the American continent, they are known in collections from Points Hope and Barrow (Mathiassen 1930a, Plate 7:11,12; Plate 14:1,2; Murdoch 1890:210, Figs. 193, 194). They are absent in the Thule culture, in the Central Eskimo area.

The same may be said of our wrist guards from the Chukchi Peninsula as of those of St. Lawrence Island and North America. They are highly variable in shape, dimensions, and material, which may be ivory, bone, antler, or baleen. We cannot even point to two entirely identical wrist guards. We are not dealing here with a standard design of the kind characteristic of many other ancient Eskimo implements. In general, the Asian wrist guards are simpler in form. We do not find among them the lyre-shaped examples that occur on St. Lawrence Island and in northwestern America.

Like compound bows, wrist guards appeared among the Eskimos relatively late. To date, we know of not a single wrist guard found in an Old Bering Sea assemblage. They are all either undecorated, when they are late, or else decorated in Punuk style. The wrist guard from the lower levels of the eastern sector of the cultural deposit at Sirhenik (Plate 21:5) stands out by its decoration, and it is probably the oldest example of this piece of equipment. At the same time, its design is by no means simple. The simplest wrist guards date from proto-historic and recent times. It may be concluded from this that wrist guards were borrowed ready-made by the ancient Eskimos from their neighbors, probably those of western Siberia.

Arrows with intact shafts or, least of all, arrows retaining their feathering have not been found in excavations on the Chukchi Peninsula. We may gain some knowledge of arrow shafts from their fragments, which are at times large. As a rule, arrow shafts are of light wood (willow), about 10 mm thick, slightly flattened but nearly round (9 mm × 11 mm) in cross-section. At the base, near the nock, they are wider and flatter (6 mm × 13.5 mm) and are sometimes provided with a row of notches on the flat surfaces (Plate 10:14; Plate 21:12,14), possibly for attaching feathers. The length of the arrow may be gauged from models in the form of small intact arrows, on the assumption that these retain true proportions (Plate 22:11,12). No variations of any significance in the size or shape of arrow shafts were noted for the Chukchi Peninsula area either in time or space. Their form apparently remained constant from earliest times to the present.

Collins has noted marked differences in the type of arrowheads in the Old Bering Sea stage, as contrasted to the later Punuk stage, paralleling the difference in harpoon head types (Collins 1937:135–137). This differentiation is supported by the data of excavations on the Chukchi Peninsula.

Arrowheads with a conical tang, two pointed barbs set close to the central shaft at the very tang, and a slit for an end-blade constitute Collins' Old Bering Sea type. They have been found on the Chukchi Peninsula in the oldest of the artifact assemblages. We have them from Kiwak (Plate 17:1), from the eastern site at Nunligran (Plate 32:19,20), where the number of closely set barbs has already increased to two pairs, and from the lower horizon of the eastern sector at Sirhenik (Plate 21:25), which, unlike other sites, has arrowheads with splayed rather than conical tangs. We also have an arrowhead of this type from Cape Bering (Plate 33:21) and, finally, one with screw-like fluting from the older site at Uwelen (Plate 2:9) which resembles an arrowhead from the Hillside site on St. Lawrence Island (Collins 1937, Plate 29:7). All these arrowheads are of bone or antler and not a single one is of ivory. Apart from the form and the material, special note must be taken of the presence on all, with the exception of the one from Cape Bering (Plate 33:21) which may be of later date, of decoration in the form of deeply cut lines. This decoration in Uwelen style, pertaining to the old Uwelen-Okvik stage, persisted as a tradition on arrowheads in Old Bering Sea times as well, in particular at the site of Kiwak and on St. Lawrence Island (Collins 1937, Plate 34:3,5).

In connection with this type of arrow, Rainey remarks, I think correctly, that we are dealing here with an arrowhead intended for warfare rather than hunting, inasmuch as the location of sharp barbs at the very tang, suitable for fighting an enemy, offers no advantages in hunting game.

Simultaneously with the type just described, quite simple arrowheads existed at the Uwelen-Okvik and Old Bering Sea stages. They were of bone or antler, light, with round cross-sections, and a sharp conical (Plate 17:3) or blunt (Plate 2:1) butt.

Apparently the most ancient type of Eskimo arrowhead on the Asian continent is one we know in two variants from the ancient site at Uwelen. The first variant includes arrowheads that are round or slightly flattened in cross-section, with a conical tang and a slit for an end-blade at the somewhat thickened distal end. Examples of this type vary considerably in length, the thickness of the arrow bearing an inverse relation to its length (Plate 2:3,5), and either lack decoration or have it in the form of deeply incised lines. The second variant differs from the first in the presence of a splayed, bifurcated tang (Plate 2:6,7,8) rather than a conical one. This variant is more consistent in size.

So far, we know of no arrowheads of this Uwelen type except on the continent of Asia. Arrowheads of similar type are known on the Lena River above Yakutsk and on the lower Lena, as a result of excavations by Okladnikov (1946:71, Plate 10) on the Bukachan River (a left tributary of the Lena). They are dated there at the beginning of the first millenium before our era. Bronze appears in burials containing these arrowheads.

It should be noted that, unlike the later arrowheads with rubbed slate end-blades, examples of the older types described above are always associated either with unground end-blades of flint or silicified tuff, or with blades that are slightly ground (Plate 21:23,25).

Bone arrowheads of later periods, from Early Punuk to recent Eskimo, differ little from one another. The specimen from Sirhenik shown in Plate 21:23 approaches Old Bering Sea types and resembles one illustrated by Collins, which differs only by the presence of a swelling near the middle of the pile (Collins 1937, Plate 34:1). The most characteristic distinguishing feature of the earlier, Punuk specimens, as compared to the later arrowheads, is the material from which they are made, namely bone, and their frequently flattened shape. Later arrowheads are usually of ivory, often triangular in cross-section, and frequently with one small barb. Judging from the context in which they occur, short and flat bone arrowheads with two symmetrical barbs (Plate 21:20,26; Plate 33:20) and flattened heads of bone with one or two barbs, shoulders, and a conical tang (Plate 21:16,21; Plate 36:17) are early in time. Bone or ivory arrowheads with one or two barbs, a conical knobbed tang and a round or triangular cross-section (Plate 22:8,9) or, finally, flat specimens with a conical or a splayed tang (Plate 21:17; Plate 36:16) are later.

Protohistoric specimens, close to the historic period in time, include: an arrow-head round in cross-section, with two sharp barbs and a slit for a stone end-blade, from Cape Chaplin (Plate 13:11), and a specimen of flattened shape, with three barbs, a conical tang, and a slit for an iron end-blade, from Nuukan (Plate 10:9). The latter bears the property mark of the owner. Judging from the groove around the slit for the end-blade, the head illustrated in Plate 10:9 held a shouldered and stemmed flint blade similar to the one shown in Plate 10:10. Similar arrow-heads are well known among the modern Asian and American Eskimos (Nelson 1899, Plate 59a:10; Plate 59b:9; Volkov and Rudenko 1910, Fig. 12a,b,h; Fig. 14g, i).

So-called bird arrowheads with blunt tips have been found in large numbers and vary in the shape of the blunt end. In this connection, I am far from certain that arrows with blunt ends were intended always for hunting birds. On the contrary, from what we know of Siberian ethnography, arrows with blunt thick-ened ends were used in hunting small fur-bearing animals to avoid damaging their pelts.

In this class, we must first note a series of arrows with a thickened, blunted distal end, lacking a separate head (Plate 5:12; Plate 21:11,13). Then, we have blunt arrowheads of bone with a splayed or conical tang (Plate 22:2,3,4). Finally, bone and especially ivory blunt heads with sockets for hafting are particularly numerous. As may be seen from the drawings (Plate 2:10; Plate 5:13,14; Plate 13:13; Plate 22:5,6,7; Plate 31:8,9,18,19; Plate 36:13), they vary considerably in size and form, and may be cylindrical, egg-shaped, acorn-shaped, or simply of walrus teeth with a drilled socket and without additional workmanship. Such arrowheads, as we know, acquired a wide distribution outside of the Chukchi Peninsula as well. We know of them on St. Lawrence Island (Geist and Rainey 1936, Plate 21:7; Collins 1937, Plate 74:72,73), in northwestern North America (Murdoch 1892, Fig. 189b; Nelson 1899, Plate 61c) and in the Central Eskimo area of America (Stefansson 1914:98).

On St. Lawrence Island, no blunt arrowheads were found in the Old Bering Sea complex. Collins has concluded from this that this trait of Eskimo culture appeared late, no earlier than Punuk (Collins 1937, 224–225). The continuous distribution of blunt bird arrows in the circumpolar area, he notes, like that of such inland traits as snowshoes, the carrying cradle, and the bear ceremony, inasmuch as we do not know them in the Old Bering Sea stage, should be considered as representing a distinct inland complex.

Collins is correct in considering blunt arrows as traits of an inland, rather than a coastal maritime culture, particularly if we consider that they were intended principally for hunting fur-bearing animals. It is possible that their penetration to the islands of Bering Sea and to North America was relatively late, though Rainey (1941d, Fig. 14:10–12) gives illustrations of blunt arrowheads from the Okvik site in the Punuk Islands. On the Chukchi Peninsula, blunt arrowheads acquired a broad distribution rather late, at the end of Punuk, but distinctive forms are known there from the older site at Uwelen (Plate 2:10) and from the lower levels of the eastern sector of the cultural deposit at Sirhenik (Plate 22:4).

BIRD BOLA WEIGHTS

The bola, used for catching birds (ducks), is widespread among the Alaskan Eskimos and persists to this day in a few places among the Eskimos and coastal Chukchi on the Chukchi Peninsula. The device consists of several (4 to 10) strings or thongs (60 cm–70 cm in length), tied together at one end. The free end of each string is tied to a bone weight. The device is thrown into a flock of birds as they pass overhead. In flight, the weights spread in a circle, the radius of which is formed by the strings, while the center is the point at which they are tied together. When the device comes in contact with a bird, the balls, acting as bola balls, became entangeld around it and it falls to the ground. Bola weights have been found on the Chukchi Peninsula at all late Eskimo sites, but not at any of the older ones. They did not occur at the older site of Uwelen, at Kiwak, in the western sector of the cultural deposit at Sirhenik or at the eastern site at Nunligran.

The shape of these weights is not consistent. The weight may be either walrus tooth, unworked except for the hole drilled in the root (Plate 13:14; Plate 22:20; Plate 31:16), an unworked walrus tusk fragment or irregular shape (Plate 13:18, 19), or a well-formed weight with a conical tip, in which a hole has been made (Plate 10:12; Plate 13:15; Plate 31:12; Plate 36:27). There are also weights in the form of balls of ivory, carefully worked, with a string hole sunk into the top of the weight, which Collins' observations show to be the predominant mode of attachment in the Bering Strait region (Plate 12:15; Plate 31:14; Plate 36:26). All our weight types are represented in the large collections of Geist and Collins from excavations on St. Lawrence Island. They are similar also to those usual for the Thule culture.

Nelson (1899, Plate 51:8), in his work on the Eskimos of Bering Strait, illustrates a bola from Point Hope, where the weights, instead of being balls, are figurines of five polar bears, a bird, and a seal. It is fully possible, therefore, that our seal gurines with suspension holes in their tail ends, of which one is from the western Nunligran site and the other two were purchased (Plate 36:28,29), served as bola weights. I will note in passing that they are all in a very good state of preservation and very late in date.

The absence of the bird bola in the early stages of Eskimo culture and the discovery of the earliest example thereof in the Birnirk complex at Point Barrow (Mason 1930:386), its absence in the Central Eskimo area, and its occurrence in the Thule culture (Mathiassen 1927; 2:54), all point to a local, Arctic origin of this device, which appeared, as already noted, relatively late.

TRAPS AND SNARES

In the ethnographic literature, we need look no further than Murdoch (1892) or Nelson (1899) to be aware of the extent to which the Eskimo made use of all kinds of traps and snares for catching animals and birds. Unfortunately, excavated material throws little light on this aspect of culture.

Excavations on the Chukchi Peninsula at Cape Chaplin have yielded a bone paddle (Plate 13:22) for erasing tracks from the snow when setting fox traps. We also have several small wooden stakes, serrated at one end and sharpened at the other, which may be viewed at the releases of traps. Finally, there are nooses or loops of baleen (Plate 22:30). It is interesting that Kiwak and Sirhenik should yield small wooden cylinders with circular grooves near the middle for a baleen strand (Plate 17:13; Plate 22:22), identical to some found by Collins on St. Lawrence Island (1937, Plate 57:18,19) and, like them, colored red. Collins believes that these were floats for baleen nooses, intended for catching birds.

SNOW GOGGLES

We shall examine snow goggles here as an object connected with spring game hunting. The device is absolutely essential under arctic conditions, when the sun is low and the snow is still on the ground, especially on expanses of sea ice, where the sun is blinding even in the beginning of summer. Because of their narrow eye slits, such goggles shield the pupils from sunlight, both direct and reflected by snow, without restricting horizontal vision. It is therefore not surprising that we should find these goggles as early as Old Bering Sea times (Collins 1937, Plate 68:1,2). The oldest snow goggles that we have from the Chukchi Peninsula are made of bone and come from the older site at Uwelen (Plate 2:14). In type of decoration, they have much in common with goggles published by Rainey from excavations at Ipiutak on Point Hope (Rainey 1941b, Plate 2:12). The ivory goggles from the Cape Dezhnev area in Plate 38:7 are of later date and are decorated in Early Punuk style. The goggles found in the excavations at Avan (Plate 18:18) in a context of Late Punuk objects are of the same type, but lack decoration.

As a pan-Eskimo trait, persisting to this day, snow goggles have undergone a certain amount of evolution. The snow goggles published by Rainey (Rainey 1941d, Fig. 17, item 12) from the Okvik site in the Punuk Islands, bearing characteristic decoration in what he terms Okvik style, i.e., Old Bering Sea Style 1, are probably roughly of the same age as the Uwelen and Ipiutak examples mentioned earlier. Their distinctive feature is the small round eye holes. The Old Bering Sea goggles published by Collins (1937, Plate 58:1,2) already have elongated, rather than round openings, though these are not so narrow as the later Punuk or slit-like modern openings.

Fishing Gear

HARPOON HEADS

Small and simple bone harpoon heads of Mathiassen's Thule 1 type, Collins' Type V, are often and, in my opinion, rightly considered as intended for catching large fish of the salmon family. Such is without doubt the function of specimens as small as that represented in Plate 22:25. On the other hand, it is incorrect to view as toys the miniature ivory harpoon heads of well-defined type that have a closed socket, usually a round line hole, a simple spur, and a lance-like fore end. The oldest specimen in this class is the bone harpoon head found at the older Uwelen site (Plate 2:19), which differs from the rest in the presence of an end-blade. Apart from this specimen, all those found on the Chukchi Peninsula at Sirhenik (Plate 22:24), Nunligran (Plate 31:5), and Enmylen (Plate 33:12) are made of ivory and are of the type described above. That these small harpoon heads were actually used for utilitarian purposes follows from the consistency or standardization, as it were, of their form, and the wear on some of them caused by prolonged use. It is quite possible that such small harpoons were shot from a bow. Harpoon heads of exactly the same type were found on St. Lawrence Island in relatively late Old Bering Sea deposits (Geist and Rainey 1936, Plate 54:18,19; Plate 59:15; Collins 1937, Plate 59:18–21).

The harpoon heads of simpler design from Cape Chaplin, shown in Plate 13:5, and from Sirhenik, in Plate 22:23, are of different type, though probably intended for the same purpose. Similar specimens are described as salmon harpoon heads by Mathiassen (Mathiassen 1927; 1. Plate 12:7) from his excavations in the Central Eskimo area, where they pertain to the Thule culture complex.

FISH SPEARS

Fish spear points occur ubiquitously and in large numbers on the coast of the Chukchi Peninsula. This indicates intensive fishing of large fish in lagoons, lakes, and at river mouths. Very large side-prongs of ivory and antler were found at Uwelen (Plate 2:26) and Sirhenik (Plate 22:39,40). Center-prongs corresponding to them, or else used separately in the manner of lance heads, are represented by outstanding examples from Sirhenik (Plate 22:31,32). Center-prongs of smaller size with blunt barbs were found in the excavations at Kiwak (Plate 17:2), Sirhenik (Plate 22:33,34), Enmylen (Plate 33:19), and on Arakamchechen Island (Plate 12:17). Side-prongs of small fish spears are found less frequently (Plate 8:11; Plate 12:18). A prong from the Cape Dezhnev area (Plate 8:12) may have been used as the point of a light fish spear; we know of analogous examples from St. Lawrence Island (Collins 1937, Plate 33:16–18).

On the Chukchi Peninsula, composite salmon spears with a lashed barb, similar to a boat hook but smaller, were used in fishing. All of them are from two localities: the older site at Uwelen (Plate 2:20,21) and Sirhenik (Plate 22:36,37, 38). They pertain to one and the same type and differ only in insignificant details. It is of interest that compound fish spear barbs of identical shape and, like ours, made of bone, were found at the Okvik site in the Punuk Islands (Rainey 1941d, Fig. 15, items 1–3).

Barbs of composite fish spears have been found in a Punuk context on St. Lawrence Island (Collins 1937, Plate 75:19), and at sites of the Thule culture in Canada (Mathiassen 1927); 1, Plate 12:10,11; Plate 43:1,3–5). Unlike the specimens from St. Lawrence Island and eastern North America, spear barbs from the Chukchi Peninsula are provided with long slots rather than round holes for lashing to the shaft. Barbs similar to our Asian examples have been found at Point Barrow in America (Mathiassen 1930a, Plate 9:11).

On the basis of finds of barbs at the older Uwelen site and in the western sector of the cultural deposit at Sirhenik, as well as the occurrence of similar examples at the Okvik site in the Punuk Islands, it may be supposed that we are dealing here with one of the oldest Eskimo implements.

FISHHOOKS AND SINKERS

In a late Old Bering Sea implement assemblage on St. Lawrence Island, Collins (Collins 1937, Plate 33:6) found a small wooden shank with a small weight in the form of a pebble attached by a strand of baleen and with a small pointed bird bone suggesting the barb of a fishhook. Similarly, the lower levels of the eastern sector of the cultural deposit at Sirhenik yielded a miniature bone point, similar to the fish spear point published by Collins, with an ivory barb lashed to it with baleen, similar to the barbs commonly found on compound fishhooks (Plate 22:14). A similar primitive fishing device has been found in excavations in the Central Eskimo area (Mathiassen 1927; 1, Plate 43:11). We will recall that we found at Avan the humerus of a dog with two holes perforated at the ends. The find of a similar bone in excavations on St. Lawrence Island (Collins 1937, Plate 79:8) with an inserted bone barb, has shown that here too we have the shank of a composite fishhook.

All these examples show that, apart from fully established types of fishhooks, casual forms were used, both in early and in late times, though the finds at Avan and on St. Lawrence Island of dog humeri worked to hold fishhooks would seemingly indicate that hooks of this kind may have had a wide distribution.

The presence of barbs, usually of ivory, at a number of sites on the Chukchi Peninsula indicates the wide distribution of compound fishhooks. Barbs of this kind are available from the later site at Nunligran (Plate 31:25), from Sirhenik (Plate 22:28), from Cape Chaplin (Plate 13:21) and from Uwelen (Plate 2:24). Simple fishhook shanks for single barbs have not been found so far. On the other hand, we do have shanks of compound fishhooks with three barbs from Sirhenik, both of wood (Plate 22:26) and of ivory (Plate 22:27). The observations of Collins show that this form of composite fishhook for catching cod appears only in Punuk times on St. Lawrence Island (Collins 1937, Plate 75:4,5). Similar fishhooks were also found on the same island in excavating late protohistoric dwellings (Geist and Rainey 1936, Plate 54:9). At the same time, Rainey believes that they were already in use at the Okvik stage of Eskimo culture (Rainey 1941d, Fig. 15, item 6).

One-piece ivory fishhooks with three barbs were found only at the relatively very late western site at Nunligran (Plate 31:36). On the coast of the Chukchi Peninsula, they persisted among the Eskimo and the coastal Chukchi until very recent times, as they did also among the Alaskan Eskimo (Bogoras 1904–1909; 1, Fig. 67e; Nelson 1899, Plate 69:2). On St. Lawrence Island, they were also found in an artifact assemblage of Punuk date (Collins 1937, Plate 75:10).

We have no fish lines from excavations on the Chukchi Peninsula, though the large number of bunches and knots of baleen strips and strands, particularly from Cape Chaplin and at Sirhenik, leaves no doubt that fish lines were made of baleen. On the other hand, quite a few fish line sinkers have been found. They include quite miniature specimens (Plate 2:22,23) and very large ones (Plate 2:27), which may coexist at the same site, as is evident in the case of the older Uwelen site. Furthermore, they vary considerably in form, though they all have two perforations, one at the upper end for the line and one at the lower end for the hook. Sinkers are even more varied at Sirhenik, where the cross-section may be round (Plate 23:15), oval (Plate 23:16) or quite flat (Plate 23:17). In some cases, they have the shape of a balance weight (Plate 36:34) with slits instead of holes for the line. All fishhook sinkers, as a rule, are made of ivory, though sometimes a walrus tooth was used for the purpose (Plate 23:18). In some cases, a sinker served simultaneously as a fishhook. Thus, the large sinker from Enmylen (Plate 34:8), oblong in form and made of whale bone, in addition to openings at the upper end, has four deep sockets for insertion of barbs in its lower third. Collins distinguishes eight types according to shape among the older sinkers alone (Collins 1937:140–142). We do not have sufficient material for such a classification.

FISH NETS

Excavations at Cape Chaplin and especially at Sirhenik have yielded many fragments of nets made of baleen. They are all of the same type and apparently belong to hoop nets of a kind that still persists among the Asian Eskimos for the winter fishing of saffron cod. This is confirmed in the finds of wooden and baleen strip hoops together with the nets, and of special sinkers of oblong pebbles with circular grooves near the middle (Plate 23:1,2; Plate 12:26; Plate 28:21). Such a net from Plover Bay is illustrated in Nelson's volume (Nelson 1899, Plate 70:12).

These nets and their sinkers were found principally at late sites. A similar sinker was found by Collins in a Late Punuk assemblage, and was described by him as the sinker of a hoop net for catching cod (Collins 1937, Plate 8:4).

A bone shuttle for the manufacture of nets from Cape Chaplin (Plate 13:24) is of the usual type, widespread among the Eskimos, in particular those of Alaska (Nelson 1899, Plate 73).

It is hard to determine the type of the larger nets and to know whether they were used for fishing only or for catching seals as well. In any event, heavy sinkers, usually of ivory, occur everywhere on the coast of the Chukchi Peninsula, though only at sites of Late Punuk and protohistoric periods. They may be divided in two types: those with one suspension hole at one end of the sinker (Plate 23:22) and those, more frequent, with two holes, one at each end (Plate 5:24; Plate 10:19; Plate 23:21; Plate 36:32). The latter type is also known from excavations on St. Lawrence Island (Collins 1937, Plate 75:16).

A scoop for skimming ice from a hole in the ice (Plate 28:3), which may be included among equipment associated with fishing and which was found in excavations at Sirhenik, is without parallel. It consists of an antler plate, intertwined with root splints.

Techniques of Working Mineral, Vegetal, and Animal Materials

FIRE-MAKING BY DRILLING

Fire-making by drilling was practised by Eskimos at all stages of development of their culture, and implements involved in obtaining fire in this manner have been found in excavations of all sites on the coast of the Chukchi Peninsula. The wooden spindles, while varying in size, are essentially of the same more or less standard form. They are somewhat thickened at the lower end, and of smaller diameter toward the top (Plate 5:17; Plate 11:6; Plate 23:23,24). The hearths that were drilled in the process apparently had no established form (Plate 11:19; Plate 18:19). Drill rests were basically of two types: the kind held in the hand and the kind held in the mouth with the teeth. The first are either deer astragali, the natural depressions of which were used as drill holders, or of casual shape, made of fragments of walrus tusk, or else damaged tools of suitable shape, in which a pit for holding the wooden spindle was drilled. The bone drill rest shown in Plate 3:14 was, apparently, specially prepared for the purpose, since it has notches for suspension at one end.

No drill rests of the kind held in the teeth were found at any of the older sites of the Chukchi Peninsula. Three of them, from Nuukan, are made of ivory (Plate 11:13,17,18) and are of very late protohistoric or perhaps even historic date. One stone specimen (Plate 5:20) purchased in Uwelen may be modern.

Drill rests of the second type were found by Collins on St. Lawrence Island in old cultural assemblages, but he notes that they were more common in Punuk times (Collins 1937:236, Plate 82:37–40). In any event, in view of the occurrence of two types of drill rests, the Eskimo must have used two drilling methods, when drilling for fire in particular: using a simple thong and drilling with the aid of a bow. Bows used for this purpose could be made of wood or bone (Plate 12:10; Plate 23:25,26).

PREPARATION OF STONE TOOLS

The techniques of preparing stone tools are known and have been described in detail in a number of special publications. With reference to the culture which concerns us, they are best treated in the work of Holmes (Holmes 1897).

The process of preparing stone tools consists essentially, as we know, of five basic steps: knocking off blades or flakes from a boulder or a core for use in preparing the tool; rough chipping of the blank to give it the required shape; fine chipping of its faces; finishing the surface and cutting edges by retouching; grinding the cutting edge or the entire tool.

So far, we do not know of a single workshop where the Eskimo made stone tools. At sites, in houses and in burials, we usually find either finished whole tools, damaged tools or, finally, fragments of tools. One also finds half-finished pieces, blanks for tools, and chips, which could have been used as tools without further processing. As far as we know, no Eskimo site has yielded the prismatic cores or the narrow blades so characteristic of the late Paleolithic of Europe, as well as of the Mesolithic and Neolithic. Neither hammers nor stone retouching tools have been found. The only obsidian prismatic core present in our collections from the Chukchi Peninsula (Plate 36:30) is a chance find, and we do not know the locality at which it was found.

It is possible that the early stages of the manufacture of stone tools took place at workshops located wherever the stone for them was obtained. Only the finishing of tools by pressure retouching would have taken place at dwelling sites, where quite a few blanks for various stone tools have been found.

I have been told by one of the maritime Koryaks of the Bay of Korfa, whose father had been a specialist in manufacturing stone tools, that in breaking up the selected pebble and in detaching flakes from it, the pebble is always held in the left hand which is wrapped in a piece of leather so as not to hurt it when striking.

According to Jochelson (Jochelson 1908:608, Fig. 134b), as mentioned earlier, the Koryaks achieve the same end by wearing a special bone ring, similar to one we illustrate from the ancient site at Cape Bering (Plate 34:2), on the thumb of the left hand.

Pressure flakers are usually in the form of slightly curved bone rods oval in cross-section. The most highly developed form is that of the composite pressure flaker set in a deer antler handle from Sirhenik, illustrated in Plate 24:31. Pressure flakers in similar handles are also known from northwestern North America (Mason 1894, Plate 39:4; Murdoch 1892:289, Fig. 281).

We know that most Eskimo stone tools, and nearly all of them at the early stages of their culture, were flaked and retouched, but lacked grinding. Grinding was used only on the bits of adzes. The material consisted exclusively of hard stones, such as basalt, nephrite, flint, silicified tuff, obsidian, and more rarely, chalcedony, jasper, and others. Flint and silicified tuff were used almost exclusively for knives, scrapers, drill bits, drills, and other small implements, as is evident from a large number of thin sections made from fragments of such implements.

Ground tools, characteristic of late stages of Eskimo culture, were made, in the Bering Sea area, mainly from argillaceous slate, more rarely of siliceous slate. They were ground, probably, on special slate whetstones, examples of which are shown in Plate 14:11 and Plate 35:13.

WORKING OF BONE AND WOOD

The stone adze was one of the most important Eskimo tools for working bone and wood. Examples occur everywhere and perhaps even in greater numbers in the early stages of their culture than later. Even as dense a material as walrus ivory had to be worked with axe-like adzes. It is therefore natural that adzes should have been manufactured of the hardest stones.

We have already indicated how the adze was used in chopping off the ends of walrus tusks in preparing blanks for harpoon heads. The adze was also used in hewing walrus tusks not to mention antler and bone, to the desired shape. An adze was used to cut out the deep hafting grooves on ivory picks and mattocks, as well as to make deep notches in all kinds of bone tools at the point of their attachment to a shaft or handle. It is self-evident, also, that the adze was used in all heavy work with wood. As we know, all timbers used in house construction were hewn with adzes until very recent times.

The form of adzes is usually rectangular and oblong. The length is usually twice the width (for example, in Plate 17:21; Plate 36:36,37). Shape is not always regular (Plate 10:11,17; Plate 18:12; Plate 24:1,2). Dimensions vary, length ranging from 7 cm to 14 cm. The working edge or bit is usually ground so that its facets come together at an angle close to 45°, the inner edge forming a larger angle with the long axis of the adze that the outer one. Long adzes, particularly large ones, could be used hafted directly to handles, while small ones, both oblong and short (Plate 17:18; Plate 24:2,3) always had to be inserted into a special antler or bone socket-piece for hafting to the handle.

Within the total sample of stone adzes, there stands out a class of specimens whose bit facets are beveled very steeply, at an angle of 75°–80° (Plate 17:17; Plate 37:1). They occur at the older sites of the peninsula, at Kiwak and in the western sector of the cultural deposit at Sirhenik. Such adzes from St. Lawrence Island have been described by Collins (1937:152–154; Fig. 16 in text) as adze-like scrapers. He justifiably considers this type of implement as characteristic of Old Bering Sea culture, while emphasizing that the type is unknown outside of the Eskimo culture. The precise function of these tools is not clear, though Collins considers reasonable the supposition that they were used for scraping hides or leather, for their working edges are too steeply beveled to make them effective for cutting. They are likewise unsuitable for scraping any hard material such as bone or ivory.

My opinion is precisely the opposite. Adzes with such blunt bits, beveled nearly at a right angle, would have been particularly effective in working a resistant material such as ivory, since they would be more durable and would not become worn or dented as fast under the impact of strong blows. Analysis of the marks on the hewn ends of walrus tusks and on all hewn surfaces of ivory reveals evidence of work with precisely such an adze. In working wood, on the other hand, adzes with sharper blades were more effective.

Two miniature, elongated chisel-like adzes (Plate 32:4; Plate 34:15), both from ancient sites, stand out among the rest. Implements of this type were most probably used in woodworking.

Adzes of ivory (Plate 28:13; Plate 34:30) are much less frequent. Sometimes, they have a stem which is lashed directly to the handle. Such adzes, of course, could have served only for woodworking.

An adze-like tool of deer antler having the form of a hoe, found in excavations at Nuukan and represented in Plate 10:8 may have been used both in wood-working and as a hoe in excavation work.

The antler and bone socket pieces in which stone adzes were set for hafting to the handle are of three types in excavations on the Chukchi Peninsula.

Type one is the oldest, since socket pieces of this kind have been found only at the older site at Uwelen and in the eastern site at Nunligran. These socket pieces (Plate 3:8 and 9; Plate 32:33) are of deer antler, and have a rectangular, sometimes square socket for the insertion of the handle. It is interesting that one of the oldest socket pieces found on St. Lawrence Island also has a socket for the insertion of the handle (Collins 1937, Plate 46:6).

Type two consists of quite simple socket pieces, likewise of antler, fittting small adzes. An excellent example of such a socket piece with a nephrite adze is shown in Plate 37:1.

The third group is that of antler or bone socket pieces with a long stem or poll, which is lashed to the handle. They are characteristic of later Eskimo settlements (Plate 6:1; Plate 24:5; Plate 37:2).

A variant of this type is represented by a socket piece shown in Plate 6:2, of late protohistoric date, with drilled openings in the poll for lashing to the handle.

So far, ivory socket pieces of Old Bering Sea or Punuk date with ear-like appendages for hafting, similar to those from excavations on St. Lawrence Island (Collins 1937, Plate 46:3; Plate 60:2) have not been found on the Chukchi Peninsula. Also lacking are the "shoe-shaped" hafts that Collins considers Late Punuk (Geist and Rainey 1936, Plate 63:9; Collins 1937, Plate 78:20,21), whereas Rainey, on the contrary, believes them to be a very ancient Okvik type (Rainey 1941d, Plate 20:10). This specialized form is known so far only from the Punuk Islands (Collins 1937, Plate 78:20,21) and from St. Lawrence Island, being found on the latter in very late protohistoric houses (Geist and Rainey 1936, Plate 43:7).

We have only two adze handles: one is of unusual form, made of ivory, and was purchased (Plate 37:4). It is an imitation of late European handles.

Wedges constitute a widespread class of tools next in importance in working not only wood, but also bone. The importance of these implements in daily life is apparent from their presence, in large numbers at that, at all ancient sites, and the stability of their forms throughout.

Wedges, as a rule, were made of the distal end of a walrus tusk, and were hewn to the required shape. The upper end or poll always bears visible marks in the form of scars due to striking the wedge with a hammer. Depending on their particular purpose, wedges vary considerably in size, from quite miniature, 4 cm to 5 cm in length (Plate 3:6; Plate 34:29) to very large, 16 cm to 22 cm long, and correspondingly wide (Plate 3:7; Plate 34:26).

As already noted, ivory wedges were the most common tool for splitting bone and ivory. Insofar as may be ascertained from numerous specimens obtained by excavation, a walrus tusk intended for any kind of artifact was never sawed through completely. It was usually provided with a saw cut of varying depth, sometimes two alternate cuts, and thus prepared was split into two pieces with the aid of a wedge. Wedge marks on such split pieces are always distinguishable as depressions at the edge of the saw cut (Plate 4:4,5).

Any boulder could serve as a hammer for striking the wedge, but in certain cases use was made of special hammers, hafted to a handle. Plate 15:7 illustrates one such hammer, made of a granite boulder with a deep encircling groove for hafting to a handle. One of its surfaces bears traces of prolonged use as a hammer. Such a hammer could be used not only in working bone or wood and in driving stakes and similar operations but also for crushing long bones to extract the marrow.

Two ivory hammers are of interest in view of their unusual shapes: one has a round socket for a handle, and is decorated in Punuk style (Plate 37:19); the other imitates the shape of an iron hammer (Plate 15:11).

The tusk of a young walrus, found in excavations at Cape Bering (Plate 35:32) was used as a hammer or, more exactly, as a mallet, to judge from its bruised surface. It has a suspension hole at its distal end.

The manufacture of all sorts of objects out of wood, baleen, antler, bone, and finally ivory, both in large numbers and in a variety of types, at times of very fine workmanship, would have been inconceivable without sets of small cutting, sawing, and scraping tools of stone. And, in fact, such tools are found in great quantities in excavations of Eskimo sites of any significant size, particularly at the older ones. Being intended for use on such resistant materials as bone and especially ivory, they were always made of very hard stone, such as flint, obsidian, chalcedony, silicified tuff, and the like.

Flat flakes with sharp cutting edges (Plate 24:9,24,27,28; Plate 34:3,4,5,6) were used as knives, as evidenced by marks of such use, clearly detectable on their working edges. Some of these flakes have unilateral retouching along the edges and may have been used as saws or scrapers for working bone or wood (Plate 24:14). Some are concave scrapers (Plate 24:23 and 30), which served to prepare such objects as bone needles and arrow shafts. We found no typical Neolithic saws, and they are likewise not known from excavations on St. Lawrence and the Punuk Islands. Nevertheless, we know that the Eskimos practised extensively the sawing of bone and ivory which, like the sawing of stone, could apparently be performed with the aid of bone tools, sand, and water.

Despite the very widespread practice at all stages of the development of Eskimo culture of incising and engraving on bone, we have no typical burins, of the kind used, for example, in the Paleolithic of western Europe. We find implements which may have served as burins (Plate 24:18,19), but only rarely. From this it may be concluded that engraving on bone was performed not with special gravers, as we think of them customarily, but simply with flint or obsidian flakes with sharp cutting edges.

Hand-held perforators were used for drilling holes (Plate 24:17,18), though drills with stone (Plate 24:21,22; Plate 32:13) and especially bone and most frequently ivory drill bits (Plate 3:4; Plate 11:8; Plate 23:3,4,5; Plate 32:24,25; Plate 35:1,2) were used much more extensively. We will recall that the excavations at Sirhenik yielded two wooden drill shafts: one of these with a bone bit, held in a socket with baleen lashing (Plate 23:10), the other without a bit. Drill rests were the same as those used in obtaining fire by drilling.

Bone and ivory objects with engraving in Punuk style often bear miniature round pits, sometimes practically points, sometimes somewhat larger in diameter, with inserted baleen plugs. A miniature drill with an iron bit for this kind of work was found in the excavations at Sirhenik and is shown in Plate 23:12.

Implements for Dismembering Carcasses and for Working Hides

The most widespread and essential implements for dressing killed animals, dismembering carcasses, and performing a variety of other tasks were knives. They are found at all Eskimo settlements and vary considerably in the material out of which they are made, in the technique of their manufacture, and in form.

More infrequent than others are relatively large knives of laurel-leaf, triangular or asymmetric backed form, made of chalcedony, flint, or silicified tuff (Plate 14:2; Plate 37:10), and originally held directly in the hand, without a special handle. Much more widespread, particularly at the early stages, are narrow stone knife-blades, which were inserted into bone or wooden handles. Excellent examples of such knives are available from the older site at Uwelen, with (Plate 3:17) and without (Plate 3:21 and 22) their handles. Judging from the bone handles of these knives, which have one or two slots or sockets for blades (Plate 3:23,24,27), knives of this type were often of great length. There were also knives consisting of rows of stone side-blades set in bone or ivory handles. Such composite knives may be two-edged (Plate 3:26; Plate 4:2) or single-edge (Plate 25:16).

We must consider stemmed specimens, fastened to the end of a long handle, as the most typical of Eskimo knives. They were used, in particular, to remove the hide from killed animals. These knives are of two types: single-edged and double-edged. Single-edged examples are the more infrequent. Their cutting edge is convex, while the back is straight, sometimes concave. Such knives, usually of flint or silicified tuff, were not ground (Plate 17:8; Plate 24:8; Plate 37:13). They are characteristic of the more ancient sites, such as Kiwak and the western sector at Sirhenik. Single-edged slate knives are always ground over their entire surface (Plate 25:13; Plate 34:20) and are characteristic of the later stages of Eskimo culture on the Chukchi Peninsula. Stemmed and non-ground blades of double-edged knives occur rarely (Plate 32:9; Plate 34:9); on the other hand, ground slate blades of this kind are numerous. They are found in especially large numbers in the late phases of the culture. Most numerous are small, relatively short blades (Plate 25:2; Plate 34:18), though we also find some of medium size (Plate 11:2; Plate 37:12,16) and, at times, very large ones (Plate 37:23). One such stemmed knife was found in its wooden handle (Plate 25:1), another in a handle of bone (Plate 37:22).

Wooden handles, similar to that represented in Plate 25:1, are very typical for thick slate blades with a broad stem (Plate 11:5; Plate 25:26). A bone handle, similar to that shown in Plate 37:22, with a row of ornamental drilled holes, was found in the excavations of the late house on the bar at Uwelen (Plate 6:7).

The most widespread type is that of flat bone handles for two-edged, stemmed blades, with a deep and narrow socket at one end, more rarely at both ends, to hold the stem of a blade. This type is known in two variants: with a closed socket (Plate 35:17,19) and with a socket one of the flat sides of which bears a longitudinal slot for extracting the stem in the event that the blade breaks and needs to be replaced (Plate 12:23; Plate 14:18,19; Plate 25:18; Plate 31:40,41,42). On the Chukchi Peninsula, this type occurs only at late sites, corresponding to the Punuk stage on St. Lawrence Island.

A rare type of wooden handle, represented in Plate 14:4, is intended, probably, for a small narrow blade of the kind shown in Plate 3:12 and Plate 37:18.

Wooden handles cut out to receive a side-blade are known on St. Lawrence Island in the Old Bering Sea complex (Collins 1937, Plate 29:11). They are also found there later (*ibid.*, Plate 38:1). This simple type of handle persisted on the island until recent times (Geist and Rainey 1936, Plate 40:5). On the contrary, bone handles of the type described above, designed to hold stemmed knives, are not known from St. Lawrence Island, though they occur in both variants among the American Eskimo at the Thule stage (Mathiassen 1927; 1, Plate 17:8,10,13, *et al.*, Plate 83:8; Mathiassen 1930a, Plate 4:1,2, Plate 10:1–3; Plate 15:2–).

The final class of knife handles deserves special attention. It is that of composite handles formed of two halves, made of ivory, and slotted at the end for the insertion of a long and thin blade. This type of handle is similar to that of a well-known Eskimo implement, in use to present times for cutting bone and ivory, the "antler chisel" of Murdoch (Murdoch 1892:173, Fig. 143) and "whittling knife" of Mathiassen (Mathiassen 1927; 1, Plate 22:1–4). These handles, generally speaking, presuppose the existence of a very narrow blade which is unlikely to be of stone and is more probably of iron or even steel. It is therefore surprising that such handles appear early on St. Lawrence Island, if not in Old Bering Sea, at least in Early Punuk (Collins 1937:145–146, Plate 38:5–7). Here, on the Chukchi Peninsula, they are well represented at the older site of Uwelen (Plate 4:5,6), though they are known also from later sites (Plate 14:4; Plate 25:21; Plate 31:39; Plate 32:30). Rainey notes the extensive distribution of knives with such handles from Old Bering Sea times to the present, basing himself on unpublished collections of the University of Alaska, and is inclined to consider them as part of the Okvik assemblage (Rainey 1941:504–505).

Semi-lunar women's knives of rubbed slate (ulu) are found in abundance at all sites, as might be expected, particularly at the later ones. They vary considerably in size, from small, 5 cm to 6 cm in length (Plate 25:30) to medium-sized measuring 11 cm to 12 cm (Plate 34:24 and 25) and, judging from the size of the handles (Plate 12:13), at times attaining lengths of 18 cm and more. Their form likewise varies considerably, from low to very tall (Plate 25:30; Plate 8:16), and from semi-lunar or triangular to nearly trapezoidal.

The handles of women's knives are made of wood, bone, antler, or ivory. They are usually low, with a slightly or at times markedly concave upper edge. In rare instances, they are decorated by means of openwork (Plate 31:36) or engraved (Plate 9:1) designs.

In general, women's slate knives from the Chukchi Peninsula differ in no way from the bulk of such implements known previously from St. Lawrence Island and North America.

Knives of bone or ivory occur at late sites on the Chukchi Peninsula, as they do on St. Lawrence Island. Knives of this kind are two-edged, long and narrow, with one flat face and one that is slightly raised to form a clearly defined ridge.

The distal end is always pointed, and the ribs are slightly sharpened. The end of the handle in this type of knife usually has a perforation for suspension.

Similar knives are known on St. Lawrence Island (Collins 1937, Plate 74:5,6) in Punuk times, and in the Thule culture of North America (Mathiassen 1927; 1, Plate 18:15).

It is possible that these knives were used not only for household purposes, but also in hunting and in warfare.

Stone scrapers for working hides are particularly characteristic of early phases, and occur principally at the more ancient sites. The material of these scrapers is most commonly flint, silicified tuff, or jasper. They are all made of massive flakes. The inner or lower face is usually worked only in part, and may be flat. The curved outer face is flaked in its entirety, and with particular care along the working edge. The most typical shape is pyriform, with a broad working edge, and a narrow end designed to fit into a handle. Scrapers range in size from small, 3 cm to 4 cm in length (Plate 24:11; Plate 32:15), to large, with lengths of 5 cm to 7 cm (Plate 24:7; Plate 34:17). Exceptionally we find small, carefully re-touched double scrapers (Plate 24:13), and large, adze-like specimens, crudely flaked on both faces (Plate 24:10).

Scraper planes differ from scrapers in their larger size, and in the fact that their working edges are not as sharp as those of scrapers. Like the scrapers, they were hafted to special handles when in use. The material out of which they were made is softer, usually siliceous or silico-argillaceous slate. Scraper planes are more characteristic of late sites on the Chukchi coast. Some of the scraper planes are large flakes which have been chipped to the desired form, in which case the working edge is ground only occasionally (Plate 37:6). Most frequently, however, the entire surface of the tool has been ground (Plate 10:20; Plate 34:22; Plate 37:7).

Bone scrapers for removing fat from intestines are a typical woman's tool of the Eskimo. Several types may be distinguished among those found in excavations on the Chukchi Peninsula.

The first and oldest of these types is always made of ivory, and is in the form of a small trough or a deep oblong scoop (Plate 4:13; Plate 35:23), sometimes with a loop for suspension (Plate 4:19). The edges taper, without being sharp, and decoration may be present on the outside (Plate 35:23). Scrapers of this kind are known both from the Okvik site in the Punuk Islands (Rainey 1941d, Fig. 21) and in later times, at the Old Bering Sea and Punuk stages of Eskimo culture (Collins 1937, Plate 30:5–7).

The second type is that of shallower gutter- or trough-shaped scrapers (Plate 12:19). This type, known in Punuk times, acquired a broad distribution through-out the area inhabited by the Eskimos.

The third type is a rare, perhaps accidental form, also trough-like, but asym-metrical (Plate 14:8), the working edge of which is sharpened. The opposite side, on which the scraper is held, is broad and blunt. Special mention must be made of a flat knife-like scraper of ivory (Plate 35:4) purchased in Enmylen, used, according to the local inhabitants, in working walrus intestines.

Sewing Gear, Articles of Clothing and Personal Adornment

Awls and punches are among the most common finds at the sites excavated and range from simple pointed splinters of bone (Plate 11:7; Plate 16:2 and 3; Plate 27:13) to specially worked examples of ivory with knobs, sharpened deer ulnas (Plate 27:20) and large walrus tusk splinters (Plate 12:24; Plate 14:20). Awls and punches were sharpened, apparently, on special whetstones, an example of which from Cape Bering is shown in Plate 35:13.

The sewing *needles* found are of two types: with eye and without. Needles without eyes which, incidentally, are rarely found, have a notch at the end for the thread (Plate 31:31). Needles with eyes include large specimens, usually of bone (Plate 27:18), and thin ones of ivory (Plate 27:19). Small needles were kept in special *needle-cases* made of bird wing bones (Plate 23:11), sometimes decorated in characteristic Punuk style (Plate 38:13), or in the form of specially carved tubes of ivory (Plate 35:28). Judging from the considerable amount of baleen fiber at the sites, we may suppose that sewing involved the use of thin strands and threads twisted out of that material, though it is possible that only gut thread was used.

Though no *thimbles* were found in the excavations, owing to the fact that they were prepared out of a piece of raw sealskin with a transverse slit on one edge (such thimbles have been described by a number of authors—Murdoch 1892:319, Fig. 326b; Nelson 1899: 109, Plate 44:11,14,18,20, *et al.*; Thalbitzer 1914:523, Fig. 252a,b), proof of their existence on the Chukchi Peninsula may be seen in the thimble holder from Enmylen, nicely decorated in late Punuk style (Plate 38:12). Illustrations of entirely similar hook-like thimble holders among the Alaskan Eskimos are provided in the works of Nelson and Thalbitzer (Nelson 1899:100, Plate 44:24; Thalbitzer 1914, Plate 35).

Apparently, toggles of special shape made of a flat piece of ivory with a central opening, such as that shown in Plate 12:14 or in the form of two crescents (Plate 29:4) constituted a different kind of thimble holder, similar to examples found by Collins on St. Lawrence Island (Collins 1937, Plate 82:23) and described by Nelson from Alaska (Nelson 1899:110, Plate 82:23). A similar form is known in the Thule culture (Mathiassen 1927; 1, Plate 52:17, Plate 63:6; 1930a, Plate 14:7).

Probably to be included among tailoring and sewing gear are carefully made and polished ivory rods, which may have served for smoothing seams and for other similar purposes (Plate 31:30).

Women's sewing bags are in general use among the modern Eskimos. No bags occurred in the excavations, though some of the handles found probably belong to such bags (Plate 29:29; Plate 38:20).

No hair *combs* in good condition were found in the excavations and those that are present in our collection are of a very late date. Yet, among the objects acquired by Sverdrup (Sverdrup 1930, Plate 25:5) on the Asian shore of Bering Strait, there is an ivory comb which, to judge from the fanciful decoration on the handle, is of Old Bering Sea date. Thus, bone combs with long teeth were present on the Chukchi coast since early times. Combs other than hair combs, intended for craft purposes such as the removal of flesh or hair from hides, for carding grass, or for combing gut or baleen in making thread, occur in great numbers. Such combs were usually made very narrow, with few teeth. They were always of ivory, and could have a long (Plate 12:11) or a short (Plate 37:20 and 21) handle. After prolonged use, these combs became so worn that only short, smooth, and polished nubbins remained of the long teeth.

Many sites also yielded *back scratchers*, in the form of flat disks with a round opening in the center for the stick on which they were set. Such back scratchers (Plate 6:20; Plate 16:10; Plate 31:20), as a rule, were made of ivory, though some were of wood or of baleen. These objects are particularly typical of the late stages of Eskimo culture on the Chukchi Peninsula.

Ornaments include only an ear pendant of ivory, found at the western site at Nunligran. The pendant is in the form of small oval disk with a stem, designed to fit through the ear lobe, and a small hole at the end of the stem (Plate 31:33). A similar ear ornament was found on St. Lawrence Island in a Punuk context (Collins 1937, Plate 82:18). According to Nelson, this same type is very common among the Alaskan Eskimos (Nelson 1899, Plate 24). Beads carved out of ivory, which may also have served as buttons or fasteners, occurred both at very ancient sites, such as Uwelen (Plate 4:11 and 12) and in a later context at Sirhenik (Plate 29:2). A single small oval ivory button, nearly circular in shape, with a loop (broken) on the inner face and a reticulate design on the outer face was found at Sirhenik (Plate 29:3). Similar buttons, though of larger size, have been found in the Old Bering Sea complex on St. Lawrence Island (Collins 1937, Plate 58:3–5).

It is clear from these finds that engraved beads—of elaborate shape, carved of ivory and used as ornaments—and buttons on clothes existed among the coastal inhabitants of the Chukchi Peninsula since ancient times.

Simple ivory buckles (Plate 29:1) may have been used with belts. One of these, distinctively carved in the shape of a bear, is decorated on its upper surface in Punuk style. The under surface bears a loop for a thong (Plate 38:5).

Containers and Household Utensils

POTTERY

Pottery vessels in the form of lamps for lighting and heating the houses and pots for preparing food were universal among the Eskimos prior to the appearance of metal containers. Pottery sherds, with rare exceptions, are common at all Eskimo sites, particularly the later ones. In our excavations, sherds were lacking only at the older Uwelen site. This is to be explained, perhaps, by the small scale of our excavations at the site.

Ethnographic information on pottery-making processes among the Eskimos is very limited. According to Nelson the Eskimos of St. Michael's Island made pottery in the following manner. A certain amount of dense blue clay was soaked and thoroughly kneaded by hand until it became plastic. To it were added short and stiff marsh grass and a small amount of fine black volcanic sand from the beach. The bottom of the vessel was shaped as a round flat cake of clay. The wall was built up around the rim of the latter using a thin strip of clay, which was coiled around the base until the required height was reached. The upper portion and rim were smoothed, and the vessel on both sides either remained smooth or was scalloped with the fingers. The walls of the vessel usually remained plain, but were sometimes decorated by simple incised lines made with a stick. After being shaped and decorated, the vessel was placed near the fire where it dried. Then fire was kindled inside and outside of it, and the vessel was fired for an hour or two at the highest temperature that could be achieved (Nelson 1899:201).

Gordon tells us that at the time he visited Alaska the art of pottery making had disappeared altogether among the western Eskimos of America, though old people still remembered the time when each village had one or two women engaged in the preparation of clay lamps and cooking pots. Gordon recorded the following pottery-making process from the words of an old man from Cape Nome. A certain quantity of clay, obtained from known locations in the tundra, was reduced to the condition of a soft paste by wetting with walrus blood and kneading. A certain amount of sand from the beach was added, together with feathers from the breast of the white partridge. From this material, the vessel was built up with the aid of a flat wooden paddle. The outer surface was smoothed and was either left that way, or else decorated with incised lines using a pointed stick. The final burnishing of the rough surface was sometimes done with a crudely carved paddle, sometimes by rubbing the unfired vessel with a grass mat, the impression of which remained. The finished vessel was then fired over an open fire (Gordon 1906:83–84).

We have noted several times already the poor quality of Eskimo pottery. No evolution toward pottery of better quality is to be seen from Old Bering Sea times to the present. All sherds, regardless of whether they are found at early or at late sites, are black in color, both on the surface and in cross-section. The firing was so poor that organic inclusions such as grass stalks were charred but not burnt out. Tempering material, for the most part, is sand and fine gravel, with grains up to pea size. As a result, the vast majority of the pots are thick-walled, 1 cm or more in thickness. In addition, hair and baleen fibers were added when making pottery at Kiwak and in the western sector at Sirhenik. Sherds with this type of tempering material are usually thinner and laminate easily. Grass stalks were added for the same purpose. Apparently, fine gravel was not used in combination with vegetal or animal fiber as temper.

Vessels were shaped by direct modelling from a lump of clay, though the thinner, laminated pottery was probably made by the superimposition of coils, as described by Nelson. Collins found only one rim sherd with clear evidence of the coiling technique (Collins 1937, Plate 50:2).

Our excavations failed to yield a single whole vessel. Judging from sherds, vessels were mainly large, often as wide as 30 cm to 35 cm at the mouth. There are no clearly defined flat bases in our collection, whence we may conclude that the vessels had round bottoms. In late times, vessels often have outside appliqué suspension lugs. There are no vessels with such lugs at the older sites.

The outer surfaces of the vessels are smoothed, but there is no trace of burnishing. The smoothing of the surface, in most cases, was performed with a bunch of wet grass, which resulted in characteristic marks.

Most of the vessels are undecorated and vessels with lugs have completely smooth surfaces. Yet, at the oldest sites, we sometimes find sherds with imprints of shallow parallel lines covering almost the entire surface of the pot, with the exception of the base. This design was applied, apparently, in the process of making the vessel, by shaping it with a special paddle (Plate 9:7) or tablet (Plate 4:25; Plate 26:19) of ivory, covered with a series of parallel ridges. Similar pottery has been found on St. Lawrence Island in the Old Bering Sea complex (Collins 1937, Plate 52). It is also known from Neolithic sites of the Japanese islands (Umehara 1934, Plate 9:1).

At the site of Miyowagh on St. Lawrence Island, Collins found a single isolated sherd with a typical "check-stamped" design (Collins 1937:169, Fig. 17 in text). The checks, 6 mm in width, were deeply impressed into the smooth surface of the vessel. Sherds with similar impressions were found by us in considerable numbers at Sirhenik. Vessels of this kind were of large size, as much as 40 cm in diameter, though relatively thin-walled (wall thickness was 0.8 cm to 0.9 cm, and exceeded 1 cm only at the rim). The checks were square or diamond-shaped (Plate 26:22,23,24), 0.5 cm to 1.0 cm in width. At the same site of Sirhenik we found an antler stamp (Plate 26:18) for applying this design.

Pottery with a similar check-stamped design, as Collins has pointed out (Collins 1928), is known in the Eskimo area only from Norton Sound and on Nunivak Island. The same author has noted (Collins 1937:349) that pottery fragments bearing this type of design are known from kitchen refuse at Japanese Neolithic sites (Kishinouye 1911, Plate 24:85) and from southeast Asia, where they have been described for Siam and Annam (Sarasin 1933, Fig. 23a; Goloubew 1930, Plate 24). At the same time, Collins believes that the principal center for this pottery lies in southeast China, judging from the finds on Lamma Island near Hong Kong (Finn 1932, 1935). Finn found there a large number of pottery sherds with check-stamp impressions, dating from 500 to 200 years before our era. In China, this pottery is known from the time immediately preceding the Yin dynasty (14th to 12th centuries B.C.). In the Amur region, it dates from the end of the Neolithic.

In northeastern Siberia, in Yakutia, pottery with this kind of decoration is known from the end of the Neolithic through the Bronze Age, and disappears at the beginning of the Iron Age (Okladnikov 1944:17).

At ancient sites on the coast of the Chukchi Peninsula we found no pottery fragments that could be interpreted definitely as pieces of oil lamps similar to those found on St. Lawrence Island. Not a single stone lamp was found. We do have a large number of fragments of heavy clay oil lamps of large size with partitions for the wicks. All of them occur at relatively late Punuk and protohistoric sites.

In connection with oil lamps, we may mention at this point the finding of a special mallet of deer antler (Plate 28:4) used in the winter to break up frozen fat on a flat stone prior to using it in an oil lamp (cf. Birket-Smith 1924, Fig. 14a).

VESSELS OF WOOD AND BALEEN

Containers with baleen sides and a wood bottom have existed among the Eskimos from Old Bering Sea times down to the present. They were in general use on the Chukchi coast and in America, from Alaska to Greenland. While they vary in size, they all have the same shape and an oval bottom, the length of which is about twice its width (Plate 15:8; Plate 28:15). The walls are made of one sheet of baleen, whose overlapping edges are sewn together with a strip of the same material.

Collins saw a connection between the baleen containers occurring only among the Eskimos, and the birch bark and wooden vessels which have a wide distribution throughout North America and Asia. He perceived this relationship both in the manner of sewing together the walls and in the shapes used. However, I fail to see any connection between the baleen containers and birch-bark vessels of northern Asia. Siberian birch-bark vessels differ substantially from Eskimo baleen containers both in their round form and the technique of their manufacture.

The containers described herein had handles of wood or bone of the most varied shapes (Plate 26:12,13,14; Plate 35:22). Wooden containers of round form were found only in the latest protohistoric dwellings.

Hooks, mainly made of segments of antler (Plate 15:15,16; Plate 18:24; Plate 28:16,17) are found as frequently as baleen containers. These hooks were used either to suspend lugged clay pots over the fire or as hooks for clothes and other objects in the home.

Among bone containers, we must note first shallow oblong whale bone platters, no more than 2 cm high, though rather large. Fragments of such platters have been found at ancient sites such as Kiwak and Enmylen. Ivory served as material for deep, oblong, trough-like containers. Such containers are likewise found at old sites, such as Uwelen and the eastern site at Nunligran (Plate 32:34).

Ladles occur in two types: those made of antler tines, which have been mentioned earlier, and those of whale or walrus scapulae (Plate 26:16).

Similar whale bone platters, trough-like basins of ivory and ladles of whale bone (lower jaw of beluga) are known from the Old Bering Sea site of Miyowagh on St. Lawrence Island (Collins 1937, Plate 47:16; Plate 51:12,13; Plate 60:1).

Spoons found in excavations on the Chukchi coast fall into two types. The first is that of thin, very shallow ovoid spoons of bone or wood, in rare cases of baleen (Plate 26:8 and 9) with short handles. These are sometimes of ivory, deeper, with a rather broad though nevertheless short handle (Plate 38:18). All these spoons are found in the older cultural deposits, belonging to the Old Bering Sea and early Punuk phases. Spoons of this kind are of the same date on St. Lawrence Island (Collins 1937, Plate 51:15). The other very stable and widespread type of spoon is made of deer antler, is round or oval in shape, and has a very long and narrow handle (Plate 14:12,13; Plate 26:10).

Such handles are characteristic of Punuk on St. Lawrence Island (Geist and Rainey 1926, Plate 33:9; Plate 73:4; Collins 1937, Plate 78:16) and of Thule in Canada (Mathiassen 1927; 1, Plate 28:9). On the coast of the Chukchi Peninsula they are known from Cape Schmidt in the north (Nordenskiöld (1882:222–223) to Cape Bering in the south.

We have yet to mention a small strainer of baleen fiber with a hoop of the same material (Plate 26:17). We do not know the specific function of this implement. It is possible that it served as a strainer, though it could have been used also to sift fine gravel to sort it for use as tempering for clay in pottery manufacture.

Means of Transportation

An excellent model of a kayak, made of ivory and covered with engraving in Old Bering Sea style (Plate 38:6) serves as indisputable evidence of the presence of this type of enclosed vessel with manhole as early as the Old Bering Sea stage of Eskimo culture. However, together with the kayak, the Eskimo made wide use of a large open boat, the umiak, of which we have good models from excavations at Sirhenik, dating back at least to Early Punuk times (Plate 27:9,10). The construction of these open boats may be understood from the wooden keel crosspieces (Plate 27:7,8) on one of the umiak models from Sirhenik. Late protohistoric sites already yield umiak keel plates of whale bone, similar to those found among the Eskimo today (Plate 6:19; Plate 12:28; Plate 15:17). We may gain some idea of the oar type from models of these (Plate 16:1). We know of boat and oar models from excavations on St. Lawrence Island as well (Collins 1937, Plate 59:1,2,6; Plate 84:2), where they have been interpreted as children's toys. With reference to the purpose of these models, we repeat what we have said already in connection with models of bows and arrows, namely, that they are of ritual significance. Bogoras tells us that toy bows and arrows (i.e., models) are brought by the Chukchi as offerings to a spirit (*kelet*). According to the same author, the Asian Eskimos hang small oars, in addition to wooden figures of birds, on a special net during the winter ceremony of the "big woman" (*kasak*). During the "going around" ceremony, the Eskimos always suspended representations of a canoe in a special frame on a pole (Bogoras 1904–1909:371).

Boat hooks of ivory are available from the Cape Dezhnev area (Plate 8:8), from Sirhenik (Plate 27:9), and from Cape Bering. These massive hooks are designed to be lashed to a shaft. While all are of the same shape, they differ substantially in details, particularly in the mode of attachment to the shaft, as may be seen from the drawings. Similar hooks have been described by Nelson as boat hooks of the Alaskan Eskimo in use from the area of the mouth of the Kuskokwim to Kotzebue Sound (Nelson 1899:222–223). Murdoch has described similar implements of the Eskimo of Point Barrow as hooks for carrying pieces of blubber or whale and walrus meat (Murdoch 1892:310). A considerable number of these hooks were found in excavations on St. Lawrence Island (Collins 1937:139–140; Plate 35:1–8). The basic function of the hooks, it must be supposed, was purely nautical: they served as gaffs when mooring on rocky coasts or on the edge of the ice floe. Independent of this, they may have served as hooks for transporting loads.

Handles of ivory for drag lines, used in boat-towing, dragging ashore boats and carcasses of killed walrus, and similar tasks, are rather numerous and varied in our collection. The typical shape of such toggles at the Uwelen and Old Bering Sea stages is triangular, with a notch at the apex and at the middle of the opposite side for the line. Such toggles are known from the Okvik site in the Punuk Islands (Rainey 1941d, Fig. 35, items 1–3) and from St. Lawrence Island (Collins 1937, Plate 30:19,20). On the Chukchi Peninsula they have been found at the older site of Uwelen (Plate 4:23), at Cape Dezhnev, and at Sirhenik (Plate 27:26).

A second type of line handle has the form of a short rod with an encircling groove at the middle. On St. Lawrence Island, this type is characteristic of the Early Punuk stage (Collins 1937, Plate 60:5). It is of roughly similar date on the Chukchi Peninsula (Plate 27:25,27).

The third type, that of long cylindrical rods, is known in two variants. One is typical of Old Bering Sea times and has a broad zone of encircling grooves at the middle for the attachment of the line (Plate 27:23). The other has a deep central groove and bears decoration in Punuk style (Plate 27:24).

We term *ice creepers* the ivory plates with spikes on their outer surface which were attached to footwear under the arch of the sole to avoid slipping when walking on ice. Ice creepers have not been found at the oldest sites on the Chukchi Peninsula and on St. Lawrence Island they are known only from the relatively late Old Bering Sea site of Miyowagh. There, they are pentagonal or hexagonal in outline and have inserted spikes (Collins 1937, Plate 37:3–5). Punuk ice creepers from the same island (*ibid.*, Plate 75:23–25) are quadrangular in shape, and have spikes which are either inserted or carved of one piece with the rest of the creeper from one slab of ivory, like those of today.

In our excavations, ice creepers were found only at Late Punuk and proto-historic Eskimo sites at Cape Chaplin and at Sirhenik (Plate 14:5,10; Plate 27:1).

The ice creepers of Punuk date from Cape Chaplin (Plate 14:5) have inserted spikes and two pairs of lashing holes. A one-piece creeper with a central opening is shown in Plate 14:10.

The ice creepers from Sirhenik and from the protohistoric site at Cape Chaplin are of modern type, elongate and rectangular in outline, with a longitudinal opening at the middle, and carved spikes or nubbins and lashing holes (Plate 27:1).

The date of the appearance of ice creepers in Eskimo culture is not clear as yet. It is important to note that they have yet to be found in the east at sites of the Thule culture, though they are known among the Eskimos of Labrador in the form of pieces of crimped sealskin sewed to the soles of shoes (Turner 1894:217, Fig. 43). The Eskimos of Point Barrow use crossed strips of hide for the same purpose (Murdoch 1892:135, Fig. 82). Ivory ice creepers of the kind described from our excavations on the Chukchi Peninsula are well known among the modern Eskimos of Asia and among the maritime Chukchi, as evidenced by ethnographic collections from the Chukchi Peninsula.

SLEDS AND DOG SLEDS

One of the important discoveries of Collins in his excavation near Gambell on St. Lawrence Island was the surprisingly late use of dogs among the Eskimos as means of transportation. It was found that remains of dog sleds and objects that may be interpreted as parts of dog harnesses appear on the island no earlier than two hundred years ago. Excavations on St. Lawrence Island and at Point Barrow have shown that dog traction was unknown in ancient times both in western North America and on the islands of Bering Sea. At the same time, Collins allowed for the possibility that such a typical trait of Eskimo culture as dog traction would be identified eventually for an earlier period somewhere in the Bering Strait area, perhaps on the Siberian coast. Our excavations on the Bering and Arctic coasts of the Chukchi Peninsula have shown that there also the use of dogs for transportation appears very late.

The Old Bering Sea site of Kiwak and the western sector of the cultural deposit at Sirhenik have yielded remains only of small ivory sleds which were drawn by hand and used to transport umiaks and loads of meat across the ice. These sleds were of two types: heavy and light. Heavy sleds, runners of which are shown in Plate 17:28 and Plate 28:19,20, were made of tusks of old walrus. Their runners were about 40 cm in length, about 7 cm in height, and up to 4 cm in width. They were joined by two cross-pieces, set in shallow notches on the upper surfaces of the runners, under which large oblong holes were provided for lashing. Similar runners have been found in Old Bering Sea contexts on St. Lawrence Island (Collins 1937, Plate 44:4; Plate 46:1,2). As indicated earlier, these heavy sleds were used for transporting umiaks and other loads over the ice.

Alongside heavy sleds, light, carefully made hunting sleds existed in several variants at the earliest stages of Eskimo culture. Among the light hunting sleds, we must first mention the specimens from the western sector of the refuse area at Sirhenik (Plate 28:21,22), with their light runners of elegant form, described earlier. Another variant of the light sled, also ancient, is one in which the narrow ivory runners have an expanded flat surface on their upper edges, as on the runners from Kiwak and Cape Chaplin (Plate 15:13). Narrow runners were decorated on the outer side (Plate 28:23; Plate 32:35).

A third variant of the sled with light, narrow runners, also found at the older sites, is distinctive in the occurrence of a continuous row of holes along the upper edge of the runner for the lashing of a large number of cross-pieces. Such sleds are represented at Kiwak, at Sirhenik (Plate 28:24), at the eastern site of Nunligran, at Cape Bering (Plate 35:21), and at Miyowagh on St. Lawrence Island (Collins 1937, Plate 45:3). We should also note that runners of light hunting sleds decorated on the outer surface were found at the Okvik site in the Punuk Islands (Rainey 1941d, Fig. 16, item 2).

Both of the types discussed, the light and the heavy, persisted in Punuk times. In Punuk times, both on St. Lawrence Island (Collins 1937, Plate 77:4,6,7,9) and on the Chukchi Peninsula, sleds appear with relatively narrow runners but having a broad, sometimes grooved, flat, upper surface. We have a good example from Cape Chaplin (Plate 15:13). Similar sleds were in use among the Eskimos until recent times both in western North America (Murdoch 1892, Fig. 358; Nelson 1899, Plate 76:1) and on the Asian shore of Bering Sea (Bogoras 1904–1909; 1, Fig. 22a).

Long and light dog sleds and dog harness equipment, even if they did appear earlier among the Asian Eskimo than on St. Lawrence Island, in any event are relatively late. Curved wooden arches of dog sleds, narrow bone runner shoes and dog harness blocks (Plate 16:5) were found only at Cape Chaplin among objects of a Late Punuk assemblage and in the uppermost levels of the eastern sector at Sirhenik. There, as at Nuukan, likewise in a Late Punuk or protohistoric context, we found swivels and blocks of dog harnesses (Plate 11:15,16; Plate 27:5,6). If the bone plates described as umiak keel plates are in reality dog sled runner shoes, their date, as we know, is very recent.

The *ice staffs* described by Nelson (Nelson 1899:214–215, Fig. 67) among the Alaskan Eskimos, who used them for traveling on thin ice and in the tundra, were in use apparently since early times on the continent of Asia. Evidence for this is to be seen in the special ivory ferrules (Plate 3:1,2) for these staffs found at Uwelen and Sirhenik, as well as in an ice staff ring found in excavations at Sirhenik (Plate 23:19).

Armor Plates

Bone armor plates were found at many sites in excavations on the Chukchi Peninsula: Uwelen, Cape Chaplin, Avan, Sirhenik, Cape Bering, or, in other words, along the entire surveyed portion of the coast. While generally of oblong quadrangular form, some of the plates are narrow (Plate 18:22) while others, on the contrary, are broader (Plate 6:17; Plate 15:19). The perforations for lashing the plates to one another are elongate, rectangular, or round. All the examples are of bone, and occur only at late sites in Late Punuk and protohistoric contexts. All armor plates from excavations on St. Lawrence Island (Collins 1937:224) are likewise of bone or else of ivory. They began to be made quite recently on the American side of Bering Strait and are known from ethnographic collections made in the last century (Hough 1895:632–633; Nelson 1899:330, Fig. 92). As on the Chukchi Peninsula, armor plates appear on St. Lawrence Island only in Punuk times.

The origin of this late element of Eskimo culture is of great importance. The problem has received the attention of Hough (Hough 1895:633 ff.), Laufer (Laufer 1914:252 ff.) and, lately, Collins (Collins 1937:325–337). As far as we know, the area of distribution of such armor includes the Alaskan shore of Bering Strait, the Diomedes, and St. Lawrence Island, and, in northeastern Asia, the Eskimo, Chukchi, and Koryak areas. Hough, in his study of the origin of this type of equipment in North America, came to the conclusion that bone plate armor arrived in America from Asia, and that its route of diffusion may be traced from Japan northeastward through the Ainu, Gilyak, and Chukchi areas across Bering Strait and the intervening islands to the Eskimos of western North America. Laufer showed that plate armor cannot be thought to have been invented by the Ainu, the Gilyak, or the Japanese. At the same time, he feels that Hough is technologically justified in relating the plate armor of Bering Strait with that of eastern Asia. Plate armor of Eskimo type attained its highest degree of elaboration in Japan, whence attempts have been made (Ratzel, Hough) to derive it. However, Laufer showed on the basis of historical considerations, that the theory of the Japanese origin of the armor in question is unacceptable inasmuch as bone armor is older in northeast Asia (among the Su Shen) than similar iron equipment in China and Korea. This view was stated by us as early as 1910 (Volkov and Rudenko 1910:190). If Japanese armor derives from some foreign source, the latter, according to Laufer, is most likely to have been the interior of Siberia though, on the whole, he is inclined to consider the development of plate armor in northeastern Siberia and northwestern North America as independent from that in the rest of Asia. Laufer was led to this conclusion by the cultural isolation of the tribes of northeastern Siberia among whom we find this trait and their close links with American tribes.

Collins has focused attention on the remarkable fact, confirmed by our own excavations on the Chukchi Peninsula, that the wrist guard, new types of ivory arrowheads, and the reinforced bow first appear among the Eskimos at the Punuk stage, together with armament, of which the most important element was plate armor. The sudden appearance of these traits may indicate either an intrusion of hostile groups into northeastern Siberia or the gradual northward diffusion of weapons and improved means of warfare.

The fact that Eskimo weapons of Punuk times are identical to recent Eskimo-Chukchi-Koryak types, which, in their basic features, resemble those of Japan, leads to the conclusion that this equipment appeared in Bering Strait after its type was already well elaborated. Collins supposes that the time of its appearance follows that of its probable adoption in China and Japan, and would be about the 7th or 8th century of our era or earlier, in the 3rd century, when the Su Shen already possessed such equipment. Collins is inclined to consider the later date as the most likely.

Ceremonial Objects

Archaeological excavations usually yield few objects that provide any idea of the world outlook of ancient peoples. Nevertheless, our collection does include a number of objects of unquestionably religious significance. They include various amulets, spirit representations, models of utilitarian objects used as offerings, and shamanistic trappings.

Amulets. Various Eskimo amulets, mostly connected with hunting sea mammals, have been described in detail by Murdoch (Murdoch 1892:435 ff.) and Nelson (Nelson 1899: 436 ff.). Some were intended to help track the animals, others to compel the latter to appear before the hunter and to approach him, others still to placate the killed animal or to serve as protectors.

We need not enumerate here the numerous and varied Eskimo amulets and guardians, and shall confine ourselves to only those that provide analogies to objects found in our excavations.

First, tusks of very young walrus (Plate 16:16; Plate 30:1,2,3) and canines of bear (Plate 16:17; Plate 30:11), dog and wolf (Plate 16:13; Plate 38:8) occur in very large numbers. They have suspension holes drilled through the root or a special lashing. Murdoch (1892:437) has described tusks of young walrus and polar bear canines used as amulets among the Eskimos of Point Barrow. The Eskimos of Kotzebue Sound (the mothers of infants in arms) wore bear canines as protective charms.

A very interesting amulet made from a wolf canine bears an eye engraved on one of its flat sides, so that the tooth resembles the head of a bird (Plate 38:8).

Another extensive class of amulets, principally from the excavations at Sirhenik, consists of single bones of animals: a walrus scapula, the tibia of a bird (Plate 30:5), the phalanges and astragalus of a walrus (Plate 30:6,7), and others, with bindings of baleen for suspension. Parry (1924:497) mentions wolf bones worn as amulets. These are also noted by Murdoch. The Asian Eskimos hang vertebral disks of whales, which have been found also in the excavations at Sirhenik (Plate 30:4,8), around the necks of children to protect them from the "evil eye." Water-worn vertebrae, available as pendants with natural openings for suspension, apparently were also used as amulets (Plate 29:19,20).

Another category of objects invested with supernatural power were representations of animals and human beings. I am not inclined to consider as children's toys all carved representations in wood or ivory of whales, seals, bears, foxes, and dogs. On the contrary I believe that most of them, if not all, had religious significance. Among them, we must first note representations of whales (Plate 29:13,17,18). Whale representations, connected with specific concepts of a religious nature (placation), are in use among the Eskimos even now. We find them as essential accessories among the Asian Eskimos at the "going around" and "whale" ceremonies (Bogoras 1904–1909). Such representations are also usual in whale-hunting umiaks in the protective bundles of these boats. A wooden whale figure, hollow inside, in which spear points were kept ("for good luck") by the western Eskimos, has been described by Nelson (Nelson 1899:439, Fig. 15). Similar representations used as amulets have been described also by Murdoch from Point Barrow (Murdoch 1892, Figs. 412,424). A very interesting representation of a two-headed dog was found in the excavations at Sirhenik (Plate 29:12). A similar two-headed figure was found at an ancient site of the western Eskimos and has been described by Murdoch (Murdoch 1892:406–407; Fig. 416). An amulet in the form of a two-headed dog has also been described by Bogoras (1907:365, Fig. 259). According to that author it is believed that the two heads protect both in front and in back. Sometimes, such "guardians" were provided with two heads and two pairs of hands.

We do not have many bear figures. One of these, from excavations at Cape Chaplin, is of Late Punuk date and is executed very schematically. It would seem that there are no grounds for ascribing to it any religious significance. Two other representations, one from the older site at Uwelen (Plate 4:8), the other from the Cape Dezhnev area (Plate 9:9), were undoubtedly not toys, but had some specific function. One of them (Plate 9:9) was worn either separately as an amulet or as part of a protective bundle, while the other was set on a shaft and had some ceremonial function.

Among representations of "masters" or "guardians," we have, first of all, the human figure from the older site at Uwelen (Plate 4:7). Typologically, it is close to a figurine published by Rainey (1941d, Fig. 21, item 1) and, especially, to a figure from the Asian shore of Bering Strait published by Hrdlička which is probably of the same date as ours (Hrdlička 1930, Plate 36). Wooden representations of "guardians" from late sites of Punuk or protohistoric date, from settlements at Cape Chaplin, and on the bar at Uwelen (Plate 6:14; Plate 16:19,20) are executed very schematically, like those of nearly modern date (Plate 38:9,10,11).

The anthropomorphic figurine of ivory which we found at the relatively late village of Nunligran (Plate 31:22) had a different significance. There is no defined head, and a suspension hole is provided in the head area. Particular emphasis is given in this figure to exaggerated female secondary sexual characteristics: the breasts, wide pelvis, and hips. We may suppose that this figurine was worn as an amulet connected with procreation.

We can also consider as an amulet, in all probability, a fish representation from Sirhenik shown in Plate 29:8, inasmuch as fish lures have suspension holes not in the head area, as in this case, but in the dorsal region.

The drums used in ceremonies and shamanistic performances among the Eskimos were, as is known, of a type different from the Siberian. Handles of such drums were found in the excavations in considerable numbers, though not at the older sites. Ivory handles with decoration in typical Punuk style are known from Sirhenik (Plate 29:25) and Enmylen (Plate 38:19). Most, however, are in the form of simple rods with a notch for the rim and lack decoration. Rims made of ivory, bone, or wood are found at very late Punuk or even protohistoric sites such as Cape Chaplin, Arakamchechen Island and Nuukan (Plate 11:23,24; Plate 12:27; Plate 16:6,7). Excavations on St. Lawrence Island yielded quite a few drum handles of Punuk date, but not a single one of Old Bering Sea provenience. The handle from Collins' excavations at Miyowagh near Gambell (Collins 1937, Plate 55:5) is unlikely to be that of a drum. In any event, it has nothing in common with the type of drum handle already fully established in Punuk times. Thus, at the present time we know of not a single handle from the Bering Sea area that we can assign to the Old Bering Sea stage of Eskimo culture. We may suppose, therefore, that drums appeared relatively late among the Eskimos, in Punuk times.

Particular attention is due to a class of objects made of baleen in the form of fishes, knives, arrowheads, and others, which have been variously interpreted. Collins, for example, who found such objects in excavations on St. Lawrence Island (Collins 1937, Plate 59:4–7), believed them to be toys. Similar objects are known from excavations in North America in the Thule culture.

On the Chukchi Peninsula, such artifacts of baleen were found at Cape Chaplin (Plate 16:8), at Cape Chukchi (Plate 17:27), and in great numbers at Sirhenik (Plate 30:12–21). Most of them are shaped like fishes, with clearly defined tail fins, though some of them have the form of the so-called "crooked" knife, with a side-blade at the end of a handle (Plate 16:8; Plate 30:19). Many have the shape characteristic of single-edged straight-backed bone knives (Plate 30:14 and 21), others are in the form of spoons (Plate 30:12). The completely uniform—we might say standard—form of these objects on the Asian shore of Bering Sea, on

St. Lawrence Island, and in the area of the Central Eskimo of North America suggests that we are not dealing here with casual objects or toys, but with objects prepared for a single specific purpose. On the other hand, the traditional fish form (Plate 17:27; Plate 30:15,16,20) and the occurrence of forms unlike those of any known Eskimo implements indicate that these are not common implements reproduced in baleen, but conventionalized renderings of various articles, models thereof intended for certain kinds of ceremonies or, perhaps, parts of a shaman's garb.

There remains to be mentioned only the serrated plaque of baleen (Plate 11:14) similar to the bull-roarer known as a child's toy among the modern Eskimos (Murdoch 1892:378–379, Fig. 377). Formerly it was used without doubt in religious ceremonies, as among many peoples of the world.

Art

A number of works have been devoted to the art of both the modern and the ancient Eskimos (Hoffman 1897; de Laguna 1932–1933; Mathiassen 1929; Collins 1929; Rainey 1937). The most detailed analysis of the art of the ancient Eskimo is to be found in Collins' volume on the archaeology of St. Lawrence Island (Collins 1937). Collins distinguishes three styles in Eskimo art of the Old Bering Sea stage, and two styles and six sequential phases of development in the Punuk stage.

Old Bering Sea Style 1, according to Collins, differs from typical classical Old Bering Sea in its relative simplicity. It is primarily a linear style, characterized by an abundance of radial lines, long and short spurs, and broken lines. It also makes use to a certain extent of concentric circles and slightly curved lines. In other words, we have the basic elements of the Old Bering Sea style, but all their possibilities are not yet realized. They are not prominent and do not serve as a basis for the elaborate and complex designs so characteristic of the latest stage of Old Bering Sea art. On the contrary, this older style is noticeably more linear. Circular elements, when they do occur, occur less predictably than other profuse decoration, consisting of long radical lines, shorter independent lines, are single or double lines to which are appended long spurs. In a special table (Collins 1937:47, Fig. 6 in text), Collins presents a synopsis of the basic elements of the oldest of the Bering Sea styles, Style 1. Its antiquity is indicated stratigraphically by the provenience of objects decorated in that style, found under the floor of the oldest dwelling on St. Lawrence Island near Gambell (the Hillside site). However, objects decorated in the style are so few that Collins felt it was highly desirable to obtain additional examples, from other localities if possible, to speak definitely of their genetic relationship with the more mature Old Bering Sea style, even though such a relationship was probably on stratigraphic grounds.

Old Bering Sea Style 2 is more varied and more consistent. A characteristic motif is the head of an animal with open jaws. Elements of design include straight, curved, and broken lines, short spurs, and hand-drawn circles between diverging lines. In this style, "eyes" are formed by wide circles or small circles with appended spurs. Decoration is more diversified, with a tendency toward the independent use of various design elements. Old Bering Sea Style 2 is highly curvilinear and stands in marked contrast to style 1, even when it uses the same design elements. Collins summarizes the characteristic motifs of style 2 in a special table (Collins 1937:96; Fig. 15 in text).

The difference between styles 2 and 3 is not as marked, and their chronological separation is not as clear. Objects decorated in style 2 on St. Lawrence Island are more abundantly represented at Hillside and in the lower levels of the Miyowagh site. This, in the opinion of Collins, indicates that they are older than objects decorated in style 3. The latter is distinctive mainly in its emphasis on "eyes," i.e., raised concentric circles and ellipses, usually so placed as to resemble the eyes of an animal. These pairs of raised concentric circles or ellipses, often with small depressions within, suggest the head of an animal within the over-all design. In some cases, the smaller circles of style 2 also suggest the "head" of an animal, though not as forcefully. In addition, the circles in decorative designs of style 3 have a tendency to simplify or subordinate the accompanying decoration, so that some of the surface remains plain. On the contrary, small circles, straight and curved lines, and spurs in style 2 are accompanied by dots or broken lines which fill in all intervening space.

The Punuk style, according to Collins, is characterized by the use of straight or slightly curved lines which, unlike those in Old Bering Sea art, are incised deeply and evenly. Circles are also characteristic, but they are completely regular and made with a compass. Small round pits and dots, alone or at the end of short lines, are also characteristic. Unlike Old Bering Sea decoration which is free-hand and executed with a stone implement, Punuk decoration is wholly the product of metal tools, and as a result is more rigid and mechanical. Collins differentiates between the older and simpler Punuk style 1 and the more varied style 2. He divides style 1 into 2 phases: (1) with shallow incised lines, and (2) with similar lines, but with the addition of incised spurs, dots, and (rarely) circles, drawn free-hand. Style 2 is subdivided into four phases: (1) using a very long spur and lightly incised lines; (2) with more deeply incised lines, and spurs, dots, and circles executed with a metal drill or a compass; (3) using short, deeply incised spurs, usually appended in pairs to lines and circles; (4) with deeply incised lines used singly or in pairs or as horizontal bands of four parallel lines.

In a recent work dealing with the Okvik site in the Punuk islands, Rainey has provided numerous examples of Eskimo art preceding Old Bering Sea (Rainey 1941d). The style which Collins considers as Old Bering Sea 1 Rainey considers to be the Okvik style, preceding Old Bering Sea. Apart from distinctive human and animal figurines carved out of walrus ivory, incised designs contain no realistic figures. The same elements that we find in the Old Bering Sea and Punuk styles (spurred lines, ovoid circles, parallel and ladder-like lines, etc.) occur here, but in quite different designs. To judge from available illustrations, typical features of this older style are deeply incised, most frequently curving lines, sometimes with spurs similar to those we have noted on our harpoon heads from the older site at Uwelen.

We will attempt to review the ancient art of the Eskimo of the Chukchi Peninsula within the framework proposed by Collins and amplified by Rainey.

First, we must deal with the distinctive and so far little known decoration characteristic of the older Uwelen site. The most typical elements of this decoration are short, deeply cut, but uneven lines, wider toward the middle and thinning out at the ends. Frequently these lines, by the use of additional strokes, are made to suggest, very schematically it is true, the appearance of an animal, perhaps a beluga. In addition, this style uses such elements as semi-circles with spurs pointing outward, series of diagonal deeply cut lines alternating with dotted or broken ones, and combinations of oblique lines meeting at an acute angle. Harpoon heads, arrowheads, and knife-handles are decorated in this style.

Decoration by means of short, deeply cut, pointed lines, sometimes suggesting the beluga or with an added side-spur, is fully adapted to the "pointed" shape of the harpoon heads on which it occurs (Plate 1:4,5,6,12,13). Apart from the beluga representations (Plate 1:4,5), the sharp and multi-prong basal spurs of harpoon heads are also shaped to suggest the head of an animal (Plate 1:4,7,9).

We know this style and these decorative motifs only on the Okvik harpoon heads and some human figurines published by Rainey (Rainey 1941d, Fig. 5, items 2–5, 7–9; Fig. 7, items 3–5,7,8; Fig. 9, item 5; Fig. 28, items 2,5; Fig. 30, item 4).

A distinctive decorative technique at Uwelen, so far not known anywhere except at the older Uwelen site, is the carving on a decorated object of a deep triangular or fusiform depression, at the bottom of which are incised sharp parallel, radiating, or zig-zag-like lines. This element is found on harpoon heads (Plate 1:8,9,10,11,13,24), on knife-handles (Plate 3:20,24), and on dart heads (Plate 2:13).

Decoration by deeply cut, short, straight, or oblique lines, sometimes with a central spur (Plate 1:5) is characteristic not only of harpoon heads, but also of a specific type of arrowhead with an end-blade (Plate 2:3; Plate 17:1; Plate 21:25) found, in addition to Uwelen, in an Old Bering Sea context at Kiwak and at Sirhenik on the coast of the Chukchi Peninsula, on St. Lawrence Island (Collins 1937, Plate 34:3), and in the Okvik assemblage in the Punuk Islands (Rainey 1941d, Fig. 14, items 1–3). Another detail characteristic of this style of decoration is the fluting of the surface of an arrowhead (Plate 2:9) or harpoon head (Plate 1:1) to suggest a twisted form. This feature is not known [on the Chukchi Peninsula?—Ed.] outside the Uwelen site. A final design motif abundantly represented on the flat surfaces of knife-handles is a combination of elements which we already know: triangles with radiating lines within them, deeply cut multiple lines with shorter interrupted lines diverging away from them at an acute angle, and dotted lines (Plate 3:18,19,20,23,24; Plate 9:1). This same motif, though not as clearly characterized, occurs on Okvik knife-handles (Rainey 1941d, Fig. 19, items 2–3).

Very interesting decoration occurs on an ivory piece purchased in Nunligran which, judging by its dark brown color and patina, was undoubtedly excavated (Plate 9:10).

Both of the broader sides of this object bear the same motif, a conventionalized representation of a "horned" and "bearded" human mask. Without analysing this representation at any length, we will point out merely that both stylistically and in the technique of its execution, this decoration obviously comes close to the Uwelen style and is probably of the same date.

We see this same decorative style clearly expressed in the decoration of sled runners from the western sector of the cultural deposit at Sirhenik (Plate 28:21).

Reviewing the entire complex of objects examined above, decorated in Uwelen style, it is essential to emphasize that we do not find a single clearly expressed feature of Old Bering Sea style, even of its earliest phase, style 1. On the other hand, if we sort out from among the many Okvik objects published by Rainey those which contain elements of Old Bering Sea and Punuk styles, we are left with objects decorated in Uwelen style.

In addition to examples of engraving, the older Uwelen site has yielded a human head and a figurine carved of walrus ivory. Both the head (Plate 4:10) and the figure (Plate 4:7) have many traits in common with the Okvik figures. The long, narrow face, sometimes pointed at the top, and a nose of exaggerated length are features characteristic of the former and of the latter (Rainey 1941d, Figs. 16–30). On the head from Uwelen, hair is indicated by dots and the deeply cut lines that are typical of Uwelen. The Uwelen figure is shaped in the manner of one illustrated by Rainey (Rainey 1941d, Fig. 29, item 1), while the decoration on its chest is identical to that of the Okvik madonna (*ibid.*, Fig. 27). The decorative technique here is again typical of Uwelen in its use of deeply incised lines.

There are two decorated objects from the Uwelen site that fail to fit in the group we have just examined. They are, first, a harpoon head (Plate 4:16), similar to one which Rainey describes as Okvik (*ibid.*, Fig. 6, item 9) and, second, a bear figure (Plate 4:8). Both of these objects are more correctly classed with those decorated in Old Bering Sea Style 1.

The snow goggles from Uwelen stand apart. Their decoration does not fit within the framework of Old Bering Sea style, and compares best in motifs and technique with decoration known from finds at Ipiutak near Point Hope on the arctic coast of North America (Rainey 1941b).

Like Collins on St. Lawrence Island, we do not have many objects decorated in Old Bering Sea Style 1. Some remarkable examples of this style include the decoration on the throwing board from Seklyuk (Plate 38:21), a harpoon head from the Cape Dezhnev area (Plate 7:1), a number of objects from Enmylen (Plate 33:4, Plate 35:26), and a "winged" object (Plate 38:3). Highly characteristic features of this style on objects from the Chukchi Peninsula are small nucleated circles with very long spurs (Plate 38:21) single or double concentric circles among solid curved lines, interrupted lines between solid ones (Plate 33:4), and large concentric ellipses with dots within (Plate 35:26). Large areas of the decorated object remain plain. We must also include among the objects decorated in this style the harpoon head from the Asian side of Bering Strait published by Sverdrup (Sverdrup 1930, Plate 25:4). We see on this object, in addition to nucleated circles and spurred curving lines, a decorative "chain" similar to that on the Seklyuk throwing board. It is characteristic of this style that lines, and especially concentric circles and ellipses, are executed free-hand, without any attempt at geometric precision. In this respect, the decoration on the upper surface of the "winged" object (Plate 38:3) is true to form. The best examples of the style under discussion is a winged object from St. Lawrence Island illustrated by Collins (Collins 1937:42, Fig. 4 in text), a number of objects also published by him from Little Diomede Island (*ibid.*:53, Fig. 8 in text) and Alaska (Collins 1929, Plate 7a–b), and objects published by Rainey from the Punuk Islands (Rainey 1941d, Fig. 10, items 1,2; Fig. 12, item 12; Fig. 17, item 12; Fig. 19, items 6,8; Fig. 24, items 6,7; Fig. 26; Fig. 35, item 12).

Stylistically, the bear figure from Uwelen (Plate 4:8) pertains, judging from the nature of its decoration, to the early phase of the Old Bering Sea stage, characterized by style 1. The decoration by clear-cut, straight rather than curved lines relates it to that of Uwelen, while the occurrence of small nucleated circles indicates relationship to Old Bering Sea Style 1. The bear figure from the Hillside site near Gambell on St. Lawrence Island, published by Collins (Collins 1937:49, Fig. 7 in text), despite the similarity in the posture of the animal and a similar rendering of the bear, differs substantially in style. The head of our bear is considerably more realistic. It has open jaws and a well outlined head, with typical short ears, eyes, and nose. The head of the bear from Hillside is rendered schematically, the ears are conventionalized and exaggerated in size, and the eyes are replaced by holes. The forward and hind limbs of our figure, though conventionalized, are rendered more completely than the rudimentary paws of the Hillside bear. Decoration on the Hillside bear consists, instead of the clear-cut, mostly straight lines of the Uwelen figure, of lightly incised, exclusively curvilinear elements, in a design characteristic of mature Old Bering Sea style. The comparison of these two figures leaves no doubt that the bear figure from Uwelen is older than the one from Hillside on St. Lawrence Island.

The bear figure from the Cape Dezhnev area (Plate 9:9) differs from the Uwelen specimen not only in posture and composition, but also in the style of its decoration. The posture here is that of an animal crouching on all four legs. The size of the head is exaggerated in relation to the body. The legs, though separate, as in the Uwelen figure, are more conventionalized. The head is less realistic and decoration is exclusively curvilinear, as on the bear figure from St. Lawrence Island. Chronologically, the bear figures from the Cape Dezhnev area and from St. Lawrence apparently belong to the same phase of Old Bering Sea culture.

Compositionally, the bear figure from the Cape Dezhnev area is similar to one from Ipiutak at Point Hope. Rainey assigns this figure to a special phase of Eskimo culture, the Ipiutak culture, older than the Old Bering Sea stage on the arctic coast of America (Rainey 1942:320). I am not convinced of this and am inclined to consider the Ipiutak figurine as later in date. While giving the appearance of being more realistic because of the treatment of the head and limbs, the Ipiutak figurine is in fact more conventionalized. The head and limbs themselves are exaggerated in size and too large by comparison with the body of the animal. If we should raise the question as to which of the two figures was the antecedent form, the one from the Cape Dezhnev area or the one from Ipiutak, all the evidence would be in favor of the former.

By our examination of the decoration of the bear figures of St. Lawrence Island and the Cape Dezhnev area, we are led to consider classic Old Bering Sea style. We have excellent examples of decoration on various objects in mature Old Bering Sea style from the entire Bering Sea coast of the Chukchi Peninsula, from Cape Dezhnev in the north to Cape Bering in the south. These include, first, harpoon heads (Plate 7:8,13; Plate 9:4,5,8; Plate 33:3), objects whose exact function is not known—in particular, "winged" objects (Plate 9:11; Plate 17:14), and a kayak model (Plate 38:6). Decoration in the same style occurs on a harpoon head from Plover Bay published by Collins (Collins 1929:5, Fig. 1) and on a harpoon head and comb from the Asian side of Bering Strait published by Sverdrup (Sverdrup 1930, Plate 25:2,5).

Our excavations on the Chukchi Peninsula failed to provide reliable criteria for the stylistic and chronological differentiation of this elaborate type of Old Bering Sea art. Yet, we may still suppose that its oldest examples are the harpoon head from Sirhenik (Plate 19:10), those objects from the Cape Dezhnev area on which paired "eyes," combined with other graphic and plastic features, suggest an animal face (Plate 9:6,8), and a number of objects whose decoration includes a specific motif in the form of a bird's head, such as occurs on a boat model (Plate 38:6), harpoon heads (Plate 9:4,5; Plate 33:3), and "winged" objects (Plate 9:11; Plate 17:14). The latest style of Old Bering Sea decoration, in the view of Collins, was one in which ornamental "eyes" are elevated in relief, par-ticularly at their centers (Plate 7:8,13); bird heads are likewise rendered in relief (Plate 33:3). This feature is clearly evident on a harpoon head from Enmylen (Plate 33:3) which acquires as a result an unusually complex form unknown in any other type of harpoon head. The relatively late date of such harpoon heads is indicated by the persistence of their form in harpoon heads of Punuk date. The objects from the Chukchi Peninsula illustrated in Plate 35:10 and Plate 38:1,2, apart from the specimens enumerated earlier, are decorated in the Old Bering Sea art style.

Inasmuch as we lack adequate stratigraphic data for a chronological and stylistic breakdown of the Punuk stage into phases, it is hard for us to analyse Punuk decoration in any detail, even in the light of the six phases distinguished by Collins.

Generally speaking, the Punuk style of decoration differs enough from the Old Bering Sea style which precedes it on St. Lawrence Island and on the Asian coast of Bering Strait to allow it to be distinguished without difficulty. First, such typical motifs of mature Old Bering Sea style as concentric circles and ellipses of various sizes, "eyes" within designs suggesting animal heads, and bird heads and beaks are entirely lacking in Punuk. Designs with straighter lines, lacking broken and dotted elements and sharp spurs, replace the earlier incised curvilinear decoration. Though incised, the precise Punuk lines are not as deeply cut as those in the Uwelen style. Important auxiliary elements, apart from solid lines, include deep pits and points (the latter often at the ends of short lines) and highly accurate circles executed by mechanical means with pits or dots in their centers.

Yet the transition from Old Bering Sea to Punuk art took place gradually, and we do have objects in early Punuk decorated in transitional style with holdovers of older designs executed in the new technique. Objects with this kind of decoration include, first, the wrist guard from Sirhenik (Plate 21:5) on which Old Bering Sea decorative motifs, already somewhat modified it is true, are combined with Punuk technique. This category also includes a remarkable handle (Plate 38:20) carved in the form of two intertwined whale heads decorated in a style distinct from Old Bering Sea, though making use of Old Bering Sea design elements that are not typical of Punuk, such as rows of dotted lines and dentated lines. The rendering of the whale heads differs sharply in its realism from the Punuk manner of carving animals. The representation of an eye on a wolf canine shown in Plate 38:8 probably also pertains to Early Punuk.

Engraving with plain shallow lines is typical of the Punuk harpoon heads from Sirhenik and Enmylen (Plate 19:14,15,16,17,18,23; Plate 33:7,8). Dots are added at the ends of the lines at Sirhenik (Plate 19:19,20,21). A plaque from Sirhenik (Plate 29:27) is decorated in the same style, with the addition of pits and rows of dentated lines. A beautifully finished drum handle from Sirhenik, decorated with deeply incised lines and nucleated circles (Plate 29:25), is of early Punuk date. Remarkable examples of later Punuk decoration by means of parallel and dentated lines combined with compass-drawn circles include a wrist guard and a thimble holder (Plate 33:25; Plate 38:12). The decoration of the handle and wrist guard from Sirhenik (Plate 29:29; Plate 21:8) by means of parallel and zig-zag-like lines is very characteristic and undoubtedly late. Objects decorated with parallel lines that are plain or elaborated with rows of short spurs (Plate 16:4; Plate 37:19; Plate 38:7,13,14) are numerous and varied.

Tridents, so characteristic of Late Punuk and found in two variants on St. Lawrence Island, are distinctive in form and decoration, and are represented likewise in our collection from the coast of the Chukchi Peninsula. One variant, apparently the older one (Plate 38:4), is decorated by parallel lines and triangles just like the trident from Seklowaghyaget on St. Lawrence Island. The other (Plate 29:24) has dots at the corners and at the ends of short lines in the manner of the trident from Ievoghiyoq on the same island (Collins 1937, Plates 68,69, Fig. 6:1).

From the Chukchi Peninsula we have a large number of carved animal figures of Punuk date representing seals (Plate 29:9,10,16; Plate 38:16), whales (Plate 29:13,17,18), dogs or foxes (Plate 29:11,12,14), bears (Plate 31:34), and birds (Plate 29:6,7; Plate 38:15,17). They all differ radically from the earlier, more realistic representations of animals in their crudeness and simplicity. As a rule, their surface is entirely plain and only in rare cases bears simple decoration by means of parallel lines (Plate 29:18; Plate 38:14). The same may be said of the anthropomorphic figures (Plate 16:20; Plate 38:9,10,11). In this respect the only somewhat unusual anthropomorphic figurine is one from Nunligran (Plate 31:22) which apparently represents a woman. Parts of the body, particularly the breasts and the hips, are rendered in bold relief.

The problem of the function and sources of Eskimo art is complex and has not received adequate treatment to date. In connection with the once current view of the resemblance of Eskimo art and the art of the Upper Paleolithic of Europe, De Laguna has undertaken a special comparative study of Paleolithic and modern Eskimo art (De Laguna 1932–1934). In comparing the two, she found only a few common traits which in turn were not found to be characteristic only of Paleolithic and Eskimo art but to be widespread among the peoples of the world in all times. De Laguna sees highly conventionalized renditions of animal forms in Paleolithic designs, particularly in curved and spiral lines combined with patterns cut into the surface and shallow bas reliefs. This feature was found to be alien to modern Eskimo art. Unlike the dynamic, flexible, youthful and as yet unformed style of the Paleolithic, modern Eskimo art was found to be hidebound and conservative, the result of slow development over many centuries. In final analysis, De Laguna was led to the conclusion that there can be no question of genetic connection between the Paleolithic art of western Europe and the art of the modern Eskimo.

Collins had the opportunity of comparing Paleolithic art with that of the ancient Eskimo. His conclusion (Collins 1940) was that greater resemblances could be found between the Upper Paleolithic and Mesolithic art on the one hand and Old Bering Sea art with its "scratchy" style 1 on the other, than between those two and modern Eskimo art. In both areas, the older style is more generalized and variable, while the more recent one is more definite and more conventional.

These comparisons do not solve, by any means, the problem of the origins of Eskimo art styles. Archaeological investigations in the Bering Sea area and, in particular, our own excavations on the Chukchi coast, indicate the existence of a number of stages in the development of the Eskimo art style. It has been found that the Old Bering Sea stage is preceded by the Okvik or Uwelen phase with its deeply cut lines, its graphically and sculpturally conventionalized animal representations, and its rendering of human and animal forms in the round with, at times, a certain degree of realism. At the Old Bering Sea stage, graphic art is enriched through the addition of a number of new decorative motifs, which attain their greatest development at the time of florescence of this culture. Sculpture in the round and in bas relief continues on a relatively high plane in Early Punuk. Mature Punuk already lacks any trace of the elaborate and accomplished style of Old Bering Sea. Graphic decorative motifs are reduced to simple, elementary forms, which are executed mechanically. Realistic sculpture degenerates until we are dealing with three-dimensional ideograms.

Thus, if our purpose now were to look for some kind of connection between the art of the Eskimo and that of the Paleolithic of western Europe, we would have to begin with the Uwelen style. However, the chronological and spatial gap between these two styles is so great that it would be futile to search for any genetic connection between them. On the arctic coast a number of elements of early (Uwelen-Okvik) Eskimo art persist through the Ipiutak, Birnirk, and, in part, the Thule stages, whereas on the Bering Sea coast they are eclipsed in the Old Bering Sea period by the temporary flowering of a special style, which develops there at the time as a result of influence from distinctive traditions whose origins are to be sought in the south. At the transition between the Old Bering Sea and Punuk stages, connections with the south are interrupted, and, along with a number of new cultural traits of undoubted western, Siberian, origin, new elements of decorative art make their appearance in Eskimo culture, and the art style of the modern Eskimo gradually takes form.

In passing, let us say a few words about the art of the so-called Ipiutak culture, discovered by Rainey and Larsen at Point Hope. The Ipiutak collection, with the exception of a small number of objects, has not yet been published, and complete information regarding it is not available to us. My general impression is that we are dealing here with materials of varying date. Some objects are decorated in the older Uwelen (Okvik) style which apparently persists there over a long span of time, to Thule-Punuk times. On the other hand, a number of objects, including a walrus ivory chain and pendants terminating in animal heads, which Rainey considers proto-Eskimo, to me seem more likely to be late, and perhaps come close to being modern.

In discussions of the function of a particular art style, the question is often raised whether we are dealing with representational art, i.e., art whose purpose is to give substance to a particular concept or image in a specific form, or with decorative art. In Eskimo art, ancient and modern, these two aspects are inseparable. In cases when, as on a harpoon head from Uwelen, we have a schematic representation of an animal, such as the beluga, rendered by means of a few strokes, we are dealing with representational art. In cases when rows of lines, as on knife-handles from the same Uwelen site, cover the surface of an object with a geometric design, we are dealing, in all probability with decoration only. In the mature phase of Old Bering Sea art, it is not always easy to differentiate pure decoration on an object from the conventional representation of a given form, such as the head of an animal, in an established style. Nevertheless, it may be said that, as a rule, representational art among the Eskimos is connected with objects of religious significance (representations of protectors, guardians, masters, and others) and objects connected with sea mammal hunting (harpoons, arrows, boats, etc.). On the other hand, objects of utilitarian nature usually bear non-objective decoration.

Social Structure

None of the numerous foreign works concerned with the past of Eskimo culture touches on the subject of socio-economic structure and of its development. This is not surprising when even ethnographic monographs dealing with Eskimo culture at the present time or in the recent past either lack a section on social structure entirely or treat the subject in a few pages. This is to be explained by the very simplistic approach of foreign investigators to Eskimo culture, caused by their disregard of the authentic scientific outlook of Marxism-Leninism. Yet, it would seem that it is among the Eskimos and particularly among the Eskimos of America, settled over the vast and inhospitable expanses of the Arctic, isolated in places from the direct influence of the capitalistic culture of the United States and of Canada, that social structure of the primitive communal type could be most easily studied.

Soviet scientists and, in particular, V. G. Bogoras, must be credited with revealing the social structure of the Eskimos. Bogoras, using materials accessible to him and gathered by Western and American investigators, formulated the problems involved in interpreting the social structure of the American Eskimo in historical perspective, in relation to the stages of development of their culture (Bogoras 1936). The importance of the subject lies also in the fact that Eskimo society is of primitive communal type in the view of all investigators, both in America and in Europe.

The body of factual material serving to describe the social structure of the Eskimos in the past and in the present has two aspects, dialectically opposed, yet related. One aspect is that of the existence of a primitive communal society, with each settlement containing only one inhabited house, occupied by several families and several generations. The household has a leader, usually oldest in age, who is not only an adviser but also a skilful hunter. The status of the leader is based on the voluntary acceptance of his authority. Food is partaken in common. However, there is no emphasis in this way of life on explicit rules in such instances, for example, as the division of game. The other aspect is that of the disintegration of primitive communal social structure.

Centripetal tendencies on the part of members of the Eskimo kin group are due, in Bogoras' estimation, to changes in the mode of production. Bogoras believes that Eskimo production, based on the hunting of sea mammals, has passed through two basic stages. The first was one in which seal hunting took place more or less constantly throughout the year, mostly close offshore, in closed or partly closed inlets and bays and on the coastal ice shelf. It is this stage that Bogoras is inclined to connect with typical primitive communal economy. The second stage is characterized by walrus and whale hunting. It involves long trips on the open sea, and requires more developed tools of production (boats and harpoons), as well as greater effort and hunting skill. The hunting of larger animals on the open sea is considerably more remunerative than seal hunting. As a result, seal hunting decreases in importance and becomes a secondary occupation. This second stage of mammal hunting also required co-operative hunting techniques, and represents the further development or even the climax of primitive production on a communal basis. At the same time, it is this very abundance of returns from hunting in this stage that leads dialectically to the decay of primitive society of the communal type.

An index of the disintegration of primitive society is the division of the communal dwelling. Families settle next to one another, and each one sets up its own dwelling. Bogoras believes that "this division of communal dwellings into smaller units became possible when blubber and oil became sufficiently abundant to allow adequate heating for each unit."

The unit dwelling naturally provided greater freedom to engage in handicrafts, and the division of the communal dwelling was thus connected not only with conditions of consumption, but also with conditions of production and technology.

"The fragmentation of the communal dwelling naturally leads to the division of consumption, as well as to the division of property rights over winter supplies of food and fuel, to the organization of their storage on an individual basis, etc."

In the course of this process, society fights such tendencies by means of public opinion and by eliminating members whose actions harm the community. The existence of such a communal judiciary mechanism, Bogoras notes, to defend community rights is evidence of the decay of social structure through the agency of coercive forces and as a result of acts by the more aggressive and unbalanced individuals. Similarly, regulations governing the sharing of game, such as occur among the Eskimos, point simultaneously to the effective strength of the communal structure and to individualistic tendencies acting to disintegrate it.

In a society structured along primitive communal lines, food is common property and does not require division. As individualistic tendencies increase, an attempt is made both to put restraints on primitive kin structure and at the same time to re-establish its effectiveness. In case of famine, the Eskimos everywhere will reinstate the ancient rule that food is to be consumed communally. The carcass of a whale thrown up on the shore likewise belongs to the people as a whole. Such is also the significance of generous hospitality to all travelers, which is observed strictly to this day.

As I. P. Lavrov and I set out from Providence Bay on a long journey along the Bering Sea coast in a chartered whaling boat, I was disturbed by the absence of any kind of provisions among the crew of the boat, who were Eskimos from Sirhenik. Our trip was organized with the help of M. G. Aristov, who had been living among the Eskimos about twenty years and was generally respected. When I asked him how the crew was to be fed, he reassured me by saying that the crew would be provided for at any settlement where we stopped. Away from the settlements, he told me, we would have to share our provisions, if we were to avoid the ill fame of "those who eat alone." We had a highly successful trip. In the villages none of us needed to worry about food. At sea, we ate the supplies of the expedition. When these supplies ran out on Arakamchechen Island, we subsisted on cormorants shot by the Eskimo crew of the whaling boat.

The division of labor within the family among the Eskimos was primarily that between the work of men and the work of women. The main occupation of the men was always the hunting of sea mammals, polar bear, deer, and arctic fox. Fishing was done both by men and by women. The gathering of vegetable food (edible roots) was always an exclusively female occupation. The care of the house and the children, the preparation of food, the working of hides, the making of clothes out of them, and the making of pottery were also women's occupations. As a matter of fact, women also participated to a degree in the hunting of sea mammals.

Increased division of labor and greater individualization of production were also accompanied by a development of patterns of ownership which differed from the primitive communal model. In this manner, three types of property arose among the Eskimos: collective (communal), family, and individual. Collective property included land and the water with everything that it contains, communal dwellings, and hunting boats or umiaks. As primitive communal structure disintegrates, the houses become recognized as belonging to individual families, and production units arise among relatives within the community and lay claim to basic means of production such as the umiak. Later, the boat becomes the individual property of the head of a family, usually the wealthiest one.

With the development of private ownership of means of production, the division of spoils becomes unequal. For example, while the meat of walrus killed by a hunting team is distributed equally among the participants, the owner of the boat who supervises the distribution gets the lion's share of walrus tusks and hides. Baleen and whale blubber are likewise distributed unequally.

In collective bear or reindeer hunts, the matter of whose arrow struck in the most vital place becomes of decisive importance in dividing the spoils. This is the basis of the custom, widespread still at the beginning of the 19th century, of putting property marks on arrowheads. This custom is well known in the Bering Sea area (Volkov and Rudenko 1910:181).

Using as a point of departure the scheme outlined above for the development of social structure among the Eskimos, let us now turn to the archaeological facts.

The first stage described by Bogoras in the development of production among the Eskimos, that of exclusive seal hunting, is not known to us, and it is possible that no such stage did exist. The oldest Eskimo sites we know of, those of the Uwelen-Okvik stage, indicate that at that time already, walrus was being hunted in considerable numbers, in addition to seal and, inland, reindeer and bear. Whales may have been hunted as well. It is hard to conceive that in those remote times, when population was relatively sparse, food should have been short, particularly if we bear in mind the accounts of our travelers in the 18th century, who were amazed at the unbelievable numbers of land and sea mammals in these regions.

We do not know enough about houses at the Uwelen-Okvik stage. As for the houses of the Old Bering Sea stage, as we have seen, they were in the form either of small isolated pit houses, in which several families lived together, or else of a system of small pit houses connected by means of short passageways, with a centrally located communal kitchen. This stage is undoubtedly correlated with collective production in hunting and communal consumption. This is the period of typical primitive communal structure. However, the decay of this type of structure began already at the end of the Old Bering Sea stage and in Birnirk times, when separate houses with separate family food storage pits appear in all settlements.

Primitive communal structure, combined with elements resulting from its decay, initiated primarily under the stimulus of inter-tribal barter and trade, has survived to this day.

Traditional and later historical accounts tell of active barter between the Asian Eskimos and the Chukchi on the one hand and the American Eskimos on the other. For the products of maritime hunting, walrus hide thongs, blubber, and others, the Eskimos obtained from the Chukchi such products of reindeer breeding as reindeer hides, suede, and fur parkas. From Alaska, where they traveled far south, they obtained beaver and martin pelts, clothing of water vole, and so on, in exchange for reindeer hides and suede. In the 17th and particularly the 18th centuries, they obtained iron artifacts, glass beads, and tobacco leaves from the fort at Anadyr through the intermediary of the Chukchi. With the establishment of the Anyuysk fair on the Kolyma, Russian goods penetrated through the Eskimos to Alaska and into America.

In the middle of the last century, foreign, mainly American, whaling boats appear north of Bering Strait, and their crews establish trade connections with the Eskimos of both shores. Inter-tribal trade is considerably modified as a result. Russian goods are forced off the market by American products. Middlemen between the whalers and the local population both coastal and inland appear among the Eskimos.

Private ownership rights to the spoils of the collective hunt or to the more valuable portions thereof appear in Eskimo society very late, after they have entered into contact with Europeans. We do find magic symbols, intended to aid hunting, on ancient harpoon and arrow heads. Property marks, however, are found on arrows and other objects only at the latest sites, already pertaining to protohistoric times. Our collection from the Chukchi Peninsula contains only two objects on which property marks have been carved: an arrowhead from Nuukan (Plate 10:9) and a netting shuttle from Cape Chaplin (Plate 13:24). Both of these objects date from protohistoric times, the 18th or perhaps even the 19th century.

Most investigators erroneously make the point that the status of women is depressed in comparison with that of men when marriage is patrilocal. It is assumed that this low status of women is connected with their slight participation in productive labor. As a result of the harsh climate, the gathering of roots, berries, etc. is of secondary importance. However, women are entirely free in their household activities, engage in fishing and often take part in the hunt by rowing the umiaks—women's boats (Shnakenburg 1932). The status of women among the Eskimos is in fact not so depressed at all. In ancient times, their status was particularly high, as a result of their exceptionally important role in magic and religion. We know of powerful and influential women shamans among the Eskimos. In this connection, the statement made to Bogoras by a Cape Chaplin Eskimo is significant:

It is wrongly that they think that women are weaker than men in the hunt. Home sorcery is more powerful than the spells cast in the tundra. The husband may go around and around, carefully searching, but those who sit by the lamp are indeed powerful, and it is easier for them to summon game to the shore.

It is also significant, as Bogoras notes, that women deities prevail over male deities in Eskimo cosmogony. The three principal Eskimo spirits are women. They are the spirit of the land (Pinga), the spirit of the air (Hila), and the most important one of all, the ruler of the sea bottom or "Great Woman" (Nulirahak among the Asian Eskimo, Sedna in America). These female spirits are definitely hostile to men.

In most folklore variants, the underwater ruler has no husband at all. According to other versions, she has a husband and a child, whom she maintains in fear and subjection.

The female ruler of the wind and lightning (Asiaq) with the horrible countenance (later version) searches for and finds with some difficulty a husband, but his role is secondary.

It is worth noting that this woman, who rules over the wind and the lightning, subsists by gathering vegetable foods, grasses, and roots. May we not suppose, in view of this, that the concepts relating to this goddess originated in ancient times when the gathering of plant foods was of substantial importance in feeding the population?

The materials presented allow the conclusion that the Eskimo were matriarchal in the remote past. Survivals of matriarchal structure may be seen also in reported cases when, upon the death of the mother and survival of the father, children were taken over by the relatives of the mother.

The pre-eminence of women under matriarchal conditions among the Eskimos may be hypothesized at the earliest known stages of Eskimo culture, the Uwelen-Okvik and early Old Bering Sea.

Lewis Morgan had rather accurate data on the Eskimo kinship system, collected in part by himself. His Eskimo materials are summarized in his work "Systems of Consanguinity and Affinity of the Human Family" (Morgan 1871: 267). Morgan clearly emphasized the basic features which distinguish the Eskimo kinship system from the Ganowanian, and concluded that it was of the classificatory type, though many of its features are those of the descriptive type. Later (1878), emphasizing that the Eskimos do not belong to the Ganowanian family, he noted that their appearance in America was late or recent relative to that of the Ganowanian family. This view now finds support in archaeological data.

GENERAL CONCLUSIONS

Excavations on the coast of the Chukchi Peninsula have confirmed the supposition, based on chance finds, that the northern Bering Sea region, which includes Bering Strait and its islands, as well as the western and eastern shores of the Chukchi Sea, constituted a single cultural area since early times. It was the focus of the lengthy development and flowering of a specialized culture of sea mammal hunters, which spread subsequently over vast stretches of the arctic coast. Despite the exploratory nature of our investigations on the Chukchi Peninsula, we were able to establish the presence there of all the developmental stages of the culture that we call Eskimo, stages which had been formulated in the researches of American and Danish scientists working on the islands of the northern Bering Sea region as well as on the arctic coast of Alaska. At the same time, the material we have gathered allows, if not the solution, at least the illumination of a number of still controversial problems relating to the history of the population of America and the origin of this remarkable culture of sea mammal hunters.

The oldest known cultural stage of the Bering Sea area is the Uwelen-Okvik. The binomial designation of this phase is due to the fact that its features were first identified at the Okvik site in the Punuk Islands, though it is represented in purer form and more completely in our materials from the ancient site of Uwelen.

The typical semi-subterranean houses and storage pits so characteristic of subsequent phases were not yet present in this period. As a result, cultural deposits dating from that time may be identified only by the greater density of the grass cover that grows over their perfectly even surface. Dwellings at this stage were either above ground or with floors only slightly sunk below ground level, probably round in outline and paved with stones. The main occupation of the inhabitants was sea mammal hunting, though the hunting of land mammals and birds, as well as fishing, were of major importance. At the Uwelen-Okvik stage, we are already faced with an elaborate harpoon complex, which includes harpoon heads of highly intricate design, harpoon floats, and ice picks. It is precisely at this stage that harpoon heads have the most complex basal spur arrangements. They are provided with both side- and end-blades of stone. Apart from sea mammals, bears were also hunted—their bones are found in kitchen refuse. Moreover, deer antler and walrus ivory are widely used in making a variety of implements, such as harpoon heads, arrowheads, fish spear prongs, adze socket pieces, etc.

Arrowheads, identical in form to those found in eastern Siberia at the end of the Neolithic and beginning of the Bronze Age, are no less numerous than harpoon heads and provide additional evidence of the importance of land hunting at this time. We already have specialized multi-prong bird darts and fish spears both one piece and composite for catching large fish of the salmon family. The occurrence of sinkers and of barbs of compound fishhooks indicates that fish were also caught with fish lines. Stone tools are almost all flaked, and rubbed slate implements constitute rare exceptions. Especially characteristic of this stage is the occurrence of stone inset blades on a large number of implements, especially harpoon heads and knives, and of long knives of flint or silicified tuff hafted in bone handles. As in later times, fire was made by drilling. There are many tools of ivory, among them picks and mattocks, wedges, etc. Ivory was the material for very carefully made containers and trough-shaped scrapers for removing fat from intestines. Apparently hunting sleds with ivory runners were already in use. Pottery, if present at all, was very scarce. Uwelen-Okvik art is highly original and distinctive. It is characterized by deeply incised linear designs, by the fashioning of certain objects, among them harpoon heads, to suggest the form of an animal, and by the especially realistic portrayal of the human form. Social organization in this period was of primitive communal type and matriarchy probably prevailed.

The area of distribution of this ancient phase includes the Punuk and St. Lawrence Islands, and, on the mainland of Asia, Cape Chaplin (at least if Rainey is correct in his reference to an unpublished harpoon head of Okvik type in the American Museum of Natural History, brought there by Bogoras from Cape Chaplin), Uwelen in the north, and the eastern site at Nunligran in the south. The collection from the eastern site at Nunligran, as we have seen, is rather small for any definite assertion as to its Uwelen age. Yet, the presence of many forms that are similar or identical to those at Uwelen and the absence of objects typical of later cultural phases such as Old Bering Sea or Punuk suggest that the Nunligran site in question does belong to the phase under discussion. On the arctic coast, this cultural stage is represented at Point Hope by some of the objects from Ipiutak and, perhaps, as far as Point Barrow in the Birnirk complex though not further east. It may have spread westward as far as Cape Baranov and the Medvezhi [Bear] Islands, judging from the harpoon heads found on Chetyrekhstolbovy Island. It is quite probable that an early phase of this culture occurs at Uwelen, and that a later one is represented at Birnirk. The early phase dates from the end of the second and the beginning of the first millenium B.C., and is coeval with the end of the Neolithic and the beginning of Bronze in the Lena River valley. The second phase may be supposed to date from the second half of the first millenium B.C.

The next Old Bering Sea stage takes shape in the last centuries before our era in the north Bering Sea area, perhaps independently, but more probably under stimulation from cultural influences emanating from the south. At this time, people were living already in small quadrangular pit houses with stone floors, log walls, and long and narrow entranceways. The subsistence basis was the hunting of sea mammals, mainly walrus. Bones found in kitchen refuse indicate that the principal food animals were ringed seal, walrus, bearded seal, and whale. The harpoon complex remained essentially the same, though a new form of harpoon head, the so-called Old Bering Sea type, made its appearance, and relatively minor changes occurred in the basic form of the harpoon head types of the preceding stage. Reindeer were hunted inland, though rarely, for artifacts of antler are few. With rare exceptions, all bone artifacts are of ivory. As before, bird darts were used in hunting birds. Dart or harpoon throwers are found for the first time. The simple bow was used, together with a variety of arrows, some intended for warfare, as well as for hunting land animals and birds. We note the first appearance of the bone arrowheads so characteristic of this stage, designed for warfare and equipped with sharp and long barbs at the very base and with stone end-blades. This form is genetically related to the arrowheads of the preceding Uwelen stage, likewise equipped with stone end-blades. To judge from the occurrence of fish spears and the abundance of sinkers, fishing was important, though no whole fishhooks belonging to this stage have been found. It is possible that these were in the form of a simple bone barb inserted in a wooden shank. As in the preceding stage, flaked stone tools of a wide variety of types definitely predominate over tools of ground stone, though the latter, particularly adzes and knives, already appear in substantial numbers. With rare exceptions, stone side-blades occur only on harpoon heads. Both the kayak and the umiak were in use. Sleds with ivory runners were of two kinds: heavy sleds for hauling loads and light hunting sleds. Ice creepers were also known. Pottery vessels and pottery lamps were in general use, though containers of bone and of baleen with wooden bottoms were also used. The Old Bering Sea stage sees the appearance of a distinctive, fully formed, and elaborate type of curvilinear decoration containing a number of design elements unknown at other stages of the maritime culture with which we are concerned. The original social organization of primitive communal type begins to disintegrate at this stage. Separate houses appear, accompanied by individual family food storage pits.

The area of distribution of the Old Bering Sea phase is limited. At the present time, we have knowledge of this phase on the coast of the Chukchi Peninsula from Cape Dezhnev in the north to Cape Bering in the south, as well as on the Punuk, St. Lawrence and Diomede Islands. Isolated objects pertaining to this culture are found along the arctic coast as far west as Cape Baranov, and on Seward Peninsula and in Kotzebue Sound in Alaska.

Simultaneously, the late phase of the Uwelen-Okvik stage continues to exist in its Ipiutak and Birnirk variants from Point Barrow in the east to the mouth of the Kolyma River in the west.

The unusual burial rites at Ipiutak, where burials have been found with artificial eyes of ivory, nose plugs, and mouth covers, indicate Chinese cultural influence in the opinion of Collins, as we have pointed out earlier. This influence would be no earlier in time than the Chou or Han dynasties. This would correspond to a date close to the beginning of our era, that is, to the time of the Old Bering Sea stage. However, there might be some question as to whether it is correct to consider the custom of providing corpses with artificial eyes, of plugging their nostrils, and of fitting them with mouth covers as due to Chinese cultural influence. Would it not be better to connect this custom with influences originating in Oceania and transmitted through the sub-arctic zone of southern Alaska? We will recall that Hrdlička found a skull with inset artificial eyes on Kodiak island. De Laguna, who has excavated in Cook Inlet, also reports this trait.

At about the 3rd or 4th century of our era, connections between the north Bering Sea area and the south apparently cease. However, close contacts are established with northeastern Asia. The appearance at that time on the Bering Sea coast and islands of new weapons and previously unknown cultural traits of clearly western, Siberian, origin is evidence of close cultural contacts. The Punuk cultural stage of the Bering Sea area begins. The mode of life at this stage continues on essentially the same basis as earlier. Houses become larger, but follow the same plan. Whale bones and especially skulls are extensively used as building material, and this, together with the appearance of indisputable whaling harpoon heads, speaks for the fact that whale hunting achieves its maximum development at this stage. In addition to whale, walrus, bearded seal, and ringed seal continue, as before, to be the principal animals hunted. Reindeer is still pursued on the mainland, small animals and a great variety of birds are hunted everywhere, and many kinds of fish are caught, particularly salmon in the lakes and cod and saffron cod ["tomcod"] at sea. Hunting and fishing gear remain essentially the same. We find the same picks and mattocks, wedges, meat hooks, specific knife forms, drills and drill rests, perforators, awls, and women's knives. However, implements of chipped stone are almost entirely replaced by ground stone tools, mainly of slate. While walrus ivory definitely predominates at the Old Bering Sea stage as material for bone objects, bone and, to some degree, antler gain favor again in Punuk. Clay pots and lamps and baleen buckets persist without change. At the same time, a number of traits are modified substantially. This applies in part to harpoon heads, whose design is simplified, as well as to bird darts, arrowheads, fish line sinkers, knives and their handles, sled runners and ice creepers. "Winged" objects, so typical of the preceding stage, disappear and are replaced by so-called "tridents." Art changes radically and, like a number of implements, becomes simpler. On the other hand, many implements of Siberian origin make their appearance. They include the reinforced bow, the wrist guard, armor, certain types of arrows, the bird bola, sealing scratchers, fishhooks, heavy net sinkers of ivory, long knives and daggers of ivory, long-handled spoons of bone and antler, shamans' drums, and engraving with metal tools. This is a period marked by the further decay of primitive communal society.

The area of distribution of Punuk culture is roughly the same as that of Old Bering Sea. On the mainland of Asia, it extends from Cape Dezhnev in the north at least as far as Cape Bering in the south. It includes St. Lawrence as well as the Punuk and Diomede Islands and Point Hope on the arctic coast of America. The Thule stage develops at Point Barrow on the basis of the Birnirk variant. It resembles Punuk in many respects, and spreads eastward along the arctic coast of Canada as far as Greenland at the turn of the 1st and 2nd millenia of our era. Our arctic coast from Cape Dezhnev to the mouth of the Kolyma is still insufficiently known, though it would seem, on the basis of casual finds, that it will yield evidence of Thule rather than Punuk culture.

The latest stage of Eskimo culture, which immediately precedes modern times and begins in the early 17th century, is characterized by the appearance of a relatively small number of new traits. Dog traction appears, and with it, dog sleds with flat bone runner shoes, swivels, and dog harness buckles. We also now get bone umiak keel plates, snow shoes, long unbarbed ivory arrowheads of triangular cross-section, fox traps and bone paddles for erasing tracks after setting them, harpoon end blades of iron, two-handed scrapers for working hides —both of stone and of iron, figures of birds, mammals, and men carved out of ivory, and beads.

Let us now return to the problem of the origin of the ancient culture of sea mammal hunters which, as we saw, developed in the north Bering Sea area and has survived to this day together with the Eskimo people.

The following features are of considerable importance to the problem of the origins of this culture as a whole: (1) bone tools with stone side-blades; (2) the harpoon complex, together with the skin boat, and (3) art.

The equipment of stone tools with stone side-blades is such a characteristic and distinctive feature of the European Mesolithic that the latter involuntarily comes to mind as soon as we come across bone tools with such blades. This parallel also struck me when I first became acquainted with harpoon heads provided with stone blades from the Chukchi Peninsula. It is only natural that Collins should point out the possible significance of the fact that the Old Bering Sea and Birnirk harpoon heads were equipped with stone blades, much in the same way as the bone tools from Maglemose in northern Europe (Collins 1935: 467). He subsequently dwells on this problem at greater length (Collins 1943).

Knives with rows of stone side-blades have been found in America at prehistoric sites in Smith Sound, in western Greenland (Wissler 1918:120–125), on Southampton Island (Boas 1907, Fig. 178), and at ancient sites of the Thule stage in the area of Hudson Bay (Mathiassen 1927; 2:70) and Baffin Island, in Ponds Inlet (Mathiassen 1927; 1, Plate 46:9; Boas 1907, Fig. 179). Knife-handles with a side-slot for a blade or a side-blade are known from Disko Bay in western Greenland (Porsild 1915, Fig. 41E), from northeastern Greenland (Thomsen 1917, Fig. 26), from the well-known Thule site of Naujan (Mathiassen 1927; 1, Plate 18:4), and from St. Lawrence Island (Collins 1937, Plate 38:2,3; Plate 71:1).

These casual finds are in no way typical of the cultural contexts in which they were made, and are not chronologically indicative. It might be supposed that knives with non-ground stone side-blades are older than those with blades of ground slate. Yet knives of the latter type on St. Lawrence Island are attributed by Collins (1943:227; Fig. 3d,e) already to the Old Bering Sea stage. Harpoon heads with stone blades are known only in the Bering Sea area and on the arctic coast of America, at Points Barrow and Hope, and from Uwelen, Point Bolshoy Baranov and the Medvezhi [Bear] Islands in Asia. The only other harpoon head with a side-blade, judging from the slot provided for it, is one described by Mathiassen (1927; 1:209, Plate 61:17) from Bylot Island in the central Arctic.

While knives with stone side-blades occur only sporadically in arctic North America, they are found together with harpoon heads equipped with stone side-blades at Point Barrow and especially at Point Hope, where they are also accompanied by arrowheads similarly armed. Even more significant is the simultaneous occurrence of harpoon heads and knives equipped with side-blades in large numbers at the ancient site of Uwelen.

Even before our discoveries at Uwelen, and basing himself on the bone implements with stone side-blades from Ipiutak and on the knives and darts with stone side-blades typical of the early Neolithic phases (Isakovo and Serovo) discovered by Okladnikov (Okladnikov 1938, 1941) in the Baykal area, Collins made an attempt to trace the diffusion of these implements across the enormous area between Scandinavia and Alaska. His Scandinavian examples include points with stone side-blades from sites of the Maglemose culture in Sweden, Denmark, Belgium, northern Germany, and Estonia, and he refers to the work of Clark (Clark 1936, Figs. 41,47,55b), Madsen (Madsen 1873, Plate 40) and Vebaek (Vebaek 1938, Figs. 1,2).

Collins considers as transitional geographically, and perhaps in time, the arrowheads, dart heads or knives with side-blades from the Pymsha river in the Urals (Tolmachev 1913, Plate 6:8–12), similar dart heads or knives from the Baykal area (Vitkovski 1881, Plate 3:4,6, Okladnikov 1938, Figs. 2,3,7,9), and knives with flint side-blades found by Andersson (1934:230,242,249; Plate 21:1) at the Neolithic site of Yangshao in Kansu and in eastern Tibet. We might add to these finds the remarkable dagger with stone side-blades from a Neolithic burial on Lake Onega (Ravdonikas 1940, Fig. 16), numerous late Neolithic knives and arrowheads with stone side-blades from Shigir and other peat bogs in the eastern Urals, and bone blades with slots for side-blades from Trans-Baykalia (Tolmachev 1929, Plate 1:1).

It would thus seem that we now have better data than before if not for establishing a direct relationship between the Mesolithic and Neolithic cultures of

Northern Europe on the one hand, and the Eskimo on the other, at least for recognizing the survival of the Mesolithic tradition of equipping bone tools with stone side-blades.

Curwen has suggested that the sickles with stone blades from the Swiss pile dwellings and from excavations in Spain, Egypt, and Mesopotamia, like modern Australian knives and spears equipped with a row of small cutting blades along the edges, are survivals among ancient agriculturists and modern hunters of the two universal implements of the Mesolithic, the knife and the spear, both provided with stone side-blades (Curwen 1941). Collins considers this conclusion acceptable with reference to the sickles, but believes that the side-blades of the Australian spears are to be viewed as a case of convergence (Collins 1943:224–225). In any event, as Collins points out, side-blades have not been recorded archaeologically from Oceania. On the other hand, he believes the Eskimo to represent an unadulterated instance of the preservation of this Mesolithic tradition among a hunting people.

First, we must point out one very important feature of stone side-blades, as we know them from the Mesolithic of Europe and western Asia and from the Early Neolithic. The vast majority of these side-blades are in the form of long and narrow flint flakes, detached from prismatic cores. Frequently, such blades, set in rows in slots provided for the purpose in bone implements, lack entirely any evidence of secondary chipping. In some cases, these thin flakes with sharp, longer cutting edges were given a trapezoidal or some other geometric outline, though the working or cutting edge as a rule was not retouched. Blades of this kind were also used to equip bone tools in the Early Neolithic of northern Eurasia, as represented at the burial ground of Oleniy Ostrov, in the Uralian peat bogs and the Angara burials of the Cis-Baykal.

The stone side-blades of Eskimo bone tools, whether harpoon heads, arrowheads, daggers, or knives, are of different form and prepared by a different technique. Long and narrow blades detached from prismatic cores, so characteristic of the Upper Paleolithic of western Europe, and of the Mesolithic and Eneolithic of Eurasia, in use until the beginning of the Bronze Age, are nowhere found among the Eskimos. All the stone side-blades of Eskimo bone tools known to us have the form of almond-shaped arrow points. Sometimes their outline is irregular, but they are always pressure flaked over their entire surface. The long and narrow knife-blades, inserted singly or in pairs so that one of their long sides fits in a rectangular bone handle are also retouched over their entire surface. In cases when bone knives were provided with rows of stone side-blades of almond-shaped or ovate outline as indicated earlier, a separate slot of corresponding shape was carved for each blade, as may be seen in examples from Southampton Island (Boas 1907, Fig. 178) and from Uwelen (Plate 4:2). On the other hand, Mesolithic and Early Neolithic implements of the Old World that are provided with rows of stone side-blades have a single continuous groove designed to hold them.

For this reason, it seems to me that the occurrence of stone side-blades on Eskimo tools in the early phases of Eskimo cultural development is not a convincing argument for connecting genetically Eskimo culture with the Mesolithic and Neolithic cultures of Eurasia. Similarly, I do not believe that these accessories of bone tools can be considered to represent a tradition surviving from the Mesolithic of Europe. Here, as in Australia, we are dealing with a distinct distribution area of the technique of equipping bone implements with stone side-blades. In this connection, it is worth keeping in mind the knife from Disko Bay, in which shark teeth serve as side-blades (Mathiassen 1934, Plate 3:21).

As noted earlier, Jenness and Collins expect to find the ancestors of the Eskimo in northern Siberia. Collins supposes that the dwellings of the direct forebears of the Eskimo will be found north or east of the Baykal, on the shores of rivers or lakes in the forest zone, whence they would have spread gradually to the shores of the Arctic Ocean and Bering Sea. At Bering Strait, an abundant food supply and generally favorable living conditions would have stimulated a sudden flowering of their culture, and the Meso-Neolithic mode of life of the inland hunters was transformed into the sea mammal hunting way of life of the Eskimo (Collins 1943:232–233).

It is curious that none of the foreign authors who have dealt with Eskimo prehistory have thrown the least light on the problem of the switch of inland hunters to sea mammal hunting on the open sea, and under arctic conditions at that.

The exceptionally important cultural traits that alone could ensure subsistence on the coast and islands of the Arctic are those of the harpoon complex, which includes the toggling harpoon and the skin boat. We know that without such devices as the sealskin float, sea mammal hunting on the open sea is unthinkable. We do know of a number of East Siberian tribes, in particular the Itelmens [Kamchadals], who used their wooden boats in hunting sea mammals at the mouths of rivers. However, they did not venture into the open sea. The Arctic does not provide materials for the manufacture of dugouts or birch bark boats with wooden frames of the kind known in the forest zone. In the Arctic, it was possible only to build boats by covering a wooden frame with skin, which replaced either birch bark, or some other kind of bark, or bast, whichever material was used for the purpose by the ancestors of the arctic population prior to their arrival in those extreme latitudes. The umiak and kayak were known to the Eskimos in the Bering Strait area at the earliest known stages of their culture. Without doubt the Eskimos already then were experienced seamen. Where then could their ancestors have perfected their skills which involved not only coastwise, but also open sea travel and, what is more, sea mammal hunting? Would it be at the mouths of rivers, or somewhere further south? In this connection, it is very important to determine the origin and distribution of the toggling harpoon outside of the area occupied by the Eskimo.

On Kamchatka, no sites have been excavated so far yielding evidence of coastal inhabitants for whom sea mammal hunting provided the basis of subsistence. Nevertheless, isolated finds of toggling harpoon heads suggest that a culture related to that of the Eskimo will be discovered in Kamchatka. Toggling harpoon heads have been found in considerable numbers in kitchen middens on the Kuriles and other islands that fringe the eastern coast of the Asiatic continent. Some of them are of simple form, with a bifurcated basal spur and invariably with an open socket. However, harpoon heads with symmetrical trifurcated spurs, similar to those of Old Bering Sea, also occur. Some of them are highly reminiscent both in form and decoration of Okvik harpoon heads and, in particular, of our specimens from the older site at Uwelen.

The oldest harpoon heads known to us from the Bering Sea area are the most complex in form and it is no coincidence that the oldest harpoon heads from the islands to the south of Kamchatka are similarly complex.

Iron toggling harpoon heads, as we know, survived until recent times among the Negritos of the Philippine Islands.

What then is the distribution of toggling harpoon heads in northern Eurasia?

Gjessing (1944:17, Fig. 4) in one of his daring distribution maps, this one dealing with the geographic spread of "Eskimo" harpoons in the arctic area, assigns to them the entire arctic coast of Siberia and Europe from Cape Dezhnev in the east to the straits of the White Sea in the west. However, we do not know of a single find of a toggling harpoon head or of any other evidence of Eskimo culture in northern Asia west of the mouth of the Kolyma River.

It seems appropriate at this point to refer to the results of investigations by A. P. Okladnikov in the Kolyma area in the summer of 1946. From a survey of the Kolyma River valley and of part of the arctic coast from the mouth of that river to Cape Baranov, Okladnikov concluded that the Eskimo culture of Cape Baranov differs in all of its specific features from ancient Koryak culture, as found in the Kolyma valley. He writes in his report:

It is remarkable that the ancient maritime (Eskimo) culture that existed for many centuries in the area of the mouth of the Kolyma should exhibit no direct relationships with the continental Arctic culture which prevailed near it on the lower Kolyma and further west in the forest-tundra zone. It may be assumed, therefore, that the Kolyma valley was the meeting place of two distinct cultures, belonging to ethnic groups of different origin.

The ancient pit houses of hunters, probably Nenets [Samoyed], discovered by Chernetsov on the Yamal Peninsula (Chernetsov 1935) failed to yield a single object typical of Eskimo culture, least of all any toggling harpoon heads.

Similarly, the bone splinters with round perforations from the excavations of Shmidt on Oleniy Island in Kola Bay (Barents Sea) have nothing in common with toggling harpoon heads (Schmidt 1930, Plate 1:6,7). As for the harpoon heads found in Scandinavia (Solberg 1909:38–40, Figs. 39–43; Björn 1930, Fig. 2; Boe 1934, Figs. 14–16), they have little in common with Eskimo types and can throw no light on the problem of the origin of the ancient culture of the Bering Sea area.

Thus, it is to the south, across Kamchatka, to the island chain fringing the continent of Asia on the east, to the area where seamanship and the harpoon complex are developed from early times that we must keep looking to solve the problem of the origin of the ancient culture of the Bering Sea area.

Let us now turn our attention to art. We know now that the fully developed elaborate curvilinear Old Bearing Sea style of engraving on bone was preceded by a simpler style of decoration, the Uwelen or Okvik. Materials are still inadequate to allow a complete characterization of the art of that period or analysis of its style. One fact is beyond doubt: the best examples of plastic art and the most realistic representations of animal and human figures are found precisely in this period. The simple and severe but highly expressive engraving found on various objects either conveys its own independent meaning, or emphasizes specific features of form in the object portrayed. It is often symbolic and even when it seems to be non-objective, it brings out the expressive qualities of the decorated object, by means of decorative techniques that are not haphazard, but rigidly patterned. It is significant that the component elements of this Uwelen decorative style are known outside of Eskimo territory so far only on harpoon heads from the Japanese islands.

The Old Bering Sea style of engraving shares a number of motifs with Uwelen, but is less expressive and more refined. Mature Old Bering Sea Styles 2 and 3 cannot be made to derive from Uwelen-Okvik. They are more elaborate and have many more features in common with the curvilinear decoration of insular Neolithic pottery and with a type of decoration current in Oceania. It is entirely possible that this style came to the Bering Sea area with a new wave of migrants from the south, together with new types of toggling harpoon heads and other cultural traits. Old Bering Sea art, which was considerably more stylized and conventional than the Uwelen style, prevailed in the North Bering Sea area for a time, but did not spread to Alaska or further east. The style gradually plays itself out and merges into Punuk.

The transition from Old Bering Sea to Punuk takes place gradually, by a process of simplification and the replacement of the thin, curvilinear, lightly incised lines with some that are more definite and eventually become quite boldly incised. Then, as metal tools come into use, the style becomes impoverished and mechanical. This process of the replacement of one style by the other is accompanied by the adoption of a number of traits undoubtedly imported from the west, from Siberia, as a result of intimate contact and perhaps of actual mixture with the aboriginal inhabitants of the mainland.

Thus, the history of Eskimo art also points to southern origins, rather than to ancient connections with the west.

As already stated on numerous occasions, the oldest known inhabitants of the North Bering Sea area, the bearers of the Uwelen-Okvik culture, hunted sea mammals, in particular walrus, but also engaged in hunting land mammals, such as deer, the antler of which was used no less than walrus ivory in the manufacture of tools. We still know nothing of the inland population of the Chukchi Peninsula at the time, though certain parallels are emerging already to archaeological finds in the Lena River valley. Therefore, even in those remote times, certain connections begin to appear with the inland peoples of eastern Siberia, though the basic and major connections were with the south, with some as yet undefined cultural center of which Uwelen was an extreme northern outlier. Southern connections are even more strikingly evident at the following Old Bering Sea stage. No evidence of metal has been found yet at either of these two oldest stages of Bering Sea culture, though we find it difficult to conceive how the slots for the socket lashings on the harpoon heads of that time could have been made without a metal tool.

The distinctive check-stamped decoration on pottery in this period occurs, outside of the Bering Sea region, at Late Neolithic and Early Bronze settlements in eastern Siberia. Its distribution is particularly extensive in the Neolithic of southeast Asia and of neighboring islands.

We have seen that the coastal population of the Chukchi Peninsula first enters into close contact with inland groups in the second half of the 1st millenium of our era. Just what events were taking place on the mainland at the time, and why contacts intensified at that time is not known. It is quite possible that it was at this time that some Paleo-Asiatic tribes of the Chukchi-Koryak-Yukagir group shifted to a reindeer-breeding economy, with the resultant acquisition of mobility and opportunities for occupying hitherto uninhabited portions of the Chukchi Peninsula. This would have led to close contacts with the coastal dwellers. Both peaceful and inimical contacts occurred. Inland weapons were adopted by the coastal inhabitants. As a result of warlike encounters and, possibly, the shift of some of the wandering inhabitants of inland regions to a settled life on the sea coast in the second half of the 1st millenium of our era the ancestors of the modern American Eskimos began moving east, and spread over the entire arctic coast of America in the Thule period.

The arctic coast of the Chukchi Peninsula has not yet been investigated archaeologically. While harpoon heads of Birnirk type are known from Chetyrekhstolbovy Island in the Medvezhi [Bear] group and from Cape Bolshoy Baranov, harpoon heads of Thule type thus far have not been reported west of Cape Schmidt.

Everything that we know at the present time concerning the early stages of maritime Eskimo culture leads us to the conclusion that sea mammal hunting culture progressed along the artcic coast of Asia from east to west, and not in the reverse direction.

Everyone is agreed on the fact that the abundance of sea mammals and, in particular, of walrus in the Bering Sea region determined the development and florescence over a long period of Eskimo culture, as we call it today. If such is the case, the distribution of the walrus and of other sea mammals should help us considerably to establish the underlying factors of the present day and former spread of sea mammal hunting groups.

In the extreme northeast of Asia, nearly all the walrus was hunted in the Bering and Chukchi seas, and only a small proportion was obtained in the East Siberian Sea. Walrus were not taken in the Laptev or Okhotsk seas or in the Sea of Japan. Bearded seals were taken in enormous quantities in Bering Sea, in small numbers in the Chukchi Sea, and in fewer numbers still in the East Siberian Sea. Only occasional animals of this species were killed in the Sea of Okhotsk, and none occurred at all in the Sea of Japan. The common seal likewise was hunted mainly in Bering Sea, less so in the Chukchi Sea and in the Sea of Okhotsk. Thus, the Bering and Chukchi seas today, and probably in the past, were the main areas yielding sea mammals. In the East Siberian Sea mammals are very scarce, and only occasional individuals wander into the Laptev Sea. On the other hand, if we turn now to the migration routes of the walrus, the most important of these animals, we see that they lead from the Gulf of Anadyr, where permanent rookeries were numerous in the recent past, along the Chukchi Peninsula between Cape Chaplin and St. Lawrence Island into Bering Strait and further to Wrangel Island in the Chukchi Sea. A permanent rookery is known not far from Uwelen (near Inchoun), and temporary rookeries occur at several points as far as Cape Vankarem. It is important to note that walrus rookeries on the ice shelf in the Bering Sea and in the Chukchi Sea as far as Cape Serdtse-Kamen are usually close to shore, while in the rest of the Chukchi Sea they occur very far out, many tens of kilometers from shore. This feature depends largely on the width of the coastal ice shelf. While the latter is narrow along the Asiatic shore of Bering Sea (usually between 1.5 km to 3 km in width), it attains widths of 30–40 km along the coast of the Chukchi Sea and increases to 120–150 km further west. It is quite obvious that low arctic coasts with shallow water with a coastal ice shelf of enormous width provide conditions for winter hunting that are incomparably worse than in the vicinity of Bering Strait, and that only stringent need could force coastal dwellers to settle on them. What is more, this settlement could take place only on a limited scale. Apparently, there was no stimulus for sea mammal hunters to move westward along the arctic coast of Siberia, and we need not be surprised that remains of Eskimo culture have not been found west of the mouth of the Kolyma River.

Excavations in 1945 on the Chukchi Peninsula and the study of the archaeological collections gathered earlier in the area allow us now to follow the cultural development of the ancient Bering Sea mammal hunters on our continent through all of its stages. A very important event has been the discovery of the Uwelen stage, the earliest known phase, corresponding to Okvik in the Punuk Islands and on St. Lawrence. Though certain connections of this maritime culture with inland groups of eastern Siberia are suggested already in this Uwelen phase, it is not only in the west, in Eurasia, that we should seek its origins. The sea mammal hunting Eskimo appeared relatively late in the Bering Sea area and did indeed constitute a wedge which separated groups, alien to them but related to each other, inhabiting northeast Asia and North America. They came, it would seem, into the Bering Sea region not from the north but from the south, not from the arctic part of Asia, but from its insular southeastern portion.

It was in early times that this culture spread from the Bering Sea region westward along the arctic coast to the mouth of Kolyma and eastward to Point Barrow. The subsequent movement of this culture eastward as far as Greenland occurred only at the end of the 1st and beginning of the 2nd millenia.

Archaeological investigations by Soviet scientists in the extreme northeast of Asia have only begun. The arctic coast between the mouths of the Indigirka and the Kolyma, and the inland portion of the Chukchi Peninsula still remain completely unexplored. Our knowledge is also defective with respect to the arctic coast from the mouth of the Kolyma to Cape Dezhnev, the Chukchi coast of Bering Sea, the coast of Kamchatka and the Kuriles. Nevertheless, it is evident already that it is only on our territory, where the remarkable culture of the daring sea mammal hunters of the Arctic first took form and developed, that the Eskimo problem can be given its definitive solution.

REFERENCES

ANDERSSON, J. G.
  1934. Children of the yellow earth; New York.
BABA, OSAMU
  1934. Archaeological investigations on Shumushu Island (Kuriles); *Journ. Tokyo Anthr. Soc.*, vol. 49, no. 556 (in Japanese).
BERG, L. S.
  1920. Izvestiya o Beringovom prolive i yego beregakh do Beringa i Kuka (Knowledge of Bering Strait and of its shores prior to Bering and Cook). *Zapiski po gidrografii*, vol. II (XLIII), no. 2.
BIRKET-SMITH, KAJ
  1924. Ethnography of the Egedesminde district. *Meddel. Grönland*, bd. 66.
  1929. The Caribou Eskimos. *Report of the Fifth Thule Expedition 1921–1924*, vol. 5. Copenhagen.
  1930. The question of the origin of Eskimo culture: a rejoinder. *Amer. Anthrop.*, n.s. vol. 32, no. 4, October–December.
BIRKET-SMITH, KAJ, AND DE LAGUNA, FREDERIKA
  1938. The Eyak Indians of the Copper River delta, Alaska. Kobenhavn.
BJORN, A.
  1930. Et eiendommelig stenaldersunn fra Serlandt. Univ. Olds. Arb.
BOAS, FRANZ
  1888. The Eskimo. *Proc. and Trans. Roy. Soc. Canada 1887*, vol. 5, sec. 2.
  1905. The Jessup North Pacific Expedition. *13th Intern. Congr. Americanists, New York, 1902*.
  1907. Second report on the Eskimo of Baffin Land and Hudson Bay. *Bull. Amer. Mus. Nat. Hist.*, 15, pt. 2.
BOE, JOHNS
  1934. Boplassen i skipshelleren pa straume i nordhordland. *Bergens Mus. Skrifter*, nr. 17.
BOGORAS, WALDEMAR
  1904–1909. The Chukchee. *Mem. Amer. Mus. Nat. Hist.*, vol. II.
  1925. Early migrations of the Eskimo between Asia and America. *21st Intern. Congr. Americanists*, pt. 2, Göteborg.
  1936. Sotsialny stroy amerikanskikh eskimosov (The social structure of the American Eskimos). *Trudy Instituta Antropologii i Etnografii*, vol. 4.
CHERNETSOV, V. N.
  1935. Drevnyaya primorskaya kultura na poluostrove Yamal (An ancient maritime culture on the Yamal Peninsula). *Sovetskaya Etnografiya*, nos. 4–5.
CLARK, J. G. D.
  1936. The Mesolithic settlement of northern Europe. Cambridge.
COLLINS, HENRY B., JR.
  1928. Check-stamped pottery from Alaska. *Journ. Wash. Acad. Sci.*, vol. 18, no. 9, May 4.
  1929. Prehistoric art of the Alaskan Eskimo. *Smithsonian Misc. Coll.*, vol. 81, no. 14, Nov. 14.
  1935. Archeology of the Bering Strait region. *Ann. Report Smithsonian Inst, 1933*.
  1937. Archeology of St. Lawrence Island, Alaska. *Smithsonian Misc. Coll.* 96 (1).

1940. Outline of Eskimo prehistory. *Smithsonian Misc. Coll.* 100.

1943. Eskimo archeology and its bearing on the problem of man's antiquity in America. *Proceedings of the American Philosophical Society*, vol. 86, no. 2, February.

CRANZ, D.
1770. Historie von Grönland. Barby.

CURWEN, E. CECIL
1941. Some food-gathering implements: a study in Mesolithic tradition. *Antiquity*, 15 (60).

DALL, WILLIAM HEALEY
1878. On the remains of later prehistoric man obtained from Caves in the Catherina Archipelago, Alaska territory, and especially from the caves of the Aleutian islands. *Smithsonian Contributions to Knowledge*, vol. 22, art. VI. Washington.

DAVYDOV, see KHVOSTOV.

DAWKINS, BOYD
1874. Cave hunting. London.

DMITRIEV
1935. Okhota i rybolovstvo v vostochnouralskom rodovom obshchestve (Hunting and gathering in an eastern Ural tribal society). *Izvestia GAIMK*, no. 106.

DUPONT, M. E.
1872. L'homme pendant les ages de la pierre.

EVANS, see STEIN.

FINN, D. J.
1932. Archeological finds on Lamma Island near Hong-Kong. *The Hong-Kong Naturalist*, vol. 3, nos. 3–4, December.

1935. Archeological finds on Lamma Island, pt. 10. *The Hong-Kong Naturalist*, vol. 6, nos. 3–4, December.

GEIST, OTTO WM. AND RAINEY, FORELICH G.
1936. Archaeological excavations at Kukulik, St. Lawrence Island, Alaska. *Misc. Publ. Univ. Alaska*, vol. 2, U.S. Dept. Interior, May 19.

GJESSING, GUTORM
1944. Circumpolar stone age. *Acta Arctica*, fasc. 11. Kobenhavn.

GOLOUBEW, VICTOR
1930. L'age du bronze au Tonkin et dans le Nord-Annam. *Bull. Ecole Française d'Extreme Orient*, 1929, vol. 29. Hanoi.

GORDON, G. B.
1906. Notes on the western Eskimo. *Trans. of the Dept. of Archeology Univ. of Pennsylvania*, vol. 2, pt. 1.

HAMY, E. T.
1870. Précis de paleontologie humaine.

HATT, GUDMUND
1916a. Kyst-og indlandskultur i det arktiske. *Geogr. Tids.*, bd. 23. Copenhagen.

1916b. Mocassins and their relation to Arctic footwear. *Mem. Amer. Anthropol. Assoc.*, vol. 3, no. 3, July–September.

HOFFMAN, WALDER JAMES
1897. The graphic art of the Eskimos. *Smithsonian Ann. Report 1895*.

HOLMES, W. H.
1897. Stone implements of the Potomac-Chesapeake tidewater province. *15th Annual Report of the Bureau of Amer. Ethnol.* Washington.

HOLTVED, ERIK
1938. Forelobing beretning om den arkaeologisk etnografiske expedition til Thule Distriktet, 1935–37. *Geogr. Tids.*, vol. 41.

HOOPER, C. L.
1884. Report on the cruise of the U.S. Revenue Steamer "Corwin" in the Arctic Ocean, 1881. Washington.

182 S. I. Rudenko

HOUGH, WALTER
1895. Primitive American armor. *Ann. Report U.S. Nat. Mus. 1893.*
HRDLIČKA, ALES
1930. Anthropological survey in Alaska. *46th Ann. Report Bureau Amer. Ethnol.*, Washington.
1933. Anthropological explorations on Kodiak island, Alaska. *Explorations and Fieldwork of the Smithsonian Institution, 1932.*
1935. Archeological excavations on Kodiak Island. *Explorations and Fieldwork of the Smithsonian Institution, 1934.*
JENNESS, DIAMOND
1925. A new Eskimo culture in Hudson Bay. *Geogr. Rev.*, vol. 15, no. 3, July.
1928a. Archeological investigations in Bering Strait. *Nat. Mus. Canada, Ann. Report 1926*, Bull. 50, Ottawa.
1928b. Ethnological problems of Arctic America. *Amer. Geogr. Soc., Special Publ. No. 7.*
1933. The problem of the Eskimo. The American aborigines, their origin and antiquity. Univ. Toronto Press.
1940. Prehistoric culture waves from Asia to America. *Journ. Washington Acad. Sci.*, vol. 30, no. 1.
JOCHELSON, WALDEMAR
1905–1908. The Koryak. *Mem. Amer. Mus. Nat. Hist.*, vol. 10.
KHVOSTOV AND DAVYDOV
1912. Dvukratnoye puteshestviye v Ameriku (A twice repeated voyage to America).
KISHINOUYE, KAMAKICHI
1911. Prehistoric fishing in Japan. *Journ. Coll. Agric.; Imp. Univ. Tokyo*, vol. 2, no. 7, Dec. 26.
KRASHENNINIKOV, S.
1755. A description of the land of Kamchatka.
KROEBER, A. L.
1923. Anthropology. New York.
KUMLIEN, L.
1879. Contributions to the natural history of America, made in connection with the Hawgate polar expedition 1877–78. *Bull. of the U.S. Nat. Mus.*, no. 15. Washington.
LAGUNA, FREDERICA DE
1932–1933. A comparison of Eskimo and Paleolithic art. *Amer. Journ. Archaeol.*, vol. 36, no. 4, Oct.–Dec., and vol. 37, no. 1, Jan.–Mar.
1934. The archeology of Cook Inlet, Alaska. Philadelphia.
1938. See Birket-Smith.
LARSEN, HELGE
1934. Dodemandsbugten. An Eskimo settlement on Clavering island. *Meddel. Grönland*, vol. 102, no. 1. Copenhagen.
1938. Archaeological investigations on Knud Rasmussen's Land. *Meddel. Grönland*, vol. 119, no. 8. Copenhagen.
LAUFER, BERTHOLD
1912. Jade. A study in Chinese archeology and religion. *Field Mus. Nat. Hist., Anthrop. Ser.*, vol. 10, publ. 154.
1914. Chinese clay figures. *Field Mus. Nat. Hist., Anthrop. Ser.*, vol. 13, no. 2, publ. 177.
MACHINSKI, A. V.
1941. Drevnyaya eskimosskaya kultura na Chukotskom poluostrove (Ancient Eskimo culture on the Chukchi Peninsula). *Kratkiye Soobshcheniya IIMK Akademii Nauk SSSR*, no. 9.
MACRITCHIE, DAVID
1912. The Kayak in northwestern Europe. *Journ. Roy. Anthrop. Institute*, vol. 42.

MADSEN, A. P.
1873. Antiquités prehistoriques du Danemark. Copenhagen.
MARKHAM, C. H.
1865. On the origin and migrations of the Eskimos. *Journ. Roy. Geogr. Soc.*, vol. 35.
MASON, J. ALDEN
1930. Excavations of Eskimo Thule culture sites at Point Barrow, Alaska. *Proc. 23rd Congr. Americanists*, New York.
MASON, OTIS T.
1891. Ulu or woman's knife of the Eskimo. *Ann. Report U.S. Nat. Mus., 1890*.
1894. North American bows, arrows and quivers. *Ann. Report Smithsonian Inst., 1893*. Washington.
1902. Aboriginal American harpoons. *Ann. Report U.S. Nat. Mus., 1900*.
MATHIASSEN, THERKEL
1927. Archaeology of the Central Eskimos. *Report of the Fifth Thule Exped. 1921–24*, vol. 4. Copenhagen.
1929. Some specimens from the Bering Sea culture. *Indian Notes Mus. Amer. Indian, Heye Foundation*, vol. 6, no. 1. January.
1930a. Archaeological collections from the Western Eskimos. *Report of the Fifth Thule Exped. 1921–24*, vol. 10, no. 1. Copenhagen.
1930b. Inugsuk, a medieval Eskimo settlement in Upernivik District, West Greenland. *Meddel. Grönland*, vol. 77. Copenhagen.
1930c. The question of the origin of Eskimo culture. *Amer. Anthrop.*, n.s., vol. 32, no. 4, October–December.
1931. Ancient Eskimo settlements in the Kangamiut area. *Meddel. Grönland*, bd. 91, no. 1. Copenhagen.
1934. Contributions to the archaeology of Disko Bay. *Meddel. Grönland*, vol. 93, no. 2. Copenhagen.
1936. (In collaboration with Eric Holtved). The Eskimo archaeology of Juliane-haab District with a brief summary of the prehistory of the Greenlanders. *Meddel. Grönland*, vol. 118, no. 1. Copenhagen.
MORGAN, L.
1871. Systems of Consanguinity and Affinity in the Human Family. *Smithsonian Contributions to Knowledge*, vol. 17.
MURDOCH, JOHN
1884. A study of the Eskimo bows in the U.S. National Museum. *Report U.S. Nat. Mus.*
1888. Henry Rink: The Eskimo tribes (review). *Amer. Anthrop.*, o.s., vol. 1.
1892. Ethnological results of the Point Barrow expedition. *9th Ann. Report Bureau of Amer. Ethnol.* Washington.
NELSON, EDWARD WILLIAM
1899. The Eskimo about Bering Strait. *18th Ann. Report Bureau of Amer. Ethnol.* Washington.
NORDENSKIÖLD, A. E.
1882. Die Umsegelung Asiens und Europas auf der Vega 1878–1880. Leipzig.
NORDENSKIÖLD, E.
1931. Origin of the Indian civilisation in South America. *Comparative ethnographic studies*, vol. 9.
OKLADNIKOV, A. P.
1935. Buret, novaya paleoliticheskaya stoyanka na Angare (Buret, a new paleolithic site on the Angara river). *Sovetskaya arkheologiya*, vol. 1.
1938. Arkheologicheskiye damnyye o drevneyshey istorii Pribaykalya (Archaeological data on the ancient history of the Baykal area). *Vestnik drevney istorii*, no. 1(2).
1939. Neolit Sibiri i Dalnego Vostoka. Sever Sibiri v pervom tysyacheletii n. e. (The Neolithic of Siberia and of the Far East. Northern Siberia in the first millenium of our era). *Istoriya SSSR*, chap. 1–4.

1941a. Neoliticheskiye pamyatniki kak istochniki dlya etnogenii Sibiri i Dalnego Vostoka (Neolithic sites as sources for the ethnic history of Siberia and the Far East. *Kratkiye Soobshcheniya IIMK Akademii Nauk SSSR*, no. 9.

1941b. Paleoliticheskiye zhilischa v Bureti (Paleolithic dwellings at Buret). *Kratkiye Soobshcheniya IIMK Akademii Nauk SSSR*, no. 10.

1944. Arkheologicheskiye pamyatniki i drevniye kultury na nizhney Lene (Archaeological sites and ancient cultures on the lower Lena). *Uchenye zapiski Yakutskogo pedinstituta.*

1946. Lenskiye drvenosti (Lena Antiquities). *Materialy po drevney istorii Yakutii*, no. 2. Yakutsk.

PARRY, W. E.
1924. Journal of a second voyage for the discovery of a northwest passage from the Atlantic to the Pacific. London.

PINART, A. L.
1875. La caverne d'Aknank, ile d'Ounga, Archipel Shumagin, Alaska. Paris.

PORSILD, MORTEN P.
1915. Studies on the material culture of the Eskimo in West Greenland. *Meddel. Grönland*, vol. 51.

PROKOSHEV, N. A.
1940. Resultaty issledovaniy pozdnikh neoliticheskikh stoyanok v ustye reki Chusovoy (Results of investigations of late Neolithic sites at the mouth of Chusovaya River). *Trudy Komissii po izucheniyu chetvertichnogo perioda*, nos. 6–7.

RAINEY, FORELICH G.
1936. See Geist.

1937. Old Eskimo art. *Natural History*, vol. 40. New York.

1941a. A new form of culture on the Arctic coast. *Proc. Nat. Academy of Sciences*, vol. 27. Washington.

1941. The Ipiutak culture at Point Hope, Alaska. *Amer. Anthrop.*, 43(3), pt. 1.

1941c. Mystery people of the Arctic. *Natural History*, vol. 47(3).

1941d. Eskimo prehistory: the Okvik site on the Punuk islands. *Anthropol. Papers Amer. Mus. of Nat. Hist.*, vol. 37, pt. IV.

1942. Discovering Alaska's oldest Arctic town. *The National Geographic Soc.*, September.

RAVDONIKAS, V. I.
1940. Oleneostrovskiy mogilnik (The Oleniy Ostrov burial ground). *Sovetskaya Arkheologiya*, no. 6.

RINK, HENRY
1887. The Eskimo tribes. *Meddel. Grönland*, vol. 11. Copenhagen and London.

RIVET, P.
1925. Les origines de l'homme Americain. *L'Anthropologie*, t. 35.

RUDENKO, S. I.
1910. see Volkov.

1947. Drevniye nakonechniki garpunov aziatskikh Eskimosov (Ancient harpoon heads of the Asiatic Eskimos). *Trudy Instituta Etnografii*, n.s., vol. 2.

SARASIN, FRITZ
1933. Recherches prehistoriques au Siam. *L'Anthropologie*, t. 43, 1–2.

SARYCHEV
1811. Puteshestviye kapitana Billingsa cherez Chukotskuyu zemlyu (The journey of Captain Billings through the Chukchi land).

SCHRENK
1883. Ob inorodtsakh Amurskogo kraya (The natives of Amur kray).

SCHMIDT, A. V.
1931. Drevniy mogilnik na Kolskom zalive (An ancient burial ground on Kola Bay). *Materialy Komissii eksp. issl. Akademii Nauk SSSR*, no. 23.

SHNAKENBURG, N. B.
  MS. Eskimosy (The Eskimo, 1932).
SOLBERG, O.
  1907. Beiträge zur Vorgeschichte der Osteskimo. *Vid. Selsk. Skrifter*, 11, Hist.
    Filos. Klasse, no. 2, Christiania.
  1909. Eisenzeitfunde aus Ostfinmarken. *Lappländische studien.* Christiania.
SOLLAS, W. J.
  1911. Ancient hunters and their modern representatives. London.
STEENSBY, H. P.
  1916. An anthropogeographical study of the origin of the Eskimo culture.
    Meddel. Grönland, vol. 53, Copenhagen.
STEFFANSSON, EVELYN
  1944. Within the Circle. Portraits of the Arctic. New York.
STEFFANSSON, VILHJALMUR
  1914. Prehistoric and present commerce among the Arctic coast Eskimo.
    C. G. S. Mus. Bull., no. 6, Anthrop. Ser. no. 3, Ottawa.
STEIN CALLENFELS (P. V. VAN) AND EVANS (J. H. N.)
  1928. Report on cave explorations in Perak. *Journal of the Federated Malay
    States Museums,* vol. 12, pt. VI.
SVERDRUP, G. U.
  1930. Plavaniye na sudne "Mod" v vodakh morey Laptevykh i Vostochno-
    Sibirskogo (The cruise of the ship "Maud" in the Laptev and East
    Siberian Seas). *Materialy Komissii po izucheniyu Yakutskoy ASSR,* no. 30.
THALBITZER, WILLIAM
  1904. A phonetical study of the Eskimo language. *Meddel. Grönland,* vol. 31.
    Copenhagen.
  1914. The Ammassalik Eskimo. *Meddel. Grönland,* vol. 39, pt. 1. Copenhagen.

THOMSEN, THOMAS
  1917. Implements and artifacts of the northeast Greenlanders. *Meddel. Grön-
    land,* vol. 44.
  1928. Eskimo archaeology. *Greenland,* vol. 2. Copenhagen.
TOLMACHEV, V.
  1913–1914. Drevnosti vostochnogo Urala (Antiquities of the eastern Urals).
    Zap. Uralskogo o-va lyubiteley yestestvoznaniya, nos. 32 and 34. Yeka-
    terinburg.
  1929. Predmety kostyanogo veka (Objects of the bone age) *Soobshcheniya
    GAIMK,* no. 2.
TORII, R.
  1919. Etudes archeologiques et ethnographiques. Les Ainus des iles Kouriles.
    Journ. Coll. Sci. Imper. Univ. Tokyo, vol. 42, no. 1.
TURNER, LUCIEN M.
  1894. Ethnology of the Ungava District, Hudson Bay Territory. *11th Ann.
    Report Bureau of Amer. Ethnol.*
UKHTOMSKIY, D. E.
  1913. Chukotskiye strely (Chukchi arrows). *Yezhegodnik Russk. Antrop. o-va
    pri SPb. Universitete,* vol. 3.
UMEHARA, S.
  1934. Official report of excavations at the prehistoric site of Kokura, Kitashira-
    kawa, Kyoto (in Japanese).
VEBAEK, C. L.
  1938. New finds of Mesolithic ornamented bone and antler artifacts in Den-
    mark. *Acta Archaeologica,* 9, no. 3.
VENIAMINOV
  1840. Zapiski ob ostrovakh Unalashkinskogo otdela (Notes on the islands of
    the Unalaska district).

VITKOVSKIY, N. M.
  1881. Kratkoye soobshcheniye o raskopkakh pogrebeniy kamennogo veka v
        Irkutskoy gubernii v 1880 g. (Brief communication on excavations of
        stone age burials in the Guberniya of Irkutsk in 1880). *Zap. Vost.-Sib.
        otd. I. Russk. geogr. o-va*, vol. 11.
  1889. Sledy kamennogo veka v doline r. Angary (Traces of the stone age in the
        Angara River valley). *Izvestiya Vost.-Sib. otd. Russk. geogr. o-va*, vol.
        20, no. 1–2.
VOLKOV, F. K. AND RUDENKO, S. I.
  1910. Etnograficheskiye kollektsii iz byvshikh rossiysko-amerikanskikh vladeniy
        (Ethnographic collections from former Russian possessions in America).
        Materialy po etnografii, vol. 1.
WEYER, EDWARD MOFFAT JR.
  1930. Archeological material from the village site at Hot Springs, Port Möller,
        Alaska. *Anthropol. Papers Amer. Mus. Nat. Hist.*, vol. 31, pt. 4, New
        York.
WILSON, THOMAS
  1897. Arrowpoints, spearheads and knives of prehistoric times. *U.S. Nat. Mus.
        Report*, pt. 1.
WINTEMBERG, W. J.
  1939. Eskimo sites of the Dorset culture in Newfoundland, parts 1 and 2.
        American Antiquity, vol. 5.
WISSLER, CLARK
  1916. Harpoons and darts in the Stefansson collection. *Anthrop. Papers Amer.
        Mus. Nat. Hist.*, vol. 14, pt. 2.
  1918. Archeology of the Polar Eskimo. *Anthrop. Papers Amer. Mus. Nat. Hist.*,
        vol. 22, pt. 3.
WONG, K. C.
  1932. Ancient Chinese jades. *China Journ.*, 16(2).
WRANGEL, F.
  1841. Puteshestviye po severnym beregam Sibiri i po Ledovitomu moryu, sover-
        shennoye v 1820–1824 gg. (Voyage along the northern shores of Siberia
        and in the Arctic Ocean in 1820–1824).
ZAGOSKIN
  1847. Peshekhodnaya opis chasti russkikh vladeniy v Amerike (A survey on
        foot of part of the Russian possessions in America).
ZOLOTAREV, A.
  1937. K voprosu o proiskhozhednii eskimosov (The problem of the origin of
        the Eskimo). *Antropologicheskiy Zhurnal*, no. 1.
  1938a. Iz istorii etnicheskikh vzaimootnosheniy na severo-vostoke Azii (Con-
        cerning the history of ethnic inter-relations in northeast Asia). *Izvestiya
        Voronezhskogo gos. ped. instituta*, vol. 4.
  1938b. The ancient culture of North Asia. *Amer. Anthropol.*, vol. 40, no. 1.

PLATES

PLATES

PLATE 1. EXCAVATIONS AT UWELEN — ⅓ size

1. Harpoon head, antler
2. Harpoon head, antler
3. Harpoon head, antler
4. Harpoon head, ivory
5. Harpoon head, antler
6. Harpoon head, antler
7. Harpoon head, antler
8. Harpoon head, antler
9. Harpoon head, ivory
10. Harpoon head, ivory
11. Harpoon head, ivory
12. Harpoon head, ivory
13. Harpoon head, ivory
14. Harpoon head, ivory
15. Harpoon head, ivory
16. Harpoon head, ivory
17. Harpoon head blank
18. Float plug, ivory
19. Float bar, ivory
20. Harpoon head blank
21. Harpoon foreshaft, ivory
22. Harpoon ice pick, ivory
23. Harpoon ice pick, ivory
24. Harpoon head blank

PLATE 2. EXCAVATIONS AT UWELEN. Nos. 1–27 — ⅓ size; Nos. 28–30 — ⅛ size

1. Arrowhead, bone
2. Arrowhead bone
3. Arrowhead, bone
4. Arrowhead, bone
5. Arrowhead, bone
6. Arrowhead, bone
7. Arrowhead, bone
8. Arrowhead, bone
9. Arrowhead, bone
10. Arrowhead, bone
11. Dart center-prong, bone
12. Bird dart center-prong, ivory
13. Bird dart center-prong, ivory
14. Snow goggles, bone
15. Dart center prong, bone
16. Side-prong of bird dart, bone
17. Side-prong of bird dart, bone
18. Side-prong of bird dart, ivory
19. Harpoon head, antler
20. Salmon spear barb, bone
21. Salmon spear barb, ivory
22. Fish line sinker, bone
23. Fish line sinker, bone
24. Fishhook barb, ivory
25. Hook, antler
26. Fish spear prong, antler
27. Fish line sinker, ivory
28. Mattock, ivory
29. Mattock, ivory
30. Mattock, ivory

PLATE 3. EXCAVATIONS AT UWELEN — ⅓ size

1. Ice staff ferrule, ivory
2. Ice staff ferrule, ivory
3. Drill end, bone
4. Drill end, bone
5. Awl, ivory
6. Wedge, ivory
7. Wedge, ivory
8. Adze socket piece, antler
9. Adze socket piece, bone
10. Reamer, bone
11. Awl, bone
12. Knife, bone
13. Stem of bone knife
14. Drill rest, bone
15. Knife-blade, slate
16. Knife-blade, slate
17. Slate knife in ivory handle
18. Knife-handle, ivory
19. Knife-handle, ivory
20. Knife-handle, ivory
21. Knife-blade, siliceous slate
22. Knife-blade, flint
23. Knife-handle, ivory
24. Knife-handle, deer antler
25. Knife-handle, ivory
26. Knife-handle, ivory
27. Knife-handle, ivory

PLATE 4. EXCAVATIONS AT UWELEN. Nos. 1–7, 9–25 — ⅓ size; No. 8 — ¾ size

1. Knife-handle, wood
2. Knife-handle, ivory
3. Knife-handle, ivory
4. Knife-handle, ivory
5. Knife-handle, ivory
6. Knife-handle, ivory

7. Human figure, ivory
8. Polar bear figure, ivory
9. Pendant, wood
10. Human head, ivory
11. Button or bead, ivory
12. Button or bead, ivory
13. Fat scraper, ivory
14. Cap, ivory
15. Tube, ivory
16. Harpoon head, ivory

17. Twister (?), ivory
18. Object of unknown function, ivory
19. Fat scraper, ivory
20. Fastener (?), ivory
21. Fastener, bone
22. Handle of woman's bag, ivory
23. Drag line handle, ivory
24. Decorated object, ivory
25. Ivory slab for decorating pottery

PLATE 5. EXCAVATIONS OF HOUSE AT UWELEN — ⅓ size

1. Harpoon head, ivory
2. Harpoon head, ivory
3. Harpoon head, bone
4. Harpoon head, bone
5. Harpoon head, ivory
6. Whaling harpoon head, ivory
7. Harpoon socket piece, ivory
8. Harpoon ice pick, ivory
9. Model of bow, wood
10. Part of composite bow, wood
11. Distal end of arrow, wood
12. Distal end of arrow, wood
13. Arrowhead, ivory

14. Arrowhead, ivory
15. Bird bola weight, ivory
16. Harpoon socket piece, ivory
17. Wooden spindle for fire-making
18. Float bar, wood
19. Butt end of arrow, wood
20. Drill rest, stone
21. Fish spear prong, ivory
22. Wedge, ivory
23. Wedge, ivory
24. Net sinker, ivory
25. Knife-blade, ivory

PLATE 6. EXCAVATIONS OF HOUSE AT UWELEN — ⅓ size

1. Adze socket piece, antler
2. Adze socket piece, bone
3. Knife-blade, unfinished, silicified tuff
4. Fragment of slate knife
5. Woman's knife, argillaceous slate
6. Boat hook (?), ivory
7. Knife-handle, bone
8. Wooden bottom of baleen vessel
9. Fragment of wooden vessel, handle
10. Wooden model of kayak
11. Bone ornament
12. Bone ornament

13. Spoon, bone
14. Human figure, cut out of larch bark
15. Figure of fox, ivory
16. Knife-handle, wood
17. Armor plate, bone
18. Armor plate, bone
19. Umiak keel plate, bone
20. Back scratcher, ivory
21. Nail (?), wood
22. Back-scratcher, baleen
23. Block of ivory, part of umiak rigging

PLATE 7. CAPE DEZHNEV AREA — ⅓ size

1. Harpoon head, ivory
2. Harpoon head, ivory
3. Harpoon head, ivory
4. Harpoon head, ivory
5. Harpoon head, ivory
6. Harpoon head, ivory
7. Harpoon head, ivory
8. Harpoon head, ivory
9. Harpoon head, bone
10. Harpoon head, antler
11. Fragment of harpoon head, ivory
12. Damaged harpoon head, ivory
13. Harpoon head, ivory

14. Harpoon head blank
15. Harpoon head blank
16. Harpoon head, ivory
17. Harpoon head, ivory
18. Harpoon head, ivory
19. Harpoon head, deer antler
20. Fragment of harpoon head, ivory
21. Harpoon head, ivory
22. Harpoon head, ivory
23. Harpoon head, ivory
24. Harpoon head, ivory
25. Fragment of harpoon head, ivory

PLATE 8. CAPE DEZHNEV AREA — ⅓ size

1. Whaling harpoon head, ivory
2. Harpoon foreshaft, ivory
3. Harpoon ice pick, ivory
4. Harpoon ice pick, ivory
5. Harpoon ice pick, ivory

6. Harpoon ice pick, ivory
7. Wound pin, ivory
8. Boat hook, ivory
9. Center-prong of bird dart, ivory
10. Center-prong of bird dart, ivory

11. Fish spear barb, ivory
12. Fish spear barb, ivory
13. Dart or fish spear point, ivory
14. Spear head, argillaceous slate
15. Spear head, silicified tuff
16. Woman's knife in ivory handle
17. Knife, slate
18. Knife, flint

PLATE 9.   CAPE DEZHNEV AREA — ⅓ size

1. Knife-handle, bone, Dezhnevo
2. Scraper plane, siliceous slate, Dezhnevo
3. Harpoon head, ivory
4. Harpoon head, ivory
5. Harpoon head, ivory
6. Whaling harpoon head (?), ivory
7. Paddle, ivory
8. Harpoon head, ivory
9. Bear figure, ivory
10. Object of unknown function. Nuukan
11. Winged object, ivory. Dezhnevo

PLATE 10.   EXCAVATIONS AT NUUKAN — ⅓ size

1. Harpoon head, bone
2. Harpoon head, ivory
3. Harpoon head, ivory
4. Slate end-blade of whaling harpoon head
5. Slate end-blade of harpoon head
6. Harpoon foreshaft, ivory
7. Harpoon foreshaft, ivory
8. Harpoon ice pick, ivory
9. Arrowhead, bone
10. Arrow point, flint
11. Adze, nephrite
12. Bird bola weight, ivory
13. Wrist guard, baleen
14. Arrow, wood
15. Sinker, ivory
16. Pick, bone
17. Adze, slate
18. Adze, deer antler
19. Net sinker, ivory
20. Scraper, slate, with wooden handle

PLATE 11.   EXCAVATIONS AT NUUKAN — ⅓ size

1. Knife, flint
2. Knife, slate
3. Knife, slate
4. Fragment of slate knife
5. Knife-handle, wood
6. Wooden spindle for fire-making
7. Awl, ivory
8. Drill end, bone
9. Harpoon float mouthpiece, ivory
10. Bird bola weight, ivory
11. Harpoon finger rest, ivory
12. Handle of woman's knife, wood
13. Drill rest, ivory
14. Bull-roarer, baleen
15. Block, ivory
16. Block, ivory
17. Drill rest, ivory
18. Drill rest, ivory
19. Hearth for fire-making
20. Dipper, wood
21. Ladle, wood
22. Float, wood
23. Drum handle, bone
24. Drum handle, bone

PLATE 12.   EXCAVATIONS AT YANDYGAY AND ON ARAKAMCHECHEN ISLAND.
Nos. 1–20, 23–25, 27 — ⅓ size; Nos. 21, 22, 26, 28 — ⅙ size

1. Arrowhead, bone. Yandygay
2. Arrowhead, ivory. Yandygay
3. Fragment of arrow, wood. Yandygay
4. Harpoon head, bone. Yandygay
5. Line sinker, ivory. Yandygay
6. Mattock, ivory. Yandygay
7. Handle, bone. Yandygay
8. Whaling harpoon head, ivory. Arakamchechen I.
9. Harpoon head, bone. Arakamchechen I.
10. Bow drill, antler. Yandygay
11. Comb, ivory. Yandygay
12. Handle of woman's knife, wood. Yandygay
13. Handle of woman's knife, wood. Yandygay
14. Fastener, ivory. Arakamchechen I.
15. Bird bola weight, walrus tooth. Arakamchechen I.
16. Wedge, ivory. Arakamchechen I.
17. Center-prong of fish spear, ivory.
18. Side-prong of fish spear, ivory. Arakamchechen I.
19. Scraper, bone. Arakamchechen I.
20. Harpoon head, ivory. Arakamchechen I.
21. Pick, bone. Arakamchechen I.
22. Mattock, bone. Arakamchechen I.
23. Handle of woman's knife, bone. Arakamchechen I.
24. Awl, ivory. Arakamchechen I.
25. Awl, ivory. Arakamchechen I.
26. Sinker of hoop net, granite. Arakamchechen I.
27. Umiak keel plate, bone. Arakamchechen I. Arakamchechen I.

PLATE 13. Excavations at Cape Chaplin — ⅓ size

1. Harpoon head, ivory
2. Harpoon head, ivory
3. Harpoon head, bone
4. Harpoon head, bone
5. Harpoon head, ivory
6. Harpoon socket piece, ivory
7. Whaling harpoon head, ivory
8. Harpoon ice pick, ivory
9. Arrowhead, ivory
10. Arrowhead, bone
11. Arrowhead, bone.
12. Twister, wood
13. Blunt arrowhead, bone
14. Bird bola weight, ivory
15. Bird bola weight, ivory
16. Wrist guard, bone
17. Part of composite bow
18. Bird bola weight, ivory
19. Bird bola weight, ivory
20. Harpoon head, bone
21. Fishhook barb, ivory
22. Paddle, ivory
23. Bone brace, part of compound bow
24. Netting shuttle, bone
25. Bone handle of woman's bag

PLATE 14. Excavations at Cape Chaplin — ⅓ size

1. Spear point, flint
2. Knife, silicified tuff
3. Woman's knife, slate
4. Knife-handle, bone
5. Ice creeper, ivory
6. Unfinished knife-blade, slate
7. Fragment of knife-handle, bone
8. Scraper, bone
9. Adze, stone
10. Ice creeper, ivory
11. Whetstone, sandstone
12. Spoon, deer antler
13. Spoon, deer antler
14. Knife, ivory
15. Knife, bone
16. Dart head, bone
17. Knife-handle, bone
18. Knife-handle, deer antler
19. Knife-handle, deer antler
20. Awl or punch, bone

PLATE 15. Excavations at Cape Chaplin — ⅙ size

1. Device for gathering seaweed
2. Pick, deer antler
3. Pick, bone
4. Mattock, ivory
5. Wedge, ivory
6. Mattock, ivory
7. Hammerstone, granite
8. Box, baleen
9. Bottom of box, baleen
10. Bow drill, bone
11. Mallet, ivory
12. Sled runner, ivory
13. Sled runner, ivory
14. Scoop of antler palm
15. Hook, antler tine
16. Hook, antler tine
17. Umiak keel plate, bone
18. Shovel, bone
19. Armor plate, bone

PLATE 16. Excavations at Cape Chaplin — ⅓ size

1. Model of oar, wood
2. Awl or punch, bone
3. Awl or punch, bone
4. Needle-case, bone
5. Block, bone
6. Drum handle, wood
7. Drum handle, bone
8. Knife (?), baleen
9. Plaited baleen
10. Back-scratcher, ivory
11. Fastener, wood
12. Bear figure, ivory
13. Dog canine pendant
14. Comb, ivory
15. Armor plate, bone
16. Walrus tusk pendant
17. Bear canine pendant
18. Float, wood
19. Human figure cut out of bark
20. Human figure, wood

PLATE 17. Excavations at Kiwak and at Cape Chukchi.
Nos. 1–19, 21–23, 27 — ⅓ size; Nos. 20, 24, 25, 28, 29 — ⅙ size

1. Arrowhead, bone. Kiwak
2. Dart head, ivory. Kiwak
3. Arrowhead, bone. Kiwak
4. Harpoon ice pick, ivory. Kiwak
5. Fragment of spear point, slate. Kiwak
6. Knife-blade, slate. Kiwak
7. Knife-blade, slate. Kiwak
8. Knife-blade, silicified tuff. Kiwak
9. Knife-blade, slate. Kiwak
10. Knife-blade, slate. Kiwak
11. Fragment of woman's knife, slate. Kiwak
12. Woman's knife, slate. Kiwak

13. Float, wood, red. Kiwak
14. Fragment of winged object, ivory. **Kiwak**
15. Pottery sherd. Kiwak
16. Spoon, bone. Kiwak
17. Adze, stone. Cape Chukchi
18. Adze, stone. Cape Chukchi
19. Pottery sherd. Kiwak
20. Hook, deer antler. Kiwak
21. Adze, nephrite. Kiwak

22. Knife, slate. Cape Chukchi
23. Handle, wood. Kiwak
24. Drill shaft, os penis of walrus. **Kiwak**
25. Mattock, ivory. Kiwak
26. Bone twister in baleen holder. Cape Chukchi
27. Fish (?), baleen. Cape Chukchi
28. Sled runner, ivory. Kiwak
29. Wedge, ivory. Cape Chukchi

PLATE 18. EXCAVATIONS AT AVAN AND IN PLOVER BAY.
Nos. 1–20, 22–24 – ⅓ size; No. 21 – ⅛ size

1. Whaling harpoon head, ivory. Avan
2. Harpoon end-blade, slate. Avan
5. Toggle, bone. Avan
6. Scraper, flint. Plover Bay
7. Scraper, obsidian. Plover Bay
8. Arrow point, silicified tuff. Plover Bay
9. Knife, slate. Plover Bay
10. Harpoon end-blade, slate. Avan
11. Knife, slate. Avan
12. Adze, sandstone. Avan
13. Sled runner, ivory. Plover Bay
14. Fragment of arrow, wood. Avan

3. Knife, slate. Avan
4. Knife, slate. Avan
15. Dog clavicle. Avan
16. Woman's knife, slate. Avan
17. Woman's knife, slate. Avan
18. Snow goggles, ivory. Avan
19. Hearth for fire-making. Avan
20. Knot of baleen. Avan
21. Pick, bone. Avan
22. Armor plate, bone. Avan
23. Pottery sherd. Avan
24. Hook, deer antler. Avan

PLATE 19. EXCAVATIONS AT SIRHENIK – ⅓ size

1. Harpoon head blank, ivory
2. Harpoon head blank, ivory
3. Harpoon head blank, ivory
4. Harpoon head blank, ivory
5. Harpoon head blank, ivory
6. Unfinished harpoon head, ivory
7. Harpoon head, bone
8. Harpoon head, bone
9. Harpoon head, ivory
10. Harpoon head, ivory
11. Harpoon head, bone
12. Fragment of harpoon head, ivory

13. Harpoon head, bone
14. Harpoon head, bone
15. Harpoon head, ivory
16. Harpoon head, bone
17. Harpoon head, bone
18. Harpoon head, ivory
19. Harpoon head, ivory
20. Harpoon head, ivory
21. Harpoon head, bone
22. Harpoon head, ivory
23. Harpoon head, ivory

PLATE 20. EXCAVATIONS AT SIRHENIK – ⅓ size

1. Harpoon end-blade, slate
2. Harpoon end-blade, slate
3. Harpoon end-blade, slate
4. Harpoon end-blade, siliceous slate
5. Harpoon end-blade, slate
6. Harpoon ice pick, ivory
7. Harpoon ice pick, ivory
8. Harpoon ice pick, bone
9. Harpoon ice pick, ivory
10. Harpoon end-blade, slate
11. Harpoon end-blade, slate
12. Harpoon end-blade, slate
13. Ice pick (?), ivory
14. Harpoon foreshaft, ivory

15. Harpoon foreshaft, ivory
16. Seal-scratcher, wood
17. Wound plug, wood
18. Wound plug, wood
19. Wound plug, wood
20. Harpoon float stopper, wood
21. Harpoon float stopper, wood
22. Harpoon float bar, wood
23. Spear point, silicified tuff
24. Spear point, slate
25. Fragment of spear point, slate
26. Fragment of spear point, slate
27. Fragment of atl atl, wood

PLATE 21. EXCAVATIONS AT SIRHENIK – ⅓ size

1. Fragment of toy bow, wood
2. Model of bow, baleen
3. Model of bow, wood

4. Wrist guard, bone
5. Wrist guard, ivory
6. Wrist guard, ivory

7. Wrist guard, bone
8. Wrist guard, ivory
9. Twister, wood
10. Part of compound bow, wood
11. Fragment of arrow, wood
12. Fragment of arrow, bone
13. Fragment of arrow, wood
14. Fragment of arrow, wood
15. Fragment of arrow, wood
16. Arrowhead, bone
17. Arrowhead, bone
18. Arrowhead, bone
19. Arrowhead, bone
20. Arrowhead, bone
21. Arrowhead, bone
22. Arrowhead, bone
23. Arrowhead, bone
24. Arrowhead, bone
25. Arrowhead, bone
26. Arrowhead, bone

PLATE 22.   EXCAVATIONS AT SIRHENIK — ⅓ size

1. Blank for blunt arrowhead, bone
2. Arrowhead, bone
3. Arrowhead, bone
4. Arrowhead, bone
5. Blunt arrowhead, ivory
6. Blunt arrowhead, ivory
7. Blunt arrowhead, ivory
8. Arrowhead, bone
9. Arrowhead, bone
10. Model of arrow, wood
11. Model of arrow, wood
12. Model of arrow, wood
13. Fish spear point, bone
14. Fishhook, bone
15. Center-prong of bird dart, ivory
16. Center-prong of bird dart, ivory
17. Side-prong of bird dart, ivory
18. Center-prong of bird dart, ivory
19. Bird bola weight, ivory
20. Bird bola weight, ivory
21. Bird bola weight, ivory
22. Float, wood
23. Harpoon head, ivory
24. Harpoon head, ivory
25. Harpoon head, bone
26. Fishhook shank, wood
27. Fishhook shank, bone
28. Fishhook barb, ivory
29. Fishhook barb, bone
30. Loop, baleen
31. Fish spear head, bone
32. Fish spear head, bone
33. Fish spear head, bone
34. Fish spear head, ivory
35. Fragment of fish spear head, ivory
36. Barb of composite fish spear, bone
37. Barb of composite fish spear, bone
38. Barb of composite fish spear, bone
39. Fish spear head, ivory
40. Fish spear head, bone

PLATE 23.   EXCAVATIONS AT SIRHENIK — ⅓ size

1. Net, baleen
2. Net, baleen
3. Drill end, bone
4. Drill end, ivory
5. Drill end, ivory
6. Knife, ivory
7. Knife, ivory
8. Handle, ivory
9. Drill stave, wood
10. Wooden drill stave, with bone drill end
11. Needle-case, bone
12. Drill stave with iron drill end
13. Knife, bone
14. Knife, bone
15. Line sinker, ivory
16. Line sinker, ivory
17. Line sinker, ivory
18. Line sinker, ivory
19. Baleen ring for ice staff
20. Net sinker, ivory
21. Net sinker, ivory
22. Net sinker, ivory
23. Wooden spindle for fire-making
24. Wooden spindle for fire-making
25. Bow-drill, wood
26. Bow-drill, bone

PLATE 24.   EXCAVATIONS AT SIRHENIK — ⅓ size

1. Adze, silicified tuff
2. Adze, siliceous slate
3. Adze, silicified tuff
4. Adze, silicified tuff
5. Adze socket piece, bone
6. Scraper, silicified tuff
7. Scraper, flint
8. Blade, flint
9. Flake, flint
10. Double end-scraper, flint
11. Scraper, silicified tuff
12. Tall scraper, flint
13. Double scraper, flint
14. Blade, flint
15. Blade, flint
16. Blade, siliceous slate
17. Perforator, silicified tuff
18. Perforator, silicified tuff
19. Perforator, silicified tuff
20. Perforator, flint
21. Drill end, silicified tuff
22. Drill end fragment, flint
23. Concave scraper, flint
24. Flake, obsidian
25. Concave scraper, flint
26. Side scraper, obsidian

27. Flake, obsidian
28. Flake, siliceous slate
29. Tall scraper, flint
30. Concave scraper, obsidian
31. Pressure flaker, bone
32. Arrowhead end-blade, siliceous slate
33. Harpoon head side-blade, siliceous slate
34. Harpoon head side-blade, flint
35. Adze socket piece, bone
36. Knife side-blade, flint
37. Knife, siliceous slate
38. Knife side-blade, flint
39. Knife side-blade, silicified tuff
40. Knife side-blade, flint

PLATE 25. EXCAVATIONS AT SIRHENIK — ⅓ size

1. Knife, slate, in wooden handle
2. Knife, slate
3. Knife, slate
4. Knife, slate
5. Knife, slate
6. Knife, slate
7. Knife, slate
8. Spear point, slate
9. Spear point, slate
10. Knife, slate
11. Knife, slate
12. Knife, slate
13. Knife, slate
14. Knife, slate
15. Woman's knife in wooden handle
16. Knife-handle, bone
17. Knife-handle, bone
18. Knife-handle, bone
19. Knife-handle, bone
20. Knife-handle, bone
21. Knife-handle, bone
22. Handle of woman's knife, bone
23. Woman's knife, slate
24. Handle of woman's knife, wood
25. Woman's knife, slate
26. Knife-handle, wood
27. Knife-handle, wood
28. Knife-handle, wood
29. Knife, bone
30. Woman's knife, slate
31. Woman's knife, slate
32. Woman's knife, slate
33. Woman's knife, slate
34. Handle of woman's knife, wood
35. Knife-handle, wood

PLATE 26. EXCAVATIONS AT SIRHENIK — ⅓ size

1. Handle of woman's knife, wood
2. Handle of woman's knife, wood
3. Handle of woman's knife, wood
4. Handle of woman's knife, wood
5. Handle of woman's knife, wood
6. Wood bottom of baleen container
7. Spoon, wood
8. Spoon, bone
9. Spoon, bone
10. Spoon, deer antler
11. Wood bottom of baleen container
12. Bucket handle, rib of ringed seal
13. Bucket handle, ivory
14. Bucket handle, wood
15. Bucket handle, wood
16. Scoop, bone
17. Strainer, baleen
18. Stamp, bone
19. Paddle for decorating pottery, ivory
20. Pottery sherd
21. Pottery sherd
22. Pottery sherd
23. Pottery sherd
24. Pottery sherd

PLATE 27. EXCAVATIONS AT SIRHENIK — ⅓ size

1. Ice creeper, ivory
2. Buckle, ivory
3. Buckle, bone
4. Buckle, wood
5. Swivel rod, ivory
6. Swivel rod, ivory
7. Cross-piece of umiak model, wood
8. Cross-piece of umiak model, wood
9. Umiak model, ivory
10. Umiak model, wood
11. Boat model, larch bark
12. Reamer, bone
13. Awl, bone
14. Awl, ivory
15. Awl, ivory
16. Awl, bone
17. Rod, ivory
18. Needle, bone
19. Needle, bone
20. Awl and reamer, bone
21. Awl, ivory
22. Awl, ivory
23. Drag line handle, ivory
24. Drag line handle, ivory
25. Drag line handle, ivory
26. Drag line handle, ivory
27. Drag line handle, ivory
28. Drag line handle, bone
29. Boat hook, ivory
30. Boat hook, ivory
31. Boat hook, ivory

PLATE 28. EXCAVATIONS AT SIRHENIK. Nos. 1–6, 8–24 — ⅛ size; No. 7 — ⅙ size

1. Hoop net sinker, granite
2. Spool, deer antler
3. Ice scoop, deer antler
4. Mallet, deer antler
5. Mallet, os penis of walrus
6. Mattock, bone

7. Mattock, ivory
8. Pick, ivory
9. Pick, ivory
10. Mattock, ivory
11. Mattock, ivory
12. Wedge, ivory
13. Adze, bone
14. Wooden bottom of baleen container
15. Container, baleen

16. Hook, deer antler
17. Hook, deer antler
18. Wooden runner of dog sled
19. Sled runner, ivory
20. Sled runner, ivory
21. Sled runner, ivory
22. Sled runner, ivory
23. Sled runner, ivory
24. Sled runner, ivory

PLATE 29.   EXCAVATIONS AT SIRHENIK — ⅓ size

1. Toggle, ivory
2. Bead, ivory
3. Button, ivory
4. Thimble holder, ivory
5. Decoration on piece of ivory
6. Bird figure, ivory
7. Bird figure, ivory
8. Representation of fish, ivory
9. Seal, ivory
10. Seal, ivory
11. Fox, ivory
12. Two-headed dog, ivory
13. Whale, ivory
14. Fox, ivory
15. Polar bear, ivory

16. Seal, ivory
17. Whale, ivory
18. Whale, ivory
19. Bone amulet
20. Bone amulet
21. Decoration on ivory plaque
22. Decorated ivory plaque
23. Ornament, ivory
24. Trident, ivory
25. Drum handle, ivory
26. Decoration on piece of ivory
27. Decoration on piece of ivory
28. Decorated handle, ivory
29. Decorated handle, ivory

PLATE 30.   EXCAVATIONS AT SIRHENIK — ⅓ size

1. Walrus tusk
2. Walrus tusk
3. Walrus tusk
4. Vertebral disk, whale
5. Bird tibia
6. Walrus phalanx
7. Walrus astragalus
8. Vertebral disk, whale
9. Baleen knot
10. Scraper of lower jaw of arctic fox
11. Bear canine

12. "Spoon," baleen
13. Strip, baleen
14. "Knife," baleen
15. "Fish," baleen
16. "Fish," baleen
17. "Fish," baleen
18. Strip, baleen
19. "Knife," baleen
20. "Fish," baleen
21. "Knife," baleen
22. Plaited baleen

PLATE 31.   EXCAVATIONS AT NUNLIGRAN, WESTERN SITE — ⅓ size

1. Harpoon head blank
2. Unfinished harpoon head, bone
3. Harpoon head, bone
4. Harpoon head, bone
5. Harpoon head, ivory
6. Harpoon finger rest, ivory
7. Arrowhead, bone
8. Blunt arrowhead, bone
9. Blunt arrowhead, bone
10. Peg of harpoon thrower
11. Wrist guard, ivory
12. Bird bola weight, ivory
13. Bird bola weight, ivory
14. Bird bola weight, ivory
15. Seal figure, ivory
16. Bird bola weight, walrus tooth
17. Unfinished arrowhead, ivory
18. Blunt arrowhead, ivory
19. Blunt arrowhead, ivory
20. Back-scratcher, ivory
21. Ivory rod of undetermined function

22. Female figure, ivory
23. Marrow extractor, bone
24. Awl, ivory
25. Fishhook barbs, ivory
26. Fishhook, ivory
27. Harpoon ice pick, os penis of walrus
28. Wedge, ivory
29. Comb, ivory
30. Red, ivory
31. Needle, bone
32. Comb, ivory
33. Ear ornament, ivory
34. Figure of rabbit, ivory
35. Spoon, ivory
36. Handle of woman's knife, ivory
37. Woman's knife, slate
38. Knife-handle, bone
39. Knife-handle, ivory
40. Knife-handle, deer antler
41. Knife-handle, deer antler
42. Knife-handle, deer antler

PLATE 32. EXCAVATIONS AT NUNLIGRAN, EASTERN SITE — ⅓ size

1. Harpoon head, bone
2. Arrowhead end-blade, silicified tuff
3. Knife-blade, flint
4. Small chisel, silicified tuff
5. Drill end, flint
6. Flake, obsidian
7. Flake, flint
8. Flake, flint
9. Knife-blade, flint
10. Knife-like side-blade, flint
11. Flake, obsidian
12. Flake, obsidian
13. Drill end, flint
14. Knife-like side-blade, flint

15. Scraper, stone
16. Scraper, obsidian
17. Harpoon ice pick, ivory
18. Center-prong of bird dart, ivory
19. Arrowhead, bone
20. Fragment of arrowhead, bone
21. Fragment of dart head, ivory
22. Awl, ivory
23. Awl, ivory
24. Drill end, ivory
25. Drill end, ivory
26. Dart head, ivory
27. Amulet, walrus tooth

PLATE 33. EXCAVATIONS AT ENMYLEN — ⅓ size

1. Harpoon head blank, bone
2. Harpoon head blank, bone
3. Harpoon head, ivory
4. Harpoon head, ivory
5. Harpoon head, bone
6. Fragment of harpoon head, ivory
7. Harpoon head, bone
8. Harpoon head, bone
9. Arrowhead, bone
10. Harpoon head, bone
11. Harpoon head, bone
12. Harpoon head, ivory
13. Harpoon head, bone
14. Harpoon head, bone

15. Harpoon socket piece, ivory
16. Harpoon socket piece, ivory
17. Harpoon ice pick, ivory
18. Dart head, ivory
19. Fish spear head, bone, unfinished
20. Arrowhead, bone
21. Arrowhead, bone
22. Arrowhead, ivory
23. Arrowhead, bone
24. Fragment of arrowhead, bone
25. Wrist guard, ivory
26. Dart head, ivory
27. Knife, ivory

PLATE 34. EXCAVATIONS AT ENMYLEN — ⅓ size

1. Fishhook barb, ivory
2. Finger ring, bone
3. Flake, flint
4. Flake, flint
5. Flake, flint
6. Flake, silicified tuff
7. Scraper, flint
8. Line sinker, bone
9. Knife-blade, silicified tuff
10. Knife-blade, silicified tuff
11. Fragment of flint knife
12. Knife fragment, silicified tuff
13. Flint end-blade of arrowhead
14. Harpoon end-blade, flint
15. Small chisel, silicified tuff
16. Scraper, flint
17. Knife-blade, slate
18. Knife-blade, slate

19. Slate end-blade of arrowhead
20. Knife-blade, slate
21. Whale lance point, slate
22. Scraper plane, silicified tuff
23. Woman's knife, slate
24. Woman's knife, slate
25. Woman's knife, slate
26. Wedge, ivory
27. Awl, bone
28. Awl, ivory
29. Wedge, ivory
30. Adze, ivory
31. Knife handle, bone
32. Knife handle, bone
33. Awl, bone
34. Awl, ivory
35. Needle, ivory

PLATE 35. EXCAVATIONS AT ENMYLEN — ⅓ size

1. Drill end, bone
2. Drill end, bone
3. Ladle, bone
4. Scraper, ivory
5. Bone splinter for extracting marrow
6. Bone splinter for extracting marrow
7. Wooden object of unknown function

8. Tube, bone
9. Pendant, ivory
10. Pendant, ivory
11. Button or fastener, bone
12. Pendant, ivory
13. Whetstone
14. Block of wood

15. Tube, bone
16. Ring, ivory
17. Dog canine
18. Buckle, bone
19. Fastener, ivory
20. Engraved plaque, ivory
21. Sled runner, ivory
22. Bone handle
23. Scraper, ivory

24. Drum handle, ivory
25. Spoon, bone
26. Engraved plaque, bone
27. Armor plate, bone
28. Needle-case (?), ivory
29. Spoon, deer antler
30. Knife, ivory
31. Spoon, deer antler
32. Walrus tusk

PLATE 36. CHUKCHI PENINSULA — ⅓ size

1. Fragment of harpoon head, ivory
2. Harpoon head, ivory
3. Harpoon head, ivory
4. Harpoon head, ivory
5. Harpoon head, deer antler
6. Harpoon head, bone
7. Harpoon head, bone
8. Harpoon head, bone
9. Harpoon head, bone
10. Fragment of whaling harpoon head, ivory
11. Harpoon end-blade, slate
12. Harpoon end-blade, slate
13. Blunt arrowhead, bone
14. Bird dart center-prong, ivory
15. Arrowhead, bone
16. Arrowhead, bone
17. Arrowhead, bone
18. Arrowhead, bone
19. Arrowhead, bone

20. Arrow point, flint
21. Arrow point, smoky quartz
22. Harpoon socket piece, ivory
23. Whaling harpoon foreshaft, ivory
24. Harpoon ice pick, ivory
25. Twister, ivory
26. Bird bola weight, ivory
27. Bird bola weight, ivory
28. Bird bola weight, ivory
29. Bird bola weight, ivory
30. Core, obsidian
31. Adze, nephrite
32. Net sinker, ivory
33. Line sinker, argillaceous slate
34. Line sinker, ivory
35. Line sinker, ivory
36. Adze, silicified tuff
37. Adze, nephrite
38. Dart head, ivory

PLATE 37. CHUKCHI PENINSULA. Nos. 1, 4–23 — ⅓ size; Nos. 3, 4 — ⅛ size

1. Nephrite adze in antler socket piece
2. Adze socket piece, bone
3. Mattock handle, wood
4. Adze handle, ivory
5. Adze, silicified tuff
6. Scraper, silicified tuff
7. Scraper plane, siliceous slate
8. Knife, smoky quartz
9. Knife, flint
10. Knife, chalcedony
11. Knife, slate
12. Knife, slate

13. Knife, siliceous slate
14. Knife, slate
15. Woman's knife in bone handle
16. Knife, slate
17. Woman's knife, slate
18. Small knife, nephrite
19. Mallet, ivory
20. Comb, ivory
21. Comb, ivory
22. Slate knife in bone handle
23. Knife, slate (whale knife)

PLATE 38. CHUKCHI PENINSULA — ⅓ size

1. Carved dowel, ivory
2. Carved dowel, ivory
3. Winged object, ivory
4. Wedge-shaped "ceremonial" object, ivory
5. Buckle, bone
6. Boat model, engraved, ivory
7. Snow goggles, ivory
8. Wolf canine, engraved
9. Human figure, ivory
10. Human figure, ivory
11. Human figure, ivory

12. Thimble holder, ivory
13. Fragment of bone needle case
14. Figure of sea otter, ivory
15. Bird figure, ivory
16. Seal figure, bitumen
17. Bird figure, ivory
18. Spoon, ivory
19. Drum handle, ivory
20. Engraved handle, ivory
21. Throwing board, ivory

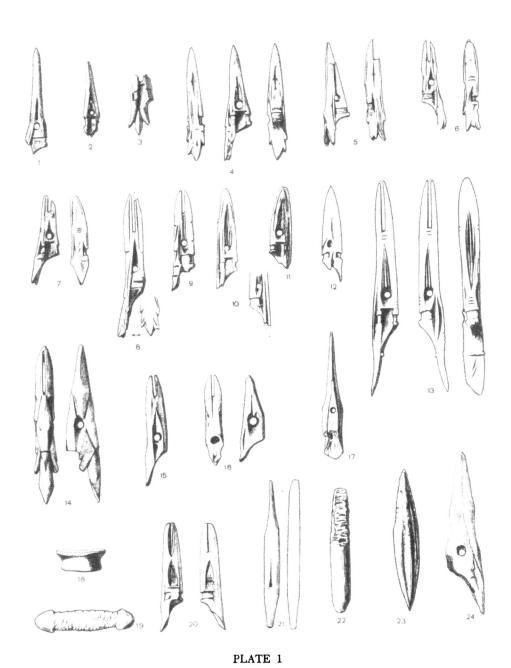

PLATE 1

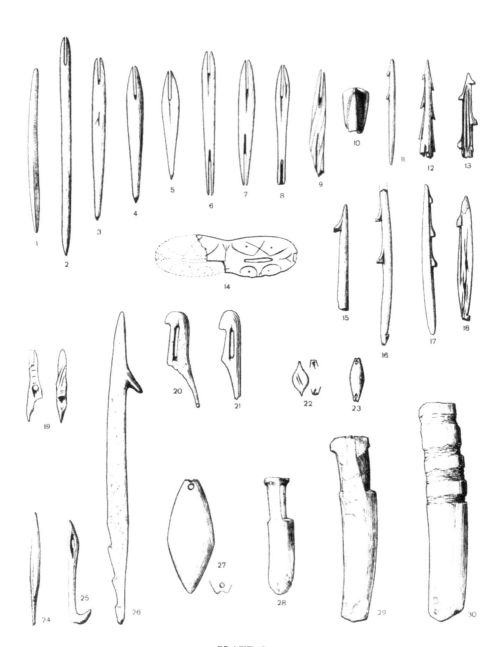

PLATE 2

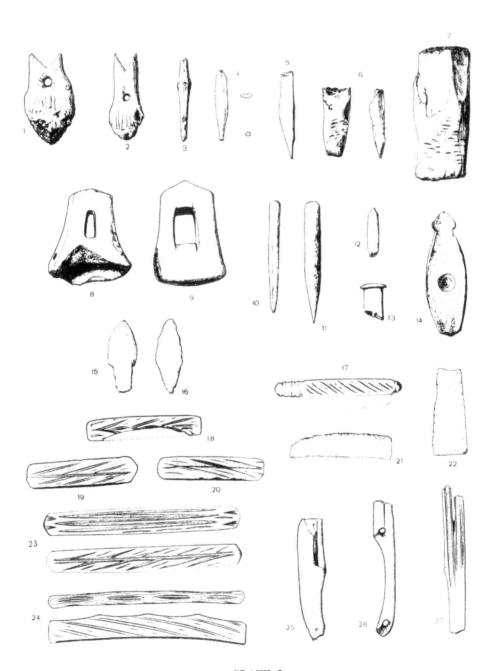

PLATE 3

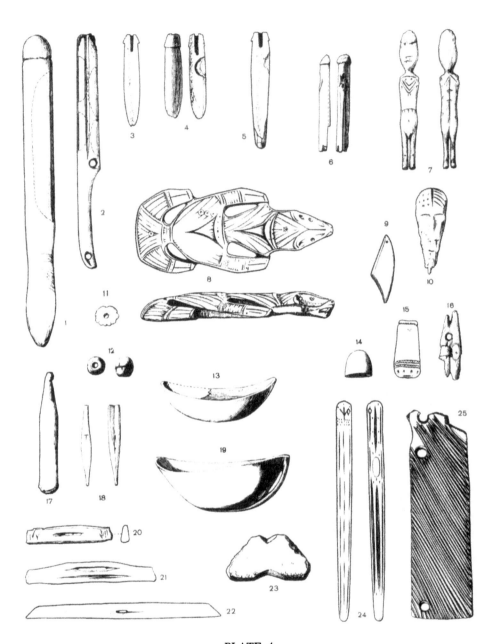

PLATE 4

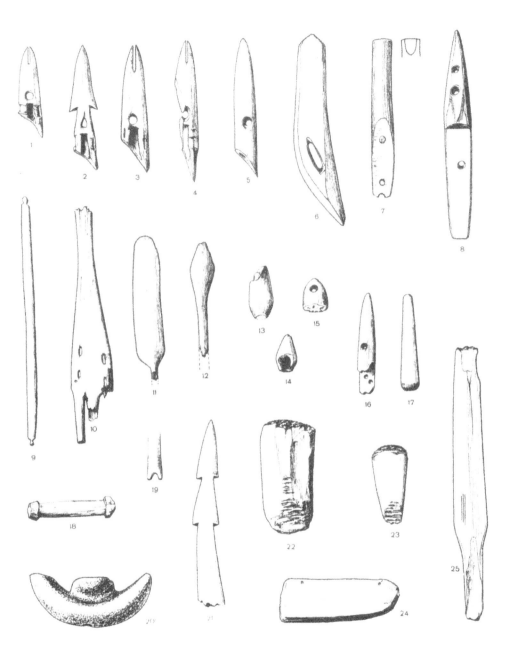

PLATE 5

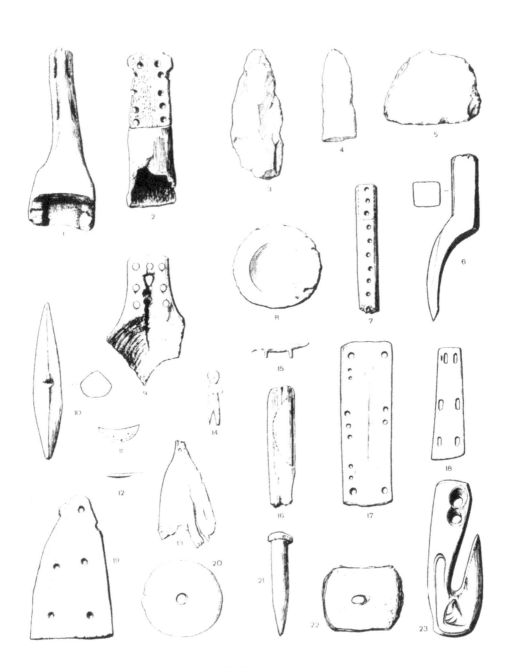

PLATE 6

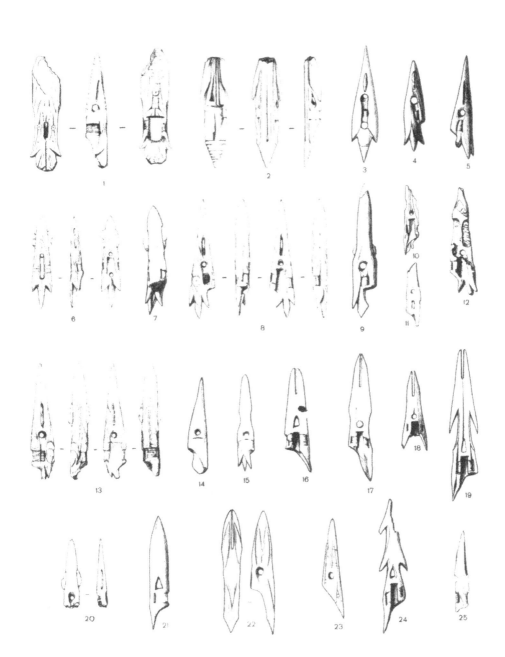

PLATE 7

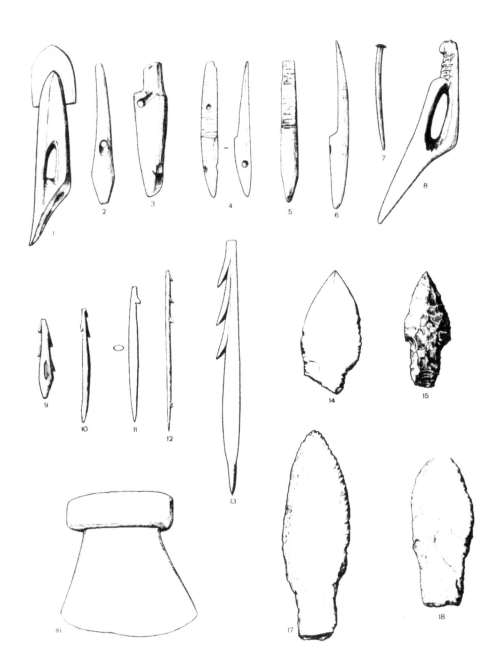

PLATE 8

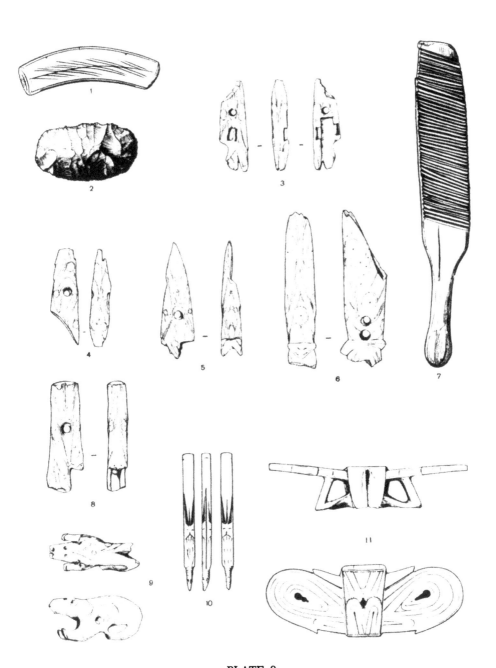

PLATE 9

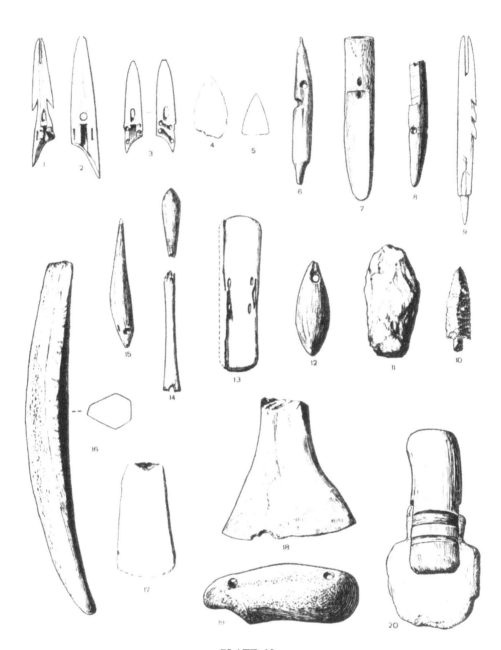

PLATE 10

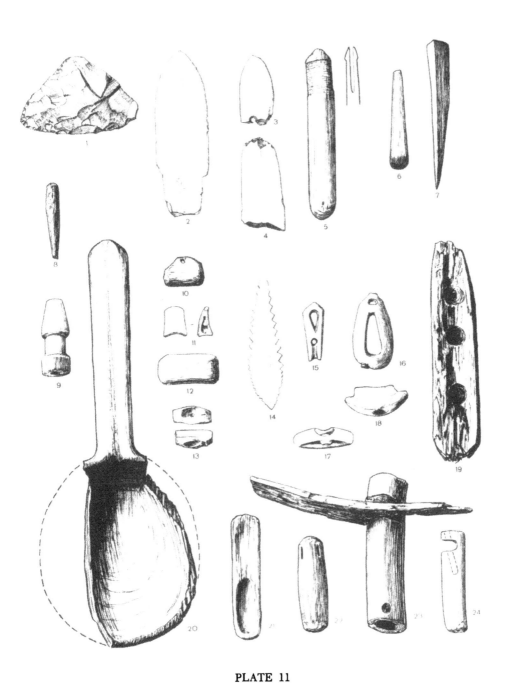

PLATE 11

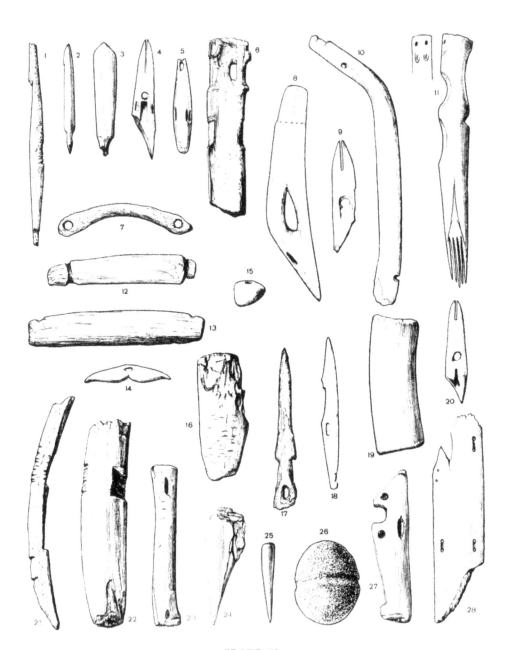

PLATE 12

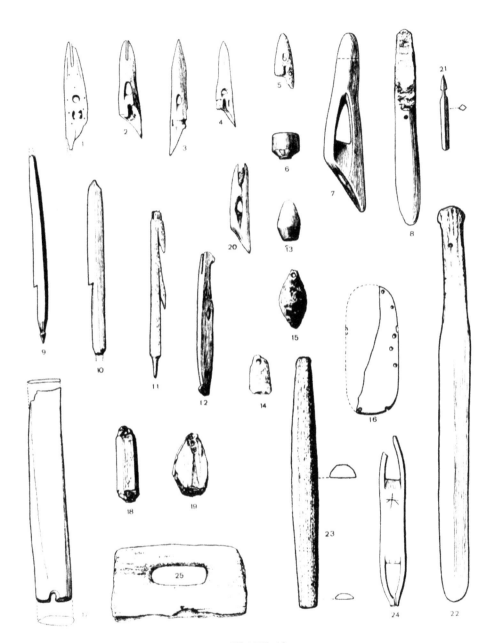

PLATE 13

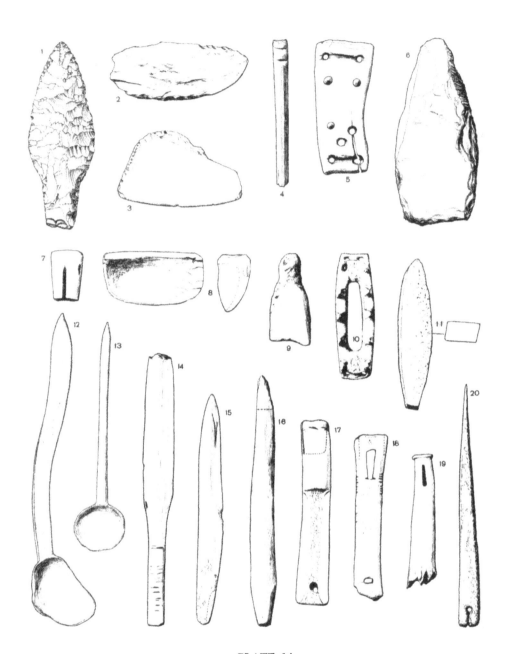

PLATE 14

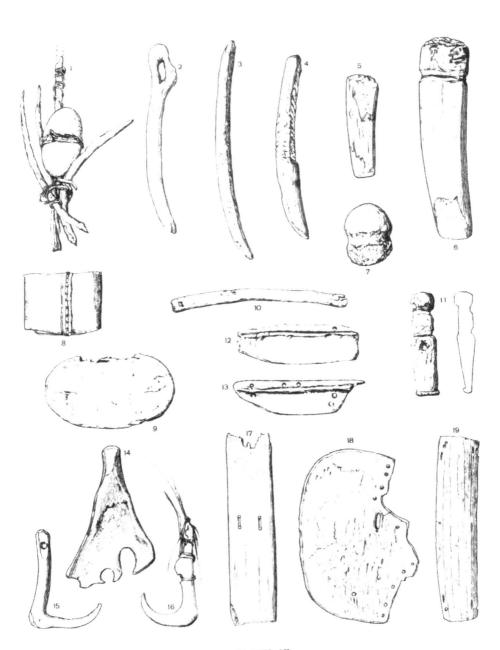

PLATE 15

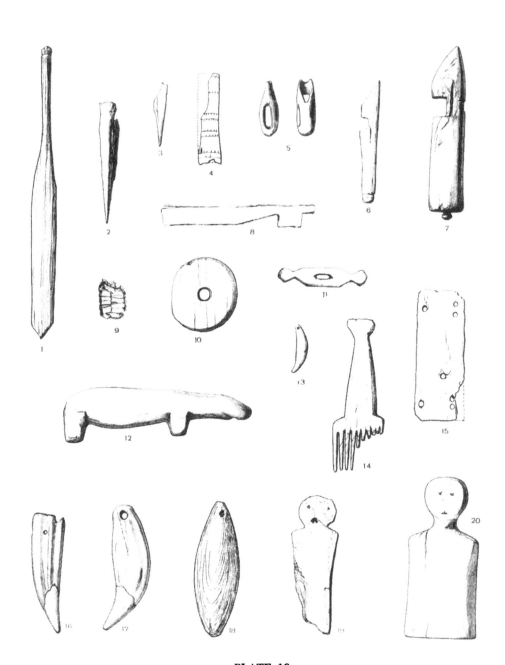

PLATE 16

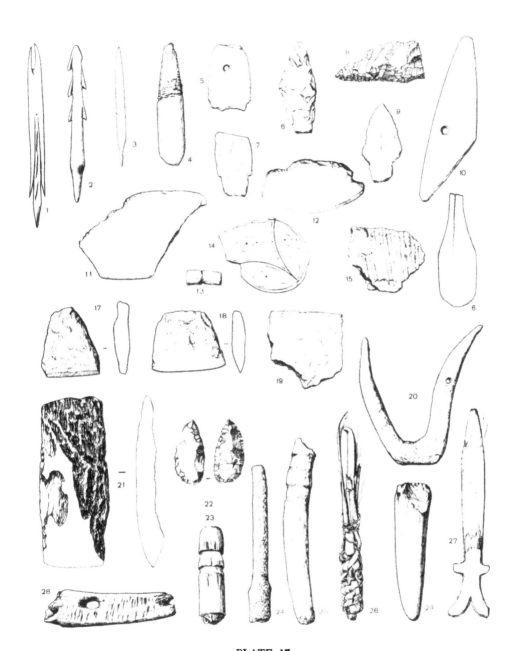

PLATE 17

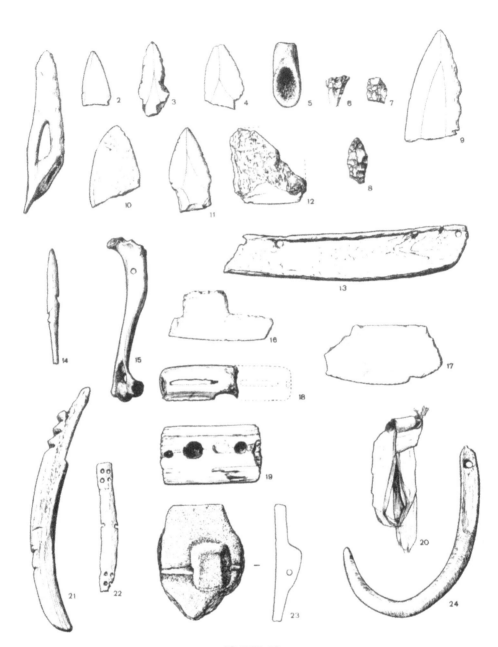

PLATE 18

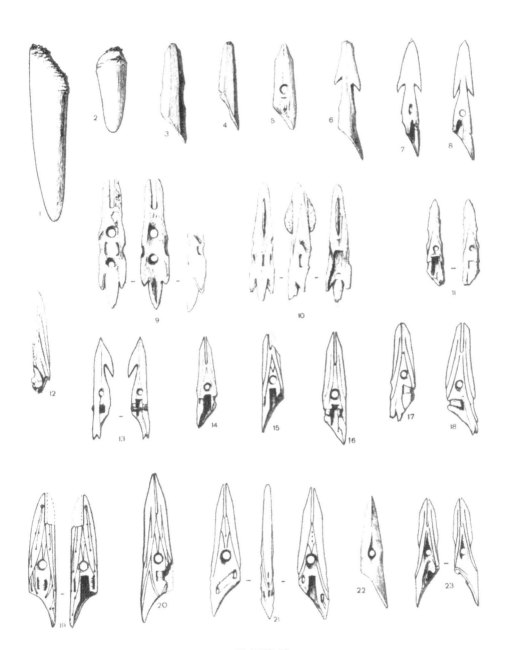

PLATE 19

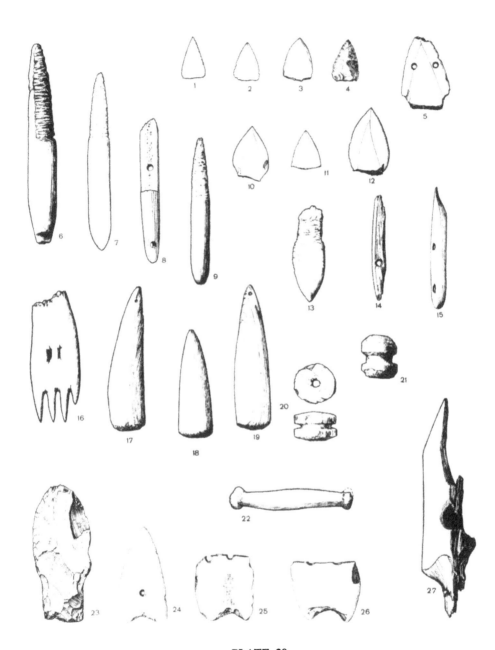

PLATE 20

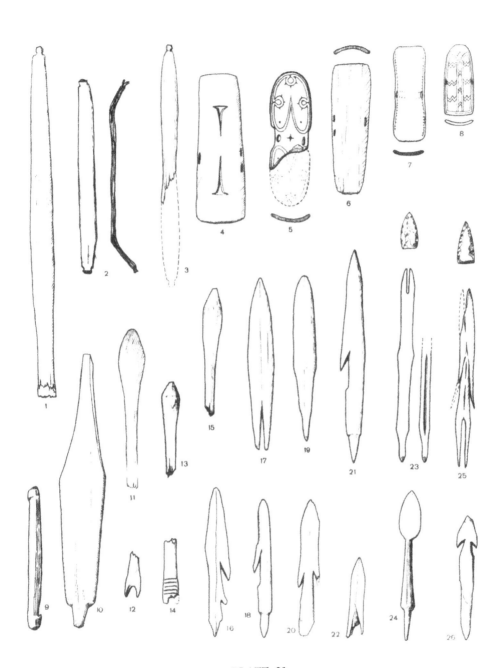

PLATE 21

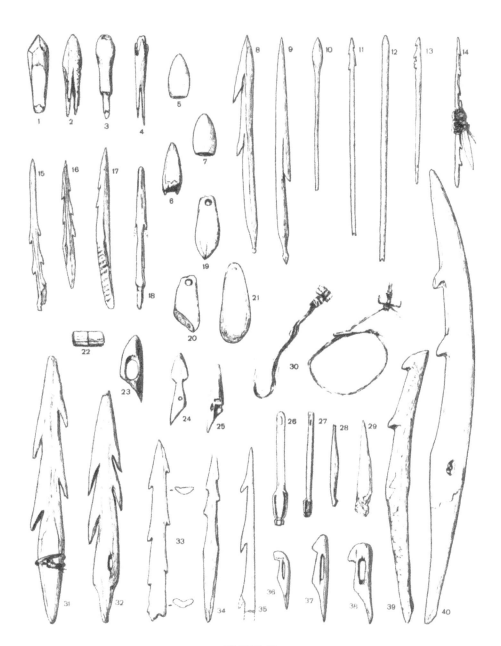

PLATE 22

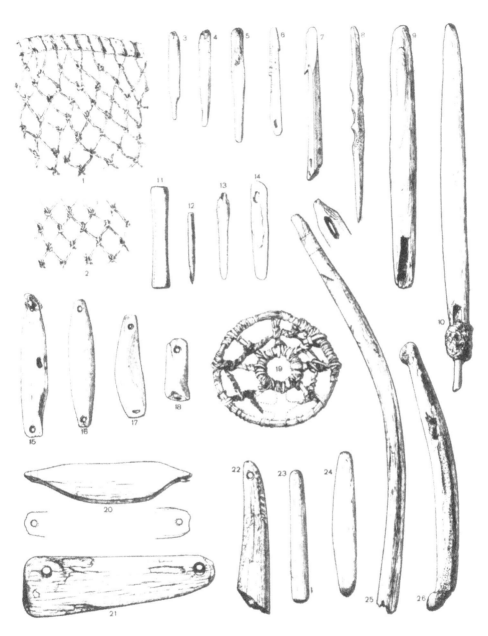

PLATE 23

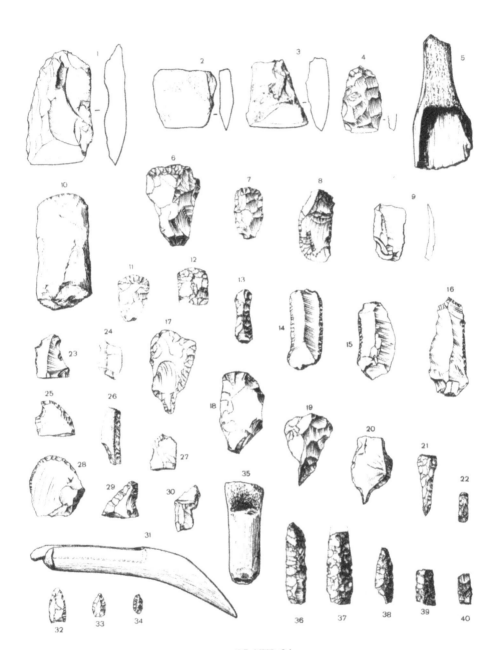

PLATE 24

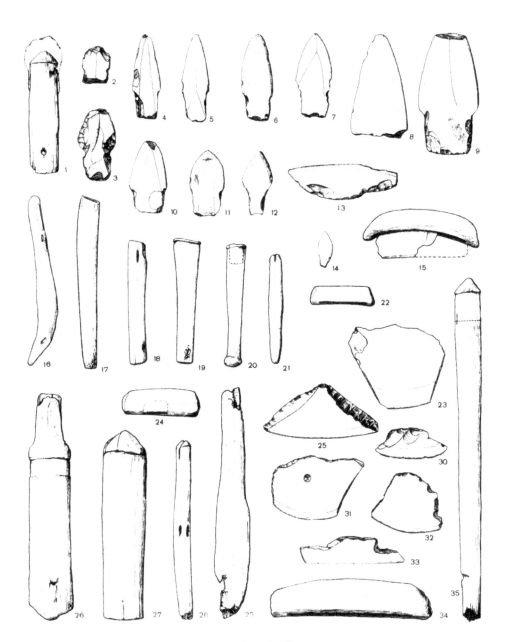

PLATE 25

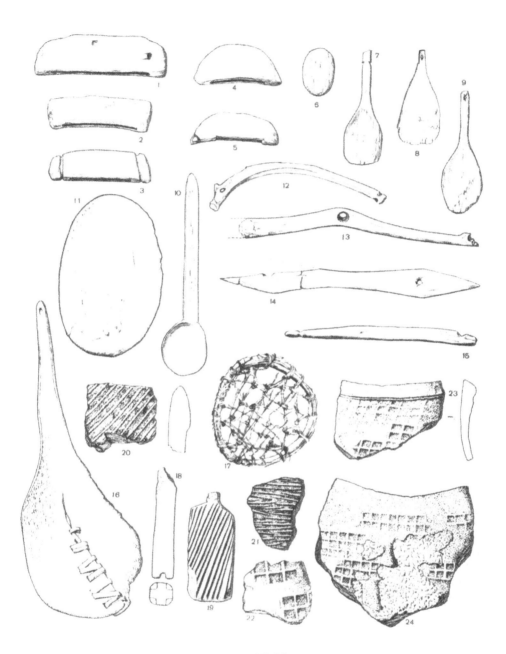

PLATE 26

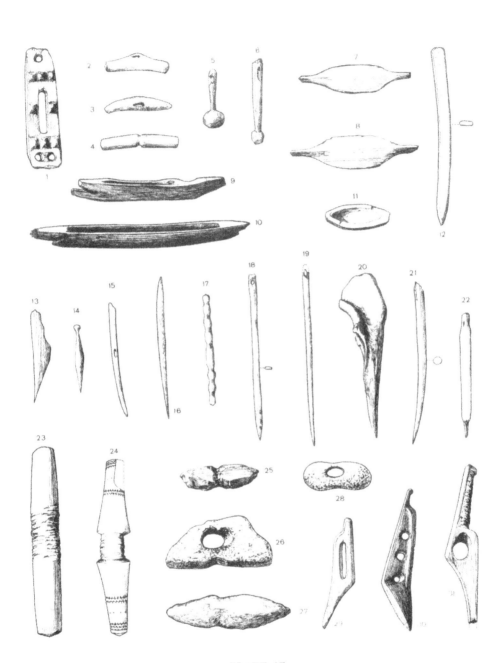

PLATE 27

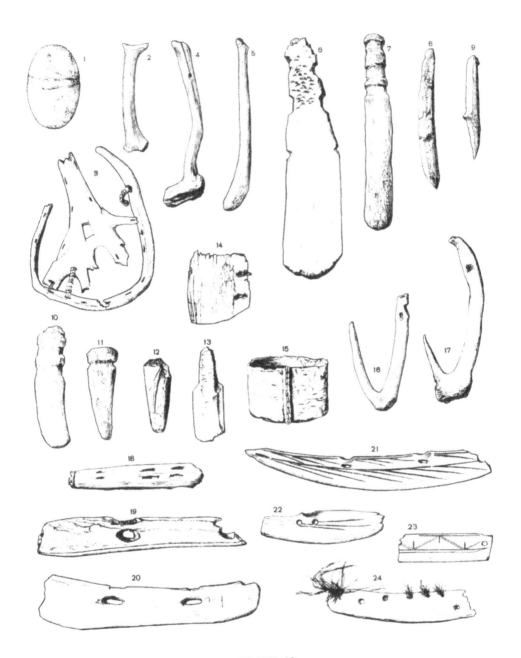

PLATE 28

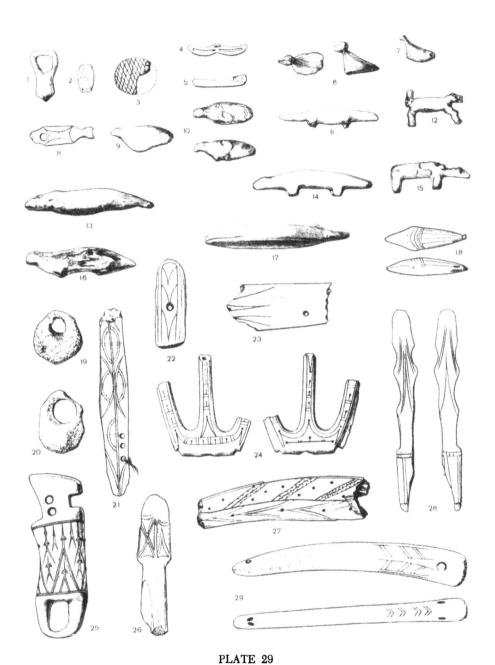

PLATE 29

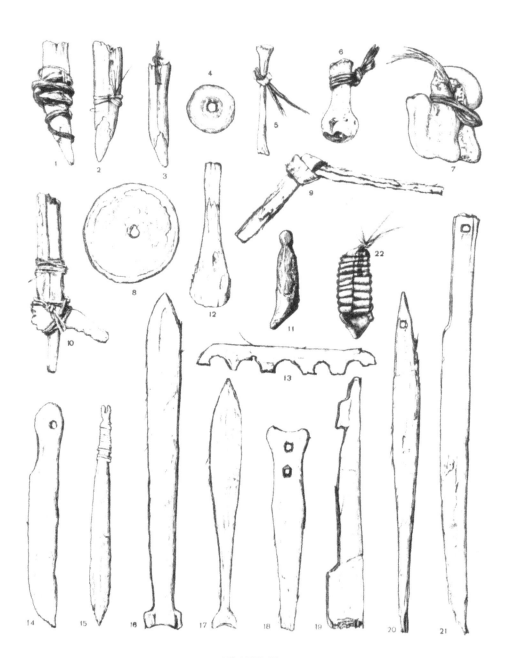

PLATE 30

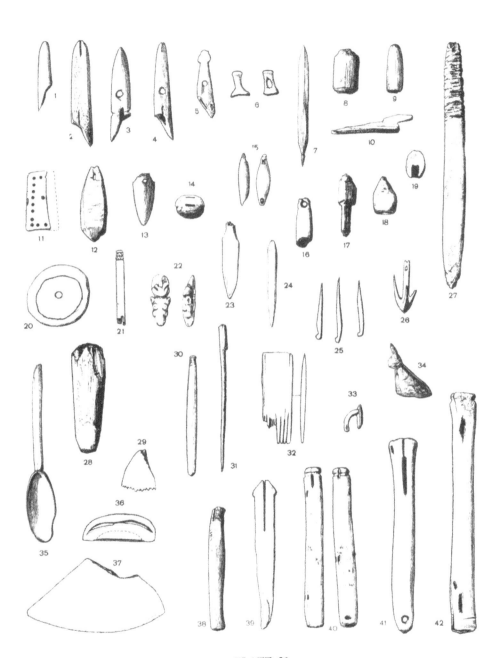

PLATE 31

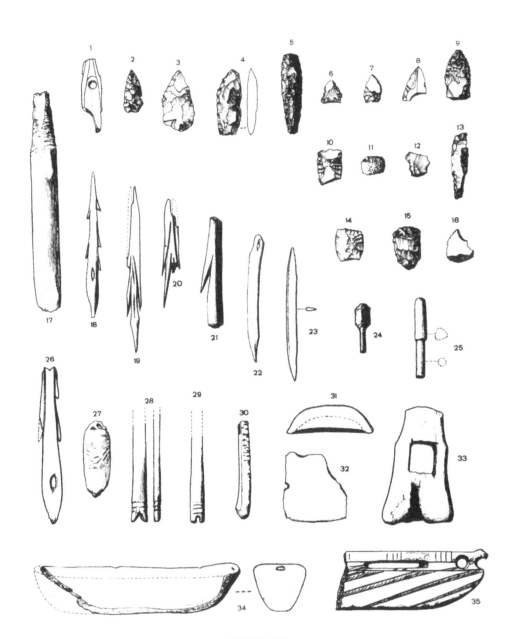

PLATE 32

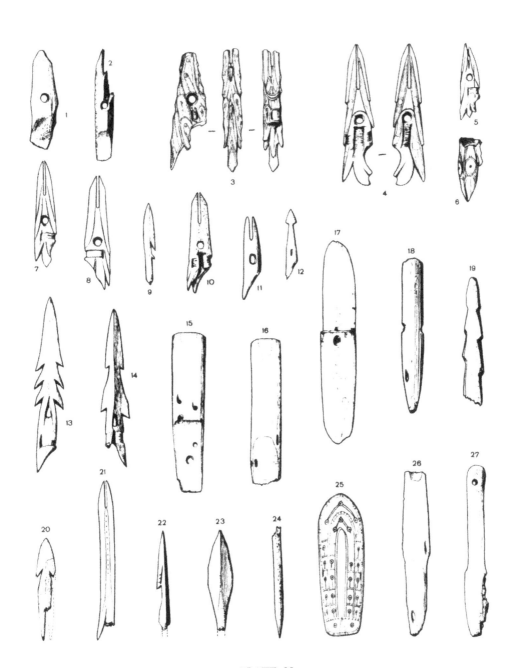

PLATE 33

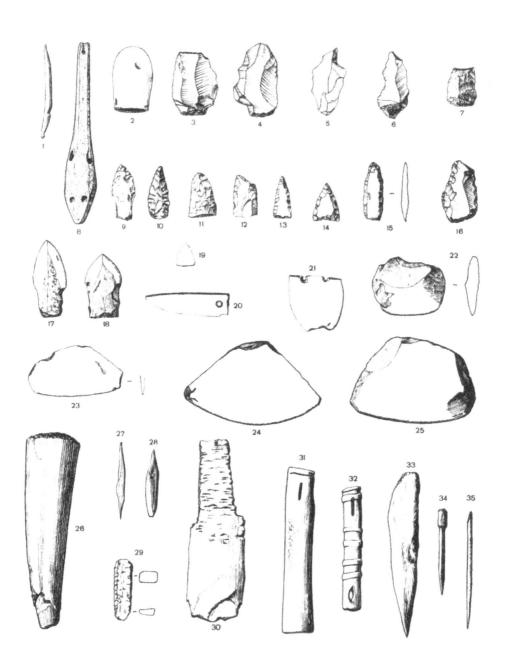

PLATE 34

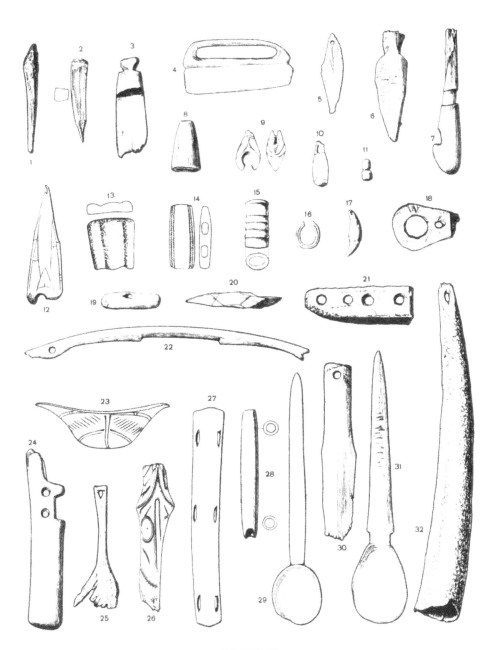

PLATE 35

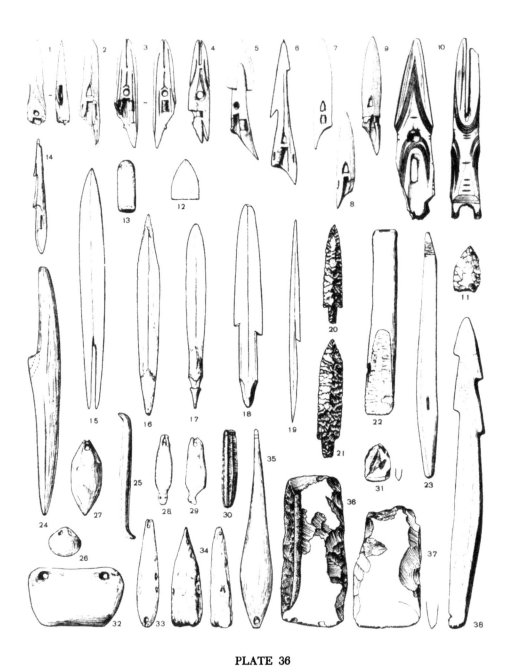

PLATE 36

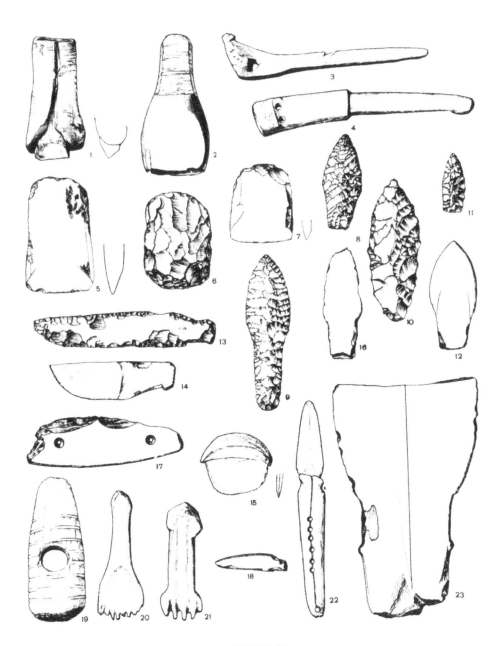

PLATE 37

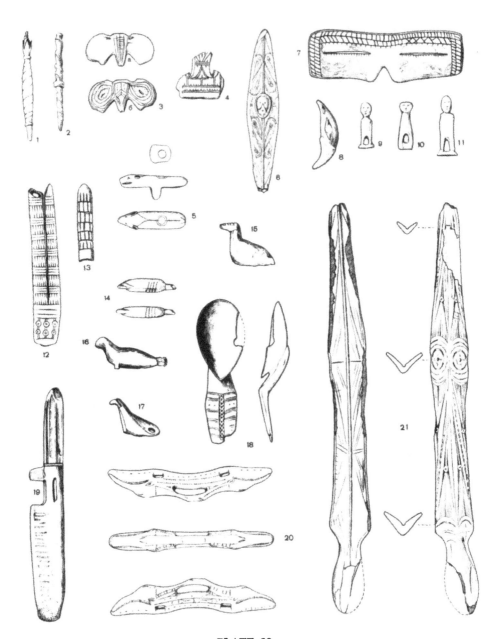

PLATE 38

THE ARCTIC INSTITUTE OF NORTH AMERICA

The Arctic Institute of North America was founded to further the scientific study and exploration of the Arctic. The Institute provides information on the Arctic through its three offices, awards research grants, and publishes scientific papers and other contributions in its journal *Arctic*. Those interested in this work are invited to become Members. Members receive all numbers of the journal. The Library and Map Collection at the Montreal office are principally for their use, and they are welcome there and at the other Institute offices.

Board of Governors

D. C. NUTT (Chairman), Hanover, N.H.
F. KENNETH HARE (Vice-Chairman), Montreal, Quebec
J. T. WILSON, O.B.E. (Secretary), Toronto, Ontario
O. C. S. ROBERTSON (Treasurer), Washington, D.C.
A. T. BELCHER, Ottawa, Ontario
W. S. BENNINGHOFF, Ann Arbor, Michigan
J. C. CASE, New York, N.Y.
HENRY B. COLLINS, JR., Washington, D.C.
FRANK T. DAVIES, Ottawa, Ontario
M. J. DUNBAR, Montreal, Quebec
RICHARD P. GOLDTHWAIT, Columbus, Ohio

DUNCAN M. HODGSON, Montreal, Quebec
TREVOR LLOYD, Montreal, Quebec
A. E. PORSILD, Ottawa, Ontario
PAUL QUENEAU, New York, N.Y.
HUGH M. RAUP, Petersham, Massachusetts
D. C. ROSE, Ottawa, Ontario
PAUL A. SIPLE, Washington, D.C.
O. M. SOLANDT, Montreal, Quebec
WALTER SULLIVAN, New York, N.Y.
W. E. VAN STEENBURGH, Ottawa, Ontario
A. L. WASHBURN, New Haven, Connecticut
IRA L. WIGGINS, Stanford, California
WALTER A. WOOD, New York, N.Y.

Executive Director: JOHN C. REED, Montreal

Director of Washington Office: R. C. FAYLOR

Director of Montreal Office: M. MARSDEN

Editor of the Institute Journal ARCTIC: PAUL F. BRUGGEMANN

Offices of the Institute

3485 University Street, Montreal 2, Quebec, Canada
1530 P Street, N.W., Washington 5, D.C., U.S.A.
2 East 63rd St., New York 21, N.Y., U.S.A.

Milton Keynes UK
Ingram Content Group UK Ltd.
UKHW051814020424
440493UK00029B/766

9 781487 592578